Modern Tim
India 1880s–1
Environment, Economy, Culture

SUMIT SARKAR

Modern Times: India
1880s–1950s

~

Environment, Economy, Culture

permanent black

Published by

PERMANENT BLACK

'Himalayana', Mall Road, Ranikhet Cantt,
Ranikhet 263645

perblack@gmail.com

Distributed by

ORIENT BLACKSWAN PRIVATE LTD

Bangalore Bhopal Bhubaneshwar Chandigarh
Chennai Ernakulam Guwahati Hyderabad Jaipur
Kolkata Lucknow Mumbai New Delhi Patna

www.orientblackswan.com

ISBN 978-81-7824-470-9

First paperback printing 2015

Second Impression 2017

Typeset in Adobe Garamond
by Guru Typograph Technology, Crossings Republic, Gbd 201009
Printed and bound by Sapra Brothers, New Delhi 110092

for
SIPRA

for

SIPRA

Contents

Preface

Much has changed in the world of South Asian history-writing over the last three decades since I wrote a book entitled *Modern India* (1983). The passage of thirty years having rendered that work thoroughly dated, the futility of any attempt to revise it became increasingly clear to me, especially as over this period my own historical perspectives took new and unexpected directions. The present work of synthesis, which is an altogether new attempt to cover the same period in the light of fresh research and rethinking, is intended as the first of two companion volumes. In it I offer an overview of political, material, and cultural processes, and of imperial administrative institutions from the mid nineteenth century to the mid twentieth. In its subsequent companion I intend providing a chronological narrative about the political developments of that period: anti-colonial nationalisms, peasant and adivasi movements, developments and problems in India's north-east, labour and Left-wing struggles, caste organizations and Dalit protests, women's activism and the politics of right-wing formations—all of these within, outside, or opposed to the framework of mainstream nationalism even as I look at the formation of regional identities and movements.

The present work begins with a study of imperial institutions and policies. Unlike the majority of post-colonial histories, I do not see the colonial state as an unchanging monolith with innate tendencies. I focus, instead, on shifts, contradictions, and movements across time, and on variations in state practices across space. This perspective is developed, however, within a framework that recognizes overarching colonial domination and exploitation. Contrary, again, to much post-colonial writing, I attend carefully to the specifically colonial experiences of the imperial state within India rather than derive its activities from Western discourses about the Orient. That allows greater scope to specific and contingent historical events and conjunctures.

Environmental histories have emerged as an exceptionally rich area of recent research and the second chapter has benefited enormously from them. In it I look closely at patterns of tribal life and peasant cultivation: not as static entities always distinct from each other, but as shifting and interpenetrating processes. Scientific discourses, laws, and the administration of forests were a major source of tensions and protests among peasants and adivasis, and I study them in some detail. I also look at irrigation and river-control projects, and at the conflicts over land use and land rights that they repeatedly stimulated.

The third chapter deals with changing patterns of agricultural practices and agrarian relations that unfolded as the aftermath to colonial revenue policies. I elaborate the links between these and processes of commercialization, rural indebtedness, and endemic famine. I focus closely on the changing countryside, tracing the new agrarian tensions and conflicts that were provoked. While I look at struggles against state policies I also attend closely to internal contradictions and tensions, and to relationships of domination and exploitation among agrarian castes and classes.

I then pass on to issues of trade, finance, and industry to outline the specific forms of emergent capitalism in India. Shifting relationships between European and Indian entrepreneurial groups are analysed as I try to identify and explain regional variations within the broad pattern. I also look at Indian and imperial debates around deindustrialization, as well as financial drain through the mechanism of trade: these came to constitute major themes in the developing nationalist critiques of colonial policies. The growth of modern sectors of so-called free and unfree labour in plantations, mines, and factories is another focus of close attention. I indicate some of the major tendencies within labour conflicts in these areas, though this is a theme developed in greater detail in the ensuing companion to the present book.

In the final chapter, the formation of modern cities, in all their internal diversity, provides the entry point into new cultural and social developments in the late colonial era. I compare and contrast cities like Delhi, Lucknow, and Ahmedabad—which had a pre-colonial urban past—with the new metropolitan centres of Calcutta, Bombay, and Madras. I then trace the different paths of development among the new urban centres. I look at their built environment, sociabilities, caste configurations, and at their public cultural activities such as theatre, cinema, and sports. There are here large sections on older forms which developed new orientations and genres: literature, dance, music, painting. Case studies of specific schools of art are given, and some representative and distinctive individuals are shown. I have within each chapter incorporated the relevant historiographical developments, changes, and debates. Separate bibliographical sections, provided in each, will I hope facilitate the work of teachers and students.

On account of a prolonged illness it took me a very long time to complete this book. I cannot sufficiently thank my ever-patient and ever-encouraging publisher Rukun Advani, without whom it may never have been written. I would also like to thank Bodhisattva Kar, Shilleima Chaunu, and Nisa for their help with books and typing. I am enormously grateful to Digvijay Kumar Singh for helping me with the bibliographical sections and for identifying visual material. Dr John Thomas and Dr Devarpit Manjit—my old students—helped me rediscover reading at a time when I was severely visually challenged. Words cannot convey what I owe to them.

A large number of dear friends and students set me on my path to recovery. I can only mention a few of them: Achin Vanaik, Mukul Mangalik, G. Arunima, Shahana Bhattacharya, Praful Bidwai, Neeladri Bhattacharya, Basudeb Chatterjee, Pamela Philipose, Rajeev and Tani Bhargava, Kamal and Anuradha Chenoy, Gargi and Sumit Chakraborty, Chitra Joshi, Hari Sen, Radhika Chopra, Aijaz Ahmad, Prabhu Mohapatra, Sambudha Sen, Tapan Basu, P.K. Datta, Tripta Wahi, Vijay Singh, Rosa and Atishi, Kunal and Shubhra Chakravarty, Anirban Bandyopadhyay—among countless others. I was most fortunate to have Ajit Bannerjee as my doctor. I am grateful to Sulekha and Beli.

My years of teaching at Delhi University lie behind this book. It saddens me to see the present swift destruction of this old institution by its new vice chancellor, but it also heartens me to see the brave efforts of students, teachers, and well-wishers to save it.

Aditya and Tanika made me write this book. Words of thanks to them and Anna will be inappropriate and superfluous. I hope they find parts of the book useful.

New Delhi, March 2014   Sumit Sarkar

1

Imperial Structures, Policies, and Ideologies

Historical studies of imperial structures have gone through several shifts in perspective. From early in the twentieth century, scholars have been attracted to this area because the archival materials on the theme—official documents and the private papers of bureaucrats—were relatively accessible. From the late 1980s, however, such work came increasingly to appear tedious because its concerns tended to be narrowly and sometimes solely focused on details of administrative policy. Especially with the efflorescence of various kinds of 'histories from below', writings preoccupied with the lives and activities of colonial bureaucrats and statesmen were branded as mere 'histories from above'. More recently, there has been yet another historiographical shift. The impact of Edward Said, and perhaps more profoundly of Michel Foucault, has stimulated a new interest in 'colonial discourses' as well as in the close details of the work of 'governmentality'—the management of bodies of subject people.

My account in this chapter will focus in the first part on official policies from around the 1880s to the partition of Bengal in 1905. This will be followed by a longer and much more wide-ranging second part, arranged thematically rather than chronologically, where I will present the broad contours of new work on Orientalism, law, census, education, print culture, Christian missions and conversions, colonial science, and colonial discourses around race and gender. Together, these comprise research that has transformed our understanding of the late-colonial era in exciting, if also sometimes controversial and problematic, ways. A short concluding third section will outline the situation in the Indian princely states via three examples.

CONSOLIDATING THE RAJ

Imperial Ceremony and Restructuring after 1857

The 'Indian Empire' that the British proclaimed at a grandiose imperial assemblage in 1877 was, and would remain for long, an autocracy veiled thinly by an ideology of paternalistic benevolence, and by occasional promises of an eventual shift to trusteeship and the training of Indians for self-government. The empire was organized as an elaborate hierarchy. It was headed by the viceroy and secretary of state, who functioned under spasmodic and largely notional parliamentary control. After the Crown takeover of the East India Company (EIC) in 1858, the personal role of this combination of viceroy and secretary of state was enhanced. The two now came into much closer contact with each other through the communication revolution epitomized by the submarine cable and the Suez Canal (1865–9). The EIC's affairs had been the subject of lively political and economic issues in England, and renewals of the Charter Act (enabling the EIC to continue) at twenty-year intervals had since 1793 provoked stormy debates in Parliament. After 1858, by contrast, annual presentations of Indian financial statements, and of the country's Moral and Material Progress Reports, were seen as routine, often quickly emptying the House of Commons. The EIC court of directors remained influential through its patronage functions. The Council of India, set up by the 1858 Act as a check on the secretary of state, never acquired much importance. It could be overruled on most matters and bypassed through 'urgent communications', or by 'secret orders' to the viceroy.

In India, too, the railway and the telegraph progressively brought local governments closer to Calcutta, making governance highly centralized. Coupland, a senior bureaucrat of the mid-twentieth century, reminds us that there was 'no trace of the federal idea' before 1919.[1] The Indian Councils Act of 1861 had strengthened the

---

[1] Coupland 1944: 10.

viceroy's authority over his executive council by substituting a 'port-folio' or departmental system for corporate functioning. Council members were now put in charge of specific separate departments and the earlier practice of collective discussions was abandoned. The Imperial and Provincial Legislative Councils, enlarged or set up by the same Act, did include a few non-official Indians, but remained largely decorative. Consisting entirely of nominated members before 1892, these councils lacked, before the reforms of that year, any statutory powers for discussing budgets or putting forward questions.

Imperial political structures now reflected an unprecedented thrust towards a comprehensive centralization and integration of the subcontinent. This was the most striking feature of late-nineteenth-century administrative developments. Indian collaborators, naturally, remained indispensable to the day-to-day governance of such a vast country. After the panic of 1857, there was an enhanced emphasis on consolidating the empire's links with princes and landed magnates. The 662 Indian princes, in particular—most of them crudely despotic in their several ways—were to remain the most loyal bulwarks of the state till the very end of the colonial era. Over time, such alliances with dependent 'feudal' elements actually became increasingly important for the Raj. Macaulay's alternative vision—of a loyal English-educated intelligentsia brown in colour but white in thought and taste (as he put it)—was beginning to turn a bit sour by the 1870s and 1880s for the modern intelligentsia had begun, by this time, to articulate more and more strident criticism of aspects of colonial governance.

The decades that succeeded the suppression of the Rebellion of 1857 were marked by very major transformations. It can be argued that it was only at this point that a colonial version of 'modernity' began to manifest itself in many spheres of Indian life, indicating clear ruptures from pre-colonial times. Railway statistics provide, per-haps, the best indicator of the advance of such change: the figure for length of railway lines shot up from 432 miles in 1859 to over 5000 ten years later, and approached 25,000 miles by the end of the century. Yet modernization went hand in hand with a considerable 'inven-tion of traditions'. The post-1857 colonial search for dependable allies among princes and landlords had its counterpart in an important strand of British Indian thinking and policies which sought to dress the Raj in Indian feudal clothes. These were borrowed, in highly transmuted ways, mainly from the heritage of the Mughals. But they also included an admixture of reinvented European medievalism. Official architecture tried to insert Oriental decorative motifs within European-style buildings. This led to juxtapositions of Indo-Saracenic with Victorian Gothic. Indian soldiers, dressed in Western uniforms before 1860, had now to put on turbans, sashes, and tunics which their masters imagined to be Mughal, Rajput, or Sikh. The new title of 'viceroy' which the governor general acquired in 1858 to imply a direct relationship with the Crown, whose agent he now became, allowed him to dispense honours in return for faithful service rendered by groups of loyal Indians. After 1858 the viceroy, Canning, went around northern India, distributing honours and titles to members of the Indian elite who had proved themselves dependable during the Rebellion. This took place amidst imitation-Mughal ceremonies. An earlier element of a symbolic 'incorporation' of the subject into the body of the sovereign was now displaced to make way for overt signs of subordination alone. 'Star of India', a non-hereditary order of knighthood for both Europeans and Indians, began to be awarded from 1861.

Efforts were made to marshal the princes into a complicated hierarchical order marked by highly regulated distinctions in the prescribed mode of their apparel, and by the number of retainers, weapons, and gun salutes allowed to each. In January 1877, at the initiative of Disraeli and Lytton, a grandiose 'imperial assemblage' was organized to proclaim Victoria the Empress of India, her formal title being Indianized to Kaiser-i-Hind. The assemblage was at Delhi, the erstwhile seat of Mughal authority, now also the scene of the British military triumph in 1857. A cult of Mutiny heroism—celebrations of British 'martyrdom' and the eventual imperial triumph over what was depicted as native villainy, violence, and rape—grew rapidly. This involved regular British pilgrimages to the Delhi Ridge, the Lucknow Residency, and the site of the 'Cawnpore massacre'. The ceremonial of the grand durbar, to be repeated in 1903 and 1911 for successive sovereigns, had also its underside—more indicative perhaps of basic colonial realities—for this colossally expensive spectacle was held in the midst of a major famine in western India. It also necessitated the eviction of peasants from a hundred villages around Delhi to make space for regal encampments. A British army officer, whose Urdu failed him, improved the occasion by addressing soldiers waiting for their decorations as 'swine' (*suar*, in place of *sowar*).[2]

Viceregal Attitudes—Liberal Rhetoric, Conservative Compulsion

New and enormous powers, concentrated in the hands of the Viceroy and the Secretary of State, make a brief discussion of their personal attitudes and political affiliations relevant. By 1885, large groups of well-informed Indians were most alert to political and party differences among Viceroys. They followed carefully, they made a black and white contrast between the authoritarianism of Lytton and the relative liberalism of Ripon. They also learnt to relate these differences to the conflict between Tories and Liberals in British politics. Some may recall Satyajit Ray's quite persuasive depiction, in the film 'Charulata', of a Bengali gentleman who celebrates a Liberal electoral victory in Britain with much pomp with his friends. Writing a history of 'Indian National Evolution' in 1915, the Moderate Congress leader Ambicacharan Majumdar counterposed 'gathering clouds' under Lytton to the 'clouds lifted' under Ripon. A more recent historian similarly contrasted the 'Conservative Adventure' of 1869–80 (under Mayo, Northbrooke, and Lytton) with the 'Liberal Experiment' of Ripon and Dufferin in 1880–8, despite his far more advanced historical sophistication.[3]

Rhetoric apart, the really significant difference lay in a short-lived attempt of the early 1880s to expand the circle of Indian collaborators from princes and zamindars to English-educated middle-class groups. Lytton had dismissed the latter as 'Babus, whom we have educated to write semi-seditious articles in the Native Press'; Ripon, by contrast, liked to talk about 'the hourly increasing . . . necessity of making the educated natives the friends, instead of the enemies of our rule.'[4] Local self-government which Ripon introduced with much fanfare was, however, related basically to a necessary measure of financial

---

[2] Cohn 1983: 204.
[3] Gopal 1965: 135.
[4] Seal 1968: 149.

decentralization. The unexpected fury that marked the reactions of resident Europeans in India to the Ilbert Bill in 1883—despite the fact that it would merely have empowered a handful of Indian officials to try Europeans in district courts—quickly ended this 'liberal' experiment. But it did invest Ripon, under whose administration the measure was sought to be implemented, with a largely unjustified martyr's halo in the perceptions of middle-class Indians.

Under Dufferin (1884–8), Lansdowne (1888–94), and Elgin (1894–8), the differences between Tory and Liberal attitudes towards India became progressively less evident. Uneasily and ineffectually, Dufferin sought to have the best of all possible worlds. He surrendered to European commercial pressure with regard to the annexation of Upper Burma, an area important for its natural resources. He introduced pro-landlord modifications in Bengal and Oudh Tenancy Bills at a time when the middle-class Indian Association wanted some concessions for tenants (*raiyats*). He briefly flirted with Allan Octavian Hume, who urged him to support the formation of the Indian National Congress, but then violently attacked the same organization at his St Andrews' dinner speech just before his departure from India. As Dinshaw Wacha pointed out to Dadabhai Naoroji in private correspondence, in the end he managed to please no one; in December 1888 Wacha went so far as to say that he could 'tolerate a Lytton but not a Dufferin'.[5] How irrelevant British party divisions were becoming in the Indian context was revealed by the promptness with which Lansdowne, appointed by the Tory Salisbury, took up Dufferin's private pleas for an elective element in provincial councils. Both argued in almost identical terms that such a move would take the wind out of the sails of the Congress.

Concessions to the Lancashire cotton manufacture lobby, in the form of countervailing excise duties on Indian cotton (after financial needs had compelled the Indian government to impose a duty on imported cloth), were made under Elgin, a viceroy appointed by Gladstone's last administration. Yet that Liberal 'Grand Old Man' himself badly let down his Indian admirers in 1892 by refusing to support an amendment to Lord Cross's Bill which sought to introduce

[5] Patwardhan 1977: 137.

elections for Indian legislatures. He did so again in 1893 when he allowed the secretaries of state, Kimberley and Lansdowne, to ignore a House of Commons resolution for simultaneous Indian Civil Service examinations in India and England.

The irrelevance of party divisions may have had something to do with the political confusion in England after the mid-1880s, when Liberals split over Gladstone's Irish Home Rule efforts. The Liberal tradition, in any case, had always been ambiguous: it included Whig admirers of aristocratic leadership, Radical advocates of greater democracy, Liberal-imperialists difficult to distinguish from Conservatives in foreign policy, and 'Little-Englanders' genuinely opposed to military expansion (though seldom to the considerable material gains for Britain from free trade). More important than political ideologies, however, were certain consequences that flowed from the overall logic of the colonial situation. It is to these long-term trends that we now turn.

British Indian Foreign Policy Before Curzon

While there was no return before Curzon's viceregal tenure (1899–1905) to the flamboyant imperialism of Lytton, colonial attitudes remained on the whole considerably more aggressive than they had been in the 'masterly inactivity' days of the 1860s. This becomes understandable in the context of sharpening imperialist rivalry, with Russia advancing towards Afghanistan and Persia, and France establishing control over Indochina. Liberals in opposition had violently denounced Lytton's Afghan adventure. Yet Ripon's policies, in the end, hardly marked a total departure. The plan for breaking up Afghanistan was abandoned, along with the insistence of the Indian government on placing a British agent in Kabul. But Abdur Rahman was allowed to continue as amir, with controls on his foreign policy which the amir had to accept in return for a subsidy. The British retained Pishin and Shibi and turned them into British Baluchistan in 1887.

In Dufferin's time the Russian seizure of the Afghan border post of Panjdeh (March 1885) led to acute tension between the two imperial powers. Eventually the issue was submitted to arbitration by the king of Denmark. An agreement concerning the Afghan frontier was reached with Russia in July 1887. With the militarist Lord Roberts as commander-in-chief from 1887 to 1892, a forward policy was followed, however, on the north-west frontier. This involved numerous expensive expeditions against Afghan tribes, the construction of strategic railways, the imposition in 1893 of the Durand Agreement demarcating the Indo-Afghan border, and the British seizure and eventual retention of Chitral despite Liberal qualms.

Dufferin's administration was also marked by the final major extension of British Indian territory: the annexation of Upper (northern) Burma in January 1886. A combination of political and commercial reasons helps to explain the decision to march British troops there in November 1885. The British were suspicious of French influence spilling over from Indo-China into neighbouring Burma, in the context of a trade treaty signed by the Burmese king Thibaw in January 1885 and a railway agreement with a French company in July. The British Chamber of Commerce in Rangoon was eager that Burma be annexed, particularly after Thibaw had imposed a heavy fine on a British timber trading company for fraudulent practices in August 1885. Randolph Churchill had assured Dufferin that in Britain, too, 'the large commercial interests', particularly Manchester, would 'warmly support annexation'. Upper Burma appeared attractive both in itself and as a possible gateway to south-west China. The Salisbury ministry had enthusiastically supported Dufferin; the Gladstone cabinet, which had come into power when annexation was formalized, displayed a few qualms of conscience but then agreed to it, albeit 'with great reluctance': a difference that just about sums up the actual distinction between Tories and Liberals on imperial matters in this period. The effete Mandalay court of Burma predictably collapsed almost without a fight, but it took five years and 40,000 troops to crush popular guerrilla resistance in that country. Meanwhile, timber, which was brought in from the new conquest, helped to build a sumptuous viceregal palace at the summer capital of Simla.

The Army and Military Policy

All such adventures meant heavier outlays on the army. To this we must add the deployment of Indian troops abroad, largely at a cost to the Indian exchequer: in Egypt in 1882 by Gladstone despite Ripon's protests, in Sudan against the Mahdi movement in 1885–6 and again in 1896, and in China against the Boxer rebels in 1900. The Panjdeh war scare was the occasion for an increase in the strength of the army by 30,000. Military expenditure accounted for 41.9 per cent of the Indian government's budget in 1881–2 and 45.4 per cent ten years later. By 1904–5, under Curzon, it had gone up to 51.9 per cent.

Military policy, in fact, provides numerous insights into the real nature of colonial rule. It was predominantly shaped by the memory of 1857. The British, Dufferin commented in December 1888, 'should always remember the lessons that were learnt with such terrible experience 30 years ago.' Two commissions, of 1859 and 1879, insisted on certain new basic principles upon the foundations of which the army should be built: it must be one-third European in its composition, as against 14 per cent before 1857; there should be strict European monopoly over the artillery (even the rifles given to Indian soldiers were of an inferior quality before 1900!); and it should have what Sir John Strachey once described as the 'policy of water-tight compartments . . . to prevent the growth of any dangerous identity of feeling from community of race, religious, caste, or local sympathies.'[6] The divide-and-rule principle had, in fact, been stated with enviable clarity by Secretary of State Wood in 1862: 'I wish to have a different and rival spirit in different regiments, so that Sikh might fire into Hindoo, Gorkha into either, without any scruple in case of need.' The 1879 Army Commission reiterated the point: 'Next to the grand counterpoise of a sufficient European force comes the counterpoise of natives against natives.'[7]

Recent research on the EIC army has highlighted the ways in which recruitment policies and assumptions had helped to consolidate distinctions of caste and ethnicity.[8] What the post-1857 era added to these was a clearer ideology of 'martial races'. This assumed that good soldiers could be recruited only from specific communities. The notion was developed particularly from the late 1880s under Lord Roberts and used to justify recruitment mainly from Sikhs and Gurkhas,

[6] Strachey 1888: 63.
[7] Singh 1963: 140, 142.
[8] See Kolff 1990; Alavi 1995.

both these being relatively marginal religious and ethnic groups less likely to be drawn to all-India nationalist movements. There was, of course, no question of racial equality or Indianization of command. Even after a slight rise in salaries, an Indian private got Rs 9 a month in 1895, while his British counterpart received Rs 24 plus a number of allowances. As late as 1926, the Indian Sandhurst Committee was visualizing a 50 per cent Indian officer cadre—for 1952!

Financial and Administrative Pressures in the Late Nineteenth Century

Foreign adventures and army expansion meant, inevitably, financial strain. From 1873 on, as the world capitalist economy began a long downturn period, the burden on the Indian exchequer was greatly enhanced by the rapid depreciation of the silver rupee in relation to gold. A big part of Indian expenses had to be paid in gold-standard-based sterling: the pensions of British Indian civilians and army men, the costs of the secretary of state's establishment in London, the interest on the India debt, and all other items that went into the so-called 'home charges'. Yet the rupee, which stood at 2 shillings in 1872, was worth little more than 1s 2d by 1893–4. Sabyasachi Bhattacharya has explored in detail the 'financial foundations of the Raj', and Cambridge-based historians have made a significant contribution towards illuminating the connections between financial problems, administrative pressures, and nationalist movements. 'The administrative grid', in Anil Seal's words, had to be 'pressed down more firmly by the heavier intervention of the Raj in local matters.'[9] In more concrete terms, this involved attempts to extend old forms of taxation and explore new ones—processes fraught with numerous problems as the government faced a number of contradictory pulls.

Land revenue remained the single biggest source of income. There had been much talk about extending the Permanent Settlement to new areas in the aftermath of 1857, the hope being that, by giving landed groups a permanently settled revenue level and near-total control over rent extraction, the alliance between the state and such groups would

[9] See Seal in Gallagher 1973: 10.

be cemented. Now, all that had to be forgotten. Receipts from land revenue increased from Rs 19.67 crores in 1881–2 to Rs 23 crores in 1901–2 despite the devastating famines of the 1890s. This provided, as we shall see, a major and continuous nationalist grievance. At the same time, too sharp an enhancement of the land tax was feared as both politically dangerous and economically unwise, for the British also urgently wanted to develop the production for export of raw cotton, jute, sugar, wheat, and other agricultural commodities. The proportion of land revenue to the total state income was, in fact, gradually decreasing: the net revenue for the years cited above was 46.86 crores and Rs 60.79 crores respectively. The persistence of the older kind of nationalist critique of colonial policy—that there was an excessive revenue burden—has obscured the significance of this relative decline. In Mughal times, and with considerable continuities into the early colonial era, the state land revenue demand had been the principal form of surplus extraction from the peasantry. A transition began from the nineteenth century that eventually made land tax an insignificant part of the income of the state. One is tempted to speculate that this long-term structural change may also have contributed to a significant shift in the nature of popular movements in the countryside. In Mughal and early colonial times alike, rural rebellions had involved communities led by zamindars against state officials. In late-colonial times, however, questions of rent, indebtedness, and tenurial claims—setting sections of peasants or sharecroppers against landlords and moneylenders—would come to acquire much greater salience.[10]

Import duties on British manufactures flooding the country would have greatly helped budget-making and also pleased politically conscious Indians. But Lancashire repeatedly dictated otherwise. Duties on cotton were bitterly attacked from the mid-1870s by the Manchester lobby, backed by Salisbury. It was alleged that such duties protected the new Bombay textile industry and violated the sacred principles of free trade. Lytton reduced these duties in 1878–9 despite the expense of the Afghan war. Ripon abolished them altogether in 1882. In the 1890s, when a restoration became inevitable in the face

[10] Sarkar 1983: 17–18, 30–6.

of massive deficits, a notorious countervailing excise on Indian cloth was imposed together with the revived import duty in 1894 and 1896. Starting with James Wilson in the 1860s, finance members of the viceroy's council had toyed with the idea of an income tax despite the opposition to it of Europeans and influential Indians alike. In 1886, after Panjdeh and Burma, Dufferin gave it a systematic and permanent shape. Two years later, the heavily regressive salt tax, a real burden for the poor, was greatly increased.

Bayly's study of Allahabad, together with Washbrook's on South India, brought out the linkages between this mid-1880s spurt in taxation and the unusually wide support for the Congress sessions in Madras (1887) and Allahabad (1888).[11] Washbrook also provided interesting data on long-term trends at the provincial level. Thus, in Madras, land revenue provided 57 per cent of the total in 1880, but only 28 per cent in 1920. Excise duties on liquor, by contrast, went up from Rs 60 lakhs in 1882–3 to Rs 5.4 crores in 1920. There was also an expansion of forest revenues, which meant restrictions on age-old customary rights to pastures and fuel for tribal and lower-caste food-gatherers, pastoralists, shifting cultivators, and poor peasants, as well as the occasional curbing of more prosperous rural interests. Provincial associations had already protested against forest laws and grazing restrictions in Madras in the 1880s and in Assam in the 1890s. The issue would be repeatedly raised, as we shall see, in early Congress sessions.

Frykenberg's study of public administration in Guntur district in the early nineteenth century revealed a picture of considerable independence and financial benefits that were enjoyed by subordinate Indian officials who were closely connected with local Indian notables in the relatively loosely organized Company administration.[12] Post-1858 financial pressures greatly reduced such autonomy.[13] We find interesting confirmation of the trend in the remote Sylhet region of East Bengal. The nationalist leader Bipinchandra Pal provided a

---

[11] See Bayly 1975; and Washbrook 1976.

[12] See Frykenberg 1965.

[13] This process is analysed in detail for Madras by Washbrook: see Washbrook 1976.

critical account of a gradual curbing of the powers of the zamindars—the 'natural leaders'—as centralized bureaucratic administration penetrated deeper into the localities.[14]

Financial pressures did not contribute to indigenous elite grievances alone. In 1890, when Moderate Congress politics of timid 'mendicancy' seemed the only kind of nationalism that existed or could exist, the Bombay governor wrote confidentially to the viceroy: 'The Forest policy, the Abkari [excise] policy, the Salt duty, the screwing up of land revenue by revision settlements, all make us odious . . . We know pretty well what the educated natives want, but what the feelings are of the uneducated I admit I don't know.'[15] A vivid awareness of possible fires underground seems aparent. Forty years later, Mahatma Gandhi forged subcontinental movements precisely around the issues of salt and land revenue, excise and forest rights.

Local Self-Government, Council Reform, and Divide-and-Rule

Financial pressures and administrative tightening had to be combined with a search for more Indian collaborators if these were not to prove politically dangerous. 'Systems of nomination, representation and election were all means of enlisting Indians to work for imperial ends.'[16] Financial and political aspects were neatly combined in the development of local self-government. The process really began under Conservative Mayo, not Liberal Ripon. The dominant motive was to tackle financial difficulties by shifting charges for local requirements on to new local taxes. But Mayo, too, felt that 'We must gradually associate with ourselves in the government of this country more of the native element.' This second political strand was displayed prominently in Ripon's famous May 1882 Resolution that promised elected majorities and local chairmen for local bodies. This remained, however, a promise implemented only slowly and incompletely because of resistance from

[14] Pal 1932/1973: ch. 8.

[15] Reay to Lansdowne, 20 February 1890. Lansdowne Private Papers, Commonwealth Relations, India Office Collection, National Archives of India.

[16] Gallagher 1973: 10.

most provincial bureaucrats: Ripon's Finance Member, Evelyn Baring, even said that 'we shall not subvert the British Empire by allowing the Bengali Babu to discuss his own schools and drains.' How important the financial aspect remained throughout the process of devolution may be indicated by a later example: the setting up of Union Boards in Bengal in 1919–20 immediately implied a 50 per cent hike in the *chaukidari* (village watchmen) tax, provoking a massive and successful nationalist protest in Midnapur.

From the late 1880s the growth of the Congress indicated to the rulers that the only antidote to serious nationalist opposition lay in collaboration with Indians at higher levels of administration. This would have to be sought mainly through successive and carefully measured doses of Legislative Council reform. Lord Cross's Indian Council Act of 1892 enlarged the non-official element in legislatures. Non-officials were to comprise 10 out of the 16 members in the Imperial Council, for instance. Without conceding elections explicitly, this did empower the colonial authorities to consult local bodies, university senates, chambers of commerce, and landlord associations in nominating members. The councillors obtained the right to discuss the budget and put questions, though not the power to move amendments, vote on the budget, or ask supplementaries.

The process of so-called 'constitutional reform' was associated in this period with two other major strands of official policy: periodic attempts to 'rally the Moderates' (the phrase was Minto's in the wake of the rise of Extremism, but the attempt existed long before him), and a skilful use of divide-and-rule techniques. Local self-government, despite Ripon's high hopes, was not particularly successful in achieving the first objective, since municipalities and district boards were given little real power and financial resources. Nationalists entered such bodies, made some use of their patronage possibilities, but in general refused to confine their energies to the improvement of drains. The 1892 reforms did possibly help to reduce the tempo of Congress agitation for a few years, as a number of prominent leaders found their way into provincial and imperial councils: Lalmohan Ghosh, W.C. Bonnerji, and Surendranath Banerjea in Bengal; Pherozeshah Mehta, Gokhale, and even for a time Tilak in Bombay; and Mehta followed by Gokhale in the Imperial Council. Demands for further council reform were not very prominent on the agenda of Congress sessions between 1894 and 1900. The effect was quite shortlived, however. The same years saw the first stirrings of Extremist nationalism. By 1904, the Congress, as a whole, was again demanding a further big dose of legislative reform.

Ultimately, the more significant instrument of policy was the encouraging of divisions among Indians along lines that were predominantly religious but which could also sometimes be language- and caste-based. Nationalists tended to exaggerate the element of direct and conscious British responsibility here, for the fissures often had deeper roots. In so far as they were constituted or sharpened under colonialism, they needed to be related to more fundamental aspects of colonial knowledge-formation and governance—notably, as we shall see shortly, law and census enumeration. And in any case, deliberate official instigation apart, conflicts over scarce resources in education, administrative jobs, and political spoils lay in the very logic of colonial underdevelopment.

Still, it can hardly be denied that the explicitly political assumptions and initiatives of British officialdom sharpened such divisions in the late colonial decades. An insistence on so-called natural and insurmountable chasms separating local communities had become the dominant trope in colonial discourses. In 1888, the year Dufferin proclaimed the Congress to be a microscopic minority, Sir John Strachey assured Cambridge undergraduates: 'There is not, and never was an India . . . no Indian nation, no people of India of which we hear so much . . . That men of the Punjab, Bengal, the North West Provinces and Madras, should ever feel that they belong to one great Indian nation, is impossible.'[17] The vehemence was related almost certainly to a growing unease over the stability of colonial governance. Official policies were already well geared towards stimulating the differences among Indians through their dispensation of favours to one or other community in ways that varied across time. Muslims, for instance, were for long held in greater suspicion than Hindus on account of the former's association with the displaced Mughal rule, their allegedly greater role in the 1857 Rebellion, and their involvement in

[17] Strachey 1888: 29.

anti-British Wahhabi militancy. W.W. Hunter's *Indian Mussalmans* heralded a significant change that roughly coincided with the beginnings of political organization among predominantly educated Hindu middle-class groups. Within an already well-established official stereotype of a homogeneous Muslim community, Muslims were now projected as imbued with dangerous memories of lost imperial splendour, as being currently in a 'backward condition' and therefore in need of special British patronage. Dufferin described them in 1888 as 'a nation of fifty millions', supposedly uniform in religious and social customs and sharing a 'remembrance of the days when, enthroned at Delhi, they reigned supreme from the Himalayas to Cape Comorin.' These were propositions as absurd as they were politically useful in subsequent years to British rule. In large parts of the country Muslims remained what they had long been: poor peasants or artisans with no pretensions to an imperial past or heritage.

Studies of the United Provinces by Francis Robinson and of the Punjab by Gerald Barrier have revealed how the introduction of municipalities elected by a limited, property- and education-based franchise immediately sharpened Hindu–Muslim tensions in both provinces. By 1885 the Punjab government under Sir Alfred Lyall was already introducing religious community-based separate representation in towns like Hoshiarpur, Lahore, and Multan. The original motive, as Barrier suggests, could have been related to a smoothening over of existing tensions. Yet it remains an undeniable fact that separate electorates tended to harden lines of division by encouraging and even forcing community leaders to cultivate primarily their own community followings. At the level of council reforms, too, Lansdowne insisted in March 1893 that representation had to be of 'types and classes rather than areas or numbers': the acceptance of demands for separate electorates lay not too far ahead in the future.

Hindu–Muslim tensions could also pose serious law-and-order problems, which meant that official policy could never be free of ambiguities. Secretary of State Hamilton's confidential letter to Elgin on 7 May 1897 perhaps best exemplifies the typical colonial thinking on the subject: 'I am sorry to hear of the increasing friction between Hindus and Mohammedans in the North West and the Punjab. One hardly knows what to wish for: unity of ideas and actions would be very dangerous politically; divergence of ideas and collision are administratively troublesome. Of the two the latter is the least risky, though it throws anxiety and responsibility upon those on the spot where the friction exists.'[18]

KNOWLEDGE AND GOVERNANCE

Orientalism, Old and New

From around the mid to late 1980s, Edward Said's *Orientalism* (1978) excited fresh research on Western discourses about the colonized. The new trajectory helped to bring about major shifts in the understanding of colonial structures, policies, and underlying cultural assumptions. Mainstream-nationalist and left-leaning varieties of anti-colonial historiography had both tended to combine denunciations of imperial economic and political domination with considerable ambiguity over its cultural dimensions. The more obvious elements of racism in colonial writings and assumptions were, of course, often pointed out, but there remained some considerable degree of approval for the unearthing of much of South Asia's past through generations of the European scholarly endeavour that began with William Jones and the Asiatic Society of Bengal (founded in 1784). An immense colonial archive on nineteenth- and early-twentieth-century India had been accumulated through a multitude of administrative files and reports, surveys and census operations, scientific observations and research. These were widely and sometimes uncritically accessed for providing source material on a scale quite impossible in earlier times. Perceptions about the apparently modernizing aspects of the colonial impact—most notably, the new middle-class culture spawned by English education— were, on the other hand, more varied. There was, still, a widespread common sense about some kind of cultural 'awakening' or 'renaissance' in the nineteenth century. Academic criticism of the 'renaissance model', developed among a Calcutta-based group of historians in the early 1970s, highlighting among other

---

[18] Hamilton to Elgin, 7 May 1897. Lord Elgin, Private Papers, India Office Library and Records, National Archives of India.

things the complicities of the modernizing literati with colonialism. It assumed, nonetheless, that the key problem was of insufficient or colonially distorted modernity. 'Modernity', or 'post-Enlightenment reason' as such, was not yet under attack.

Said's work brought in moods of systematic methodological suspicion about Western images of the non-West. These have proven particularly attractive to students of English literature when reacting against the dominance of Western literature and canonical Western literary criticism. Such scholars now tried to go against the grain of the existing widespread assumptions concerning supposedly timeless and universal 'humanist' values. From this starting point there developed a larger and more generalized critique of colonial and Western discourses of all sorts. These now came to be primarily animated by the inseparable connections between power and knowledge, elaborated most strikingly by Michel Foucault. There was, moreover, a still broader context for the new turn. An academic counter-orthodoxy soon developed which was, at times, loosely termed 'post-modernist': a stance sharply critical—occasionally to the point of the complete rejection—of 'modernity' as a whole. The 'Enlightenment rationality' in which modernity was supposedly grounded appeared to many now to be incorrigibly Western, male, and inhospitable to the recognition of cultural differences.

Colonial discourse analysis is nowadays often sought to be comprehended under the rubric of 'postcoloniality'. This has provoked much controversy in turn. The opposition to postcoloniality can occasionally be rooted in a sheer conservative desire to stick with past celebrations of modernity, but there is also considerable and legitimate unease about the many simplifications that postcolonial scholarship has brought in its train to South Asian historical studies. The Saidian—and perhaps even more the Foucauldian—turn, however, has inspired much valuable research, and this has at times been helpful in overcoming some of the inadequacies and initial simplifications of an earlier historiography that preceded the postcolonial turn.

'Orientalism', before Said, referred to the kind of modern European knowledge about Asia that based itself on studies of Asian languages, particularly the ones termed classical ever since William Jones discovered affinities between Sanskrit and ancient Greek and

Latin. The term tended to connote a highly respectful attitude to the cultures and religions of that ancient or classical era, though often much less so to those of more recent times. Saidian frames have vastly expanded the meaning of Orientalism, signifying, at times, virtually all Western representations of the Orient in the era of European domination. Such extensions have helped to bring out linkages and imbrications with power relations within works of Western literature, scholarship, and colonial documentation, as well as elements in them of implicit ethnocentrism and racism. This has meant a systematic questioning of canons and archives previously considered more or less 'objective'. The value of such exposure is undoubted: our sources and frames of analysis for not only the colonial but also for much of the precolonial past has been constituted precisely in this era of dominant colonial power-knowledge regimes, by European scholars and administrators, and by Indians trained in such ways. We will need to confront and go beyond many such Orientalist constructs in subsequent sections. To take only the most obvious instance: Orientalist scholarship contributed decisively to the formation of a hugely influential stereotype whereby an ancient time of 'Hindu' achievement was followed by one of medieval 'Muslim' decline, and then, possibly, an 'awakening' or 'renaissance' under colonial aegis. The resultant tripartite periodization of Indian history into Hindu, Muslim, and British has often had fairly disastrous academic and political consequences. Academically, the division cannot strictly be sustained. Politically, it has tended to demarcate Hindu histories and Muslim ones, thus stimulating communal stereotypes.

Yet the expansion of the category of Orientalism by Said has also created major problems. The term can now simplify and homogenize significant distinctions in alarming ways. It is in danger of reproducing through inversion the simplistic dichotomy of West and non-West, both implicitly assumed to be uniform and unchanging: precisely that which Said had rightly set out to demolish. William Jones, James Mill, and Thomas Babington Macaulay are all nowadays sometimes collectively denounced as Orientalists, though Mill's *History of British India* was extremely critical of antiquarianism of the Jones variety, while Macaulay's denigration of the worth of all Indian knowledge and literature in his Education Minute of 1835 is, of course, notorious and contrasts greatly with the views of William Jones. To point out these distinctions is not to suggest that connections between British Orientalist and Indological studies on the one hand, and the colonial project on the other, are not fairly obvious, but only to suggest that differences can be erased and complexities sidestepped in the interest of arriving at a singular political argument. To give another and related example: EIC officials in late-eighteenth-century Bengal needed an entry into religious-cum-legal traditions and revenue documents maintained in Sanskrit as well as Persian—to mention only the most obvious linkage. Indology, however, came in the course of the nineteenth and early twentieth centuries to flourish most of all in German universities, i.e. in a part of Europe which, for a long time, had virtually no colonial possessions. So, the terms 'Western' and 'European' do not carry the weight of the distinctions that are necessary when applying to them the charge of 'racism', even if racism's close bond with the expansion of the West since the sixteenth century is undoubted.

Ethnocentric arrogance is fairly cross-cultural, but what has been qualitatively new in the modern era is the power developed by dominant groups in one section of the world to impose their values and assumptions on others, and even get them internalized on a global scale. Still, the Indo-European, or 'Aryan', racial myth inaugurated by William Jones did suggest a sense of kinship between the British overlords and some, at least, of their Indian subjects. As such, the Orientalism of this earlier time does not entirely fit with the more aggressive subsequent varieties of European racism. It may be helpful also to distinguish between the Macaulay–Mill (as well as missionary) variety of cultural ethnocentrism or racism, which assumed the superiority of one or other set of Western values, and subsequent varieties of biological racism. The Macaulay–Mill views visualized the gradual spread of supposedly superior white values among non-white peoples through processes such as Christian conversion, Western education, and modernizing reform which would eventually eradicate cultural differences between races. These perspectives stood in sharp contrast with the more blatant biological racism during the high noon of European imperialism. Racism of the second kind came to be buttressed by selective appropriations of Darwin which were then deployed to create a dominant assumption—the eternal inferiority of 'lesser breeds'. This variety of racism was interested not in imposing 'modern' institutions and values, nor 'Enlightenment rationality', but in shoring up what it considered 'traditional' in Indian society. I have already indicated that it was this latter set of attitudes that, on the whole, came to predominate in the late-colonial era. They manifested themselves, for instance, in the widespread 'invention of traditions' that has been touched upon at the beginning of this chapter.

Colonial discourse analysis also needs to be brought into closer relation with both global histories and internal developments within metropolitan countries. Many of the stereotypes about the non-West actually had close affinities with assumptions about inferiorized Western groups—women, ethnic minorities (such as Irish immigrants), troublesome workers, and the 'undeserving' or criminalized poor in Britain. Shifts in such discourses of domination were also interrelated. Recent research indicates connections with eras when the established order felt particularly threatened by radical solidarities with non-racial, internationalist politics. The panic inspired by the French Revolution—which in its radical Jacobin phase preached international revolution and freed slaves in Haiti—produced more aggressive brands of Christianity and conservative nationalism in England. It dispelled the cosmopolitan moods of the Enlightenment era. It was hardly an accident, again, that biological racism developed rapidly in the wake of the failed European revolutions of 1848—that 'springtime of the peoples and seedtime of the racists'. The London-based *Ethnological Journal* began its first (June 1848) number with the categorical assertion, 'in the name of science', that the notion of 'the natural equality of men', responsible for so much disorder, is *'false'*. And in 1866—when memories of the 1857 Rebellion were still fresh, a revolt of ex-slaves took place in Jamaica, and militant demonstrations were held in London's Hyde Park demanding the democratization of Parliament—the ethnologist Robert Knox was violently abusing John Stuart Mill for adhering to a 'false daydream of racial equality'.[19]

A further set of problems that has troubled many about Saidian critiques is their excessive culturalism: their abstraction from the more

---

[19] Guha 1999: 12; Susan Bayly in Robb 1995: 179.

material processes of colonial domination. Reduction into the purely discursive has sometimes led to exaggerated notions of an absolute rupture between pre-colonial and colonial times, the former in some danger of romanticization as a time virtually free from internal tensions and structures of domination. A reader of Ronald Inden's *Imagining India* (1990), for instance, might get the impression that caste in Indian history has been little more than a colonial discursive construct. An important corrective to such a position has been provided by the work of C.A. Bayly and scholars associated with him. These works have tried to integrate some of the insights of colonial discourse analysis with close attention to socio-economic and political processes that go beyond the narrowly discursive.

Much of what has come to be widely assumed as 'traditional' in Indian society does seem to have come into existence in the colonial era. The processes of 'construction' or 'invention', however, were more complicated than a mere imposition of alien colonial-Western categories on a helpless, passive, and undifferentiated mass of the colonized. The burgeoning discipline of environmental history has added important new insights here. As the next chapter will indicate in more detail, colonial pacification, pressures for more revenue and exportable products, and, somewhat later, demographic growth, combined to bring about large-scale deforestation. Settled peasant agriculture expanded at the cost of communities of often migratory food-gatherers and pastoralists, helping to consolidate, and in some regions to constitute, the image of India as overwhelmingly a land of unchanging villages. There was a simultaneous and related expansion of the sway of the 'classic' brahmanical model of firmly hierarchized castes, well entrenched for many centuries, in the more prosperous agricultural tracts—it was, however, not universal. Knowledge about both high-Hindu and high-Islamic norms spread through 'Orientalist' research, vernacular translation, and the vastly improved communications networks developed in the colonial era: above all, with the coming of print culture and the railways. The influence of 'traditional' elites, as we shall see shortly, was consolidated also by the specifics of colonial law, census enumeration, and 'modern' education.

Initial applications of Saidian ideas to colonial India had suggested a one-way flow of power-knowledge, a nearly complete acculturation of Indians by the West. The colonized middle-class educated Indian was thereby thought to have been rendered incapable of more than what one influential historian termed a 'derivative discourse'.[20] We shall have occasion to note many instances where the reach and impact of colonial knowledge remained limited, and where its role may have been necessary to producing—through maps, surveys, and masses of apparently rigorous statistical 'facts'—what were only comforting illusions of total imperial-bureaucratic control. The idea of 'derivative discourse' seems to have been quickly recognized as the most vulnerable part of Saidian readings, for it was abandoned, or at least significantly modified, fairly soon.[21] Clearly, indigenous inputs—'material' and 'cultural' or 'discursive'—are vital to the more complicated historical narratives that have emerged through recent research, in which it is recognized that early Orientalist scholarship was heavily dependent on indigenous literati and translators. C.A. Bayly made an impressive study 'from below' of colonial knowledge, relating it to already operative, pre-colonial information networks: pandits and the ulema were indispensable for colonial courts till well into the nineteenth century; the census and other forms of systematic late-colonial information-gathering obviously required masses of Indian collaborators and subordinates. The power relations involved in such connections should, of course, not be forgotten, and it seems best to avoid the idea of a 'dialogue', suggestive of equality in the relationship between the informant and the informed.[22] Yet a degree of autonomy was surely often possible. Indian elites did have ideas and projects of their own: pandits nudged their foreign masters towards readings of texts more conducive to brahmanical hegemony, for instance. Indians also read Western texts through a grid of their own kinds of cultural meanings.

Not just indigenous inputs, however: multiple, often highly diverse and mutually conflicting appropriations are an important part of any comprehensive study of 'colonial power-knowledge'. If the general thrust of colonial, and particularly late-colonial, assumptions and

[20] Chatterjee 1986.
[21] Chatterjee 1993.
[22] Irschick 1995.

practices was towards alliances with dependent elites, counteracting tendencies were nonetheless often activated precisely by such consolidations. The sections that follow on law, the census, education, science, and missionary activity will have occasion to repeatedly indicate the operation of such divergences. The general pattern, we shall see, is one that will recur on many different registers throughout this history of late-colonial times: the consolidation of structures of power, and their occasional questioning and subversion.

A Legal Basis for Communalism? Law and the Creation of Religious Domains

Colonial law has attained a sudden and exciting prominence in recent history-writing about modern South Asia. Earlier, legal history was assumed to be a rather dull and minor area—a narrative of administrative evolution and successive codes which were of interest primarily to lawyers. But legal history in its more expanded form as history of law is now recognized as a privileged entry point into two key areas. It can illuminate basic questions of continuity and change in state ideology and practices through colonial times. Moreover, law often played a critical role in the consolidation of identities along deepening faultlines of religion, caste, gender, and race.

In formal terms, EIC authority over the Bengal subah rested on the Mughal grant of diwani in 1765. Early Company administration had to necessarily relate itself to the Mughal tradition of a demarcation between faujdari (or nizamat) and diwani: roughly, the maintenance of order and criminal justice, as distinct from revenue collection and civil justice. Sadr Nizamat and Sadr Diwani adalats remained separate till their amalgamation into high courts after the Crown takeover. There was also, up to that point, a separate supreme court to administer English law to Europeans who resided in India.

Criminal law, closely connected with processes of pacification, came to be an area where a modernizing and centralizing thrust was most evident. Radhika Singha's study of early-colonial criminal law has revealed the ways in which the state tried to establish a new monopoly over legitimate violence and power of punishment. This concentration sought to displace the partial dispersal of legal authority among many diversely hierarchized social institutions persisting from pre-colonial times. The new legality was crucial to the EIC's bid to enforce a modern notion of indivisible sovereignty. Earlier Islamic criminal law permitted relatives of the victim of the crime to exact restitution or retribution for offences from the offender: patterns of punishment such as this, which had generally governed Mughal criminal justice, were gradually eliminated in colonial times. Criminal law, as reformed and systematized by Macaulay's draft Penal Code of 1837 and finalized in the early 1860s, was 'territorial': applicable equally to everyone living under British Indian jurisdiction, and not differentiated along lines of religious community or caste. Singha has argued that this conception of legal equality, of 'abstract and universal' subjects irrespective of differences in social status and community affiliation, emerged in colonial conditions essentially as the byproduct of a ruling framework which she terms a 'despotism of law'. This was not the consequence of any benevolent application of Western liberal principles, nor, at least initially, of deliberate pressures from below. Jörg Fisch, too, had questioned the earlier assumption that reforms in specific laws made from the time of Cornwallis onwards were noticeably marked by a higher level of humanitarianism. Mutilation largely disappeared as a form of punishment. But the eighteenth-century British practice of awarding death sentences for even minor property-related crimes—protecting limbs while cheapening lives—was extended to all of India and could well have appeared much more barbaric to many Indians. Singha has also shown the many limits to this theoretically modernizing and homogenizing thrust. These limits occurred because of the need to accommodate alien rule to pre-existing patterns of social authority or prestige. In 1795, for instance, Benaras Brahmans were exempted from the death penalty for homicide, and numerous concessions were made to 'rank and respectability . . . the authority of husband over wife, and master over servant. . .'[23] The other barrier to legal equality was racist privilege. As we saw earlier, this became most crudely manifest in the 1880s when Europeans in India hysterically opposed the Ilbert Bill, which had empowered Indian magistrates to serve as judges in legal cases against Europeans.

Modernizing moves became discernible also in that part of civil justice which related to questions of landed or business property,

[23] See Singha 1998: xv, *et passim*; and Fisch 1983.

contract, and commerce. There were some developments in this domain in the direction of bourgeois norms of unrestricted private property, and the 'liberty' and 'equality' of the marketplace. One expectation that underlay the making of the Permanent Settlement of 1793 with Bengal zamindars was that 'the magic touch of private property' would set in operation a 'productive principle': if zamindars were given absolute rights to landownership, they would be encouraged to invest in agricultural improvement. Colonial revenue settlements, however, came to vary widely across regions and times in accordance with shifting theoretical assumptions, state financial needs, and the pressure of local circumstances. We see almost everywhere a search for a definitive location of property rights, inheritable and freely saleable. State regulation also occasionally prodded business life towards more modern capitalist forms: notably through the series of Company Acts made between 1850 and 1862 which ensured limited liability for shareholders of joint-stock enterprises. And yet even here, as David Washbrook has pointed out, significant limits were set once again by power structures among Indians. Washbrook has drawn attention to the persistence in many regions of differential rates of revenue or rent on land held by different castes.[24] A glance at the Rae Bareli District Gazetteer of 1923, for instance, confirms that Brahmans and Rajputs who were tenants (and not landlords) usually paid rent at much lower rates than their Ahir (Yadav) or Kurmi lower-caste neighbours. Above all, there were numerous unresolved contradictions: between a 'public' law based on territorial principles which sought to foster the freedoms of the individual in the marketplace, and the colonial retention and development of a parallel domain of 'personal', 'private', or 'family' law that enforced religious and community obligations specific to Hindus and Muslims. Even today, to take a familiar instance, Indian income tax returns make a distinction between the individual and the 'undivided Hindu joint family' assessee.

This has been a critical dualism, underlying the whole evolution of colonial law and persisting to some extent into postcolonial times. It has had extremely significant social consequences. Its origins go back to Warren Hastings' decision in 1772, soon after the Company had decided to 'stand forth as the Diwan', and it was reiterated several times

[24] Washbrook 1981.

subsequently. It was decided that matters concerning 'inheritance, marriage, caste, and other religious usages and institutions' were to be regulated, for Hindus, 'according to their Shaster', and for Muslims by the 'Shariat'. The EIC no doubt thought that they were following Mughal precedents: it had been customary in the diwani branch of administration to consult Brahman pandits and Muslim legal experts in disputes concerning Hindu or Islamic laws. J.D.M. Derrett has suggested, in addition, that the British in the late eighteenth century may have found such a division quite natural. There was still a distinction in their own country between 'courts temporal' and 'courts Christian'. The latter were run by clergymen and dealt with disputes concerning marriages, wills, and religious discipline. Following precedents drawn from both Mughal and British practices, pandits and the ulema played a key role in Company courts, adjudicating disputes in matters of personal law. Gradually, however, colonial officials became suspicious about nepotism or corruption in their interpretations of custom and scripture. This quickly became a major impetus for the codification of personal laws so as to make them independent of conflicting interpretations among Indian legal experts. Early British Orientalists like Halhed, Colebrooke, and Macnaughten produced successive digests of Hindu law. In 1864 their Indian assistants—court-employed pandits and maulvis who advised judges about tricky points of custom and scripture—were formally dropped from court employment. It was assumed that courts and modern lawyers now possessed sufficient knowledge of indigenous legal texts to render the mediation of traditional experts unnecessary.

Legal historians have pointed out that the corpus of 'Anglo-Hindu' and 'Anglo-Muhammadan' law that resulted from this evolution was on many matters considerably more orthodox, rigid, and geared to high-caste, elite-Muslim, and patriarchal assumptions than pre-colonial legal practices probably had been. The colonial claim to continuity with indigenous traditions was in fact accompanied by significant change. This produced a pattern that combined a centralization of laws which were, nonetheless, bifurcated along community lines. Homogenizing tendencies were combined with a strong insistence on an absolute distinction between Hindu and Muslim laws. In Mughal times, the administration of civil justice with the help of pandits and Shariat experts had been confined to major centres of imperial power. The absence of any systematic structure of appeals meant that the vast majority of disputes were likely to have been settled at local, village, or small-town levels in accordance with immensely varied local customs. Even twentieth-century administrative reports from remote regions often make it clear that the dharmashastras or the shariat remained virtually unknown and irrelevant. Nor were distinctions between Hindu and Muslim particularly clear. The more relevant identities could be based on affinities of locality, caste, or sect. Colonial civil law, which progressively developed a hierarchized and uniform structure of courts of appeal, and tended to prioritize 'classical' texts over local custom, thus helped to bring about significant extensions in the influence of orthodox Brahmans and Muslim religious experts and practices. It needs to be noted, further, that the legal changes made it increasingly incumbent for people to declare themselves definitively as Hindu or Muslim in numerous everyday disputes. In this sense, the impact of law on the consolidation of religious distinctions was probably greater than that of the census—which was, after all, only a decennial affair. The codified and communally bifurcated structures of colonial personal or family law also set the terms for indigenous middle-class religious and social reform efforts: from Rammohan Roy—the first major modern Indian reformer—onwards. Each reformer directed his efforts only at his own community. Textual support from the scriptures had to be found if changes, such as a ban on widow immolation and the sanctioning of widow marriage, were to be made legal. Public spheres that emerged through debates around questions of reform thus remained trapped in bifurcated Hindu and Muslim domains.

Instances abound of British Indian civil courts modifying local customs through an application of brahmanic texts, in the process frequently consolidating and providing a legal basis to caste and patriarchy. In 1864, for instance, the Bombay High Court struck down a local practice whereby a deserted wife could marry again, on the grounds that 'such a caste custom—even it be proved to exist, is invalid, as being entirely opposed to the spirit of the Hindu law.'[25] Restrictions on inter-caste marriages were similarly made more rigorous.

[25] Cowell 1870: 167, 169.

The colonial shoring-up of caste hierarchy and discipline also took a second form. Courts of civil law recognized castes as being to some extent 'self-governing' bodies that had powers to make and enforce rules of their own. The social boycott of recalcitrant members (*nai-dhobi bandh*, in North Indian parlance) was, therefore, considered non-justiciable. Yet courts did intervene at times—with a systematic bias towards the preservation of high-caste privilege. The exclusion of lower castes from temples was upheld in Bombay in 1883, defending Chitpavan Brahmin privilege; by the Privy Council in 1908, rejecting Shanar (Nadar) claims to the wearing of the breast cloth by their women; and in Nagpur in 1924, when Mahars were convicted for entering a village temple enclosure. As late as 1945 a Madras court ordered low-caste Ezhavas, who had bathed in a tank adjoining a temple used by dominant caste Nairs, to pay the costs of the necessary 'purificatory' ritual. By this time, judges and lawyers in Indian courts would have been overwhelmingly Indian and predominantly high caste.[26]

But one needs to keep in mind the question of important regional variations, both in Orientalist scholarship and in related legal practices. The standard model, among admirers and critics of colonial law alike, has tended to emphasize the state's valorization of Sanskrit texts and its consequent alliance with brahmanical orthodoxy. This possibly generalizes overmuch from the Bengal situation. In the South, in contrast, the work of Company offiicials and missionaries like Francis Ellis and Robert Caldwell helped to constitute notions of 'Dravidian', and specifically Tamil, distinctiveness. The claims, over time, were appropriated by powerful anti-Brahmin movements.[27] The specifics of the Punjab situation, where there was a significantly different stress on non-textual village or 'tribal' custom, have also been highlighted.[28] Colonial officials in these regions tried to consolidate customary practices through discussions with villagers. Such an 'ethnographic dialogue', however, was also power-driven. Bhattacharya's analysis brings out the making of an unequal duet of colonial masters and native informants. The latter came from the village 'proprietary body

[26] Kikani 1912; Galanter 1968.
[27] Trautmann 2009.
[28] Bhattacharya 1996.

speaking against the rights of non-proprietors, females, and lower castes.'[29]

Yet the impact of colonial law, particularly in terms of its unintended consequences, was not always or entirely in the direction of the consolidation of conservatism. Promises held out but largely withheld often turned out to be the most dangerous, for they whetted desires but did not satisfy them. This, in effect, is what happened with the colonial discourse of law. Couched in a language of equal and impartial justice, it promised a rule of law and equal weight to testimonies of white and brown, men and women, rich and poor, high caste and low. But in practice it was shot through with inequities of race, caste, class, and gender. The contradictory implications of colonial law will follow us all along this history: there is space to touch upon only a few instances here.

British Indian justice was bound up with the development of a rapidly expanding and multi-layered profession of law that was more independent, on the whole, of the state than were most other segments of the educated middle class. From the late nineteenth century onwards, it produced a large number of nationalist leaders and activists. Racist abuse and official repression were resisted very visibly in the courts in terms of a previously unknown liberal language of rule of law, legal equality, and civil rights. This became an early and important dimension of anti-colonial struggles.

The courts were very profitable for successful lawyers. But they were also alien, time-consuming, and expensive. They promoted principles of absolute and freely alienable property rights. They thus became a nightmare for very many of the poor and the underprivileged. And yet the novel and dramatic paraphernalia of law courts and of publicly enacted legal proceedings could be seen and heard by large crowds. Reports of legal matters spread among large groups of ordinary readers through cheap print culture, newspapers, pamphlets, and plays that were written around celebrated or scandalous court cases. This helped to stimulate the emergence of an Indian public sphere of open discussion and debate around matters of public concern.[30]

[29] Ibid.
[30] See Sarkar 2001.

Restricted severely by the constraints of literacy and class, this partially autonomous public domain had a tendency to expand over time. It may not have been utterly dissimilar from the Western European prototype that Habermas has analysed.[31] Later, in times of popular nationalist struggles in the twentieth century, public trials of noted nationalists spread political consciousness—the trials of Tilak and Gandhi being spectacular instances.

Let me conclude this section with two specific instances, both taken from nineteenth-century Bengal. The elements of drama and spectacle in court proceedings quickly attracted vernacular playwrights and farce-writers whose works began to proliferate from around the mid-nineteenth century. A scandal in 1873 that involved the chief priest of a major pilgrimage site near Calcutta produced a spate of plays which suddenly made profitable the first, hitherto struggling, public theatre in Bengal—that now ran on the sale of tickets and not upper-class patronage. The theme that excited public interest, both in the legal proceedings and in plays based on them, was the way in which the law convicted, sentenced, and imprisoned the powerful priest, treating him like any other common criminal. At a very different social level, but by coincidence in that same year, a group of untouchable 'Chandals' (who would subsequently gain for themselves the more prestigious caste-name of Namasudras) in the Central Bengal district of Faridpur embarked on a struggle against landlord and high-caste oppression. One of their grievances was that, unlike higher-caste convicts, they were ordered if arrested to clean prison latrines. This, they argued, went against the government claim 'to treat all castes on terms of equality'.[32]

Surveying an Empire: The Census and the Constitution of Social Realities

The history of colonial governance seems to provide an almost copy-book illustration of the links between 'power' and 'knowledge' that Foucauldian analysis has highlighted. As early as 1769, the fifteen

---

[31] Habermas 1989.

[32] See Sarkar 2001; and Government of Bengal, Judicial Proceedings, March 1873, n. 179.

'supervisors' appointed by the Company's Governor Verelst to oversee revenue collection had been instructed to collect information not just about rent rolls, but also concerning local history, manners, and customs as well as agricultural and craft production.[33] Every step in the expansion of British political and economic control was accompanied by the interrelated accumulation of administrative knowledge. Distinct from the Indological concentration on ancient texts in its apparent reliance on empirical observation, such knowledge culminated in decennial census reports from 1871 onwards, and the late-nineteenth and early-twentieth-century series of district gazetteers, survey and settlement reports, and 'tribes and castes' volumes for the various British Indian provinces. Thus came to be constituted an enormous archive, far more extensive and detailed than any pre-colonial equivalents. The Mughals, the most bureaucratized of the preceding empires, come next. And though postcolonial states have no doubt accumulated even more impressive data holdings, access to most of them remains closed or difficult.

The colonial administrative archives constitute the single most important data bank for historians of modern India: the sign of 'modernity' among such scholars being, indeed, in major part both enabled and limited by its presence. Ways of looking at these indispensable sources, however, have changed significantly in recent years, and the census provides the best illustration for the historiographical shift. Census data had been tested often enough earlier for bias and degree of reliability, and their information had been calibrated to assess changes in colonial policies and attitudes across time by looking at the changing categories that were used for classification.[34] Starting with the work of Kenneth Jones and Bernard Cohn in the late 1970s and early 1980s, and stimulated by the Saidian turn, historians became much more aware of the dimensions of power, and power-related assumptions, lying concealed within even the apparently most objective, statistical, and scientific of the colonial administrative knowledge apparatus. Much more important, there has developed a

[33] Cohn 1987: 231.

[34] The next chapter will have occasion to mention one striking instance of such efforts, made by Daniel and Alice Thorner in 1962.

new emphasis upon the ways in which such knowledge actually came to constitute social realities. For, any enumerative procedure needs to homogenize the units being counted, and so classification, imparting fixed and firm boundaries to such units, becomes indispensable. If the census authorities decide to count the numbers of 'Hindus' and 'Muslims', for instance, the boundary lines between the two must become definitive: a census respondent cannot claim that s/he shares in a bit of the rituals and beliefs of both. Again, enumeration can stimulate competition, rivalry, and conflict, for a new awareness may dawn about the existence of imbalances in the respective shares of communities within a population—their access to education, jobs, and political influence. The official choice of classificatory categories, therefore, becomes important. There were significant differences between census procedures in Britain and the colony. Religious differences and conflicts were by no means unimportant in nineteenth-century Britain, yet they hardly figured in British census operations, which concentrated on territorial location and occupation. The basic building blocks of the Indian census, in striking contrast, were religion and caste.

The specificities of the colonial census have been highlighted by Arjun Appadurai.[35] The Mughals had measured land for revenue purposes, but they were not interested in counting heads. So, estimates of pre-colonial populations remain uncertain. Earlier regimes acknowledged group identities but made little effort to enumerate each. Censuses in the modern West have generally taken as their basic unit the citizen or individual and classified them primarily by territorial location (borough or county, in Britain), gender, age, and occupational class. The key colonial distinction, Appadurai argues, lay in the assumption of 'incommensurable group difference' along lines of religion and caste. This set the ground 'for group difference to be the central principle of politics' in late-colonial as well as, quite often, post-colonial times. This is an important point, but one that needs to be pressed further: Appadurai's explanation for this colonial difference seems to stop short, restricting itself to references pertaining to the exoticizing Orientalist gaze. In fact, more 'material' considerations

[35] Appadurai 1993.

and distinctions could also have been relevant. The capitalist state in Britain had needed to break up the rebellious popular eighteenth-century cultures and communities of poor peasants and artisans that derived from customs held in common.[36] It also needed to resist the emergent community solidarities of workers. Notions of bourgeois individualism, and about the undifferentiated abstract citizen, were helpful in both these contexts. 'Traditional' solidarities were being undercut, meanwhile, by the pressures of rapid capitalist growth and the emergence of new forms of democratic and labour politics. The patterns of colonial development, as subsequent chapters will try to outline, were significantly different. Here, too, many solidarities of resistance, old or new, were sought to be repressed: 'thugs', criminalized tribes,[37] non-sedentary groups, rebellious adivasis and peasants, and eventually anti-colonial mass movements. But the tiny foreign ruling elite needed, always, shifting alliances with more or less privileged indigenous strata. These would be most useful when they could draw upon reserves of 'tradition' and 'community', whether truly old or freshly minted. With the advance of anti-colonial nationalist movements that sought to ground themselves in notions of Indian patriotism and equal citizenship, there also grew the colonial need to play off, against each other, varied kinds of alternative community identities: of religion, caste, ethnicity, language, region, or class.

British officials often showed considerable awareness that their pursuit of empirical knowledge through statistics and classification was fundamentally political, and did not so much reflect ground realities as help to reshape them through the ordering devices that they tried to impose on refractory human material. H.H. Risley's *Tribes and Castes of Bengal* declared that ethnographic survey and a record of the customs of the people were 'as necessary an incident of good administration as a cadastral survey of the land and a record of rights of its tenants.'[38] Not all officials were in agreement that religion and caste should be the basic units for arranging census data. There was even greater dispute about what should be taken to be

[36] Thompson 1991.
[37] See Radhakrishna 2001.
[38] Risley 1891: vii.

the crucial determinant of caste distinctions. Risley developed an argument based on an extreme biological racism. This grounded caste in an Aryan–non-Aryan racial distinction, claiming that this could be proved by the physical (anthropometrical) measurement of heads and noses. From this followed his famous formula that was incorporated in his all-India census report of 1901: that 'the status of the members of a particular group varies in inverse ratio to the mean relative width of their noses.'[39]

There were alternative views among officials. J.C. Nesfield presented ample data about physiological resemblances that cut across high and low castes. He stressed the importance of occupation rather than race. But Risley was able to clinch his highly dubious case by reminding fellow officials of the 'political value [that] may attach to the demonstration that a given population either is or is not composed of homogeneous ethnic elements.'[40] As for the gap between census categories and reality, G.A. Gait, Bengal Census Commissioner in 1901, made the interesting admission that 'the more ignorant classes have very little idea as to what caste means—.' Ten years later, now heading the census for the whole country, the same official was confronted by a suggestion from the Bombay Census Superintendent that he be allowed to classify some communities in Gujarat who refused to return themselves as definitively either Hindu or Muslim. The superintendent said he preferred the term 'Hindu-Muhammadans'. Gait's angry reply was that the official would have to relegate 'the persons concerned to the one religion or the other as best he could.'[41]

Three instances taken from census operations between 1891 and 1911 provide particularly clear evidence of official classification and enumeration helping to mould social realities, as well as the limits of such impact. In 1891 C.J. O'Donnell, on the basis of some data indicating a faster growth rate among Muslims as compared to Hindus, made the sensational prediction 'that if this rate continued, the faith of Muhammad would be universal in Bengal Proper in six and a half

[39] *Census (India), 1901*: 498.
[40] Risley 1891: xx.
[41] *Census (Bengal), 1901*: 347; Census (India), 1911: 118.

centuries.' His own report, however, admitted that part of the Hindu relative decline was on account of skewed definitions: many followers of 'animistic religions' (i.e. tribals) had been classed with Hindus in 1881.[42] A later chapter will indicate how, some years later, this prediction became a principal foundation of highly emotive arguments concerning Hindus as a ' Dying Race'—the title of a very influential tract by U.N. Mukherji in 1909. The temporal gap of more than a decade, though, is a reminder that the development of what became, and still remains, a standard trope of Hindu communalism can be attributed only in part to census discourse. It was more a product of the growing communal imperative that conveniently used census data.

In 1901 Risley instituted a classic instance of census classifications moulding social reality. He ordered a new arrangement of caste entries that had been previously presented (as in his 1891 *Tribes and Castes* volumes) in alphabetical order: 'classification by social precedence, as recognised by native public opinion at the present day.' This unleashed a flood of claims and counter-claims regarding relative ranking and varna status from numerous spokesmen and associations of jatis, thus vastly stimulating upward mobility efforts as well as conservative responses from higher castes. 'Caste associations' and caste-based conflicts proliferated on an unprecedented scale in the wake of the 1901 census.

During the run-up to the 1911 census, Commissioner Gait issued a circular (July 1910) suggesting a more restricted definition of 'Hindu' to exclude those who were not allowed access to Brahman priests and to high-Hindu gods and temples, and whom the upper castes would refuse to touch or take water from. This was violently denounced in the Indian press, overwhelmingly dominated by high-caste Hindus, who feared that the measure would if implemented lead to a major statistical decline of Hindus relative to Muslims and so might affect their employment and electoral prospects. It would also, they feared, encourage movements among subordinated castes. The circular was quickly withdrawn. But the controversy stimulated a prolonged debate about the correct definition of a Hindu. Distant echoes can be traced in V.D. Savarkar's *Hindutva/Who is*

[42] *Census (Bengal), 1891.*

a Hindu? (1923), a foundational text for the contemporary Hindutva
movement.

Yet an overdeterministic view of causal links between census classification and enumeration on the one hand, and caste movements
and tensions on the other, would be untenable. Research on caste
increasingly reveals ideological and organizational antecedents that
often precede the 1901 innovation, and even the institution of the
census itself.[43] It is not always remembered that Risley's principle of
arranging of castes by regionally-determined social precedence was
tried out only once, in the 1901 census. Gait abandoned it in 1911 and
returned to simple alphabetical order because officials were alarmed by
the flood of status claims and counter-claims: Bengal Census Commissioner O'Malley complained about 'one-and-a-half maunds' of
petitions.[44] No reduction in caste conflict was visible either then or,
for that matter, after caste itself disappeared from census questionnaires
in post-colonial times. Upper-caste Hindu communal consolidation,
too, had much wider contexts than a single, quickly abandoned official
initiative. Threats posed by lower-caste pressures would explain them
better, as we shall later see.

The more significant implications of the census perhaps lay in other
directions. Census details repeatedly indicate the importance of links
between colonial power-knowledge and Indian social forms: in this
case predominantly brahmanical or high-caste. For his 1891 volume
on tribes and castes, Risley appointed 190 local correspondents and
instructed them 'to go for their information to—priests, marriage-
brokers, geneaologists, headmen of caste panchayets, or the like':
all but the last will have been entirely high-caste.[45] In 1901 Gait,
as head of the Bengal census, added an important gloss to Risley's
order to classify caste in each region by precedence as recognized
by 'native public opinion'. He said 'the decision must rest with enlightened public opinion, and not with public opinion generally',
as a Hindu often knew 'little of any caste other than his own', and
was content to use terms like Bania or Malla for others as vague

[43] Deshpande 2007.
[44] *Census (Bengal), 1911.*
[45] Risley 1891: xiii.

indicators of occupation-cum-social status.[46] 'Enlightened' opinion would inevitably mean the views of highly educated Hindus, i.e. overwhelmingly, upper-caste men. Not surprisingly, therefore, both the 1901 and 1911 census reports indicate that the vast majority of claims to higher status were rejected. One must not, also, forget the importance of alternative possibilities and appropriations. The census emphasis on religious and caste differences was obviously made with an eye on their potential for divide and rule. It is not irrelevant to recall that Risley, after directing the 1901 census, soon became Home Member in Curzon's administration. In this capacity he played a very notable part in the partitioning of Bengal in 1905.

Unmasking Conquest: Education, Print, and the Early Public Sphere

Colonial education, unlike law and the census, has always occupied an important niche in the more conventional narratives of modern Indian history as well as in recent postcolonial studies. Value judgements have differed sharply, however. What has been variously termed Western or English or modern education has been alternately hailed as harbinger of cultural 'awakening', perhaps even a 'renaissance', or denounced as instrument of colonial hegemony, a 'mask of conquest'.[47] Both stereotypes oversimplify and ignore important distinctions. Either way, the focus on colonial education, in praise or blame, has been simultaneous with a surprising neglect of a significant and far-reaching innovation of colonial times: the transition—with its manifold implications—from manuscript to print.

It is helpful to start with some distinctions. Writings that are critical of English education often do not make clear whether their central target of criticism is the importance within Indian curricula of English literary texts, or the imposition of English as the medium of instruction at higher levels of learning, or the structures introduced and values sought to be inculcated by colonial education in general. Quantitatively, it was only a small and slowly expanding minority that obtained the new education. Even this was received not through

---

[46] *Census (Bengal), 1901.*
[47] Viswanathan 1989.

English but was transmitted through the vernacular languages. English, in most cases, became the medium only in the penultimate phase of high school education, and in colleges. The striking thing about the culture produced by the nineteenth- and early-twentieth-century colonial intelligentsia is the fact that its medium was overwhelmingly the vernacular languages of the country. In fact these, in most cases, attained their modern forms, and developed prose literatures, in the colonial era. Even the most successful of the English-educated chose their particular vernacular as the medium for creative expression. In contrast, what is today termed Indo-Anglian literature has attained literary significance entirely in post-colonial times, eclipsing, almost, the value of vernacular writings.

Colonial educational policy should not be equated with Macaulay's 1835 Minute on Education, though that is done quite often. The Minute had denounced Indian cultures for their alleged poverty and suggested that Western texts alone should be taught at the higher levels of education, primarily through the English language. There were, actually, numerous variations across time and space. The medium of the English language was established only after a bitter debate among Company officials who struggled hard to overcome the opposition of the Orientalists (in the narrower sense of that word) among them. The latter had wanted the not particularly lavish sum of Rs 1 lakh, assigned to education by the Charter Act of 1813, to be spent on Sanskrit and Perso-Arabic institutions alone. The best-known Indian intervention in that debate, by Rammohan Roy in 1823, clearly wanted a combination of the English medium with emphasis upon scientific education in ways very different from Macaulay's preference for 'liberal', literary training. There were also some advocates for a development of the vernacular media. Notable instances would include William Adam in late 1830s Bengal, he being the author of a famous report on indigenous education; the Company-funded Delhi College in pre-1857 Delhi, which used the Urdu medium and encouraged vernacular translations of books on Western science; the effort to promote vernacular primary education in Urdu and Hindi by Lieutenant Governor Thomason of the North-Western Provinces in the 1850s; and the initial support given by some Bengal officials to Iswarchandra Vidyasagar's drive for popular education through the Bengali medium and his founding of some girls' schools in that decade.

The main reason why state funding was directed towards higher education in English, more or less closing off other alternatives, had little to do with ideology and much to do with considerations of administrative economy. The expanding colonial bureaucracy, as well as British mercantile firms, needed subordinate and low-paid Indian employees with some knowledge of English. That need could be met most cheaply by confining direct funding to a small number of English-medium government colleges and high schools, and to a literary rather than scientific thrust. There was, moreover, a reliance on a 'filtration' effect as concretized by Charles Wood's Minute on Education in 1854. Wood preferred to develop Indian private investment for lower levels of education, with limited grants-in-aid to private schools and colleges set up by educated middle-class Indians as well as by Christian missions. Mass primary education under state auspices would have been very much more expensive: it was started in England from 1870, shortly after the 1867 'leap in the dark' which enfranchised the bulk of the male British working class. It was never felt to be necessary or advisable to follow suit in a colony governed mainly in despotic ways.

English literature departments were started in major universities in Britain very late in the nineteenth century, in most cases after their colonial Indian counterparts had already come into existence. There is some evidence of a hegemonic motivation in their introduction within Britain, particularly in the context of early-twentieth-century labour militancy. English literature, in the words of a 1921 Report on high school education, could help close the gulf between 'the mind of the poet and that of the young wage-earner', and bring about the 'much-desired spiritual unity of the nation'. The few detailed studies of colonial Indian university syllabi that have been attempted so far do not establish political motivations with anything like such clarity: thus, three out of five questions in an MA examination paper at Allahabad University in 1893 were set on John Stuart Mill's *Liberty*, 'which scarcely suggests that the University was acting as an instrument of imperial thought control.'[48] One could still legitimately suspect

---

[48] Harrison 1996: 165, 177–8; McDonald 1966: 453–70.

the presence of colonial acculturing desires, in the broader sense of inserting beliefs in the superiority of Western liberal cultural values. But two vital caveats remain. It is well known that Macaulay's dream of producing natives who would be brown in colour but white in tastes and values boomeranged within a couple of generations once English-educated Indians pioneered nationalist protest: so much so that the Anglicized 'babu' (Kipling's 'bunderlok') became a standard figure of ridicule and abuse in the more blatant of racist and imperialist writings. The fundamental fact remains that only very niggardly sums were invested in education throughout the colonial era. So, notwithstanding Macaulay's pronouncements, acculturation could not have been a priority. It is stretching credulity to make too much out of the emancipating or acculturing role of English education: both eulogy and critique have vastly exaggerated its impact. Between 1864 and 1885 a grand total of 5108 Indians attained BA degrees in all of India, which, in the 1881 census, had a population of over 250 million. 'Public expenditure on education in India was a miserable 0.2% of the national income in the nineteenth century, and never much above 0.5% in the twentieth.' Not surprisingly, even vernacular literacy for those ten was only 6 per cent in the 1890s, and no more than 15 per cent even in 1941.[49] Only a very elitist reading of history can postulate pervasive hegemonization amidst such parsimony.

The debate around English as the medium and British literature has obscured certain other more significant and structural changes in education under colonialism. There was, first, the vastly enhanced importance of formal education as the channel of upward mobility. It could be so for those with some economic resources, though not for all. Under Pax Britannica, it was no longer possible to carve out a petty kingdom or lordship through military adventure: the earlier, pre-colonial routes to upward mobility, for which education and even literacy was not particularly relevant. The British monopolized the top levels of the army and the bureaucracy. In some regions, particularly Bengal, a successful ascent through business became very difficult due to what has been called a collective European monopoly over the higher reaches of commerce, finance, and industry. What remained, or came to be constituted in their recognizably modern forms, were the

[49] Anil Seal in Gallagher 1973: 18; Kumar 1983: 935–7.

'respectable' professions: law, teaching, medicine, and journalism, all requiring higher education. There were, moreover, intermediate- or lower-level jobs in the administration and foreign mercantile firms. Starting with the Indian Civil Service from around 1856, recruitment through patronage alone—previously the standard practice in Britain and early-colonial India alike—began to give place to competitive examinations: one more instance, incidentally, of the British rulers trying out in their colony what came to be instituted only later in their own country. An immediate consequence was the foundation of universities, for long purely examining structures, in Calcutta, Madras, and Bombay in 1857–9. An educational hierarchy governed by a definite and uniform sequence of examinations was indispensable if recruitment was to be through tests of academic merit and not patronage connections.

It is this clear-cut educational ladder that had been conspicuously absent till well into the nineteenth century. Pre-colonial education possessed a markedly segmentary character, with little connection or relation between different types of institutions. Adam had found elementary village schools surprisingly numerous in Bengal in 1835, with a very considerable lower-caste component among pupils and even sometimes teachers. The education imparted in such pathshalas (which had afternoon breaks, and holidays at harvest times, and so were better tuned than their successors to South Asian conditions) was fairly well tailored to the immediate needs of better-off peasants, traders, and petty zamindari officials. It was confined to writing, arithmetic, and a bit of revenue and commercial accounting. Reading was less important, since textbook manuscripts were scarce and expensive before the coming of print: pupils did not have their own textbooks, they had to take down what the teacher dictated and memorize it. Romanticizing a pre-colonial world of widespread rural education would be misplaced, however, because the village schools had virtually no connection with the centres of higher learning in Sanskrit, Persian, and Arabic. The tols, chatuspathis, and madrasas were the preserves of Brahmans and other largely hereditary learned groups. Systems of higher education remained exclusive, with the English medium adding to existing hurdles of economic and/or social disadvantage. But the new theoretical equality, which provided no respect to inherited status and promised a uniform educational ladder, stimulated important new desires among hitherto illiterate groups. It opened up some opportunities for a small but growing number of subordinate castes and middle-class women. It needs to be emphasized that pre-colonial education, even at elementary levels, seems to have excluded girls almost totally. This was due to a very strong taboo which associated the woman who could read—and, more dangerously, write—with immorality: she could then be expected to develop extra-marital liaisons by writing letters to lovers.

Despite several thousand years of scribal literacy, brahmanical culture had retained an exceptionally strong oral bent, even refusing to write out its most sacred texts. Orality, far from being always a realm of greater freedom, as is sometimes imagined, was in fact associated much more with strict, if personalized, hierarchies which often tended to veer towards sacral forms of power–knowledge. The guru–shishya relationship, obtaining both in village schools and in centres of higher religious training, had its homologous counterparts across the entire gamut of cultural transmissions, Islamic as well as Hindu: murshid and murid in the Sufi silsilas (lineages), for instance, or ustad and shagird in the world of Indian classical music.

In an essay confined to Indian Islam, but capable of wider extension, Francis Robinson has argued that this interlinked scribal-cum-oral transmission of sacred learning may help explain why print culture did not develop in India till the colonial period.[50] Print, as everywhere else, came to be associated very quickly with the development of vernacular writings or texts in regional languages. It was particularly associated with the development of vernacular prose. Mechanical reproduction, which vastly cheapens texts, requires a significant widening of markets for profitability, and so attaches a premium to popular, as distinct from classical, languages. The need for memorization declines with the multiplicity of copies, stimulating prose forms even further. The connections of print with educational changes also need to be remembered: thus, school textbooks became a primary market for printing and publishing concerns, stimulating the proliferation of small-scale but numerous capitalist ventures. It was by setting

[50] Francis Robinson, in Crook 1996.

up a printing press and writing school primers that Iswarchandra Vidyasagar attained financial independence—something fairly rare for men like him, born into very poor rural Brahman families.

In sheer quantitative terms, the impact of print was very much more extensive and significant than that of the more written-about English education. In what is today the Uttar Pradesh region (then called North-West Provinces and Oudh)—to take an instance from an area where both developed somewhat later than in the presidencies—there were only 272 graduates clearing BA examinations between 1864 and 1885. But already by 1871 there were 33 newspapers, most of them in Urdu. That year, 317 books were published in the province, in a total of over 440,000 copies.[51]

As with so many other colonial developments, education and print, taken together, carried extremely contradictory implications. Higher education through English had obvious alienating effects. But it also enabled easy access to political ideals, Western in origin, which soon came to be effectively deployed against colonial domination. Its initial beneficiaries have been, of course, high-caste Hindu men along with ashraf Muslims in parts of North India. Anil Seal cites some relevant official figures: the three bhadralok castes of Brahmans, Baidyas, and Kayasthas comprised 9.41 per cent of the population of Bengal Presidency in 1881 but comprised 84.7 per cent of college students in 1883–4. The disproportion was even more staggering in Madras: Brahmans, 3.9 per cent of all Hindus in that Presidency in 1881, constituted 74.6 per cent of college students in 1883–4. Print, and the vernacularization associated with its coming, have never been emancipatory or democratizing in any unambiguous manner. Their immediate consequences included a vast broadening of the reach of orthodox or conservative brahmanic and high-Islamic texts, and a tendency towards fixing more authoritative single meanings. The proliferation of sectarian publications often acted as a stimulus to conflict. The most obvious instance of the latter was the 'one language, two scripts' situation in the Urdu–Nagari controversy, central to the emergence of modern communalism in northern India: the dispute was clearly related to the sudden enormous expansion of the importance of the written word. More generally, the colonial

[51] Lelyveld 1978: 82.

combination of print with low levels of literacy obviously sharpened the literate/illiterate divide, stimulating social and cultural arrogance at one pole, and feelings of deprivation and resentment at the other.

The new education and print theoretically open to all irrespective of caste or gender, did nonetheless come to mean some limited but radically new opportunities. The cheapening and multiplicity of texts, together with the enhanced portability of books, extended the range of subjects and genres which could be written about and read. It opened up new possibilities not just for reading but for authorship as well: for small but growing numbers of women, lower castes, and the underprivileged in general.[52] These were openings which were often bitterly resisted by sections of the dominant groups, most of the time with considerable British backing: the image of colonial rule as modernizing in intent is curiously persistent but in fact very dubious. Work on nineteenth-century Maharashtra, for instance, indicates how local English officials connived with high-caste school authorities to exclude Dalit children from government primary schools. Only after much protest did they agree to allow them to sit on the school veranda, open to sun and rain and far removed from the teacher and other pupils.[53] Yet the public and written protests which such exclusion provoked help to confirm that print was helping to bring into existence, even in colonial conditions, some limited forms of what Habermas has termed the modern public sphere: a realm of open discussion and debate around a variety of public issues concerning religion, gender, caste, forms of literature, and eventually nationalist and many other kinds of politics. This has become in recent years a central focus of much research in social and cultural history and provides a recurrent theme for our subsequent chapters.

The Missions of Empire—Christianity and the State

Education, to the extent that it was directly promoted by the colonial state, was necessarily non-denominational in government-funded institutions, since the religion of the rulers was shared by only a

---

[52] See Venkatachalapathy 2011 for a detailed account of this development in Tamilnadu.

[53] Constable 2000: 383–422.

small minority of their subjects. Like the structures of law and census enumeration, it tended on the whole to bolster Hindu and Islamic socio-religious hierarchies and not subvert them in the interests of either modernity or Christian proselytization. But what, then, of Christian missionary activities and conversions under British rule?

In a widely read general survey of the 'Vasco da Gama era' of South Asian history, K.M. Panikkar in 1959 branded Christian prose-lytization as a drive for 'mental and spiritual conquest . . . supplementing . . . political authority.'[54] This reflects a fairly widespread common sense, and one that has been appropriated in recent years by Hindu chauvinist groups to strengthen a virulent anti-Christian campaign. Such perspectives often propagate the view that Christianity is a foreign and culturally alienating faith, an absurd charge since the religion has existed in parts of the subcontinent for almost two thousand years—it is older, in fact, than Islam and most varieties of living Hindu traditions. Christianity came earlier to India than to most parts of the West. Much more important for a survey of modern Indian history, however, is the fact that a substantial and growing body of recent research has enormously complicated the question of missionary–state relations in the colonial era. It is no longer possible to assert that the relationship was always symbiotic, each acting as a support for the other.

The connections between colonial conquest and an aggressive form of Catholic Christianity had certainly been close in Portuguese-ruled Goa. Later colonial histories, however, indicate that this closeness was exceptional rather than the norm for the subcontinent as a whole. The Inquisition was active in Goa between 1560 and 1812: its targets, though, as everywhere, were primarily Christian 'heretics' suspected of Protestant leanings, not adherents of non-Christian religions. Among the latter, the victims of persecution were usually Muslims, not Hindus, for there was an old religious-cum-commercial rivalry between the Muslim 'Moors' and the Catholic Portuguese—it had animated the early Portuguese expansion down the west coast of Africa in the fifteenth century. But the considerable expansion of Christianity in other parts of the South during the sixteenth to early eighteenth

[54] Panikkar 1959: 314.

century had little to do with the presence of Christian political power. Because they had to operate without the protecting umbrella, Jesuit missionaries engaged in extensive debates about how best to approach Hindu and Muslim cultures. Working in early-seventeenth-century Hindu-ruled Madurai, the highly educated upper-class Italian Roberto Nobili pioneered a technique, 'accomodatio', which sought to build bridges with brahmanical ideas, norms, and customs, to the extent of advocating living like a sanyasi, observing pollution taboos, and seating low-caste converts separately in church. Such an implicit separation between the 'religious' (polytheism and idolatry, which Nobili of course rejected) and the 'social' was unacceptable to his rival, Gonzalo Fernandes, a Portuguese of more plebeian origin. Fernandes preferred a more aggressive proselytization directed towards winning over victims of high-caste oppression. Interestingly, the Vatican endorsed Nobili's relatively tolerant and syncretic, if also socially conservative, approach. The choice was conditioned by the rivalry between two missionary outfits: the Portuguese state-controlled Padroado and the Vatican Propaganda Fide. Christian missions have never been anything like a homogeneous bloc, even within a single denomination. Such tensions and disagreements had a tendency to recur in later times.[55]

Missionary relations with the colonial state were varied, and shifted across time and space. On the whole, they were not particularly mutually supportive; in fact they were even, occasionally, conflictual. There could be no question for a long time of state patronage for Catholics in British India. They suffered from numerous disabilities in England till the Catholic Emancipation Act of 1829. The late-eighteenth-century decades, during which the Company established its control over parts of India, coincided with a nadir in Christian piety among the British upper classes, who were at the time considerably influenced by the Enlightenment notions which questioned the churches. This situation changed rapidly with the European religious revivals that appeared in the wake of the French Revolution as a reaction against revolutionary ideas. A large number of colonial officials nonetheless feared proselytization as an unnecessary provocation. The Baptist missionary group of Carey, Marshman, and Ward was not at first

[55] Zupanov 1999.

allowed to establish a mission within Company-ruled Calcutta and had to set up its headquarters in Danish-controlled Serampore. There was a strong element, moreover, of class suspicion or snobbishness among colonial officials which closed off the possibility of social relations with missionaries. Many missionaries, particularly those who belonged to non-conformist groups like the Baptists, came from lower-middle-class or artisanal backgrounds in Britain. High-ranking colonial bureaucrats, often from quite plutocratic backgrounds, shunned their company.

Missionaries were allowed to settle in British India under a licence system only from 1813, and such controlled entry remained the rule till 1833. A brief spell of state–missionary interaction and closeness did follow the lifting of such restrictions, particularly in the frontier areas of mid-nineteenth-century British expansion in northern India. Anglican missionaries, affiliated to the established church in Britain, now tended to include a stronger component of university-educated 'gentlemanly' recruits. What came to be termed the 'Punjab School' of administrators and army officers was often characterized by Evangelical piety and an aggressive, muscular brand of Christianity.

The rebellion of 1857 sent shock waves across colonial officialdom. Analysing its causes, many thought it had much to do with the excessive religious zeal that missionaries had displayed. In Indian perceptions, the state had got too closely linked with their proselytizing agenda. Officials advised a marked distance between the state and missionaries in the future. The Queen's Proclamation promised strict religious neutrality which was, on the whole, much more faithfully observed than other such pledges (as, for instance, equality before the law irrespective of race). It is arguable, in fact, that colonial state support and patronage were more consistently available to non-Christian— most notably brahmanical Hindu—religious establishments than to Christian missionaries. The state's observance and toleration of Hindu and Muslim personal or family law have already been noted. Till the 1840s, the EIC collected pilgrim taxes on behalf of the Jagannatha temple as well as many others, even though missionaries were denouncing this all the while as direct collusion with idolatry. British officers participated in Hindu festivals in Company regiments. Regimental posts were instituted for pandits and maulvis in the pre-1857 Bengal army, which was predominantly high-caste, and sepoys could even be dismissed at times for converting to Christianity: this happened in 1819 with a soldier of the 25th Regiment.[56] Brahmanical Hindu practices in the army became less evident under the Crown as recruitment shifted focus to other groups. But there was no basic change in policies: some of the cultural signs that we today take to be characteristically Sikh, for instance, seem to have developed through British Indian army customs.[57] Till the 1870s there was a general suspicion in official circles about Islam, particularly in the wake of 1857 and Wahhabi conspiracies. The bid for rapproachement with Muslims followed some years later. The new process had interesting sidelights: English teachers at the Aligarh Muhammadan Anglo-Oriental College enforced student attendance at Islamic rituals 'with a determination unmatched by their pious Muslim predecessors.'[58]

Just as missionary relations with the colonial state varied, Christian missions and communities cannot be considered monolithic. Strategic differences, reminiscent of the Nobili–Fernandes rift, continued into the nineteenth century. Some missionaries, such as Alexander Duff in Bengal, sought to win over the urban-educated elites. Others, on the whole with greater success, worked primarily in the countryside, among peasants, subordinate castes, and tribals. A related debate, which Antony Copley has revealed through a study of late-nineteenth-century missionary conferences, occurred between 'education' and 'itinerating' as methods of work: i.e. whether missionaries should concentrate on higher-level elite instruction, or function mainly through public preaching and extensive proselytizing tours.

Missions, moreover, should not be equated with the entire Christian community of Indians. The successful conversion of large Indian groups could, in fact, produce elements of racial tension among Christians. The highly educated ex-Derozian Krishnamohan Banerji—Duff's best-known convert who became a clergyman—came to develop sharp differences with his mentor over questions of 'native' status and salaries within the Mission. In Maharashtra Pandita

[56] Alavi 1995: 85.
[57] Notably, it appears, the turban: see Cohn 1996: 106–62.
[58] Lelyveld 1978: 276.

Ramabai, the remarkable proto-feminist Maharashtrian woman, developed her own very individual interpretation of theological doctrines that were greatly at variance with what her Mission taught. European missionaries became worried that implicit demands for equality such as Krishnamohan's could make the 'Native Ministry very nearly as expensive as a European one.' Krishnamohan had suggested that Mission expenses could be reduced by making Europeans live on less. European missionaries regarded this as an indication of an 'infidel democratic spirit'. Krishnamohan would later become a major figure in the early nationalist Indian Association.[59]

The important point about Christian missions is that their impact went much beyond the fairly limited numbers that they were able to convert. This consisted often in a wide range of largely unintended consequences. Missionary schools and colleges came to provide high-quality education to a significant and growing section of the Indian elites, very few among whom became Christians. Mission hospitals came to cater to Indians, most of whom did not convert. Missions simultaneously helped to open up windows of opportunities for wide sections of the local populace which had been almost totally excluded from formal education: women, lower castes, Dalits, and adivasis. Mission schools, health centres, and effective philanthropic and famine relief activities did lead to considerably large numbers of conversions among the underprivileged. The late-nineteenth-century spurt in Christian conversions in the South—described in Mission histories as the era of mass movements— coincided with a series of major famines and led to the coining of the pejorative term 'rice Christians'.[60] Missionaries themselves deplored the fact that many poor famine victims converted in order to procure subsistence. But the actual beneficiaries of their famine relief included larger numbers than converts. A second major contribution was their energetic promotion of print and vernacular languages. These, being cheap and accessible

[59] Copley 1997: 218–28.

[60] Catholics related to the old Jesuit Madurai Mission numbered 169,000 in 1880 and 260,000 in 1901. The 75,000-odd Protestants in Madras Presidency in 1851 had gone up to 300,000 by 1891: Henriette Bugge in Oddie 1997: 97.

to ordinary people, were vital for the missions as indispensable aids to mass-scale proselytization. The consequences, intended or otherwise, proved wide-ranging. The Serampore Baptist Mission Press, set up around 1800 by Carey and his companions, started one of the earliest Bengali newspapers, the *Samachar Darpan*, and soon began to print non-Christian material, including the sacred texts of other religions. Missionary scholars, among whom Robert Caldwell (the author of *A Comparative Grammar of the Dravidian Languages,* 1856) is only the best known, helped to stimulate modern Tamil culture and identity.

Most missionaries who worked among the poor must have been motivated primarily by the desire for conversion. They are unlikely to have been pro-peasant or socially radical as a matter of principle. Yet their presence could still be a resource for the underprivileged: as, for instance, when French Catholic missionaries of the Pondicherry-based Societes des Missions Etrangeres helped agricultural labourers who had been beaten up by landlords to launch a court case at Alladhy in 1874–5. This incident stimulated a wave of mass conversions in that area.[61] Missionary lobbying with the state occasionally helped to bring about pro-tenant legal reforms: notably in connection with the Bengal Tenancy Act of 1859 and the Chhota Nagpur legislation to protect adivasi land rights in 1911.

Christian attitudes towards caste varied widely in practice. Caste discrimination was often practised even by converts. On the other hand, a study of anti-Brahmin movements in early-twentieth-century South India has emphasized the imaginative impact of church ritual practices upon subordinated groups. The basic ritual of a collective sharing of the communion bread across caste lines in the congregation galvanized those 'who for centuries . . . had been considered unclean and polluting.'[62] Missionary intervention on behalf of the under-privileged was not necessarily directed only against Indian dominant groups. There is a striking instance of the role of foreign missionaries in Bengal during the 1850s, when, led by Reverend James Long, many of them took a public stand against European indigo planters during and after the Blue Mutiny. James Long even went to prison,

[61] Ibid.: 105.
[62] Geetha and Rajadurai 1998: 84.

accepting responsibility for the publication of the English version of Dinabandhu Mitra's play *Neel Darpan*, which had exposed planter excesses. Peasants celebrated his role in folk songs.

The missionary mode of preaching was often extremely abrasive in its denunciations of 'heathens' and their 'polygamous' and 'idolatrous' ways. Among adivasi converts of the north-eastern regions, American Baptists insisted on a whole-scale abandonment of traditional community customs and festivals. Missionaries have been blamed for greatly enhancing, sometimes even creating, intra-religious hostility.[63] However, Hindu and Muslim anti-Christian polemics in the nineteenth century were often equally abusive towards Christianity. Swami Dayanand, for instance, dismissed Christ as a mere carpenter's son living in a wild and poor country: 'This is why he prays for the daily bread.'[64] On the other hand, mutual criticism often tended the proponents of one faith to learn more about others. A very lively tradition of public debate, both oral and in print, developed in the nineteenth century among spokesmen of various Islamic groups, Hindu reformers (Brahmo or Arya Samajist), orthodox Hindu Sanatanists, and Christian missionaries. However acrimonious, this carried the possibility of serious and important discussion around questions of theology, belief, and practice. Such doctrinal discussions declined markedly from the early twentieth century with the rise of large-scale communal identity politics.

Along with instances of interaction, there was a simultaneous hardening of community identities that were earlier overlapping or crosscutting. At the same time, the hardening of community boundaries occasionally also produced an affirmation of individual rights: a key dimension of the modernity which colonial structures and policies otherwise actively discouraged. A theme that will figure prominently in several later chapters can be entered briefly here through the question of religious conversions explored by Gauri Viswanathan.[65] She analyses legal disputes that arose out of one of the few colonial laws that seemed to favour conversions: the Lex Loci of 1850, enabling converts to

[63] Bayly 1989 and 1995.
[64] Cited in Jones 1992: 63–4.
[65] Viswanathan 1998.

pursue their inheritance claims even after converting. Her study reveals that such preservation of inheritance rights was actually grounded in a religious/social distinction by which converts were classified as still partially tied to their abandoned religion. Their new religious identity was not, therefore, completely acknowledged. She also shows that, even after they had converted, women were legally bound to many of the rules of Hindu caste and patriarchal discipline. In 1876 a Christian convert named Huchi was restored by the court to her Hindu husband, to whom she had been married before she converted. This was ordered despite her vehement opposition, repeatedly voiced in court, and even though the husband explicitly declared before the judge that he intended to treat his apostate wife as no better than a prostitute, sleeping with her but never accepting food from her.[66]

Conversion could occasionally open up new spaces, for it was not necessarily a movement from one stable identity and discipline to another. Pandita Ramabai retained and developed after converting a restless, enquiring, and argumentative spirit. This deeply worried the missionary sisters who had brought about her conversion in England in 1883. She developed doubts about the Trinity, was angered by signs of racist contempt in her mentors, and insisted on freedom of individual belief and choice: 'I have a conscience, and a mind and judgement of my own. . . . I have with great effort freed myself from the yoke of the Indian priestly tribe so I am not at present willing to place myself under another similar yoke by accepting everything that comes from the priests as authorized command of the Most High . . .'[67]

Western Science, Colonial Practice

The criticism of colonial modernity has been extended by historians to an interrogation of the nature and impact of Western science. This has helped to make the history of science a part of mainstream narratives of modern Indian history for the first time. Earlier accounts of a benign and slow diffusion of modern European technological

[66] Ibid.
[67] Viswanathan 1998: 126; see also Chakravarti 1998: chapter 6; Kosambi 2000: Introduction; Kosambi 2007: Introduction.

and scientific knowledge are now largely replaced by an image of science 'groaning under a colonial framework', its scope and operations determined and constrained by the requirements of colonial domination and shot through with racist discrimination. David Arnold, for instance, emphasizes that 'denial was as important as diffusion' in shaping the technology and science of British-ruled India.[68]

A limited degree of diffusion of Western science and technology was combined with serious lags in their spread.[69] As for scientific research and its institutionalization, the involvement of the colonial state has been described as little more than 'a fitful flirtation'.[70] Most of the striking early achievements came about through private or autonomous initiative: as when James Prinsep, officially managing the Calcutta Mint in the 1830s, transformed methods of ancient Indian studies. He moved from an earlier concentration on literary sources alone to archaeology, epigraphy, and numismatics. An army engineer and a surgeon discovered the rich fossil remains of the Siwalik region. Though they were state officials, their intellectual ventures happened outside the scope of their official activities. The four main areas where systematic state initiative was visible—maps and surveys, botany, geology, and medicine—were all related to British economic or politico-military interests. The sciences with less immediate practical application—notably mathematics, physics, and chemistry—tended to be neglected by the state. Interestingly, these domains were developed by Indians from around the turn of the nineteenth century into the twentieth.[71]

Modern medicine was evidently necessary for the sheer survival of British traders, officials, and soldiers who now existed in an unfamiliar climate and amidst frequent wars. The beginnings of what became the Indian Medical Service (something uniquely colonial, with no metropolitan or Indian predecessors) actually go back to the 1760s in Bengal. Recruiting through examinations from 1855, this remained

[68] Arnold 2000: 92; see also Kumar 1982: 63–82.

[69] A theme addressed below, in the chapter on environments and economies.

[70] Arnold 2000: 25.

[71] Chakrabarti 2004; Phalkey 2013.

overwhelmingly European in its composition till the early twentieth century. However, the need for 'native' assistants in subordinate capacities led to the early founding of medical colleges, starting with one in Calcutta in 1835. There was some initial interest in indigenous medical systems, but it came to be largely displaced through the development and the long preponderance of a new environmental paradigm for the diagnosis of illness and epidemics.[72] Indigenous medical experience and knowledge fell into disregard, yet full, even excessive, weight was given to the supposed peculiarities of Indian climate which supposedly bred unhealthy miasmas. Consequently, there came into being the notion of a very different and exclusive order known as tropical medicine, applicable to India alone. This considerably delayed the acceptance of the germ theory of disease in British India: thus, Koch's identification of the cholera bacillus in a Calcutta water tank was dismissed by the medical establishment for some years. Malaria was explained by the peculiarities of climate. The supposedly emasculated physique of many Indians (more particularly Bengalis, who appeared especially vulnerable to 'Burdwan fever') was similarly explained away by climatic features. Ronald Ross received little encouragement or recognition for his major discovery, in 1899, of the link between a particular kind of mosquito and malaria. Meanwhile, the state invested very little in the area of Indian public health. The modern hospital was dreaded as a death trap by most people, uncaring towards the poor and insanitary for all.

Colonial investment in botany, typified by the foundation of the Sibpur Botanical Gardens near Calcutta as early as 1786, was followed later by research centres at Saharanpur in north UP and elsewhere. These were related to an interest in exportable agricultural products. The foundation of the Geological Survey of India in 1851 was similarly connected to a growing need for mineral resources, above all coal, essential for the railways. The demand for timber by the railways was a major factor behind the creation of a Forest Department in 1864 which ultimately came to control or regulate around 20 per cent of the land area of British India.[73] By far the biggest single land manager

[72] See Alavi 2007; Sivaramakrishnan 2006.
[73] Guha 1989; Rangarajan 1996.

on the subcontinent, the Forest Department's administration and interpretation of state policies had manifold ecological, economic, socio-cultural, and political implications which will engage our attention in subsequent chapters.

It is possible, however, to oversimplify the links between colonial scientific policies and their material, pragmatic, or ideological determinants, especially in the interests of colonial power–knowledge. Matthew Edney's study of colonial geography shows that the development of cartographic techniques and surveys of physical space were a prerequisite for the effective control and exploitation of a vast subcontinent. Beginning with Rennell's maps of Bengal, and then of India, in the 1770s and 1780s, the mapping endeavour went through two phases. Route surveys, based on the physical measurement of distances covered by foot, were combined with compass readings. These gave way from the early nineteenth century to the more abstract, scientific trigonometrical survey. The need for physical traverses was now overcome by fixing angles from hill-tops or towers, measuring a base line, and then calculating the other sides of an expanding series of imagined triangles. Triangulation clearly had affinities with a panoptic vision of total control that Bentham had imagined in the nineteenth century and that Foucault described as an ideal instrument of disciplinary control: in our case, the British surveyor occupying high points to produce a dominating, controlling view of spaces from above. Edney shows, however, that there were frequent gaps and conflicts 'between the desire and the ability to implement the perfect panopticist survey': the modernist gaze 'could never be so totalizing . . . so effective'. Funds were often inadequate for these very expensive triangulations. Frequent adjustments and compromises had to be made with local informants. The all-India Great Trigonometrical Survey (1818–43) was actually less useful than the earlier ground surveys for generating detailed data that were required for military campaigns and land revenue survey settlements. The shift to trigonometry, Edney argues, had therefore a compulsion perhaps more ideological than pragmatic. It was related, above all, to British self-images, helping to boost their self-confidence as the ruling elite, placing them in a situation of total surveillance and control. At least in the early nineteenth century, there may not have been much difference between on the one hand such modes of control which guided colonial assumptions about Indians, and on the other the attitudes of the metropolitan male ruling class towards workers and women in the home country. For all these numerous qualifications, Edney still assumes a fairly sharp 'modernizing' break in cartographic practice through the imposition of colonial-Western scientific knowledge. His view has been questioned by Kapil Raj, who argues for elements of hybridity through an interpenetration of conjoint developments in metropolis and colony. Raj points out that no uniform or detailed map of the British Isles existed when Rennell started his large-scale survey map in Bengal in the 1760s; so, there was no ready-made Western model being imposed from above. He emphasizes the role of indigenous informants and even methods within a pattern he calls 'assymetric reciprocity'.[74]

There are many indications that science became more important for imperial governance around the late nineteenth and early twentieth century. The deepening thrust towards a more centralized bureaucratic administration led to efforts to import, and in one striking case even to invent, more scientific procedures. One study traces the development of numerous new methods for a much more individualized surveillance, felt to be necessary precisely because late-colonial rule was marked by an enhanced fluidity in the movements of people across space through migration. This evoked fears of a possible loss of control; people's mobility had been comprehensively revolutionized by the railways, for instance. This enabled vast labour flows to cities, mines, plantations, and abroad. Verifications of personal identity came to be required in more and more administrative situations. The registration of births and deaths was introduced in big towns in the 1870s, especially as the more structured educational and administrative patterns often demanded proofs of age. The photographing of indentured labourers was introduced in the 1860s, and for transported convicts in 1875. Most strikingly, the Bengal police invented the method of fingerprinting for crime detection and proof in the 1890s. They used it for the first time in 1898, to establish

---

[74] Edney 1997: xiii, 25, *et passim*; Kapil Raj in Markovits, Pouchepadass, and Subrahmanyam 2003: 23–54.

guilt in a case where a Jalpaiguri tea-planter had been murdered.[75] Meanwhile, a wave of epidemics and famines in the 1890s and 1900s prodded the colonial state to become more energetic—often oppressively and unimaginatively so—in matters of public health. The plague panic, in particular, led to the immediate use of the serum that had just been invented by Haffkine. This was combined with draconian methods for segregating the infected, which produced widespread resentment and occasional violence among Indians. This did not stop Curzon—never known as being easy to stop—from proclaiming the ideological virtues of Western science in India. He proclaimed before a medical conference in 1899 that the British 'gifts' to India of law, Christianity, and literature might perhaps be questioned, but never that of science, particularly medicine. That, he declared, was based on 'the bedrock of pure, irrefutable science', and it could lift the veil of purdah and break down the barriers of caste without 'irreverence' or 'sacrilege'. Medicine, he believed, was the best justification for British rule.[76]

The imperial scientific structure was deeply racist, practising discrimination and exclusion, and expressing a sneering contempt for Indian scientific knowledge and methods. This became an increasing irritant with a growing number of Indians managing to get some scientific training. Instances of obvious discrimination became apparent when some of these tried to join state scientific institutions. Their failure in turn fuelled patriotic resentment among educated Indians. A well-known case was that of Pramathanath Bose, who had returned from London with a geology degree, but who found employment in the Geological Survey of India difficult because its superintendent had doubts whether as 'a Bengali he . . . may be physically unfit for our work.' Superseded as director by an Englishman ten years his junior in 1903, Bose resigned and went on to discover iron-ore deposits in Keonjhar in Orissa for the Tata steel plant in Jamshedpur. Educated Indian responses to Western science in the era of anticolonial nationalism could not but be highly varied, rather than a total rejection—as we shall see.

[75] Singha 2000: 151–98.
[76] Arnold 2000.

Racist and Gendered: Facets of the Empire

The preceding sections have concentrated on links between and interpenetrations of colonial power–knowledge with indigenous hierarchies. Ranajit Guha designated the colonial state 'an *absolute externality*', exercising 'domination without hegemony', a method of rule that never struck any roots whatsoever in Indian minds, or acquired any real and felt acceptance among its subjects. Guha's conclusion is important, but it needs some modification.[77] British rule was alien to Indians in ways that distinguish it from preceding patterns of imperial domination in two crucial respects. First, it had a racist aspect that deepened over time. The racism often fed into, and was fed by, evolving British stereotypes about gender. Moreover, the ultimate controlling power over the exploitative structures basic to its rule was located not within India but among dominant groups in the metropolitan country. These dimensions are crucial to explain the mass appeal and power that anti-colonial nationalism acquired over time.

Nonetheless, some qualifications are necessary, and this brings us to the second crucial fact about racism in the Indian colony. European racism in India could never attain the levels of control that it reached in the settler colonies. Europeans always remained too thin on the ground to even think of a New World-style physical extermination of natives. Nor was racism in India ever as systematically institutionalized, as it was in South Africa by apartheid. There was, of course, no lack of everyday racist behaviour, and formal or tacit double standards in the law courts. It is generally agreed that such things got noticeably worse in the latter part of the nineteenth century. Many new historical ingredients constituted this refashioned racism. Memories of 1857

---

[77] Guha 1989. To be fair to Guha, his essay also draws attention to inter-actions with indigenous traditions: between 'order' and 'danda', for instance: ibid.: 237–8. See also Neeladri Bhattacharya's helpful argument that though Gramscian hegemony in the sense of internalized cultural-moral consensus through democratic forms could not develop in colonial India, the degree of 'legitimacy' that colonial rule often enjoyed through adjustments and shifting accommodations should not be underestimated: Bhattacharya 1992: 113–49.

worsened mutual relations, breeding a perpetual anxiety and suspicion of Indians in general. There was also an avoidance of Indian women as possible sexual partners, especially after the opening of the Suez Canal allowed memsahibs to come to India in large numbers. A sharper 'biological' racism grew at this time, to which certain readings of Darwin significantly contributed: his theory of the survival of the fittest among the animal species was extended to imply that Indians colonized by Europeans represented an inferior species.

All this combined to produce in the late-nineteenth–early-twentieth century an aggressive imperialism and enhanced European arrogance. The British in India were now more conscious than ever before of being a master-race, as even the tallest in 'native' society sometimes learnt to his cost when he blundered into reserved compartments in trains or steamers, or faced discrimination and barriers to promotion in his job or profession. In 1878 the appointment of Muthuswamy Iyer to the Madras High Court was opposed by the *Madras Mail* (an organ of European businessmen) explicitly on the grounds that 'native officials should not draw the same rate of pay as Europeans in similar circumstances.'[78] The consequent uproar led to the foundation of a famous nationalist newspaper, *The Hindu*. Racism, predictably, could take on much cruder forms in relation to the 'lower orders', where it was overdetermined by class. It regularly manifested itself in kicks and blows by easily aggravated Europeans rupturing numerous Indian spleens. There were large numbers of shooting 'accidents' as the sahib disciplined his punkah coolie or bagged a native by mistake when out on shikar. Eighty-one shooting such accidents leading to Indian fatalities were recorded between 1880 and 1900. European-dominated courts regularly awarded ridiculously light sentences for such incidents, and a glance at contemporary Indian journals and private papers immediately reveals how important such things were for the rise of nationalism. Dinshaw Wacha complained to Dadabhai Naoroji on 30 October 1891 that 'European murders of natives are daily on the increase. Soldiers chiefly are the brutal offenders . . . [they are] always acquitted on some plea or another.'[79] The treatment of

[78] Suntharalingam 1974: 151–2.
[79] Patwardhan 1977: 265.

coolies on Assam tea plantations figured prominently in the work of the Indian Association in the 1880s. The question of indentured labour in Assam, as well as across the seas in the West Indies, Natal, Mauritius, and Fiji remained a very live issue even for the most moderate of nationalists till the abolition of the indenture system in 1916. Racial discrimination and brutality were, indeed, themes which could momentarily unite the highest in Indian society with the lowest within a common sense of deprivation and injustice.

The classic instance of European racism was the outcry over the Ilbert Bill which, in itself, was no more than a minor change in the Code of Criminal Procedure. All that had been proposed by the Ripon administration in February 1883 was that certain limited categories of Indian magistrates should be given the power to judge Europeans living in mofussil towns. Only three Indians in the whole country (all of them, as it happened, Bengalis) had risen high enough in the civil service to exercise this new criminal jurisdiction immediately.[80] Yet the ensuing White Mutiny was so intense that Ripon beat a hasty retreat. The compromise, eventually reached in January 1884, retained the new provision but diluted it drastically: Europeans being tried on criminal charges by Indian magistrates in the mofussil were given the right to demand trial by a jury of whom at least half would have to be Europeans.

The alarm and anger set off by the Ilbert Bill obviously had much to do with the fear that henceforward it would be less easy to get off so lightly in courts from assaults on Indian labourers or servants, or hunting accidents that maimed or killed villagers. The furore drew on the kinds of racist stereotypes that had been constituted in the post-Mutiny era, to which Ashis Nandy has drawn attention. Nandy illuminates the links between racial and sexual hierarchization—which he assumes to be more or less invariant across the history of modern Western colonial domination—whereby European and colonized stood to one another as masculine to feminine. This was often added to a further stigmatization on the grounds of immaturity or infantilism.

[80] They were Satyendranth Tagore, an older brother of Rabindranath; Romesh Chandra Dutt, the later Moderate Congressman and economic historian; and Biharilal Gupta.

For the white male, the native appeared congenitally immature, either on the one hand 'childlike', innocent, open to improvement through education, and occasionally attractive in a romantic manner; or on the other incorrigibly 'childish', impossible to reform, worthy only of repression.[81] Recent feminist scholarship has added to and historicized such insights considerably. The work of Mrinalini Sinha, in particular, has explored the multiple ramifications of the moment of extreme racism represented by the Ilbert Bill backlash. She highlights the interconnections between processes of ethnic, gender, and class stereotyping both in British-ruled India and in Britain. H.H. Risley, the future Census Commissioner, who was then a junior official, argued that Indians (more particularly the Bengali, already branded as peculiarly non-martial in army and other discourses) were, as a race, too effeminate: being no sportsmen, they would be unable to understand what he described with much affection as 'the thoughtless schoolboy spirit' which was all that lay behind the shooting of natives by mistake. The Indian male was simultaneously accused of gross patriarchal oppression. This was an appropriation of the theme of gender injustice in India for the cause of colonial domination, enabling the Englishman (and the Englishwoman, too) to appear to others, and to themselves, as benevolent guardians of oppressed Indian womanhood. The 1880s were also a time of incipient feministic activity within Britain, and some of the energies of this movement could now be neatly diverted into channels of what some have called 'maternal imperialism'.[82]

The more humane or farsighted among British Indian statesmen did occasionally try to restrain the grosser crudities of racism. Not only Ripon, even Curzon risked some unpopularity among his compatriots on this score, taking disciplinary action against British soldiers in two notorious cases. One was of collective rape of a Burmese woman, the other the murder of an Indian cook for refusing to act as a procurer. The regiment involved in the second case was given a defiant, hero's reception at the Delhi Durbar in 1903. But what needs emphasis is that, excesses apart, a measure of racism had a functional and neces-

[81] Nandy 1983: 4–16.
[82] Sinha 1995: chapter I; see also Burton 1994.

sary role in the political and economic structures of colonial India. It helped, in the first place, to unite the European ruling caste across divisions of class and gender. Two instances may be cited. The anti-Ilbert Bill agitation saw an unusual degree of public activism among white women in India. Some of them organized a Ladies Committee to organize a social boycott of the minority of Europeans who supported Ripon and Ilbert. Soon afterwards, during the Panjdeh war scare of 1885, non-elite Anglo-Indian clerks and railway employees were welcomed into the volunteer groups that had been set up to assist the army, while offers by Indian elites to raise a native volunteer force were firmly rejected.

The Indian empire was an important provider of 'jobs for the boys' in Britain. After recruitment through examinations became the rule, within certain limits colonial employment cemented the ties of different groups within Britain through the projection of a common 'British masculinity'.[83] It should be emphasized also that there was nothing irrational, from the British point of view, about excluding Indians for as much and as long as possible from the senior and key posts in the military and administrative cadre. So, an apparently trivial demand like the holding of simultaneous ICS examinations in India was bitterly opposed for fifty years. Elgin argued in a letter to Rosebery in July 1895 that 'we could only govern by maintaining the fact that we are the dominant race . . . Though Indians in the services should be encouraged, there is a point at which we must reserve the control to ourselves, if we are to remain at all.'[84]

Even more crucial were the economic dimensions of racism that have been shown in, particularly, the work of Amiya Bagchi. Colour played an important role in preserving the unity of European businessmen in India against possible Indian competitors. The functioning of the various European chambers of commerce, trade associations, and organizations of jute, tea, and mining interests often reveal something like a 'collective monopoly' of European businessmen that was particularly formidable in the eastern part of India. 'European traders

[83] Sinha 1995: 54–60, 95, 131–2.
[84] Elgin to Rosebery, July 1895: Lord Elgin, Private Papers, India Office Library and Records, National Archives of India.

and businessmen were great believers in reasonable compromise and mutual accommodation among themselves, however much they might believe in the virtues of competition for others.'[85] And, despite the occasional conflict and a certain aristocratic disdain for trade affected by some bureaucrats, there always existed innumerable personal and 'club-life' ties between the white businessman and the white official in India. Lord Curzon, in a speech to British mine-owners in Barakar in 1903, summed up with admirable frankness this crucial link between government and business: 'My work lies in administration, yours in exploitation: but both are aspects of the same question and of the same duty.'[86] As late as in 1944, an Indian manufacturers' association complained about 'the silent sympathy from the mystic bond of racial affinity with the rulers of the land, which procures them [European businessmen] invisible, but not the less effective, advantages in their competition with their indigenous rivals.'[87]

THE PRINCELY STATES

British-ruled India consisted of directly ruled provinces and a large number of princely states of diverse sizes. These included big states like Hyderabad, Mysore, and Jammu and Kashmir, and tiny princely states sometimes difficult to distinguish from the larger zamindaris. Even estimates of their numbers varied: thus the Imperial Gazetteer of 1909 listed 693, while another official report of 1929 reduced that number to 562.

Why did the British keep such an untidy political map of their possessions when they could have swept many of these kingdoms away and absorbed the domains into their direct rule? In part this was a product of a change in British policy after 1857. Prior to that, an aggressive policy of annexation had been generally followed, but the experience of the Great Rebellion of 1857 created a new need to consolidate an alliance with dependent princes, and with the upper classes in general. Preserving the princely domains also suited British

[85] Bagchi 1972: 170.
[86] Cited in McLane 1977: 37.
[87] Bagchi 1972: 166.

purposes, since in most princely states petty despotism flourished. The princes were, by and large, servile with the paramount power and oppressive with their subjects.

Let us look briefly at three of these states.

Mysore

Mysore under Hyder Ali and Tipu Sultan had been the most formidable enemy of the EIC in the late eighteenth century, and the Company was able to defeat Mysore only as late as 1799. Perhaps because of this earlier history, a period of direct British rule from 1831 was followed in 1881 by a form of indirect rule under an Indian dynasty. Indirect rule, of course, still meant overall control by the British paramount power. But Mysore was exceptional in one way. Under an unusually efficient and dynamic dewan, Visvesvaraya, a policy of state-sponsored economic development was promoted. This has sometimes been hailed as a partial anticipation of later state-sponsored economic development, which would become the policy of independent India in the Nehruvian era. Visvesvaraya's policy was based on promoting three areas for development: coffee and tea plantations in the Nilgiris, cotton textiles in centres like Bangalore, and the gold fields in Kolar. However, textiles apart, the areas of development were mostly under British ownership, and in this matter differed from post-colonial Nehruvian policy. Mysore under Visvesvaraya also remained generally compliant with the overall British political control, so there were no open clashes with the paramount power. This was possibly helped by the fact that there was, on the whole, little nationalist or popular militancy except for some small-scale labour unrest in and around Bangalore. Later, the Congress came to dominate popular politics and this helped bring about a transition to independence without much upheaval. There was, however, a powerful development of non-Brahmin politics against brahmanical power, especially among Lingayats and Vokkaligas.

Jammu and Kashmir

There has been a persistent dualism in tribal accounts, and in Mughal and British sources alike: ecstatic descriptions of the beauty of Kashmir have coincided with a profound silence on the misery and exploitation of its people.[88]

After the disintegration of the Sikh kingdom of Punjab under Ranjit Singh, the British lumped together different parts of that kingdom under Gulab Singh, the Dogra ruler of Jammu, with which the Kashmir valley was integrated in 1846. Gulab Singh and his successors, like native princes in general, combined servility towards the British with a rule that was oppressive in relation to their subjects.

Jammu and Kashmir were distinctive in having a Hindu king ruling over an overwhelming majority of Muslim subjects. The situation here was just the opposite of the one in Hyderabad, where a Muslim dynasty of nizams ruled over a mass of Hindu peasants. Despite the communal implications of both these situations, open communal clashes, while not entirely absent, remained relatively rare in both. For Kashmir, this has been explained in Indian nationalist accounts, with some exaggeration perhaps, as the product of a unique sense of regional identity or 'Kashmiriat'. Such accounts sometimes tend to play down the elements of tension, conflict, and oppression under Dogra rule. In Hyderabad, by contrast, opposition to the rule of the oppressive nizam and his landlord allies was spearheaded by left-wing groups, particularly Communists who led the Telangana peasant rebellion in the late 1940s and early 1950s on entirely secular lines.

Gulab Singh and his successors ruled mainly through an alliance with a literate minority of Kashmiri Hindu pandits. Their rule, generally oppressive, proved specially so for the majority of peasants and artisans, who were largely Muslims. Heavy rents were extracted from peasants, including the occasional use of forced labour; and the prices of the best-nown product of Kashmir, woollen shawls, were arbitrarily fixed by the maharaja. In 1846, for instance, the shawl weavers in a collective protest migrated in large numbers out from Kashmir. In 1877, again, peasant oppression contributed to a terrible famine in the Kashmir valley.

The tradition of Kashmiriat, however, if not entirely a myth, has a long literary heritage in medieval Kashmiri poetry, notably that of the

---

[88] Zutshi 2003 and Rai 2004 are among the best recent works on Kashmir over the century spanning Gulab Singh and Indian Independence.

poetess Lal Ded, and of Nooruddin. Their verses mingled devotion to Allah with Shiva and were marked by a sense of fluid religious boundaries. In partial contrast to this tradition, the Dogra rulers tried at times to consolidate their somewhat uncertain legitimacy by claiming mythic Rajput ancestry. This went along with an increasing emphasis on Hindu ceremonial, the patronage of Hindu temples, and the encouragement of pilgrimages to Hindu sacred places in the subcontinent. By the early twentieth century such policies led to occasional clashes between Hindus and Muslims over Hindu shrines and mosques. A major riot occurred in 1931 because of such conflicting claims over sacred sites.

Dogra oppression and the dynasty's widespread unpopularity created the possibility of communal conflict as well as of Hindu–Muslim collective popular resistance. In the 1930s and 1940s a united movement demanding democratic rights developed under the leadership of Sheikh Abdullah and the National Conference party led by him. This generally supported anti-British movements in India because the British, as elsewhere in princely India, backed feudal rulers against their subjects. Protest movements, notably those led by Sheikh Abdullah, also combined a general sympathy for Indian nationalism and Hindu–Muslim unity with the desire for autonomy for Kashmir in any future Indian dispensation. This was the setting in which, soon after Independence in 1947, the new Kashmir state decided to accede to the Indian Union but on condition of considerable autonomy. The desired autonomy has been whittled down over time, contributing to an intense alienation from India of increasing numbers of Kashmiris.

Manipur

Manipur's strategic location near Burma and China had contradictory implications for British policies. The British wanted to control this fertile valley surrounded by mountains, but instead of total incorporation they generally preferred to keep Manipur as a buffer state. So Manipur was never integrated with British India.

Till the early nineteenth century Burma claimed a vague kind of authority over Manipur. After the first Anglo-Burmese war, however, in 1826 the British and Burma both recognized the independence of Manipur. Unlike the mountainous areas that surrounded Manipur which was inhabited by tribal groups like the Nagas, Mizos, and Kukis, this fertile land had already had a long tradition of being a small independent kingdom.

In 1885 the British defeated and annexed Burma, making it a part of British India. However, it was still convenient for the British not to fully incorporate Manipur into their empire, but keep it as a buffer frontier state, since by the 1880s there was also the possibility of French penetration into neighbouring Indochina. So, British authority over Manipur was exercised through a political agent without it becoming formally a princely state. The Manipur maharaja was, like other native rulers, allowed to exercise despotic authority over the people of Manipur. The resentments that developed as a result of this situation led to the murder of some British Indian soldiers in 1891 and to a widespread popular rebellion. Manipur was annexed the same year.

In much of the popular unrest against the dynasty, and against British political and military controls and changes, women producers and traders played a significant role. Women have traditionally enjoyed a position of independence in Manipur society quite different from the situation of women in most parts of India. In particular, they were extremely prominent in trade, and the major rice bazaar was a place where large numbers of women gathered and exchanged information. This therefore became the centre for political and social gatherings. The tradition of women's militancy in Manipur culminated in the two Nupilans or 'women's wars' of 1904 and 1939. These were provoked by Marwari penetration into the rice trade, and the colonial cornering of the rice market during the Second World War alongside the despotic behaviour of the maharaja operating under British protection.

By the 1940s economic tensions helped a movement for democratic reforms. This was led in part by Irawat Singh, who had developed links with both the Congress and the Communist Party of India. Pressures for democratic reform culminated in the late 1940s in a remarkable development. Between 1947 and 1949 Manipur was able to briefly evolve a democratic constitution based on an assembly elected via a democratic franchise. It is seldom remembered today that this anticipated by a number of years the establishment of democracy in the rest of the subcontinent. However, the democratic autonomy that Manipur briefly enjoyed was soon snuffed out by its integration with independent India.

Bibliography

Alavi, Seema, *The Sepoys and the Company: Tradition and Transition in Northern India 1770–1830* (Delhi: Oxford University Press, 1995)

———, *Islam and Healing: Loss and Recovery of an Indo-Muslim Medical Tradition 1600–1900* (Ranikhet: Permanent Black, 2007)

Appadurai, Arjun, 'Number in the Colonial Imagination', in Carol Breckenridge and Peter van der Veer, eds, *Orientalism and the Postcolonial Predicament* (Philadelphia: Pennsylvania University Press, 1993)

Arnold, David, *Science, Technology and Medicine in Colonial India* (Cambridge: Cambridge University Press, 2000)

Bagchi, Amiya, *Private Investment in India 1900–1939* (Cambridge: Cambridge University Press, 1972)

Barua, Sanjib, *Durable Disorder: Understanding the Politics of Northeast India* (Oxford: Oxford University Press, 2005)

Bayly, C.A., *The Local Roots of Indian Politics: Allahabad 1880–1920* (Oxford: Clarendon Press, 1975)

Bayly, Susan, *Saints, Goddesses and Kings: Muslims and Christians in South Indian Society, 1700–1900* (Cambridge: Cambridge University Press, 1989)

———, 'Caste and Race in the Colonial Ethnography of India', in Peter Robb, ed., *The Concept of Race in South Asia* (Delhi: Oxford University Press, 1995)

Bhattacharya, Neeladri, 'Remaking Custom: The Discourse and Practice of Colonial Codification', in R. Champakalakshmi and S. Gopal, eds, *Tradition, Dissent and Ideology* (New Delhi: Oxford University Press, 1996), pp. 20–51

———, 'Colonial State and Agrarian Society', in Burton Stein, ed., *The Making of Agrarian Policy in British India* (Delhi: Oxford University Press, 1992)

Breckenridge, Carol and Peter van der Veer, eds, *Orientalism and the Postcolonial Predicament* (Philadelphia: Pennsylvania University Press, 1993)

Burton, Antoinette, *Burdens of History: British Feminists, Indian Women, and Imperial Culture, 1865–1915* (Chapel Hill: University of North Carolina Press, 1994)

Census (Bengal), 1891 (Calcutta: Bengal Secretariat Press, 1893)

Census (Bengal), 1901 (Calcutta: Bengal Secretariat Press, 1903)

Census (India), 1911 (Calcutta: Bengal Secretariat Press, 1912)

Chakrabarti, Pratik, *Western Science in Modern India: Metropolitan Methods, Colonial Practices* (Delhi: Permanent Black, 2004)

Chakravarti, Uma, *Rewriting History: The Life and Times of Pandita Ramabai* (New Delhi: Kali for Women, 1998)

Champakalakshmi, R., and S. Gopal, eds, *Tradition, Dissent and Ideology* (New Delhi: Oxford University Press, 1996)

Chatterjee, Partha, *Nationalist Thought and the Colonial World: A Derivative Discourse* (London: Zed Books, 1986)

——, *The Nation and Its Fragments: Colonial and Postcolonial Histories* (Princeton, NJ: Princeton University Press, 1993)

Cohn, Bernard S., 'Representing Authority in Victorian India', in E.J. Hobsbawm and Terence Ranger, eds, *The Invention of Tradition* (Cambridge: Cambridge University Press, 1983)

——, *An Anthropologist among the Historians and Other Essays* (Delhi: Oxford University Press, 1987)

——, *Colonialism and Its Forms of Knowledge: The British in India* (Princeton, NJ: Princeton University Press, 1996)

Constable, Philip, 'Sitting on the School Verandah: Ideology and Practice of "Untouchable" Educational Protest in Late 19th Century Western India', *Indian Economic and Social History Review*, 37 (IV), 2000

Copley, Antony, *Religions in Conflict: Ideology, Cultural Contact and Conversions in Late Colonial India* (Delhi: Oxford University Press, 1997)

Coupland, Reginald, *The Constitutional Problem in India, Parts I–III* (Oxford: Oxford University Press, 1944)

Cowell, Herbert, *The Hindu Law: Being a Treatise on the Law Administered Exclusively to Hindus by the British Courts in India* (Calcutta: Thacker, Spink, 1870)

Crook, Nigel, ed., *The Transmission of Knowledge in South Asia: Essays on Education, Religion, History, and Politics* (New Delhi: Oxford University Press, 1996)

Dena, Lal, *British Policy towards Manipur 1762–1947* (Imphal: Nongeen Publications, 2008)

Deshpande, Prachi, *Creative Pasts: Historical Memory and Identity in Western India, 1700–1960* (Delhi: Permanent Black, 2007)

Edney, Matthew, *Mapping an Empire: The Geographical Construction of British India, 1765–1843* (Chicago: University of Chicago Press, 1997)

Fisch, Jörg, *Cheap Lives and Dear Limbs: The British Transformation of the Bengal Criminal Law, 1769–1817* (Wiesbaden: F. Steiner, 1983)

Frykenberg, R.E., *Guntur District, 1788–1848: A History of Local Influence and Central Authority in South India* (Oxford: Clarendon Press, 1965)

Galanter, Marc, 'Changing Legal Conceptions of Caste', in M. Singer and B.S. Cohn, eds, *Structure and Change in Indian Society* (Chicago: Aldine, 1968)

Gallagher, J., *et al.*, *Locality, Province and Nation: Essays on Indian Politics, 1870 to 1940* (Cambridge: Cambridge University Press, 1973)

Geetha, V., and S.V. Rajadurai, *Towards a Non-Brahmin Millennium: From Jyothee Thass to Periyar* (Calcutta: Samya, 1998)

Gopal, S., *British Policy in India 1858–1905* (Cambridge: Cambridge University Press, 1965)

Guha, Ramachandra, *The Unquiet Woods: Ecological Change and Peasant Resistance in the Himalaya* (Delhi: Oxford University Press, 1989; new edn rpnt Ranikhet: Permanent Black, 2009)

Guha, Ranajit, 'Dominance without Hegemony and its Historiography', in Ranajit Guha, ed., *Subaltern Studies VI: Writings on South Asian History and Society* (Delhi: Oxford University Press, 1989)

Guha, Sumit, *Environment and Ethnicity in India 1200–1991* (Cambridge: Cambridge University Press, 1995)

Habermas, Jürgen, *The Structual Transformation of the Public Sphere: An Inquiry into a Category of Bourgeois Society* (Cambridge: Polity, 1989)

Harrison, J.B., 'English as a University Subject in India and England: Calcutta, Allahabad, Benaras, London, Cambridge, and Oxford', in Nigel Crook, ed., *The Transmission of Knowledge in South Asia: Essays on Education, Religion, History and Politics* (New Delhi: Oxford University Press, 1996)

Hettne, Bjorn, *The Political Economy of Indirect Rule: Mysore 1881–1947* (London: Curzon Press, 1978)

Inden, Ronald B., *Imagining India* (Oxford: Blackwell, 1990)

Irschick, E.F., *Dialogue and History: Constructing South India, 1795–1895* (Berkeley: University of Berkeley Press, 1995)

Jones, Kenneth, ed., *Religious Controversy in British India: Dialogues in South Asian Languages* (New York: State University of New York Press, 1992)

Kikani, L.T., *Caste in Courts: Or, Rights and Powers of Castes in Social and Religious Matters as Recognized by Indian Courts* (Rajkut: Printed at the Ganatra Printing Works, 1912)

Kolff, D.H.A., *Naukar, Rajput and Sepoy: The Ethnohistory of the Military Labour Market in Hindustan, 1450–1850* (Cambridge: Cambridge University Press, 1990)

Kumar, Deepak, 'Racial Discrimination and Science in Nineteenth-Century India', *Indian Economic and Social History Review*, XIX (I), 1982

Kumar, Dharma, 'The Fiscal System', in Dharma Kumar, ed., *The Cambridge Economic History of India, Volume 2 c.1750–c.1970* (Cambridge: Cambridge University Press, 1983)

Kosambi, Meera, *Ideals, Images, and Real Lives: Women in Literature and History* (Mumbai: Orient Longman, 2000)

———, *Crossing Thresholds: Feminist Essays in Social History* (Ranikhet: Permanent Black, 2007)

Lelyveld, David, *Aligarh's First Generation: Muslim Solidarity in British India* (Princeton: Princeton University Press, 1978)

Markovits, Claude, Jacques Pouchepadass, and Sanjay Subrahmanyam, eds, *Society and Circulation: Mobile People and Itinerant Cultures in South Asia, 1750–1950* (Delhi: Permanent Black, 2003)

McDonald, Ellen, 'English Education and Social Reform in Late 19th Century Bombay', *Journal of Asian Studies*, XXV (3), 1966

McLane, J.R., *Indian Nationalism and the Early Congress* (Princeton: Princeton University Press, 1977)

Nandy, Ashis, *The Intimate Enemy: Loss and Recovery of Self Under Colonialism* (Delhi: Oxford University Press, 1983)

Oddie, G.A., ed., *Religious Conversion Movements in South Asia: Continuities and Change* (Richmond, Surrey: Curzon Press, 1997)

Pal, Bipinchandra, *Memoirs of My Life and Times* (Calcutta: Yugayatri Prakashak, 1932, rpnt 1973)

Panikkar, K.M., *Asia and Western Dominance: A Survey of Vasco da Gama Epoch of Asian History, 1498–1945* (1953; London: George Allen & Unwin Ltd, 1959)

Patwardhan, R.P., ed., *Dadabhai Naoroji Correspondence*, vol. II (New Delhi: Allied Publishers, 1977)

Parratt, Saroj Arambam, and John Parratt, 'The Second Women's War and the Emergence of Democratic Government in Manipur', in Sumit Sarkar and Tanika Sarkar, eds, *Women and Social Reform in India: A Reader* (Delhi: Permanent Black, 2008)

Phalkey, Jahnavi, *Atomic State: Big Science in Twentieth-Century India* (Ranikhet: Permanent Black, 2013)

Radhakrishna, Meena, *Dishonoured by History: 'Criminal Tribes' and British Colonial Policy* (Hyderabad, A.P.: Orient Longman, 2001)

Rai, Mridu, *Hindu Rulers, Muslim Subjects: Islam, Rights and the History of Kashmir* (Delhi: Permanent Black, 2004)

Raj, Kapil, 'Circulation and the Emergence of Modern Mapping: Great Britain and Early Colonial India, 1764–1820', in Claude Markovits, Jacques Pouchepadass, and Sanjay Subrahmanyam, eds, *Society and*

Circulation: Mobile People and Itinerant Cultures in South Asia, 1750–1950 (Delhi: Permanent Black, 2003)

Ramusack, Barbara, *The Indian Princes and their States* (Cambridge: Cambridge University Press, 2004)

Rangarajan, Mahesh, *Fencing the Forest: Conservation and Ecological Change in India's Central Provinces, 1860–1914* (Delhi: Oxford University Press, 1996)

Risley, H.H., *Tribes and Castes of Bengal: Ethnographic Glossary* (Calcutta: Bengal Secretariat Press, 1891)

Robb, Peter, *The Concept of Race in South Asia* (Delhi: Oxford University Press, 1995)

Said, Edward, *Orientalism* (New York: Vintage Books, 1978)

Sarkar, Sumit, *Modern India: 1885–1947* (Delhi: Macmillan, 1983)

Sarkar, Tanika, *Hindu Wife, Hindu Nation: Community, Religion and Cultural Nationalism* (Delhi: Permanent Black, 2001)

Savarkar, V.D., *Hindutva / Who is a Hindu?* (Ahmedabad: Loksanghara, 1923)

Seal, Anil, *The Emergence of Indian Nationalism: Competition and Collaboration in the Later Nineteenth Century* (Cambridge: Cambridge University Press, 1968)

Singh, Hiralal, *Problems and Policies of the British in India: 1885–1898*, Asia Historical Series No. 1 (London: Asia Publishing House, 1963)

Singha, Radhika, *A Despotism of Law: Crime and Justice in Early Colonial India* (New Delhi: Oxford University Press, 1998)

———, 'Settle, Mobilize, Verify: Identification Practices in Colonial India', *Studies in History*, 16 (2), 2000

Sinha, Mrinalini, *Colonial Masculinity: The 'Manly' Englishman and the 'Effeminate' Bengalis in the Late 19th Century* (Manchester: Manchester University Press, 1995)

Sivaramakrishnan, Kavita, *Old Potions, New Bottles: Recasting Indigenous Medicine in Colonial Punjab 1850–1940* (New Delhi: Orient Blackswan, 2006)

Stein, Burton, ed., *The Making of Agrarian Policy in British India* (Delhi: Oxford University Press, 1992)

Strachey, Sir John, *India* (London: Kegan Paul, Trench & Co., 1888)

Suntharalingam, R., *Politics and Nationalist Awakening in South India, 1852–91* (Tucson, Arizona: University of Arizona Press, 1974)

Thompson, E.P., *Customs in Common: Studies in Traditional Popular Culture* (New York: New Press, 1991)

Thorner, Daniel, and Alice Thorner, *Land and Labour in India* (Bombay: Asia Publishing House, 1962)

Trautmann, Thomas R., *The Madras School of Orientalism: Producing Knowledge in Colonial South India* (New Delhi: Oxford University Press, 2009)

Venkatachalapathy, A.R., *The Province of the Book: Scholars, Scribes, and Scribblers in Colonial Tamilnadu* (Ranikhet: Permanent Black, 2011)

Viswanathan, Gauri, *Masks of Conquest: Literary Studies and British Rule in India* (New York: Columbia University Press, 1989)

———, *Outside the Fold: Conversion, Modernity, and Belief* (Delhi: Oxford University Press, 1998)

Washbrook, David, *The Emergence of Provincial Politics: The Madras Presidency 1870–1920* (Cambridge: Cambridge University Press, 1976)

———, 'Law, State and Agrarian Society in Colonial India', *Modern Asian Studies*, 15 (3), 1981

Zupanov, Ines G., *Jesuit Experiments and Brahmanical Knowledge in Seventeenth-Century India* (New York: Oxford University Press, 1999)

Zutshi, Chitralekha, *Languages of Belonging: Islam, Regional Identity and the Making of Kashmir* (Delhi: Permanent Black, 2003)

2

Woods and Trees
The Environment and the Economy

From around the 1870s British India began to suffer repeated famines. The obvious contrast between British or Western prosperity and persistent, possibly worsening, Indian poverty became ever more evident. A significant section of the Indian intelligentsia now began to develop a powerful critique of the economic consequences of British rule.[1] This was a discourse built around a series of interrelated concepts and themes which we will soon discuss: the 'drain of wealth' through an artificially maintained and harmful export surplus; an alleged devastation of indigenous handicrafts through 'deindustrialization'; excessive land revenue burdens which, together with forced commercialization, kept the countryside backward and poor; and unfair tariff policies alongside measures encouraging foreign capital to dominate, which severely restricted the possibilities of indigenous capitalist industrial development. Endlessly propagated through newspapers, pamphlets, speeches, and patriotic literature, these views—of which Dadabhai Naoroji and R.C. Dutt became the major exemplars—would remain more or less standard

---

[1] Dadabhai Naoroji stands at the head of this intellectual tradition, with his lectures to the East Indian Association entitled *The Wants and Means of India* (1870) and *Poverty of India* (1876); and his magnum opus, *Poverty and UnBritish Rule in India* (1901). The other major figures include R.C. Dutt, author of a pioneering two-volume *Economic History of India* (1900, 1902), M.G. Ranade, G.V. Joshi, and some Indophile Englishmen (notably W. Digby).

for all anti-colonial nationalist ideologies, Moderate, Extremist, Gandhian, or Left-nationalist-Marxist. They provoked many rebuttals from apologists for 'England's work in India'. All this led on to an extraordinarily persistent academic debate, which for very long—perhaps too long—has occupied the core of modern Indian economic-historical research.[2]

Many of the questions raised by that debate remain relevant: particularly in today's era of triumphant neo-colonialism, neo-liberal orthodoxy, and rapidly intensifying disparities of wealth on a global scale. In their own ways, the nationalist critics had questioned the universal applicability of some of the dogmas of neo-classical economics based on laissez-faire, especially the argument that free trade invariably brings universal prosperity. At the same time, the analytical framework of economic nationalism was somewhat constricted as it posited an oversimplified opposition between colonial oppression and Indian suffering, ignoring for instance the collusion between Indian elites and colonial power, or the oppression of Indian subalterns by authorities of local origin.

In new historical research, three kinds of thrusts have developed to complicate and take us beyond the old framework. Critics and defenders of colonial economic policies and structures had for long argued alike about the subcontinent as a whole, their underlying assumption suggesting a single territorial unit. Regional and local variations inevitably became evident as detailed economic-historical research began to develop from around the 1950s and 1960s. The extent—sometimes even the reality—of deindustrialization, or the allegedly negative and forced nature of the commercialization of agriculture, came to be seen to differ widely across regions, times, and in relation to the specificities of handicrafts and crops. Nationalist

---

[2] Well after Independence, the embers of that old debate have been re-stoked on at least three notable occasions: by Morris David Morris's efforts to demolish the deindustrialization thesis in the 1960s; through the controversial parts of Dharma Kumar, ed., *The Cambridge Economic History of India, Volume 2, c.1750–c.1970* (Kumar 1983); and by Tirthankar Roy's thesis (Roy 2000), at once provocative and stimulating, concerning the survival-cum-growth of small industries through the colonial era. An early exploration of this idea is in Roy 1993.

frameworks, in the second place, had a built-in tendency to play down internal tensions and conflicts, and indigenous power relations, in order to establish their case for the overall exploitation and immiserization of the entire colonized world through alien domination. But the most far-reaching historiographical transformation is the coming into being from the 1980s of an entirely new sub-discipline—environmental history. It seems most convenient to begin with this, for so far it has hardly entered the world of textbook historical accounts. A survey of environmental studies bearing on the late-colonial era can provide a necessary setting for subsequent sections on the economy, and indeed also for many aspects of the history of the popular movements which are the subject of later chapters.

Environmental Histories: Origins and Core Issues

The historical interest in environmental questions related in part to the deepening of research on regional and local agrarian conditions. Scholars moved beyond the earlier concentration on top-level decision-making and institutions (above all, revenue policies) towards micro studies based on district and sub-district archives. Consequently, the 'earthier' details of production—soil conditions, water resources, and other such issues with clear ecological dimensions—could no longer be ignored. Research on the precise catchment areas for labour migration towards plantations, overseas British colonies, and mines as well as other emerging capitalist industries, also revealed significant environmental variables.[3] A more general input was the worldwide spread of a growing concern with issues of environment and ecological devastation alongside the emergence of 'Green' movements. But probably the biggest factor was the rise of numerous movements of peasants and adivasis around questions of community rights to forests—as against commercial and state intrusions—which stimulated historical interest in colonial forest policies and led to popular protests. This would subsequently extend to the politics of water use and big dams. From around the 1970s a new kind of middle-class social activism expressed

[3] For two early indicators of this emerging change in emphasis, see Chakrabarti 1978: 249–327; and Bhattacharya 1985.

itself in the formation of decentralized non-governmental groups rather than through established political parties. These groups worked at local, grassroots levels, and aroused interest in, and sometimes mass enthusiasm over, such movements—Chipko and Narmada Bachao being the most obvious landmarks for the intelligentsia and academia. Chipko was both stimulus to and the subject of the early work of a pioneer of Indian environmental history, Ramachandra Guha.[4]

Prior to the environmental turn agrarian historians, irrespective of their other differences, had assumed that rural India meant overwhelmingly a multitude of peasant villages engaged in settled agriculture. Other, non-sedentary ways of relating to environments were relegated to 'marginal' areas or situations. Mughal chronicles and revenue records and British archival material buttressed such presuppositions. Settled villages were easier to control, measure, and tax. Hence they left behind a great deal of documentation for later historians. Pre-colonial and colonial ruling groups alike assumed that extending cultivation to 'cultivable wastes' (the nuances of this colonial and post-colonial term need to be unravelled) was synonymous with the advance of civilization.

Into this environmental histories brought about something like a paradigm shift via their emphasis on communities of hunters, food-gatherers, pastoralists, and shifting or swidden cultivators. These now appear to have had an extremely significant and far from marginal presence down to late-colonial times, when there was a comprehensive tightening up of communicational, politico-military, administrative, and economic integration. The new focus, and associated empirical research, raised important questions. These related to whether significant elements of what had come to be considered quintessentially traditional—e.g. countrywide hierarchies of varna and jati rooted in settled villages, along with sharply distinct 'tribals' at the margins—may not have been constituted by colonial modernity.

But the new historiographical turn also brought problems of its own. Sedentary modes of life had long been valorized against the nomadic. Environmental history, in sharp contrast, tended to reread narratives of 'progress' through agrarian expansion as 'deforestation'.

[4] Guha 1989; Gadgil and Guha 1992.

It has, in practice, virtually banished the settled peasant cultivator from its concerns. The older dichotomy persisted: between forests and pastures on the one hand, and settled agriculture on the other. Environmental history concentrated on the first alone, inverting rather than overcoming this dualism. One collection of essays has drawn attention to the need to overcome this rift between environmental and agrarian history by establishing 'links between the studies of pastures, forests, fields and farms'—we might add: 'of towns and factories'—for no sphere of human labour and history can avoid mediation in varying ways through changing relationships with nature.[5]

The dichotomy is also related to other commonly assumed polarities. Much environmental history, in India as well in many other countries, has been inspired by what is aptly termed the 'arcadian principle'. This means romanticizing the pastoral and rendering it pristine, idyllic, and generally more virtuous than other domains. As Neeladri Bhattacharya puts it, from this vision the world of forests and other common property resources tends to be seen 'as domains that are free of sharp inequalities and internal tensions, insulated and totally distinct from the settled, hierarchized, and conflict-ridden life of peasants and townsmen.'[6] Given the importance and undoubtedly oppressive nature of much of the environmental impact of colonial policies and transformations, such romanticization added to temptations in history-writing towards 'exaggerated contrasts between precolonial and colonial, modern Western and indigenous traditional.'[7]

Despite such necessary qualifications, it is undeniable that a series of late-colonial developments were critical for Indian environmental history. We will begin with a glance at two kinds of subcontinental

[5] Bhattacharya 1998: Introduction.

[6] The other kind of locus for romanticization—peasant 'community consciousness'—had of course figured prominently in the early phase of the *Subaltern Studies* project, but is no longer so visible. Evocations of peasant community then, however, had not been much alive to environmental questions. But Ramachandra Guha's early work can be read as combining elements from both.

[7] For an analytically and empirically rich analysis of these problems, see Sivaramakrishnan 1999a.

pressures: first, from British forest policies; and second, from multiple efforts by colonial officialdom to control local populations through sedentarization. This will be followed by a brief look at some recent regional studies.

Regulation and Protection as Appropriation: Forests and 'Wastes' in Late-Colonial India

The colonial state extended its regulation over vast areas which it defined as 'forest'. This often abrogated a very wide range of customary practices and claims, and constituted the most dramatic and controversial aspect of colonial environmental policies. The two key legal landmarks here were the Forest Acts of 1865 and 1878. The first merely empowered the state to assert control over forest resources that it immediately required, while still acknowledging a need to respect what it vaguely described as the 'existing rights' of forest users. The more precise and definitive 1878 Act established the basic categories of 'reserved' and 'protected' forests. The management and resources of the first were made an exclusive state monopoly; in the second, particular types of trees were protected from felling even while access to firewood, grazing, and other resources could continue to be allowed to villagers—such everyday practices from antiquity now becoming at a stroke, by state fiat, special privileges granted by the Forest Department and regulated by it. The state also retained, and widely exercised, the power to transfer land under the second category to the first. The area classified as reserved forest, 14,000 sq miles in 1878, had shot up to 56,000 sq miles by 1890. In that same year, 20,000 sq miles had been declared protected forests. The amount of land reserved rather than protected approached 100,000 sq miles on the eve of Independence. The Forest Department thus came to control about one-fifth of the British Indian land area, making it the biggest land manager on the subcontinent.[8]

The colonial justification for such extensive state control—so contrary to the usual assertions of the virtues of laissez-faire—was propounded via terms such as 'scientific forestry', which would

[8] Gadgil and Guha 1992: chapter 4; Rangarajan 1996: Introduction.

supposedly end the destruction of forests by rapacious private interests and ignorant peasants. Indian environmental history, beginning with the work of Ramachandra Guha and Madhav Gadgil, rejected—with considerable justice though perhaps also the occasional exaggeration—this official 'conservationist' plea as little more than an ideological cover for military and economic motivations. The first British attempt at state regulation was in Malabar in 1806. During the Napoleonic wars, the teak of the Western Ghats came to be seen as important for building ships for the Royal Navy. British timber resources were already getting exhausted, while the Continental System blocked access to Baltic timber. The post of conservator of Malabar forests was, however, abolished by 1823, and the real leap in colonial forestry was clearly related to the needs of railway construction after the 1850s. Massive amounts of timber were required for railway sleepers, as well as for fuel prior to the complete shift of steam engines to coal. Other forms of new or enhanced demand came from cantonments, hill stations, and paper manufactures in the new era of print. Since extraction was largely made through private contractors, there were growing fears over uncontrolled commercial logging, which might lead to deforestation in more and more areas. The shift towards state regulation began at the all-India level when the Forest Department was set up in 1864 under a German expert, Deitrich Brandis. The change could thereby also be explained as necessary for the extraction of forest resources in ways that were more efficient and sustainable.

Some environmentalist scholars, notably Richard Grove, however, feel that this line of interpretation is economically deterministic and guilty of some nationalist oversimplification. Conservationist ideas did not emerge with or because of colonialism alone. They have had a long and autonomous pedigree in the West, going back to some Greek thinkers. They were revived during the era of the Renaissance and the European 'discovery' of countries and peoples hitherto unknown to them. They were stimulated particularly by the experiences of early colonization in small tropical islands like St Helena and Mauritius, where the disastrous ecological consequences of deforestation quickly became evident within the small space of the islands. In early-colonial India it was a group of amateur naturalists, often surgeons in the Company's service, who began to press for conservation measures during the 1830s and 1840s, after the Malabar effort had petered out and well before the coming of the railways. Their major impetus could have been a genuine concern over environmental degradation, sparked off by a persistent agricultural depression, droughts, and widespread famine in North India in the late 1830s. Grove and others also suggest that a school of 'Nationalist Political Economy', typified by Guha and Gadgil, has somewhat exaggerated the sharpness of the precolonial–colonial rupture in attitudes and policies regarding forests. Neither exploitation nor a degree of conservation was entirely novel. Boundaries between arable and forest had continually shifted in the past, trade in timber and other forest produce was not unknown, rulers sometimes cut down woods as a part of military strategy or planted them for protection. In the early nineteenth century the amirs of Sind had even deliberately planned afforestation in the interests of elite shikar. What changed in the course of the nineteenth century was, perhaps, not so much the outlook of ruling groups, but a progressively enhanced 'ability to enforce'. This led to an inexorable roll-back of forests in many areas in the late-colonial and post-colonial era, along with efforts at more 'rational' use through control-cum-scientific conservation.[9]

Grove's Indian data is taken mainly from before the 1850s. It does not quite confront Guha's argument about a very direct link between economic determinants, especially the connection between railway needs and forest policies in the late-colonial era. But work of Grove's kind has had the salutary effect of drawing attention to variations in official motivations and the need to avoid assumptions of a single, unilinear thrust in all colonial environmental policies. In one of his early papers, Guha had himself drawn attention to multiple strands, analysing the 1878 Act as the outcome of years of intensive intra-official debate. Baden-Powell, the most aggressive advocate of total state control, claimed that under pre-colonial 'Oriental Despotism' all land not actually under cultivation had belonged to the state anyway. Madras revenue officials, in total contrast, emphasized the many hardships that the state monopoly would inflict on villagers. Sometimes they

[9] Grove 1993: 318–51; Sivaramakrishnan 1999b: 1–31; Guha 1999: 135.

amassed impressive local detail. One of them argued that traditional community claims on forests represented village property, not village privilege. Brandis tried to occupy a midway, pragmatic position. The final draft, however, which the Madras government resisted for several years, basically reflected Baden-Powell's views.[10] In more general terms, too, British forest policies remained always open to several different, and quite often contrary, pressures. The expansion and tightening of control over areas designated 'forest' was clearly beneficial for the Forest Department, and is likely to have seemed attractive to those who had conservation in mind. But there was also a primary interest in an extension of settled peasant cultivation to enhance land revenue and boost the export of agricultural commodities, thereby maintaining the export surplus vital for the basic structures of colonial rule and exploitation. Such contrary pulls could produce inter-departmental conflict. There was a third variable as well: it came from considerations of law and order, from the need to keep within manageable limits the popular discontent and protest that arose out of the harsh implementation of forest regulations.

A diversity of views on origins and pressures notwithstanding, there does exist a general historiographical consensus in relation to the administration of forests in late-colonial India: that this had extremely adverse consequences for varied sections of the rural population. A Bombay governor had given it first place among the reasons for British unpopularity among the uneducated. How far the new administration of forests really promoted the conservation of forest wealth along scientific lines also remains, by consensus, dubious.

The consequences of late-colonial forest policies were far-reaching, precisely because the restrictions they imposed did not affect only, or even primarily, isolated and marginal groups of forest-dwelling tribal hunter-gatherers living in extreme backwardness and/or arcadian simplicity. What came to be disrupted were multifarious connections among forests, pastures, and settled peasant agriculture. The disjunctures among these categories were actually products of colonial material and discursive processes.

Let us enumerate the main areas of conflict. The Forest Department's

---

[10] Guha 1990: 65–84.

primary interest was in the exploitation-cum-maintenance for timber of specific kinds of trees—above all, Himalayan deodar, which was best suited for the making of railway sleepers; and teak and sal (roughly west and east of 80 degrees longitude). It wanted such trees to grow to their full stature, and at times tried to promote a—not necessarily ecologically advantageous—monoculture of these commercially profitable species. But villagers in many parts of the country had freely used wood from these forests for dwellings, tools, and fuel, and were habituated to often cutting the more accessible branches of trees not fully grown. The Forest Department now branded this a crime: the crime of lopping. Second, the forest administration banned or drastically restricted age-old patterns of popular grazing facilities in ways that adversely affected both settled villagers as well as nomadic pastoral communities who often had symbiotic relations with peasants. Their herds, allowed entrance at specific times in the harvest cycle, had provided manure to the cultivators, for instance. It must be recalled here that 'forest' could quite often be more a legal than a strictly geographical classification, for the state put under that label many uncultivated tracts not thickly wooded by designating them 'wastes'. The characteristic colonial combination of state control over areas defined as forests, alongside sharper definitions of private property rights in settled agriculture, disrupted older, more fluid, and interrelated usages and ways of life in the countryside.

A third major—and particularly unpopular—thrust was constituted by determined efforts to end slash-and-burn shifting, or swidden, cultivation. Known by a variety of local names,[11] and obviously very widely practised, swidden was not at all merely the practice of supposedly primitive tribes ignorant of civilized agricultural practices. Often vital for the survival of poorer peasants who could not afford ploughs and cattle, it could also be sometimes finely tuned to conditions of soil and the logic of seasonal cycles of cultivation with hunting and food-gathering. Thus the Hill Maria of Bastar practised the shifting cultivation of millets on poorer soil, annually apportioning the plots for penda. At the same time, they had individually-owned

---

[11] E.g. 'jhum' in eastern India, 'bewar' in the upper Narmada forests, 'penda' in Bastar, 'podu' in Andhra, and 'kumri' in South Kanara.

permanent wet-rice fields. Among the Baiga of the Central Provinces there was a well-worked-out seasonal rhythm of hunting, gathering, and bewar.[12] And then there were the many monopoly appropriations or restrictions on a variety of what the officialese came to term 'minor' or 'non-timber' forest products. The harvesting of non-timber forest produce was relatively harmless and in this sense different from swidden, which could result in forest fires (even though debates continue about whether the fires were, ecologically, entirely harmful). The motivation for restricting even such an activity was clearly the enhancing of Forest Department profits, not conservation.

Collectively, these regulations disrupted everyday life and reduced incomes already slender. People had felt connected to the use of such 'minor' resources in multifarious ways, and the trade in them had often developed into a major resource for even the apparently most 'backward' of communities. Bastar villagers had depended on forests for a variety of roots, fruits, and medicinal herbs; they had used creepers to make ropes, leaves for plates and cups, bamboo for fencing and baskets and arrows; they had extracted oil and liquor from sal and mahua trees. The Baiga had well-established networks of commodity exchange with settled village and urban artisan communities, supplying them with, among other things, lac for jewellery, wood for toys, and dyes from tree-roots.[13] Colonialism disrupted these old links in many areas, thus engendering the twentieth-century image of 'remote jungle tribes' which has tended to be either looked down upon or romanticized.[14]

An interesting subplot within forest policy is constituted by the theme of hunting, or shikar. This had been, of course, a major pre-colonial royal or aristocratic pastime and one recalls some famous Mughal paintings on this theme. What the British introduced was not so much new desires or ideologies as greater reach and efficacy.

[12] Sundar 1997; Prasad 1998: 325–48.

[13] Sundar 1997; Prasad 1998. The multifarious popular use of forests, down to present times, is vividly indicated by a three-page list of trees and their uses, appended to Amita Baviskar's case study of Anjanvara village in the Narmada valley in the 1990s: Baviskar 1995: 259–61.

[14] A point made very effectively by Sumit Guha, in Guha 1999: 130, *et passim*.

State forests became a vast hunting estate for Europeans and favoured 'natives', particularly the Indian princes.[15] Meanwhile those who were excluded from these newly privileged areas included many for whom hunting had been a livelihood, and/or a necessary form of self-defence, or a measure to protect their crops from wild animals. Unlike timber, the motivation with respect to fauna was not profit, but a grotesque variety of pleasure, and the maintenance of a regal lifestyle in which the often obscene massacre of mostly harmless wild animals and birds was trumpeted as a manly sport. Only occasionally did the requirements of big-game hunting and villagers' needs coincide, as in the celebrated instance of Jim Corbett and the man-eating tigers of Kumaon.[16] There was little or no thought for the preservation of threatened species: thus the cheetah, as well as the lion outside Kathiawar, were hunted to extinction.[17] Visitors to the Bharatpur bird sanctuary can still see a triumphal plaque recording the slaughters by particular viceregal or Indian princely visits. And, once again, the price had often to be paid by villagers. Excluded from their old hunting grounds and disarmed by Lytton's Arms Act of 1877, their labour and time were freely requisitioned for organizing 'beats' and providing for the sahib's pleasure.[18] More generally, too, the oppressive nature of forest laws was aggravated by multifarious petty demands extracted by ill-paid underlings of the Forest Department. Some of all this was quite institutionalized, as with the Kumaon and Garhwal practice of forest officials on tour who extracted forced labour (known variously in local parlance as 'utar', or 'begar', or 'coolie pratha') from villagers and got free supply of provisions from them as 'bardaish'.[19]

The overall impact was well summed up by an admission made once by a British forest officer to the anthropologist and activist for tribal welfare Verrier Elwin: 'Our laws are of such kind that every villager breaks one forest law every day of his life.' Annual Forest

[15] The panoply, prestige, and paraphernalia of the royal hunt and of colonial shikar has grown into a sub-discipline within Indian ecological history. See Rangarajan 2000–2; Rangarajan 2001; Hughes 2013.

[16] See Rangarajan 2002.

[17] Divyabhanusinh 2002; Divyabhanusinh 2008.

[18] Rangarajan 1996: chapter 4; see also Rangarajan 2001.

[19] Guha 1989: 101–2.

Department reports are replete with statistics of forest law violations, and the income derived by the state from the fines extracted for such 'crimes'. In 1939 Elwin recorded this Baiga song:

> In this Raja's reign we are all dying of hunger,
> He robs us of our axes, he robs us of our jungles . . .
> He beats the Gond,
> He drives the Baiga and the Baigin from the jungle.[20]

Emergent middle-class nationalists occasionally took up forest grievances, even though they came from a social milieu far removed from that of adivasis and peasants. The Poona Sarvajanik Sabha complained about the proposed Forest Act in March 1878, and resolutions on the subject were sometimes passed in Congress sessions during the 1890s. But the sharpest and most concrete early criticism came in 1883 from Jyotirao Phule, the Maharashtrian pioneer of modern radical anti-Brahmin and anti-caste movements:

> In the past, those farmers who had very little land and could not survive on its produce, would go into the nearby forest and would gather wood, fruits and leaves from trees like palash and mahua. By selling these things they managed to collect enough money for their basic needs . . . But now the cunning European employees of our honourable government have spent all their foreign and multifaceted intelligence to establish a massive Forest Department, including all mountains and hills and valleys. This culminates in the inclusion of unused lands and . . . pastures as well. Now our poor and handicapped farmers' sheep and goats have no place to feed even on air in the forest.[21]

It would be simplistic, however, to present a narrative of the inexorable advance of colonial and post-colonial state-cum-commercial control over forests and wastes, irresistibly appropriating traditional 'common property resources'. Much before Gandhian nationalists took up the question in a significant way and integrated the forest satyagraha into civil disobedience, resistance at local levels occasionally burst into open rebellion. Most of these took the forms of what

[20] Cited in Sundar 1997: 113; and Rangarajan 1996: 95. See also Elwin 1936/1992.

[21] Jyotirao Phule in Deshpande 2002: 132.

officials described as 'forest crimes'—illicit lopping, felling, trespass, and deliberate arson. Such protests sometimes compelled adjustments, relaxations, and partial retreats by the state. But the important point is that the conciliatory moves tended to be directed towards relatively privileged groups who possessed what the British recognized as some variety of proprietary right. Concessions and partial co-options, as has been pointed out, 'meant a strengthening of the position of the village proprietary community *vis-à-vis* agricultural labourers, poor tenants, artisans, and nomadic graziers.'[22]

Sedentarization, Property, and Order

The British wanted to control and conserve forests for a more rational extraction of timber and other resources as well as for the pleasures of shikar. But a second, somewhat contradictory, and major imperative was the expansion of arable farming, of settled peasants at the cost of nomadic communities of pastoralists and hunter-foragers. These were ways of living that colonial officials often wrongly assumed to be rigorously distinct from each other, but which their own policies actually helped to disaggregate. Surplus extraction, directly or indirectly from settled agriculture, had always been the foundation of pre-colonial state finances. Land revenue would remain, till well into the late-colonial era, a major though diminishing asset. In the late nineteenth century the more critical need was to maintain and enhance an export surplus in foodgrains and cash crops, for that was the principal channel of remittances to Britain of official savings, pensions, and business profits from India. These, moreover, were quite vital for the maintenance of overall British trade balances. Repeated famines also posed problems to the state and they became more frequent and devastating in the closing years of the century. This called for the enhancing of food production.

Recent historians have emphasized the resultant processes of 'sedentarization' or 'peasantization' of erstwhile nomadic groups under British rule. This theme has partly questioned or displaced an earlier focus in much nationalist and Left agrarian studies on 'depeasantization': the alleged transformation through colonial

[22] Bhattacharya 1992: 135.

pressures of many peasants into landless semi-proletarians.[23] Sedentarization was associated with modern Western notions of the 'naturalness' and worth of private property in land as firmly defined, stable, and above all marketable. Only 'the magic touch of property', the makers of the Permanent Zamindari Settlement had assumed in 1793, could set in motion a 'productive principle' and stimulate agricultural growth. The location of that property right became a subject of much debate and variations across regions. But the basic assumption of what Ranajit Guha felicitously termed the 'rule of property' continued to persist. Economic, political, and ideological considerations were inextricably intermingled. A precise and definitive location of saleable property right was felt to be indispensable for stable revenue collection, because defaulters or improvident owners would be displaced through market forces by more efficient categories. Sedentary ways of life were also valorized for being much more orderly and manageable. There developed, therefore, a powerful thrust towards branding those who refused to settle down to regular farming as vagrants, even criminals: most notoriously, that strange and savage late-colonial construct, 'criminal tribe', was applied to many categories of the population.

Irrigation works—more precisely, canal irrigation—represented by far the most visible form of late-colonial interest in the improvement and extension of arable farming. Experiments with improved seeds or cultivation methods, by contrast, were virtually absent. The Pusa Agricultural Institute was set up under Curzon only in 1906.[24] Irrigation initiatives were not uncommon in precolonial times. Some of them had been fairly big and state-sponsored, like the anicuts in the Kaveri delta and the canals in the Ganga–Jumna Doab associated with Feroz Shah Tughlaq. More common were small-scale works with a strong element of local community management, as in South Bihar, or in the Sahyadri region of western Maharashtra.[25] Many works of both kinds seem to have declined or vanished in the late eighteenth

[23] For an influential early statement of this thesis of a colonial 'creation' of peasants, see Bayly 1987: chapter 5.

[24] Curzon, that same year, started the Indian Agricultural Service—forty years after the Indian Forest Service had been inaugurated.

[25] Sengupta 1980: 157–89; Hardiman 1996: 185–209.

and early nineteenth century. The Company merely tried to repair or extend the old structures, notably the Kaveri barrage or anicut, and the system of Jumna canals that had been built in the wake of the North Indian famine of 1837–8. The major spurt in British construction of dams and canals occurred only in the last quarter of the nineteenth century. These were focused on the western United Provinces and above all in the Punjab. A grandiose system of canal irrigation had come into being in the latter province by the early twentieth century, opening up large tracts of what the British termed 'waste' to state-organized agricultural settlements: the Canal Colonies. These were considered invaluable for boosting the production and export of wheat.

Unlike most aspects of British Indian state policies, the investment in irrigation tended to be quite favourably viewed by early nationalists like R.C. Dutt. They often counterposed it to the railways, which were built through the guaranteed interest system that, to them, represented one of the forms of the 'drain of wealth'. More recent evaluations have tended to be much more critical, though debates continue. The state judged the worth of irrigation projects primarily from a narrow, revenue-generating point of view. Payments extracted from peasant users of canal water could prove oppressive, even prohibitive for the poorer sections among these. The burden was often enhanced by local official extortion. Excessive bureaucratic controls provoked a major protest movement in the Punjab Canal Colonies around 1907.

During the most recent generation of scholarship in this area, there has been a more fundamental questioning of the value of vast systems of canal irrigation constructed by damming rivers. The British Indian state (and, on a much grander scale, its post-colonial successor) clearly preferred such big projects, to which hydro-electric and other multi-purpose dimensions were added in the twentieth century. Unlike locality-centred and managed small dams, wells, and tanks, these offered much greater prospects for centralized bureaucratic control, revenue extraction, and vistas of 'modernity' and 'development'. Beginning with Elizabeth Whitcombe's pioneering work on UP canal irrigation,[26] the possibly adverse environmental fallout from these

[26] Whitcombe 1972; see also Whitcombe 1983, and Whitcombe 1995: 237–59.

large and ecologically questionable projects began to attract historical attention. Whitcombe suggested that irrigation based on big dams, reservoirs, and extensive canals had been beneficial only where they had fitted in with local ecological conditions. Elsewhere, as in large parts of the western United Provinces, significant immediate gains in production and improved cropping had been offset over time by problems, such as excessive waterlogging on account of a disregard for natural drainage flows, the salinity of the soil, and the spread of malaria. Only recently, however, has the negative fallout—in terms of the dispossession and displacement of large numbers of human beings through big dams and reservoirs—arrived centre-stage. This has been a consequence of popular resistance; above all, of the Narmada Bachao Andolan.[27]

Environmental historians have also come to pay increasing attention to the disruption of nomadic–pastoral population flows and ways of living. These were interrupted by the potent combination, from late-colonial times, of state control over loosely defined forests, the expansion of settled agriculture (whether through state-constructed artificial irrigation, or as the 'natural' fallout of growing populations), and the sharper definition of property rights in land. In reserved or protected forests, as we have seen, pastoralists were either totally excluded, or were allowed entry only on payment of a heavy grazing fees. Simultaneously, numerous, and probably very old, patterns of interdependence between pastoralists and peasants were disrupted. Those who lost out were usually nomadic groups and the poorer cultivators. In the old pattern of transhumance in the Kulu-Kangra region, shepherds and cowherds would come down from the higher mountains at the onset of winter. They were allowed to pass freely through cultivated fields after the harvest. In the process, their livestock manured the fields. But with the greater consolidation of property rights, such rights of passage came under legal pressure. Even where a sense of village collectivity persisted—notably in the Punjab where colonial law claimed to base itself on local customs—the right

---

[27] There had however been some late-colonial precedents: see below for the Mulshi Petha Congress-supported peasant satyagraha in Maharashtra in 1921–2 against a Tata hydro-electric project. A detailed account of the satyagraha has been translated from the Marathi into English: see Vora 2009.

to pasture came to be appended to the right to revenue-yielding agricultural land. British land settlements continued to allot some open grazing land to villages as their 'shamilat deh'. However, only proprietors of land (those with ancestral shares in the village 'community') were allowed to use these pastures: 'nomadic pastoralists, people without property, could have no access to the shamilat.' Ideologically, this entailed a valorization of settled agricultural life over the nomadic and pastoral, which, though not without some pre-colonial precedents, was made much more unambiguous under colonial and post-colonial modernity. Even British administrators like Malcolm Darling, who romantically extolled the virtues of rural life, celebrated peasant culture as opposed to that of the pastoralist.[28]

A general conclusion emerges. British rule worsened the lives of many, but not entirely indiscriminately. Substantial groups benefited, gaining new opportunities for upward mobility, at least up to a point. Many native princes were able to get a share of forest revenues in return for allowing entry to the Forest Department. The consolidation of marketable property rights fitted well with the interests and aspirations of the more enterprising or fortunate landlords, richer peasants, traders, and moneylenders. The colonial era helped consolidate and sharpen many already existing inequalities. For instance, Kangra's shepherd headmen ('waris') had previously combined certain privileges with much reciprocity in their relations with other shepherds. Now they began to claim more wide-ranging powers as maliks. One needs to avoid positing an over-sharp dichotomy between traditional common property resources—sometimes assumed to have been marked by near-total reciprocity and harmony—and the inequities and conflicts inseparable from modern capitalist development. This has to be acknowledged, even if the dream of a lost commons has often been a resource for popular movements in many parts of the world. How egalitarian community claims would have been depends on the absence or otherwise of internal hierarchies, whereas most

[28] Malcolm Darling (Darling 1947) contrasted the 'smiling' wheatfields in the Canal Colonies with the same countryside in the 1890s: 'an endless waste of bush and shrub, with little sign of life beyond the uncertain footmark of camel, buffalo, and goat, and the movable dwelling of the nomad grazier . . .' See Bhattacharya 1995: 68, 75, *et passim*.

communities in the subcontinent have been more or less hierarchized since much before the colonial era. Village community rights in uncultivated or wastelands can, on occasion, be used against the less privileged and the landless. A Japanese historian, who has studied village common lands in unirrigated parts of Tamilnadu, has unearthed data to indicate the ways in which dominant landholders 'opposed the cultivation of . . . waste lands by landless people, in particular by Dalit agricultural labourers, since it might have led to an insufficient supply of obedient labourers.'[29] Regions and times which were marked by a degree of lower-caste empowerment, like parts of Tamilnadu and Maharashtra, have witnessed Dalit encroachment on village commons to take over land for cultivation.

The pattern of restrictions, alongside partial opportunities, which was constituted by forest laws, sedentarization, and rigorous notions of private property quite possibly worsened already skewed gender equations. Women would have been quite prominent in many of the wide range of activities associated with food-gathering, collection, and sale of 'minor' forest products. The criminalization of such practices, alongside the tightening of legal notions of private ownership—which were in any case based on an amalgam of Western, brahmanical, and elite-Islamic assumptions—further slanted the social ethos in favour of male dominance. There are, naturally, the dangers of romanticization here, of exaggerating or imagining pre-modern gender equality and harmony. Nonetheless, the burden of the increased attack on many usages and 'customs in common' (to borrow E.P. Thompson's phrase) fell on women to a very considerable degree. More specifically, feminist scholars have highlighted the erosion in late-colonial times of the matrilineal inheritance practices of groups like the Garos and Khasis of the north-east, and the Nayars and Tiyyars of Kerala. And strikingly, post-colonial land reforms even in Left-ruled West Bengal and Kerala, have looked very reluctant when it has come to giving land rights to women alongside 'their' menfolk.[30]

The British preference for settled agriculture as against nomadism

---

[29] Yanagisawa 2001: 98–104. See also Chakravarty-Kaul 1992: 393–436.

[30] See, for these and related themes, the important study by Bina Agarwal (Agarwal 1994).

and foraging led towards conceptualizing the nomad as vagrant, even criminal. In severe regimes of private property food-gathering can be redesignated as 'theft' or 'robbery', bolstering the generalized construction of an ethos of inequity through the creation of forest crimes via forest laws. In addition, the establishment of Pax Britannica in the first half of the nineteenth century had in the interior of the subcontinent been associated with the large-scale demobilization of an earlier vast and volatile military labour market. The subsequent revolution in communications, along with the state monopoly on salt manufacture and trade, disrupted many networks among nomadic traders, especially of Banjara communities that had been ubiquitous in the inland trade for many centuries. The panic over thuggee in the second quarter of the nineteenth century helped to stimulate a widespread colonial notion that roving bands of criminals must, on the analogy of the caste system, have a hereditary basis. The apogee of such tendencies was the Criminal Tribes Act of 1871, applied mainly to the North-West Provinces (UP), Punjab, and later to parts of Bengal. A similar Act was enforced in Madras from 1911. These were truly draconian laws, under which groups notified (by administrative fiat, with no right to appeal) as hereditarily criminal could be moved to 'reformatory settlements' where their movements would be restricted by a system of passes and rollcalls. The violation of these pass or other rules could be punished by fines, whipping, and six months' rigorous imprisonment for the first and a year for the second. In some instances, surveillance was later sought to be combined with schemes for 'reformation and employment'. Christian missions, most notably the Salvation Army, helped with these projects.

British rule was most blatantly repressive here. Scholars of the criminal tribes policy have been tempted to identify it as a uniquely and quintessentially colonial development. However, mid-Victorian Britain around 1860–75 was similarly engaged in trying to identify its own groups of 'habitual criminals', as distinct from the 'respectable' labouring poor. Colonial rule, moreover, operated often in and through indigenous collaboration and structures of domination. A major aspect of the criminal tribes policy seems to have been the creation of pools of semi-servile labour for the benefit of property-holders, both foreign and Indian. For instance, a landlord from UP, who was earlier suspected of harbouring a band of Bawarias for criminal purposes, employed them after they had been tied down to a settlement to dig a canal and open up uncultivated land on his estate. He then rented out the improved land at higher rents to better-off tenants, leaving the Bawarias with no option but to go back to their lawless ways. The zamindar profited as well. He was suspected of taking a share of the plunder, thus more or less reproducing the earlier pattern. In Madras, a generation or so later, 'criminal tribes' were constituted through processes such as the destruction of old channels of salt trading through the new colonial monopoly over that item, and, as we have seen, forest laws which ended free grazing for nomadic groups. The dispossessed now became reserves of controlled labour, to be used in British plantations and Indian-owned textile mills. The well-known nationalist newspaper, *The Hindu* (29 April 1916), went so far as to praise the Madras Criminal Tribes Act of 1911 for providing a 'large and efficient addition . . . to the mill labour supply . . . out of . . . cattle lifters, thieves, and petty pilferers.'[31]

Seeing the Wood through the Trees: Regional Studies

Subcontinental perspectives on late-colonial environmental change are based on a large and growing number of regional studies. A brief glance at some of these may help sharpen the focus.

Ramachandra Guha's study of Tehri and Pauri Garhwal (the former a princely state, the latter British ruled) was published a decade or so after the Chipko movement, when village women, children, and men started hugging trees to protect them from forest contractors. This made international headlines. It presented a cataclysmic picture of late-colonial developments as an 'ecological watershed'. Guha saw the village structures of that area as fairly egalitarian. The large majority of peasants had occupancy rights and enjoyed high-caste status, a degree of gender equality,[32] well-developed village communities, no intermediate landlordism, and a

[31] Nigam 1990: 131–64; Radhakrishna 1989: 269–95.
[32] A minority of untouchable Doms did exist, but allegedly also as 'an integral part of the village community', while an anthropologist was quoted

long established symbiotic relationship between settled agriculture and the community's collective use of forests. All this was disrupted by British forest laws. Guha suggested a sharp contrast between on the one hand princely Tehri, ruled by the same dynasty allegedly for 1200 years and acknowledged by its subjects as the protector of the sacred Badrinath shrine as well as marked by elements of paternalist rule; and on the other the onset of much harsher and impersonal British administration in the adjoining Pauri region. Forest laws had similarly adverse consequences in both areas. In 1865 the British leased rights to the very rich deodar forests of Tehri in return for hefty payments to the raja. But resistance movements in Tehri and Pauri remained significantly different in nature for quite some time. Tehri was marked by periodic, limited, non-violent protests utilizing a traditional dhandak form by which subjects appealed to the raja to act against oppressive officials. In British-administered Pauri, where from the 1890s the chir pine was reserved and ruthlessly exploited for resin, rebellion quickly turned into 'confrontation', involving massive 'deliberate and organized incendiarism' in 1916 and 1920–1 in the forests of the Naini Tal division. Interestingly, Guha suggests a pattern that persisted into the post-colonial Chipko movement. The strand associated with the strictly Gandhian, somewhat anti-modernist and religious Sunderlal Bahuguna was strong in Tehri, while more militant figures like Chandi Prasad Bhatt had greater appeal in the Pauri and Kumaon area to the east.

Chetan Singh's study of the Himachal region, to the west of Ramachandra Guha's area of research, gives a much less cataclysmic account. It emphasizes continuities across the precolonial/British/postcolonial divides alongside change, and focuses on wider, longer-term ecological themes rather than on forest policies and administration alone.[33] More than Guha, Singh emphasizes the conjoint role of indigenous princes and the British in the late-colonial intensified appropriation of forests.

---

with approval for his assertion that women in this Himalayan region 'work equally with men in the fields, help them in looking after domestic animals, *and, of course, take physical care of husband and children*': Guha 1989: 20–2; my emphasis.

[33] Singh 1998.

By the early twentieth century, for instance, the petty rajas of Bashahr, Chamba, and Mandi derived half or more of their revenues from the lease of their forests to the Forest Department: income from the forests became for them considerably more important than taxes from land.[34] Singh's wider time perspective (he is also a major historian of Punjab in the seventeenth and eighteenth centuries) enables an important questioning of the categories normally used to characterize the 'intermediate spaces' between settled cultivation and forests. 'Waste', as used by the British and their successors, is certainly a misnomer. These tracts have, in various ways, been essential for the survival and reproduction of peasant societies. The recent environmental-populist alternative term, 'common property resources', however, implies, according to Singh, a somewhat romanticized and excessively sharp disjunction between pre-modern community management and the subsequent capitalistic individualization of land use. He cites Chamba Raj land grants in the tenth and eleventh centuries: as early as this, they gave 'grass, grazing and pasture land . . . fallow . . . fruit trees and waters' to individuals without any mention whatsoever of 'village community' or 'common property'.[35] A much more multiple, oscillating, and fluid history has to be imagined, and this, rather than unilinearity, is in general Singh's overall analytical thrust in assessing late-colonial processes. The gradual growth of a market economy, and the associated sharpening of notions of private property, have been more crucial, according to Singh, than colonial legal administrative interventions and forest laws in the intermittent and gradual erosion of 'waste' or 'common lands' in the western Himalayan region, and perhaps elsewhere.

Interactions between settled agriculture and nomadic pastoralism become more important than forests as one goes up the Himalayas into the regions of possibly age-old transhumance, or descends south-westwards into the vast Punjab plain. These were potentially fertile areas, but they were marked by insufficient and uncertain rain.

---

[34] A similar situation is mentioned by Ramachandra Guha (in Arnold and Guha 1995) with regard to Tehri, but this does not become central to his analysis.

[35] Singh 1998: 93.

Neeladri Bhattacharya's study of colonial Punjab relates the varied patterns of continuity-cum-change in pastoralism to specific forms. Thus, the long-distance seasonal migratory flows of Pathan powindahs in armed kafilas, linking Central Asia with the plains of Hindustan across the centuries, were utilized by the British initially for trade and intelligence-gathering. But there was also a long-term decline as the Central Asian trade became less vital. British grazing taxes tripled between the 1870s and 1920s, access to pastures diminished through the spread of settled agriculture and tighter notions of property, and curbs came to be imposed on the money-lending activities of the 'Kabuliwalas'. The processes affecting, on the whole adversely, Kulu-Kangra transhumance, the Punjab shamilat deh open grazing land, and pastoral–agriculturalist interchanges across the Punjab plains with the rise of the Canal Colonies, have been mentioned already. But, like Chetan Singh, Bhattacharya rejects any unilinear model, emphasizing a multiplicity of patterns, resistance, and survival along with change. 'I can see no simple, smooth process of displacement and dispossession', nor of an irresistible and uniform 'peasantization' of nomads.[36]

The ecological dimensions of South Indian history have long been recognized by scholars. Tamilnadu, in particular, has been marked for many centuries by the contrasts and shifting balances between on the one hand 'wet valleys'—the Kaveri delta, above all—together with those of Tambraparni and Vaigai to the south and Palar and Cheyyur to the north; and on the other the drier 'plains'. In parts of the plains, prior to the late nineteenth century, permanent cultivation had been difficult and the livelihood of most had depended on combinations of swidden, the herding of cattle, the transport of goods by moving Banjara-type communities, and considerable warfare-cum-plundering. We have already seen how the British, by disarming such groups, contributed to the formation of 'criminal tribes'. Settled and intensive cultivation on these plains required resources to dig wells or tanks, collect manure from animal-droppings or from leaves obtained from forests and wastes, and, of course, cattle. It depended, in other words, on a coexistence with communities of herders and easy access to forests. Here, as C.J. Baker pointed out in his study, late-colonial

[36] Bhattacharya 1995: 84–5, *et passim*.

developments proved acutely contradictory. The export boom from the 1860s in raw cotton and groundnuts stimulated settled agriculture by better-off or upwardly-mobile groups in the plains. However, the resultant expansion of arable cut into pastures, while the British were simultaneously fencing in the forests: 'just at the time when the forests were being ploughed up or reserved . . . the advent of cash-crops was increasing their importance as sources of leaf-manure, grazing for work-animals, and timber for implements.'[37] Small wonder then that Madras was perhaps the first province where criticism of the forest laws was articulated, and even contributed to a sharp intra-official debate in the 1870s. The affected people were not just the poor or the landless, but upwardly-mobile agriculturists who flooded the government with demands for freer access to forests when the latter instituted an enquiry in 1913.

Apart from certain Himalayan regions, the main focus of environmentally-aware histories has been the highlands, plateaus, and valleys of Central India. These had extensive forests which now came under threat and produced significant mobilizations by restive adivasis. The British came to control forests in such areas by arbitrarily designating their inhabitants 'primitive' or 'backward'. Sometimes this strategy originated in sheer trickery. In 1842, leases for timber rights were obtained from three Bhil chiefs of the Dang region (in south-east Gujarat and north-west Maharashtra) in return for a payment of less than Rs 5000. Control was gradually tightened over the Dang forests: 34 per cent of these tracts were reserved and closed to shifting cultivation by 1893, even though the original lease had said nothing about any such prohibition. This led to three Bhil rebellions, in 1907, 1911, and 1914. The last of them was associated with rumours that the British had got involved in a faraway big war and this was the right time for a revolt.[38]

Ajay Skaria makes an interesting attempt to enter Bhil history and mentalities 'from within', through a collection and analysis of their vadilcha goth, or stories about the past. These, Skaria tells us, are structured around a contrast between on the one hand 'moglai', a

---

[37] Baker 1984: 157, *et passim.*
[38] Hardiman 1994: 89–147.

time of freedom or 'chhut' when Bhils had been 'kings of the forest', free to move and hunt in it and raid the surrounding plains without restrictions; and on the other 'mandini', its conceptual opposite, full of restrictions, associated roughly with 'gora' (white) rule as well as its Indian successor. Skaria's method provides us with exceptionally vivid and revealing details, particularly stories that illuminate the ways in which Bhils consider themselves to have been subordinated through a combination of deceit and superior power-knowledge.[39] More problematic is his claim to have recovered a distinct Bhil conception of wildness. This, he says, developed in what conventionally has been thought to be the time of anarchy during the breakdown of Mughal and Maratha power, before the establishment of the British peace. Bhil 'wildness' is a notion that Skaria occasionally romanticizes, making it seem almost a 'counteraesthetics of modernity'.[40] The problem with this is that the reconstruction is based on a leap backwards across almost two centuries, on the basis of stories collected now. Other scholars working on the same or neighbouring areas, notably David Hardiman and Sumit Guha, have paid greater attention to distinctions and changes over time. The Bhil claim to have ruled the forests and plundered them at will must have been fairly oppressive, for instance, for Varli and Konkani peasants in the Dang area who actually had a more advanced, settled agriculture. It is noteworthy that such groups did not join the Bhil risings against British rule.[41]

Moving eastwards, we have already had several occasions to refer to the work of Mahesh Rangarajan on the British Central Provinces, Archana Prasad's on the Baigas in the eastern part of the same region, and Nandini Sundar's on Bastar. Sundar's is a less adventurous but

---

[39] Two examples: the Bhil rajas were offered the choice between three sacks—of earth, bark, and money. They chose the last, since they thought they had more than enough of the others in the forests—after which they were told that now 'you shall get the money and we shall take away the forests and the land' (a reference probably to the 1842 leases). Again: a sahib was once given shelter for a night by a raja. He went out and measured all the trees and forests around, and so the Bhils lost these all. In a variant, a sahib looked at a forest through a durbin (telescope) and grabbed it. See Skaria 1999: 176–8, *et passim*.

[40] Skaria 1999: 23.

[41] Hardiman 1994: 140; Guha 1999: *passim*.

perhaps more convincing effort than Skaria's to combine anthropological fieldwork and readings of oral memory with archival research. She, understandably, has to focus on moments of rebellion which, consequently, have also produced much more in the way of records: notably the clashes of 1876 and 1910 (which will figure in our later survey of late-colonial popular movements). Prasad has been particularly meticulous in her exploration of the seasonal rhythm of food-gathering, hunting, and shifting cultivation among the Baiga till their disruption under colonial policies. Hers is an analysis unusually strong in its interlinking of ecology with the history of production and production relations. She warns us against the danger of idealizing tribal gender relations. Even in food-gathering, Baiga men monopolized the sale of the more lucrative items, while women were even prohibited from touching the axe in shifting cultivation. Rangarajan's work brings out important distinctions between the Central Provinces and Garhwal. The meeting point of teak and sal belts, the former saw less British effort to promote the kind of monoculture of deodar and pine which had caused much discontent in the Himalayas. But there were numerous conflicts over multiple uses, and questions of timing. Villagers in Hoshangabad, for instance, needed to use teak for wheels and yokes, and it was more convenient for them to lop off parts from young trees. The Forest Department wanted large logs for railway sleepers. By the early twentieth century, however, various kinds of 'everyday resistance' compelled officials to go in for adjustments and compromises. Rangarajan questions the notion of excessive unilinearity in domination. There was also the complication of private forests of landlords (malguzars) in many parts of the CP, providing a fruitful source of multiple conflicts and adjustments over forest claims between the state and malguzars as well as between the latter and their tenants.

Private zamindari forests were most widespread in permanently settled Bengal. They constitute an important element of the empirically rich and theoretically acute analysis developed by K. Sivaramakrishnan.[42]

---

[42] Sivaramakrishnan 1999a; see also Sivaramakrishnan 1998: 237–64; and Sivaramakrishnan 1999b: 1–34. There has been relatively little work on environmental history for Bengal and even less for Assam and north-east India, but see also Samaddar 1998.

His primary focus is on the upland region along the Bengal–Bihar border, 'a patchwork forest-savannah transition zone that took the character of woods and then of fields in a somewhat unpredictable seasonal sequence.'[43] Here the standard dichotomies of colonial forestry, as well as of much of environmental history-writing with its proneness towards a nature/culture division, were particularly inappropriate. Sivaramakrishnan traces in meticulous detail the non-unilinear ebbs and flows through which a shifting landscape of 'aman' (embanked wet-rice lowland), 'dahi' (unembanked, occasionally cultivated upland), and sal forest came to be gradually remoulded into more ' sharply etched compartments of fields and forests'.[44] The zamindari forests were a further complication. Some British officials occasionally tried to regulate them in the interests of conservation, as around 1909–14. These attempts were repeatedly blocked by temporary coalitions of officials who had other inclinations, influential raiyats afraid that the Forest Department would be more intrusive, and landlords eager to preserve a lucrative source of income. The property principle under colonialism, Sivaramakrishnan argues, could be enacted only 'through coalitions cutting across elements in the heterogeneous state and a differentiated society.'[45] Such environmental studies join the critique of the homogenized binaries deployed by some analyses of colonial discourses. *Modern Forests* emphasizes in particular the need to not 'conflate policy intent with practical outcome', and seeks to 'question the simple divide often instituted between universal Western modernity and its indigenous Other.'[46]

Bibliography

Agarwal, Bina, *A Field of One's Own: Gender and Land Rights in South Asia* (Cambridge: Cambridge University Press, 1994)

Arnold, David, and Ramachandra Guha, eds, *Nature, Culture, Imperialism: Essays on the Environmental History of South Asia* (Delhi: Oxford University Press, 1995)

[43] Sivaramakrishnan 1998.
[44] Sivaramakrishnan 1999a.
[45] Sivaramakrishnan 1998: 244.
[46] Sivaramakrishnan 1999a: 147, 243, *et passim*.

Baker, Christopher J., *An Indian Rural Economy, 1880–1955: The Tamilnad Countryside* (Delhi: Oxford University Press, 1984)

Baviskar, Amita, *In the Belly of the River: Tribal Conflict over Development in the Narmada Valley* (Delhi: Oxford University Press, 1995)

Bayly, C.A., *Indian Society and the Making of the British Empire* (Cambridge: Cambridge University Press, 1987)

Bhattacharya, Neeladri, 'Colonial State and Agrarian Society', in Burton Stein, ed., *The Making of Agrarian Policy in British India 1790–1900* (Delhi: Oxford University Press, 1992)

———, 'Pastoralists in a Colonial World', in David Arnold and Ramachandra Guha, eds, *Nature, Culture and Imperialism: Essays on the Environmental History of South Asia* (Delhi: Oxford University Press, 1995)

———, ed., *Forests, Fields and Pastures,* Special Issue, *Studies in History,* 14 (2), 1998

Bhattacharya, Sabyasachi, ed., *Essays in Agrarian History: India, 1860–1940, Studies in History,* NS (3), Special Number, 1985

Chakrabarti, Lalita, 'Emergence of a Labour Force in a Dual Economy', *Indian Economic and Social History Review,* 15 (3), 1978

Chakravarty-Kaul, Minoti, 'The Commons, Community and the Courts of Colonial Punjab', *Indian Economic and Social History Review,* 29 (4), 1992

Darling, Malcolm, *The Punjab Peasant in Prosperity and Debt* (1925; rpnt London: Oxford University Press, 1947)

Deshpande, G.P., ed., *Selected Writings of Jotirao Phule* (New Delhi: LeftWord, 2002)

Divyabhanusinh, *The End of a Trail: The Cheetah in India,* 2nd edn (New Delhi: Oxford University Press, 2002)

———, *The Lions of India* (Ranikhet: Permanent Black, 2008)

Dutt, R.C., *Economic History of India,* 2 vols (London: Kegan Paul, 1900, 1902)

Elwin, Verrier, *Leaves from the Jungle: Life in a Gond Village,* 2nd edn (1936; rpnt Delhi: Oxford University Press, 1992)

Gadgil, Madhav, and Ramachandra Guha, *This Fissured Land: An Ecological History of India* (Delhi: Oxford University Press, 1992)

Grove, Richard, 'Conserving Eden: The (European) East India Companies and their Environmental Policies on St. Helena, Mauritius, and in Western India, 1660 to 1854', *Comparative Studies in Society and History,* 35, 1993

Guha, Ramachandra, *The Unquiet Woods: Ecological Change and Peasant*

Resistance in the Himalayas (Delhi: Oxford University Press, 1989; new edn Ranikhet: Permanent Black, 2009)

————, 'An Early Evironmental Debate: The Making of the 1878 Forest Act', *Indian Economic and Social History Review*, 27 (1), 1990

Guha, Sumit, *Environment and Ethnicity in India 1200–1991* (Cambridge: Cambridge University Press, 1999)

Hardiman, David, *Power in the Forests: The Dangs 1820–1940*, in David Arnold and David Hardiman, eds, *Subaltern Studies VIII* (Delhi: Oxford University Press, 1994)

————, 'Small Dam Systems of the Sahyadris', in David Arnold and Ramachandra Guha, eds, *Nature, Culture, Imperialism: Essays on the Environmental History of South Asia* (Delhi: Oxford University Press, 1995)

Hughes, Julie, *Animal Kingdoms: Hunting, the Environment, and Power in the Indian Princely States* (Delhi: Permanent Black, 2013)

Kumar, Dharma, ed., *The Cambridge Economic History of India, Volume 2, c.1750–c.1970* (Cambridge: Cambridge University Press, 1983)

Naoroji, Dadabhai, *Poverty and UnBritish Rule in India* (London: S. Sonnenschein, 1901)

Nigam, Sanjay, 'Disciplining and Policing the "Criminals by Birth": The Making of a Colonial Stereotype—the Criminal Tribes and Castes of North India', *Indian Economic and Social History Review*, 27 (2–3), 1990

Phule, Jyotirao, *Shetkaryacha Asud / Cultivators Whipcord* (April–June 1883), in G.P. Deshpande, ed., *Selected Writings of Jotirao Phule* (New Delhi: LeftWord, 2002)

Prasad, Archana, 'The Baiga: Survival Strategies and Local Economy in the Central Provinces', *Studies in History: Forests, Fields and Pastures*, 14 (2), 1998

Radhakrishna, Meena, 'The Criminal Tribes Act in Madras Presidency: Implications for Itinerant Trading Communities', *Indian Economic and Social History Review*, 26 (3), 1989

Rangarajan, Mahesh, *Fencing the Forest: Conservation and Ecological Change in India's Central Provinces, 1860–1914* (Delhi: Oxford University Press, 1996)

————, ed., *The Oxford Anthology of Indian Wildlife*, 2 vols (New Delhi: Oxford University Press, 2000–2)

————, *India's Wildlife History: An Introduction* (Delhi: Permanent Black, 2001)

————, 'Five Naturalists', in Arvind K. Mehrotra, ed., *An Illustrated History of Indian Literature in English* (Delhi: Permanent Black, 2002)

Roy, Tirthankar, *Artisans and Industrialization: Indian Weaving in the Twentieth Century* (New Delhi: Oxford University Press, 1993)

————, *The Economic History of India 1857–1947* (Delhi: Oxford University Press, 2000)

Samaddar, Ranabir, *Memory, Identity, Power: Politics in the Jungle Mahals—West Bengal 1890–1950* (New Delhi: Orient Longman, 1998)

Sengupta, Nirmal, 'The Indigeneous Irrigation Organisation in South Bihar', *Indian Economic and Social History Review*, 17 (II), 1980

Singh, Chetan, *Natural Premises: Ecology and Peasant Life in the Western Himalayas 1800–1950* (Delhi: Oxford University Press, 1998)

Sivaramakrishnan, K., 'Conservation and Production in Private Forests: Bengal, 1864–1914', *Studies in History*, 14 (2), 1998

————, *Modern Forests: Statemaking and Environmental Change in Colonial Eastern India* (New Delhi: Oxford University Press, 1999a)

————, 'Transition Zones; Changing Landscapes and Local Authority in South-West Bengal, 1880s–1920s', *Indian Economic and Social History Review*, 36 (1), 1999b

Skaria, Ajay, *Hybrid Histories: Forests, Frontiers and Wildness in Western India* (Delhi: Oxford University Press, 1999)

Sundar, Nandini, *Subalterns and Sovereigns: An Anthropological History of Bastar, 1854–1996* (Delhi: Oxford University Press, 1997)

Vora, Rajendra, *The World's First Anti-Dam Movement: The Mulshi Satyagraha 1920–1924* (Ranikhet: Permanent Black, 2009)

Whitcombe, Elizabeth, *Agrarian Conditions in Northern India: The United Provinces Under British Rule, 1860–1900* (Berkeley: University of California Press, 1972)

————, 'Irrigation', in Dharma Kumar, ed., *The Cambridge Economic History of India, Volume 2: c.1750–c.1970* (Cambridge: Cambridge University Press, 1983)

————, 'The Environmental Costs of Irrigation in British India: Waterlogging, Salinity and Malaria', in David Arnold and Ramachandra Guha, eds, *Nature, Culture, Imperialism: Essays on the Environmental History of South Asia* (Delhi: Oxford University Press, 1995)

Yanagisawa, Haruka, 'The Decline of Village Common Land in the Context of the Changing Internal Structure of Village Society: Unirrigated Land of Tamilnadu since the 1850s', paper presented at a Jawaharlal Nehru University Seminar, December 2001

3

Fieldwork
Agriculture and Agrarian History

Despite the new historiographical prominence given to forests and pastures by the environmental turn, the importance, and indeed growing centrality, of peasant cultivators and agricultural labourers in late-colonial India cannot be seriously questioned. Census data, often controversial in relation to detail but useful for conveying orders of magnitude, returned 69.4 per cent of the work-force as 'cultivators' and 'agricultural labourers' in 1901; by 1951 this had risen to 73.3 per cent. The primary sector thus employed around 70 per cent of the economically active population throughout the colonial era, and its output largely determined trends in national income. We start, therefore, with agricultural production, followed by revenue, rent, and tenancy, then commercialization and indebtedness, and finally agrarian structures, forms of labour, and conditions of famine.

Agricultural Production

An all-India database for estimates of agricultural production emerged only from the 1890s, once the state became keen on statistics in the wake of repeated famines. For the preceding decades of colonial rule, environmental histories and a number of regional agrarian studies often give the impression of a significant expansion in sown area at the expense of forests and cultivable wastes. Such instances include Bengal, as its population recovered from the devastating famine of 1770 and cultivation extended deeper into the floodplains, marshes, and forests of the Ganga–Brahmaputra delta; parts of Punjab, western UP, and Madras, where the British proceeded with canal irrigation as early as the mid-nineteenth century; and periods and regions of intense, though at times short-lived, agrarian booms directly connected with exports: cotton in the Maharashtra Deccan in the 1860s, Narmada wheat from the 1860s to the 1890s, East Bengal jute from the 1870s till the 1920s. At the same time, when quantification became possible, it indicated a much more depressing overall picture: of stagnation and partial decline with regard to acreage, gross and per capita output, and per acre yield. The figures have been much debated, however.

The standard work on this remains that of George Blyn. His meticulous all-India analysis in the *Estimates of Area and Yield of Principal Crops* series indicated, over 1891–1946, an annual per cent growth in output of all crops of only 0.37: non-foodgrains registering +1.31, but foodgrains lagging behind with +0.11. This was related to a very small annual growth in acreage of 0.40, suggesting that the bulk of cultivable waste had already been brought under the plough by the 1890s. Even more significant are the figures for per acre yield: a negligible annual growth rate of 0.01, with non-foodgrains at +0.67, but foodgrains actually at -0.18. Commercialized non-foodgrain figures recorded significantly higher growth rates than foodgrains. There is a major contrast also within the latter category between wheat, with large-scale exports from Punjab and elsewhere (+0.84), and rice, exported from Burma but not Bengal or other Indian provinces (-0.09). Output of poor peoples' food stagnated markedly. Ragi went down by 0.37. Such expansion as did take place often took the form of an extension of commercial crop acreage at the cost of foodgrains, rather than aggregate growth. The other important, and obviously related, variation was across provinces: Greater Bengal growth rate in output of all crops at -0.45, but Greater Punjab at +1.57. Per capita foodgrain output went down catastrophically in Bengal, where population was growing at around 1 per cent per annum over 1921–41, while food output declined annually by 0.7 per cent.[1]

Clive Dewey and Alan Heston tried to controvert Blyn's pessimistic findings since the available statistics do show major problems. Blyn's

---

[1] Blyn 1966: Appendix, Table 5A, cited in Roy 2000: 56–8.

output figures were arrived at only indirectly, through multiplying the 'standard yield' per crop (estimated through occasional sample crop-cutting in a 'normal' season) by area cultivated (as reported annually by village officials). The standard yield, again, was modulated annually by a 'condition factor', depending supposedly on good or poor crop conditions in a particular year. The responsibility for data collection rested mainly with village accountants and watchmen (patwaris and chaukidars), who tended to be somewhat thin on the ground in Permanent Settlement areas, and not entirely reliable anywhere. More specifically, critics of Blyn suggest an administratively generated systemic downward bias, since local officials would understate yields and acreage in order to please influential landholders and help them get revenue remissions. But a counterbalancing tendency towards overassessments may also have operated, since that would please superior state officials. On the whole, the basic tendencies diagnosed by Blyn do not seem to have been convincingly controverted, while one detailed statistical study of trends in Punjab, based on a different official series, suggests that growth even in that region has been exaggerated.[2]

At the most basic and long-term level, the distribution of crops across the subcontinent has been obviously conditioned by patterns of average annual rainfall, with 80E longitude roughly separating the wheat from the rice zone. On this must be superimposed regional and local variations of terrain, and soil and water availability. The latter, in particular, has come to constitute what both colonial officials and later scholars have often construed as a basic distinction, most evident in the South, between wet and dry lands. The former is defined by the presence of adequate and reliable water supply through effective irrigation (by canals, wells, or tanks), or in some areas by the sheer abundance of natural precipitation. The dry areas (usually in the interior, and away from major rivers), by contrast, were necessarily dependent on uncertain and inadequate rainfall. The distinction has had long-term significance, going much beyond narrowly conceived agrarian or economic history. The core wet areas, like the Ganga valley

---

[2] Islam 1988: 319–32. For a survey of the entire debate around Blyn, see Guha 1992: Introduction.

and the deltaic regions in the South (most famously the Thanjavur region), have been characterized by stable settled agriculture for many centuries. On this have rested well-developed caste-cum-class hierarchies appropriating the surplus produced by subordinated groups. These constitute the classic centres of the brahmanical caste order, with a broadly tripartite structure of predominantly high-caste landlords, intermediate- or backward-caste peasants, and Dalit agricultural labourers. Beyond these, across the drier interior of the subcontinent from peninsula tip to Rajasthan, Sind, and the Punjab, life seems to have been much more migratory and mobile, with shifting patterns of extensive rather than intensive cultivation, swidden, pastoralism, and hunter-gatherer communities. This was also the domain of migratory trading communities like the Banjaras, and of a volatile military labour market of actual or potential soldiers or marauders. British rule, with its built-in assumptions of stable and marketable property rights in land, tended to consolidate the already hierarchized societies in the wet regions, while extending similar patterns into the interior through policies of pacification and sedentarization. The changes, therefore, may have been more marked in the dry zones. Parts of the latter, notably the Punjab after major irrigation inputs, became more dynamic than the old centres of agrarian civilization. These were now increasingly burdened by demographic pressures and shortages of fertile land.[3]

It is tempting to suggest at this point some possible correlations of the expansion of sedentarized agriculture with a series of social developments that will occupy us in our next chapter: in particular, a tightening of caste structures and patriarchal norms. Even many of the non-brahmanic sanskritizing movements that became increasingly visible by the late nineteenth and early twentieth century tended to combine, in varying proportions, elements of protest with an ultimate strengthening of the ladders of hierarchy, since protesting castes tried to move up the latter, not break them down. Such movements simultaneously helped to extend, down the social scale, upper-caste norms requiring the greater seclusion of women and prohibiting widow marriage.

[3] A point emphasized in Ludden 1994: Introduction.

The other major, more directly economic, change was associated with the leap in communications and associated commercialization of agriculture from the third quarter of the nineteenth century. The qualitatively higher level of subcontinental integration, in particular the development of a unified market for bulk agricultural produce, enhanced regional specialization at the cost of a greater variety of produce and relative self-sufficiency. Cotton, to take a specific example, had been previously grown also in regions like Bengal. It now came to be concentrated in areas of most favourable soil and climate, notably the northern part of interior Maharashtra. Commercialization certainly promoted growth in a range of agricultural commodities—wheat, sugarcane, cotton, jute, groundnuts, oilseeds, and tobacco, along with the new plantation crops of tea and coffee. The consequences, though, were not free of considerable ambiguity, as we shall see.

The basic macroeconomic fact, however, is that of a remarkable near-stagnation across the late-colonial decades. A relevant factor would have been the fairly negligible state investment, except in irrigation. The proportion of irrigated land did go up considerably, rising from 12.4 per cent to 22.1 per cent of the cultivated area between 1885–6 and 1938–9, with the acreage served by government-constructed canals (mostly in the Punjab, western UP, and Madras) quadrupling during these decades. The benefits for many of these projects, though, are controversial. Agricultural implements and other technological inputs changed very little, though some belated efforts were made from the early twentieth century to set up a few government agricultural research stations, notably at Pusa in 1906. But the more fundamental constraints on development lay probably in structures of agrarian relations and the specific forms of commercialization. It is to these that we now have to turn.

Revenue, Rent, and Tenancy

Research on Indian agrarian history began with studies of revenue policies, a choice explained by the easy availability of top-level official pronouncements and archives. Early accounts therefore fastened on the apparently obvious contrast between the zamindari, raiyatwari, and mahalwari settlements made during the first couple of generations of Company rule, roughly located, respectively, in the presidencies of Bengal, Madras, and Bombay, and what later became the United Provinces. The distinctions pertained to three questions: (1) who paid revenue directly to the state (landlords, peasants—or, rather, the relatively privileged among them—or village 'communities'); (2) how would the amount be fixed (on the basis of old assessments, as a proportion of the gross agricultural produce, or by the Ricardian net produce criterion); (3) and for how long would it be fixed (in perpetuity, in Bengal by the 1793 enactment, or on what eventually became a thirty-year basis elsewhere). What attracted a lot of attention was the apparently dramatic shift in British policy, around the turn of the eighteenth century into the nineteenth, from zamindari to raiyatwari. The major studies around this theme by Ranajit Guha and Eric Stokes sought to explain it in terms of changing ideologies and intellectual currents in a West that was itself going through an era of dramatic transformation. Others preferred to concentrate more on the nitty-gritty of regional or local circumstances as more important, pragmatic, determinants of Company policy. Such studies tended to emphasize continuities with pre-colonial rural structures rather than dramatic change: factors like big revenue collectors being already prominent in the Bengal landscape and much less so in most parts of Madras, for instance.

The continuity arguments were strengthened as research increasingly shifted downwards into regional and district records, while the contrast between the three revenue systems also began to seem less crucial. A quest for stable and marketable property rights was one common element. The British everywhere sought to ensure security of revenue through immediate sale for arrears, in place of the occasionally physical coercion of earlier regimes. A second change, across different revenue regimes, was the extraction of revenue from the entire property, and not just on the basis of cultivated area. In other ways, too, the distinction between zamindari and raiyatwari zones becomes less sharp when looked at in terms of ground-level realities, as well as over time. Thus, the anti-intermediary slant outside Bengal went along in practice with numerous adjustments with quasi-landlord figures like holders of tax-free inams in the West and the South. More significantly, the raiyat, in practice, was quite often not really an actual cultivator or peasant, and the phenomenon of 'raiyatwari landlordism' soon became almost ubiquitous. As early as December 1820, in the very process of finalizing the raiyatwari settlement, the Madras Board of Revenue had clarified that 'It never was intended that the ryotwar settlement should go lower than the landholders or meerasidars . . . It would appear, however, that in some cases this mistake has been actually made, and it seems to have been supposed that under a ryotwari settlement the collector is to settle with the actual cultivators . . .'[4]

Landlordism developed also because there was never any legal barrier to the revenue-paying raiyat renting out a part or the whole of his land to subordinate tenants. Meanwhile, a contrary tendency became visible through the progress of research on the zamindari settlement in Bengal Presidency. Rajat Ray and Ratnalekha Ray emphasized elements of continuity through their 'jotedar thesis'. Zamindars both before and after the Permanent Settlement, they argued, were basically revenue collectors and not organizers of agricultural production. Below them, and in practice often more crucial, was the stratum, already noticeable in the eighteenth century, of jotedars: 'dominant landed village groups in effective possession of land and commanding the labour of poor villagers.' Zamindari power was enhanced for a while in the wake of 1793, notably by new powers of the distraint of raiyat property in cases of non-payment of rent. The British armed zamindars with such powers through regulations made in 1799 and 1812, for they were initially nervous about security of revenue. There is little doubt, also, that in the permanently settled regions zamindars as a social group benefited throughout the colonial era on account of the gap between fixed revenue and flexible rents. But the massive fragmentation of estates and the proliferation of intermediate tenures (which became a principal economic base of the Bengali Hindu bhadralok) meant that by no means all individual zamindars were always particularly well off. From the 1850s the British began to introduce some provisions

---

[4] Madras Board of Revenue, 4 December 1820, cited in Yanagisawa 1996: 196. 'Mirasidar', along with terms like 'kaniyatchi', referred to dominant-caste joint holders of land, particularly prominent in wet areas like Thanjavur, a southern and western Indian counterpart to the so-called 'village communities' of parts of North India with whom the mahalwari settlement was made. Thus, the distinction between raiyatwari and mahalwari was always fairly tenuous.

for tenancy protection, again in practice reducing the distinction between zamindari and raiyatwari systems through a curtailment of the authority of intermediary landlords.[5]

The late-colonial era was characterized by one very significant shift in agrarian history that has been somewhat obscured by a persistent tendency in nationalist writings to underline and emphasize British efforts at maximizing land revenue. That charge, classically made by R.C. Dutt, for instance, was valid enough in the earlier decades of colonial rule, particularly the Company phase. As in pre-colonial, and notably Mughal, times, the state, till around the mid-nineteenth century, remained the principal appropriator of surplus from the countryside. Even the Permanent Settlement had been fixed at a level significantly higher than the highest level of assessments of which Company officials had found records, while early accounts of raiyatwari are full of evidence of overassessment. But a combination of factors began to push down the proportion of state demand to gross agricultural produce after the 1850s. The panic of 1857 made the conciliation of landed groups, and more generally of the rural upper strata, a political imperative. Colonial state policy, it needs to be emphasized again, was seldom a monolith, it was always open to contradictory pressures. Thus the desire to enhance revenue to meet state expenses increasingly clashed with the need to stimulate the export of agricultural commodities. At the same time, the encouragement of rural purchasing power by reducing revenue could also help expand markets for British manufactures.

Steps were taken immediately after 1857 to extend the Permanent Settlement which, it was felt, had kept Bengal loyal. These, however, proved abortive, and revenue enhancement still led to occasional peasant unrest and nationalist criticism till the 1920s. But, on the whole, land revenue steadily fell below agricultural prices.[6] The share of land revenue in gross Government of India tax receipts fell from 43 per cent in 1880 to 23 per cent in 1920. In Madras Presidency,

---

[5] Ray and Ray 1992: chapter 7.

[6] Relevant here also was the general upward curve in the latter, from the 1860s till the global Depression—an important secular trend to be taken up in the next section.

between 1860 and 1920, grain prices rose between 120 per cent and 180 per cent, but average assessment per acre went up only from Rs 1.7 to Rs 2.1. The decline in the state's share was most evident in the permanently settled areas where revenue, however high initially, remained fixed while prices and rents rose. But the trend was increasingly evident everywhere. It benefited zamindars, as well as the upper stratum of raiyats who could now become petty landlords. The contradictions between such strata and subordinate rural elements were simultaneously sharpened. The former now displaced the state as the major appropriator of the agrarian surplus.

A very important consequence followed. Under Mughal and Company rule alike, and down to the 1857 upsurge, peasant rebellions had been directed in the main against state officials. They were frequently led by local zamindars or chiefs with whom the upper strata of raiyats could be associated by clan or caste ties and paternalist traditions. Along with the shift in surplus share, such patterns also tended to get eroded by the advance of the harsher logic of commercialization and the full-scale market economy. As the lords of the land were transformed into mere landlords, Awadh (Oudh)'s peasants (as one instance), who had loyally followed their talukdars in 1857, now began to consider them their principal enemies. We shall later see that this development often caused considerable embarrassment to middle-class nationalists. Many among them had rentier connections which gave them a stake in the agrarian power structure. Nationalism, moreover, was motivated by the desire to maintain the unity of all Indians against foreign rule, the tendency thus being to avoid or suppress class issues and other social contradictions with a disruptive potential. Revenue extortion consequently figured much more prominently than rent exploitation in standard nationalist economic thinking.

The sharpening tension between landlords and the peasant upper stratum over questions of rent and security of tenures prodded the British to search for a balance between continued support to landlords alongside some protection for sections of tenants. In Bengal the tenancy acts of 1859 and 1885 brought into being a legal category of occupancy raiyats. Tenants who could establish continuity of tenure for twelve years could not be evicted, and limits were placed on rent enhancements pertaining to their land. In practice, landlords successfully evolved strategies for getting around most such restrictions. In the Oudh portion of the United Provinces, for instance, the broadly similar Rent Act of 1886 was evaded by extorting unpaid labour (begar), a variety of abwabs (illegal cesses), and by charging a premium (nazrana) for the renewal of tenancies by threats of bedakhli (eviction): issues which would be central to the major peasant movement under Baba Ramchandra in that region in 1920–1.

The other major limitation of tenancy legislation was that no effort was ever made to ensure a link between the legal right of occupancy and actual cultivation. As in raiyatwari areas, subordinate unprotected tenancies quickly developed below the occupancy tenant, while the latter right could pass by sale to people who had neither any connection with agricultural production nor even village residence. A second major development, markedly more prominent from the early decades of the twentieth century, was an increasing centrality in large parts of the country of the phenomenon of sharecropping or produce-rent. Landlords and better-off raiyats who leased out parts of their land were not sure that in the future tenancy protection would not be extended to tenants-at-will. So they often preferred arrangements with sharecroppers (or bargadars or bhagchasis, to use the Bengali terms: there were equivalents in other areas) under which indebted or otherwise downwardly mobile peasants were allowed to retain their holdings but had to surrender a much higher share of the crop as rent than the sum they may have earlier paid in cash. More crucially, produce-rents would benefit rent-receivers and adversely affect rent-payers in an era of rising agricultural prices, as in the early decades of the twentieth century. This thus became an arena of sharp class tension. Erstwhile occupancy raiyats in the eastern Bengal districts, for instance, tried to take advantage of Section 40 of the Bengal Tenancy Act of 1885 under which the commutation of produce into money rent could be applied for in certain circumstances and times. Politically influential landed bhadralok groups bitterly resisted such efforts, and the clause was repealed in 1928.

What has often been assumed to be the logical succession of economic forms—from labour to produce to money rents through deepening commercialization and movements in a capitalistic direction—

was often reversed in colonial India. Micro studies of regions as diverse as the jute belt of eastern Bengal, Bihar's districts south of the Ganga and north of Chhota Nagpur, and lands newly benefiting from irrigation in Punjab all indicate this inverted correlation.[7] Over the long time span, one might suggest, the focus of agrarian struggle has been shifting 'downwards': from issues of revenue, to rent and tenancy protection, and then to the forms and conditions of sharecropping (along with agricultural labour). But it took time for even the Left-led kisan sabhas of the 1930s, who led tenant-cultivators in movements against landlords, to become sensitized to bargadar exploitation.

Our brief sketch of revenue, rent, and tenancy points to numerous other themes, in particular to questions of agrarian stratification: how far did this change over time, and in what ways did rural production relations possibly contribute to overall agricultural stagnation? Late-colonial efforts at balancing their continued support to landlords with a degree of tenancy and rent protection to the upper strata of peasants, for instance, could have unwittingly made for the worst of both worlds from the point of view of any agrarian breakthrough in a capitalist direction. It may have stymied the possibilities of landlord enterprise, which would have had to be based on entrepreneurial control over extensive estates constituted through a large-scale eviction of peasants while still maintaining a situation where it made more sense for the raiyat to become a petty rentier and not a proto-capitalist farmer. The paths of capitalist development 'from above' and 'from below' both remained full of pitfalls. The risks of cultivation, particularly in the zamindari areas, tended to be passed down the expanding chain of intermediaries: the burden to be eventually placed, often, on sharecroppers or poor peasants whose resources were obviously quite inadequate for significant productive investment.[8] But a fuller

[7] E.g: 'In general, with the extension of irrigation, increased production of more valuable crops, and a long-term price rise, there was a shift from cash rents to share-cropping (*bata*).' Cash rents were more common in the arid and poorer south-eastern parts of the Punjab, and not the fertile, river- or canal-watered richer central districts: Narain 1965. For similar trends in parts of Bengal and South Bihar in the same period, see Nakazato 1994: chapters 6, 7; and Prakash 1990: 111ff.

[8] See, for instance, Chatterjee 1982: 113–224. Studies like these used terms

discussion of such issues requires a close look, first, at the impact of late-colonial commercialization, and the closely related theme of rural indebtedness.

Commercialization and Indebtedness

The myth of the golden age of pre-colonial rural self-sufficiency has long been shattered. The Mughals extracted a heavy land tax mainly in cash, necessitating peasant–market linkages: European traders were purchasing a few agricultural commodities, like indigo, even in the seventeenth century. The major part of subcontinental exports, however, were of manufactured goods, notably cotton and silk textiles. For all this there can be little doubt that a qualitative break took place in the latter half of the nineteenth century in the level or intensity of agricultural commercialization, above all through external trade. The value of exports from India went up by about 600 per cent between 1860 and 1925, along with a trebling of prices, and 70–80 per cent of these exports consisted of non-manufactured, mainly agricultural, products. The commodity composition of the latter underwent many changes. The decline in indigo and opium was heavily compensated by a rapid growth in the exports of raw cotton and raw jute, wheat, cane sugar, oilseeds, and the new plantation product, tea. Factors which contributed to the leap in exports included British pacificatory measures: the 'anarchy' of the late eighteenth and early nineteenth century has been grossly exaggerated, but in some regions it was not entirely a myth. Internal trade duties were removed following the Trevelyan Report of 1835; there was a gradual decline in the land tax; and, above all, there was a revolution in communications: improved roads, railway construction, the shift to steam navigation, and the opening of the Suez Canal in 1869. All this vastly enhanced speed and reduced the costs of transport in the bulk of commodities. Railways constituted the most dramatic new input: only 850 miles in 1860, 16,000 in 1890, 35,000 by 1920, and 40,000 by 1946. The freight carried by railways, 3.6 million tonnes in 1871, had soared to

---

taken from the then-contemporary Marxian debate on the transition from feudalism and capitalism in Europe, notably the contribution of Takahashi.

143.6 million in 1945–6. The alignment of the main railway routes was also significant. Apart from a north-western network of strategic lines determined by the fear of Russian expansion, most of the lines connected the major port cities with regions important for agricultural exports.[9]

Yet any history of late-colonial commercialization has to confront a central paradox. Export booms coincided with devastating famines, notably in the 1870s in western India and in the late 1890s in the interior regions of the South. Contrary to conventional economic theory, expanding markets, far from stimulating 'export-led growth', went hand in hand with an overall stagnation in agricultural production. Some have sought to explain the anomaly by factors such as excessive population growth, which, however, was hardly evident prior to the post-1921 demographic upturn. Inadequate natural-resource endowments, or socio-cultural barriers to economic development (caste, or alleged Indian otherworldliness), are also cited as contributory factors. For many others, above all for nationalist and Left critics of colonialism, the paradox was one of 'forced' commercialization.

In its early nationalist depiction, predictably, forced commercialization was explained as flowing primarily from the excessive land revenue demand which compelled peasants to sell their produce even while they starved. The responsibility for what was often depicted as a uni-linear and absolute process of immiserization could then be placed squarely on the colonial state, while the contributions of indigenous exploiting groups (landlords, moneylenders, traders) were slurred over. The theory in this simplistic form clearly has many problems. Pre-colonial revenue demands had also been extremely heavy and early Company rule had only continued older traditions, perhaps in an aggravated form. Early-nineteenth-century extortionate assessments seem to have often acted as a constraint on commercialization. And by no means were all sections of rural society adversely affected: some gained substantially from the processes unleashed or accelerated by colonialism.

[9] I am taking the statistics from Tomlinson 1998: 51–63; and Roy 2000: 60–9.

In the 1980s, however, a much more sophisticated model of forced commercialization was worked out by a group of Indian economists, influenced by Marxism, and led by by K.N. Raj, Krishna Bharadwaj, and Amit Bhaduri. They questioned the neo-classical tendency (even more prevalent today) to abstract the so-called free market from specific historical circumstances and assume that all exchange is by definition entirely voluntary, operative between individuals functioning on the same level and so entering into transactions only up to the point where it is gainful for all participants. But, Bhaduri pointed out, a poor tenant might have to take regular consumption loans to tide over the lean pre-harvest season from his landlord—who would double up as moneylender. In return, the latter might extract repayment in grain at a predetermined price, or in labour at an unduly low wage; in such a situation the landlord could also impose less favourable tenurial conditions. Under these constraints, which were fairly typical in colonial and post-colonial India as well as in many other underdeveloped societies, market relations in credit, output, labour, and land can become intertwined, dependencies and inequalities in one feeding into those in others. Increasing commoditization would then be quite unrelated to any expansion in producer surplus.[10]

This has proved to be a rich vein of analysis, largely free of the old nationalist tendency to concentrate solely on specific policies of the colonial state, and highlighting, instead, the dependence of small agricultural producers on world-market fluctuations, big foreign export–import firms and banks, and indigenous groups of merchants, moneylenders, landlords, and rich peasants. One should add that the word 'forced' should not be taken too literally, or as necessarily implying that commercialized agriculture was always unremunerative for the peasant.[11] The point, rather, is that relationships of dependence and

[10] Bhaduri 1999: 74–85 (the essay was first published in 1986). See also Bharadwaj 1985; and Raj 1985: Introduction.

[11] Thus Dharm Narain was able to establish, statistically, a positive correlation between relative crop prices and variations in acreage, indicating 'normal' profit-maximizing behaviour (Narain 1965). But gross statistics like these do not of course prove that all or even most peasants were behaving in this manner, for the big producers may have been tilting the scale in that direction.

inequality continued to be reproduced, and agricultural production stagnated in many (though not all) regions despite rapidly expanding markets. In the mid-1950s Daniel Thorner coined the term 'built-in depressor' to denote the 'complex of legal, economic and social relations' that made it more profitable for superior right-holders 'to rent out their land than to manage them personally . . .'[12] It needs to be emphasized, however, that the progress of detailed research on regional and local material—very impressive in the late 1980s and early 1990s though declining somewhat subsequently—has brought out significant variations in the degree of forced commercialization, and the extent to which the 'depressor' produced overall immiserization and/or stagnation, or could be compatible with some growth and relative prosperity. The variations that demand particular attention are those of times, crops, regions, and social strata.

Late-colonial commercialization went through several phases. The 1860s saw first a dramatic boost through the surge of raw cotton exports to Lancashire mills from western India when the American Civil War (1861–5) disrupted supplies from the seceding southern states. This was followed by an equally sharp decline. Then followed a long period of growth in agricultural exports from the 1870s which lasted, with a brief hiccup in the early 1880s, till the mid-1920s. Indian raw cotton built up a market in Continental Europe, and then after 1900 the country became the chief source of supply for emerging Japanese textiles. The Suez Canal made bulk shipments of Indian wheat and oilseeds cheaper and more practical, while much of the world's grain trade came to be transported in jute bags, creating an enormous market for Bengal's jute manufacture. Particularly in the 1870s and 1880s the currency ratio also favoured Indian exports. The silver rupee was depreciating against gold-based British, European, and American currencies, and this made Indian export prices highly competitive.

These then were the decades when benefits probably did accrue to some from commercialization, and many historians think there

---

[12] Thorner 1976 (reprinting a 1950s lecture in Delhi): 16, cited in Patnaik 2001: 17–57. Patnaik's was the first Thorner Memorial Lecture, delivered in 1985.

is evidence of the growth of rich peasant groups in regions like the wet deltaic areas of the South, parts of Gujarat, Maharashtra, and western UP, the Punjab canal colonies, and the jute-growing districts of Central and Eastern Bengal.[13] Much of the gains probably went to foreign export–import, shipping, banking, and insurance firms. Indian producers remained throughout dependent on world-market fluctuations over which they could have little or no control, or even knowledge. How uneven the gains were even during these decades of export and price upturn is revealed when we recall that the last quarter of the nineteenth century was also marked by a succession of devastating famines, mostly in the 'dry' regions. Everywhere the poor were adversely affected by the shift in acreage towards higher-priced, exportable crops (e.g. wheat, cotton, sugar, or tobacco in place of millets).

From the mid-1920s, world trade in primary products began to stagnate and then decline, leading on to the catastrophic Depression of the early 1930s. In India, the prices of agricultural produce went down by 44 per cent between 1929 and 1931, becoming on average half what they had been for much of the 1920s. Some have seen in the consequent plight of large sections of the peasantry (including the better-off strata that had benefited from the preceding regime of rising prices) one reason for the massive rural rally around Gandhian Civil Disobedience in 1930–1. What made the crisis worse was that the 1920s had also ushered in a marked demographic upturn, while—given the very low investment in infrastructure—there was less and less new land available for cultivation. The recovery was slow, and in terms of agricultural prices it came only after 1939, when wartime inflation displaced the Depression of the 1930s. This may have benefited, to some extent, a few regions like Punjab. The flip side was represented by Bengal, where in 1943 British rule drew near its end amidst a famine comparable in scale with the one of 1770 that had symbolized its beginning.

---

[13] We shall see in later chapters that such upward rural mobility had possibly interesting correlations with developments such as the intermediate- and lower-caste assertions in Tamilnadu and Maharashtra, and the rise of Muslim identity politics in East Bengal.

Of the new commercial crops, tea fell into a special category, the only one (apart from a variety of coffee in South Indian uplands) to be grown in full-fledged plantations. Migrant labour was brought in, through semi-servile indentures from distant parts of the country, to work on tea gardens located on largely vacant lands along the Assam–North Bengal Himalayan foothills.[14] Opium was also a special case: it was cultivated mainly in parts of Central Bihar under a direct state control that periodically regulated acreage and prices. Very important during some decades of the mid-nineteenth century in the context of the notorious opium–tea connection with China run by the EIC and then British private traders, it declined rapidly from a peak point around 1860–1, when its sales were bringing in more than 30 per cent of the aggregate export value.

The 'forced' aspects of commercialization were most evident with regard to indigo. The old European purchases from centres in the Mughal subahs of Agra and Gujarat had declined in the eighteenth century following the rise of slave-based plantations in the West Indies and the American South. But then there was a major revival following the shift of the latter to sugar and then cotton, the successful slave revolution in San Domingo (Haiti) in the 1790s, and the abolition of slavery. Indigo, though, was always a fluctuating and uncertain proposition, and the European planters who went in for it on a large scale in Central Bengal during the early and middle decades of the nineteenth century were not allowed to purchase land by the Company till 1833. So what they did was resort to a variety of crudely coercive measures to terrorize peasants, otherwise subordinated to Indian land-lords, into taking advances and then forcing them to grow what was for the growers an often unremunerative crop. Peasant resistance in 1859–60 (the so-called Blue Mutiny) got substantial Indian zamindar and middle-class sympathy as well as missionary help. There seems to have been some unhappiness even among some colonial officials at peasant distress. After 1860, indigo was largely shifted away from Bengal to some north Bihar districts such as Champaran. There, for a generation, planters were able to strike a mutually profitable

---

[14] Its history forms a part of indentured migration, and will be considered later.

accommodation with zamindars. They entered the local hierarchy of land rights through taking out rent-paying 'thika' leases from zamindars, kept the latter happy through regular payments, and went in for 'zerat' cultivation of indigo by sub-tenants whom they directly controlled. This was different from the earlier Bengal system of raiyati, where advances had been forced on peasants over whom planters had no legal powers except for the imposed indigo contract. A sharp market decline, however, followed the German invention of the cheaper and more efficient synthetic aniline dye in 1897 which doomed indigo to extinction (though there was a brief surge in demand when the War disrupted Continental European supplies). The contrast between falling indigo and rising foodgrain prices made peasants—particularly those among them with resources to produce for wider markets—increasingly restive, and this would provide the longer-term foundation for Gandhi's first intervention on Indian soil, in Champaran in 1917.[15]

In general terms, the commercialization of most crops was based not on literal coercion but on a hypothecation of crops prior to harvest through advances. The crucial element, in other words, was the peasant's need for loans, and this fits rather well in Bhaduri's model. The receipt of loans—mid-century indigo apart—would be mostly 'voluntary', but overdetermined by the specifics of ecological conditions, agricultural production processes, and pre-existing structures of dependence and power. And it is here that variations entered, in terms of the degree of imposition and the existence or otherwise of productivity gains: themes illustrated by a rich literature of crop-cum-region-oriented studies.

Jute, for instance, proved considerably more attractive than indigo, for its early growing season meant that peasants got advances towards its cultivation during the leanest part of the year. Indigo could never occupy more than 6–7 per cent of the total cultivated area even in Champaran, and the poppy proportion was only 3 per cent even in the district where it had spread the most, Shahabad. But in 1901–2 jute was grown on 30 per cent of the land in Rangpur and 27 per cent in Tippera. Districts like the latter constituted part of the fertile or active

---

[15] Chaudhuri 1967: 237–336; Pouchepadass 1999: chapters 1–5.

delta region of central and eastern Bengal: land with abundant rains, towards which the river system was shifting, away from the moribund delta of the western part of the province. But research also indicates that the big purchasers of raw jute were predominantly British-owned Calcutta jute mills and foreign export firms who operated along a complex hierarchy of indigenous intermediary traders through which advances went down to the peasants. They tended to appropriate the major share of the gains. Finally, world market fluctuations, above all the late 1920s and early 1930s Depression, spelled total disaster for the small producers at the base of the hierarchy. East Bengal would be particularly severely affected by the famine of 1943.[16]

Shahid Amin's study of sugarcane in the Gorakhpur region of eastern United Provinces was pathbreaking in its focus on the internal complexities of small-peasant production. It sought to locate sugar cultivation within the totality of agricultural practices in their temporal sequence and pointed out that the peasant would not normally sow sugar alone. It drew attention to a want of congruence between the rhythms of farm production and surplus appropriation that often helped to provide entry points for mercantile, and eventual sugar-capitalist domination. Agriculture, Amin pointed out (drawing on a little-known passage in Marx), is generally characterized by a long working period and an even longer production period when the crop has been sown but is not ripe for harvest. Small peasants tend to require advances or other sources of income to tide over the lean months. This is particularly true for sugar, as the harvest time for some varieties spilled over into sowing time for other crops. The peasant therefore had often to sell it very quickly to itinerant dealers even at a below-market price in order to clear his land for other crops. What made matters worse was that the bulk of revenue collections was made around the time of the main (kharif) harvest, when prices would be low due to the new supply. In Gorakhpur, there were zamindar intermediaries between the cultivators and the state and the former were careful to demand their rents a month or so before the time they had to pay revenue—that is, when peasants would have exhausted their stock from the previous year. All these time disjunctions contributed to

[16] Chaudhuri 1967: 247–54; Mukherji 1982.

the peasant's dependence on loans, which again led to a hypothecation of the otherwise most profitable crop of the area, sugar. Amin went on to argue that the big indigenous capitalist sugar mills that had emerged in UP by the 1930s did not create new networks but went on to procure cane from peasants through the existing quasi-feudal exploitative structures: mill domination of cane-growing peasants remained contingent 'on the former's prior subordination to the landlords, moneylenders and the richer peasants.'[17]

It needs to be emphasized that there has been no invariable or inevitable link between commercialization and either stagnation and immiserization, or growth. The key variables usually seem to have been the specificities of ecology and agrarian structure. Space permits reference to only a few instances, among many. David Washbrook and Christopher Baker highlighted the contrast between the 'dry' interior areas of Madras Presidency, and the Andhra coastal region watered by the Godavari and the Krishna as well as, from the mid-nineteenth century, by canals. In the first, the scanty and uncertain rainfall, the poor and uneven soil, and a skewed rural structure combined to perpetuate sharp divisions between 'big men' and 'little men'. Village elites in precolonial times had commandeered the labour of dependent villagers for military service in what had then been a politically fluid region. With British demilitarization and the subsequent expansion of external markets, similar relationships of domination were reproduced for intensive cultivation on the relatively better-endowed lands, which were of course controlled by that same elite. But commercialization did lead to significant expansion, notably through the cultivation of groundnuts and cotton (the latter would provide the basis for the important twentieth-century rise of cotton mills and handloom factories in towns like Coimbatore, Madurai, and Salem). Parts of coastal Andhra indicate a different pattern: here commercialization (e.g. tobacco farming) could lead to a somewhat broader prosperity and the development of what Washbrook described as a middle-peasant stratum. The Kaveri delta (Thanjavur) reveals yet another kind of history. Traditionally rich and much more densely populated

---

[17] Amin 1984, as well as two essays by Amin which conveniently summarize the core of his argument: Amin 1982: 39–87, and Amin 1994: 182–206.

than the uplands and plains of interior Tamilnadu, its capacity for high agricultural surplus had produced a society sharply divided on class-cum-caste lines. This comprised Brahmin or Vellala mirasidars or kaniyatchikarans who appropriated the labour of sharecroppers and semi-servile or 'bonded' low-caste agricultural workers (the pannaiyal). The sheer ease of exploitation may have made the region less dynamic, though some changes began to take place, as we shall see, by the turn of the nineteenth century.[18]

Studies of the Punjab, as well as of central and western India, similarly highlight variations that are explicable in terms of specific, and often inter-related, ecological and agrarian structures. Neeladri Bhattacharya's seminal essays on pastoralism, tenancy cultivation, credit and markets, and agricultural labour in late-colonial Punjab repeatedly link these facets of rural life with one another. His analysis is grounded in a basic ecological contrast between the central districts, watered by the five rivers and by British-constructed canals, and the semi-arid, for long part-nomadic, south-east.[19] T.C.A. Raghavan's study of the Narmada valley has explored the ways in which peasants cultivating poorer soil tended to suffer much more from erratic monsoons, making them more dependent on landlords, moneylenders, and traders: factors contributing to rural inequality in fact often tend to enhance each other. The promising Narmada valley wheat boom, which had followed railway construction in the 1880s and early 1890s, quickly petered away, in part because of the excessive burdens imposed on cultivators by state-backed malguzari high landlordism. The Nimar district in the same valley, with a ryotwari system, however, came to enjoy what has proved to be a relatively stable prosperity resting on a more widely-based rich peasant agriculture (this is threatened now, though, by post-colonial 'development': the region may be flooded by the Narmada valley project). An important cotton belt emerged in Nagpur and Berar, where, too, rural society seems to have been relatively less differentiated. But it has to be added that the growth of

[18] Washbrook 1976: chapter 3; Washbrook 1978: 68–82; Washbrook 1993.

[19] Bhattacharya 1995: 49–85; Bhattacharya 1983: 121–70; Bhattacharya 1994: 197–247; and Bhattacharya 1985: 105–52.

this bloc of commercialized agriculture, fairly distant from the coast, had a lot to do with abundant supplies of cheap seasonal adivasi or low-caste labour from nearby uplands as well as Chhattisgarh: once again, a pattern that continues in an aggravated form today.

Crispin Bates has emphasized the intermeshing of many of the processes surveyed in this chapter. Colonial forest laws began in relation to the woods and affected shifting cultivation: pastoralists, food-gatherers, and adivasis lost land through the operation of stringent colonial laws of property and alienation in cases of a failure to repay debts. The resultant imposed mobility made seasonal labourers come every year to gather wheat and cotton harvests in relatively prosperous areas for the upwardly-mobile beneficiaries of commercialized agriculture. 'Development' and 'underdevelopment' thus fed each other, not just globally, but also with regard to relationships within the colonized country.[20]

Further west and south, Sumit Guha's work reveals that the Bhaduri model of interlocked and skewed land-labour-credit-output markets that blocked development and produced immiserization was also evident in the mid-nineteenth century in the Khandesh region. This began with a heavy initial colonial assessment, low prices, and poor communications. But commercialization did bring growth here subsequently, loosening the gridlock. As in the pockets in the Maharashtra Deccan where canal irrigation had been introduced, a rich peasant stratum emerged, benefiting from the cultivation of cotton and sugarcane. That the central and southern Deccan dry areas, however, did not on the whole share this relative prosperity till much later is indicated even by the more optimistic study of Neil Charlesworth.[21]

Rural indebtedness has already figured repeatedly in our surveys of agrarian relations and commercialization, but the subject is crucial enough to demand a closer look. It was hardly a new, specifically colonial, or modern phenomenon. The statement by a Madras official in

---

[20] Raghavan 1985: 169–200; Bates 1985: 573–92. Both are reprinted in Ludden 1994.

[21] Guha 1985: 210–46.; Charlesworth 1988. These essays provide helpful previews of later books by the same authors.

1895 that small ryots in the dry region 'could not begin to cultivate without borrowing seed, cattle, grain for maintenance, etc.' is open to much wider extension in space and time alike.[22] But British rule did make a difference, in two ways. Tighter laws of property, contract, and alienation for non-repayment of loans meant that indebtedness could have much more serious economic consequences than earlier. The results were devastating, particularly in the less settled areas, where notions of strict private ownership had hardly developed. Several historians, moreover, have drawn attention to a probable shift from 'usurer' towards 'merchant-moneylender' with intensified commodity production and commercialization. The usurer would be concerned primarily with interest, and with the eventual return of the loan that he had advanced; the merchant-lender would be more in control over the product made by the indebted artisan or peasant. The former would be inclined to charge very high rates of interest and extract compliance, sometimes with physical threats (like the archetype of the Pathan or Kabuli moneylender). The latter would be more interested in organizing capitalistic putting-out forms in manufacture, and establishing domination over peasants through a pre-harvest hypothecation of crops. Putting-out and hypothecation had had earlier manifestations but were much intensified under colonial rule. No doubt, the transition remained incomplete, uneven, and open to varied combinations.[23]

British officials tended to attribute most of the ills of Indian rural society to the depredations of the mahajan or sahukar, often conceptualized as an external urban force impinging on village society. This ploy shifts responsibility from colonial revenue burdens and

---

[22] Cited by Washbrook 1978: 70–1.

[23] Prasanna Parthasarathi provides important details of such a transition towards tighter control over artisanal production in early-colonial Madras, emphasizing the ways in which it helped to constitute a Company alliance with Indian cloth merchants and mirasidars 'to discipline weavers and agrarian producers': Parthasarathi 2001: 5–6, *et passim*. Benoy Chaudhuri drew attention to the same phenomenon in Bengal agriculture (Chaudhuri 1967), while there is a detailed study in Bhattacharya 1994. Bhattacharya points also to the less developed areas of south-east Punjab being more subject to the older, more purely usurious forms of moneylending, with higher interest rates, by contrast with the central districts.

forced commercialization which nationalists used as the staple of their critique. It also suggests that the peasant could at times be responsible for his own suffering because of extravagance during social and religious occasions. In the context of attacks on Marwari and Gujarati moneylenders—aimed at the destruction of debt bonds—in 1875 in the Pune–Ahmednagar region of the Maharashtra Deccan, the Deccan Agriculturalists' Relief Act tried to restrict the sale of land for indebtedness to outsiders. Similar laws were made later in several other provinces, most famously the Punjab Land Alienation Act of 1901 which banned the transfer of land to 'non-agriculturalist castes'. This was followed in 1904 by legislation to facilitate cooperative credit societies among peasants. But there was nothing to prevent the oppression of upwardly-mobile peasant groups and land-grabbing moneylenders in relation to their less successful or fortunate fellow villagers. Legislations like these seem to have ultimately benefited rich peasants, who often also managed to dominate the cooperative societies.

Middle-class nationalist opinion was ambivalent about the figure of the moneylender. They were critical of Curzon's Punjab Act, for in that region the Congress had connections mainly with Hindu urban trading groups. Subsequently, Gandhian nationalism was able to attract substantial support in many areas from small-town and rural Bania groups. But there has also been a widespread stereotype, very visible in Bengali literature for instance, of the moneylender as an upstart with money and urban connections who comes to disturb the 'natural' rural harmony; dispossessing the cultured, old-fashioned, and paternalistic zamindar, he rack-rents peasants and tribal communities.[24] There are elements of validity in such images, but also considerable romanticization. The figure of the benevolent zamindar presiding over a harmonious rural society somehow is always located in a just-vanished past, whereas real-life landlords have often been rack-renters and usurers.

How crucial, and how disastrous, was the burden of rural indebtedness? There is little doubt about its massive aggregate volume, or about

---

[24] For two memorable literary representations, one might recall Satyajit Ray's early film *Jalsaghar*, and the novel *Paraja* by Orissa's Jnanpith Award winner Gopinath Mohanty.

the fact that it was probably growing from the late nineteenth century till the Depression years. In 1929, the Provincial Banking Enquiry Report found annual interest charges in the Central Provinces, for instance, to be 2.5 times the land revenue. A central argument of Sugata Bose's work on twentieth-century Bengal agrarian society is that credit exploitation had become more important than landlord rent in the surplus appropriation from peasant producers.[25] But some problems remain. Neeladri Bhattacharya's essay on indebtedness in Punjab emphasizes the need to disaggregate. Statistical estimates of the total volume of debt do not help much beyond a point, for lenders and borrowers came in all sizes and shapes, with transactions taking place in widely varied circumstances: 'Apart from the professional *sahukars,* one could find peddlers and vendors, big landlords and rich peasants, village drummers, Mochis . . . even *faqirs* and widowed women lending out money.'[26] Conversely, the rich and/or upwardly mobile could borrow as much, or in fact often much more, than the poor. The 1929 Report found the rich central districts of the Punjab to be more in debt than the poorer south-east: per capita debt in the former was Rs 51, as compared to Rs 31 in the latter. Such data seems to provide some basis for Malcolm Darling's optimistic assertion, in his *The Punjab Peasant in Prosperity and Debt* (1925), that indebtedness indicated prosperity rather than poverty.[27] But then Darling too emphasized one tendency among several others—which would have included the opposite and more widespread view which stressed immiserization. Once again, there is a need to distinguish across regions and times. Bhattacharya suggests that in Punjab by the 1920s there had been 'a general weakening' of the power of merchant-moneylenders over the better-off wheat farmers: in partial contrast perhaps to the continued monopolistic control over production and marketing diagnosed by Amin for sugar producers in eastern UP.[28]

'Mahajan' literally translates as 'great man', and in his field study of south Gujarat villages Jan Breman found Dubla bonded labourers

---

[25] Bose 1994: Introduction; Bose 1986: chapter 4.

[26] Bhattacharya 1994: 198.

[27] In his book *The Punjab Peasant in Prosperity and Debt* (1925): see Darling 1947 in chapter 2 above.

[28] Bhattacharya 1994.

tied for life, or across generations, by advances received from their Patidar overlords-cum-creditors, still commonly referring to the latter as 'dhaniamo': those who provide riches.[29] Unlike the extraction of revenue or rent, debt relationships were related commonly to necessities of subsistence and/or production. Notions of reciprocity or paternalism, while not absent in relations of subordinates towards state officials and landlords, were much more evident here. Where exactly one should locate the balance within this patronage/exploitation amalgam depends on times and contexts. It will tend to vary, too, with the values and ideological presuppositions of the observer. Interesting homologies can sometimes come in. Consider, for instance, the following appeal in a local Gandhian news-sheet, during the Bardoli satyagraha of 1928 in Gujarat, that associated class with gender relations: 'The government wants to divide you and the *sahukar,* but for you your *sahukar* is everything . . . It is just like saying to a *pativrata* [devoted wife] that she should change her husband. How can you leave the *sahukar* who has helped you in your difficulties?'[30]

It had been common at one time to assume a linear connection between indebtedness and depeasantization through loss of land. The advance of research has made this assumption largely untenable. Creditors, by and large, have been interested not in outright dispossession and the consequent taking over of the risks of direct farming, but in exploitation through lowering the status of the tenant-cultivator to sub-tenant or sharecropper. Questions of indebtedness thus lead on to a more general theme, to which we now turn.

Agrarian Structures, Changes, and Continuities

Efforts at bringing together the different strands of agrarian history into more holistic models necessitate a focus on questions of rural—more precisely, peasant—stratification, and the extent to which that changed in late-colonial times. Statistical data collected by National Sample Surveys in the early 1950s indicate a highly skewed pattern of control over land and other agricultural inputs, and one in which there was also a broad correspondence of class with caste. In 1953–5,

[29] Breman 1979.
[30] *Satyagraha Patrika,* quoted in Dhanagare 1983: 103.

around 9 per cent of the operational holdings contained more than half of the total cultivated area. Small peasant holdings, three-fourths of the total, extended over less than a third of the latter; and around 20 per cent of rural households consisted of agricultural labourers. Only 7 per cent of the total number of Hindu rural households were defined by the Sample Survey as farmers tilling mainly with hired labour, but a fourth of the higher castes fell within that category. Conversely, 36 per cent of scheduled caste families were agricultural labourers, as compared to only 1 per cent higher caste. (Only 1.5 per cent of scheduled caste households qualified under the farmer category.) There was considerable cross-cutting, however, at intermediate levels, once again statistically confirming what was, and remains, the common-sense perception.[31]

There was once a widespread understanding that such inequalities were primarily a product of colonialism, which had destroyed the traditional self-sufficient, unchanging, and relatively egalitarian and harmonious village community. Traces of these assumptions can still be encountered at times, but they are no longer accepted in serious scholarship. The one apparently solid argument was that which was put forward by S.J. Patel in 1952. He sought to establish from census data a growth in landless labour between 1871 and 1951, and related it to deindustrialization, revenue pressure, and forced commercialization. We shall see in the next section how this, too, had to be abandoned in the 1960s. By the early 1980s, Irfan Habib had come to emphasize the existence of a substantial population of landless labourers in medieval India as well. He sought to explain their coexistence with a land surplus in terms of caste: the widespread taboo against high castes touching the plough, and social barriers preventing landholding by untouchable groups. Habib also pointed to seventeenth-century documents like a firman of Aurangzeb, describing the reza ri'aya (small peasants) as those cultivators who 'depended wholly upon borrowing for their subsistence and for seed and cattle.'[32] Not so fundamentally different, it seems, from the late-colonial situation, though of course we have no means for precisely estimating how spatially extensive such dependence had been in those times.

[31] Raj 1985: xi, xix.
[32] Habib 1982: 221.

Peasant stratification and its implications lay at the heart of the vigorous 'mode of production' debate in the pages of the *Economic and Political Weekly* during the 1970s and early 1980s. As in the near-contemporary 'transition debate' concerning the evolution of capitalism in the West, it was a dialogue principally among Marxists who started from a common understanding about a three-tiered peasant stratification emerging through market expansion and development along capitalist lines. The 'rich' peasants, in this framework, were those marketing most of their crops and using hired labour; the 'poor' were those with holdings inadequate for subsistence who, therefore, had to work for others; while at the core were 'middle' peasants growing subsistence crops with family labour. The peasantry, in the Marxist framework that had been canonized by Lenin, would sooner or later disintegrate, producing petty capitalists at one pole and landless labourers at the other. But this process, in colonial India as well as quite often elsewhere (e.g. France, till well into the twentieth century), seemed to be almost endlessly prolonged. The need was felt, therefore, to formulate categories to characterize and explain rural societies like the Indian, where many decades of intensive commercialization and some urban industrial capitalist growth had still not radically transformed the major part of the countryside.

Broadly, three kinds of positions emerged, with many variants for each. Some emphasized the colonial dimension as principal barrier (even occasionally suggesting a distinct colonial mode of production), linking up with the widely current 'dependency' theories that sought to directly relate growth in the core capitalist world to the 'development of underdevelopment' (Gunder Frank's much-quoted phrase) in the subordinated colonial or semi-colonial periphery. Others, while not denying the evidently crucial nature of overall imperialist domination, felt that class relations within the colonized world also required more attention. The favoured formula, put forward for instance (with some internal differences) by Utsa Patnaik and Amit Bhaduri, was 'semi-feudal'. This stressed the continued domination of the Indian countryside by elements that needed to be characterized as basically pre-capitalist. Phenomena which we have already seen to have been widely prevalent—indebtedness, the hypothecation of crops, sharecropping— were interpreted in this framework as representing trader-moneylender 'mercantile profit', not the full-scale capitalist appropriation of surplus value through a mastery of the production process. The semi-feudal model had affinities with the theoretical positions of Mao Zedong, and it became the most widely-held view. But there was also an alternative with a somewhat Trotskyist ambience, put forward notably by Jairus Banaji in an influential paper in 1977. This used empirical details from the Maharashtra Deccan in the late nineteenth century to argue a case for a particular kind of capitalism in the countryside: one that amounted to a 'formal subsumption' of labour (where the production process has come under capitalist control, but has not been internally transformed), as distinct from 'real subsumption' (which happens when the labour process is technologically revolution-ized). Both, in his view, could be meaningfully considered capitalist: an emphasis which allowed Banaji to be readier to accept the possibility that colonial commercialization could sometimes enable a significant degree of upward mobility among some rural groups. It spelt out a political message. The essay ended with a demand that contemporary agrarian movements should be directed towards the 'abolition of the system of wage slavery', i.e. they should target capitalism, not primarily 'semi-feudal' elements, and concentrate more on energizing the landless strata.[33]

Political subtexts were in fact implicit among all positions on the mode of production debate. The varied categorizations tended to be associated with alternative strands in existing Left thinking about effective agrarian programmes. The backdrop, at once enabling and self-limiting, was the widespread hope in rural revolution aroused above all by China and Vietnam. The fading of such hopes after the 1970s, along with perhaps a widespread feeling that the debate was becoming somewhat scholastic and economically determinist, led to moves away from concentration on peasant stratification.

[33] 'Formal' and 'real' subsumption were terms taken from a then little-known passage in Marx. The article suggested that the greater penetration of the Khandesh–Berar region by European capital in quest of raw cotton made for a relatively prosperous and independent peasant upper stratum, whereas less developed regions remained more subject to moneylender domination: Banaji 1977: 1375–1404. The major *EPW* articles that contributed to the mode of production debate may be accessed most conveniently in Patnaik 1990.

This shift, described by Tomlinson as one from 'stratifiers' to 'populists', took two forms.[34] There were attempts to apply an alternative framework to India, associated in its beginnings with Russian Narodnism and developed particularly by the dissident Soviet scholar of the 1920s, Chayanov. This argued a case for sustainable peasant stability as against inevitable disintegration. Peasants using family labour may not be guided always by capitalistic motivations of productivity and profit. And the rich peasant could be, not a stable stratum, but a kind of biological or demographic incident within peasant family cycles. An upwardly-mobile family might take in more land, but, given a surplus land situation (as in much of Russia) and the likely expansion in family size over time, it could then split up into several units or, alternatively, sink back into poverty because of there now being too many mouths to feed. Such cyclical patterns could leave the overall distribution of peasant households into rich, middle, and poor more or less unchanged. There were clearly major problems in applying Chayanov to twentieth-century India with its growing land scarcity. Still, the framework helpfully questioned some of the rigidities which had come into the efforts at classifying peasants into categories which were neat but often difficult to correlate with the ground data.[35] There was, moreover, the widespread reaction against excessive economism and the turn towards more culturalist analysis, this being heralded by Ranajit Guha's major effort to study forms of peasant insurgent consciousness cutting across distinctions between better-off, poorer, tribal, or even at times including quasi-landlord elements.[36]

As with many other aspects of colonial Indian history, studies of agrarian stratification have found it difficult not to get involved in perennial continuity/change debates. An overall shift away from the

---

[34] Tomlinson 1998.

[35] A recurrent problem was the difficulty of translating the terms in which much of the statistical data was collected into meaningful class categories. Operationally, a landholding 'peasant' could also be an occasional sharecropper, while a poor peasant needing supplementary income from city employment might lease out his plot and become, formally, a petty rentier.

[36] Guha 1983.

initial assumptions of cataclysmic change under British rule is easily discernible. The entire mode of production debate, after all, had turned around the felt need to explain lags, hindrances, or apparent blockages of capitalist development. Both poles of the peasant differentiation model have come under question. If the downwardly-mobile peasant was less often evicted than kept on under inferior, subordinate-tenurial or sharecropping terms, theories of stable rich peasant development (once put forward, for instance, by Ravinder Kumar for the Maharashtra Deccan and by David Washbrook for some parts of the Madras dry zone) have also provoked controversy. But disagreements persist about how far the opposite argument of continuity should be extended, and here the advance of detailed regional or locality-based research has thrown up interesting combinations which helpfully complicate and open up the very categories termed 'change' and 'continuity'.

Two instances will have to suffice. Bengal is notable among the regions where research on agrarian history has been particularly intensive and long-lasting, and consequently a rich variety of alternative schemas have been thrown up. The initial assumption of very big changes through the Permanent Settlement had, it was assumed, introduced a totally new conception of rigorous and alienable private property in land, and had been followed by the large-scale auction sale of estates by old-fashioned zamindars unable to pay their revenue strictly on time. A consequent passage of land to new moneyed people from Calcutta had thus enhanced peasant oppression. But then detailed research revealed that the land market had developed only slowly, with purchasers tending to come from circles already close to zamindari management. Relatively little urban capital got diverted from trade towards land till Bengali business enterprise declined around mid-century. Such diversion, it had been widely assumed earlier, had been one motive-cum-consequence of the 1793 decision.

A more basic change of emphasis towards continuity then came through Rajat Ray and Ratnalekha Ray's jotedar thesis. This argued a case for power in the countryside that rested not so much with zamindars, whose quasi-proprietary rights really pertained to revenue collection and not land management even after the 1793 enhancement of their privileges. It rested more with the jotedari stratum of 'dominant landed village groups, in effective possession of land and commanding the labour of poor villagers'—in significant part because they tended to be also the suppliers of credit.[37] The subsequent peasant movements that contributed to the tenancy laws of 1859 and 1885 fundamentally benefited the jotedars alone. Some rather fragmentary evidence was then presented from Buchanan's early-nineteenth-century survey of parts of north Bengal to suggest a basic continuity also at the level of jotedar–sharecropper relations.

In the 1980s, however, an important ecological slant came into the discussion through the work of Partha Chatterjee and Sugata Bose. Rural differentiation, it was now suggested, was much more evident in frontier zones like north Bengal, where absentee landlords leased out large blocs to jotedars (who would then deploy sharecroppers or sometimes labourers), as well as in the 'moribund delta' of western and central Bengal. In significant contrast, the long-term shift of river flows eastwards led to the formation of the 'active delta' of eastern and south-eastern Bengal, which now emerged as a zone of relatively stable and undifferentiated peasant agriculture, with a modicum of prosperity particularly during the long jute boom from the 1870s till the mid-1920s.

But this triadic model, too, has recently come under some questioning in the work of Nariaki Nakazato. The threefold distinction in levels of differentiation between east, west, and north Bengal had been based mainly on Settlement Reports data. These had been compiled at various times, with the eastern districts being surveyed first and the northern last: so the contrast in levels of differentiation could be a function of later investigation. Nakazato made a detailed

[37] Zamindari estates tended to be widely scattered, unlike jotedar holdings, reducing the effective power of the former on the ground. The zamindars as a whole of course benefited massively over time through revenue having been fixed in perpetuity, while no such permanence was ever extended to the rents they were extracting. But the fruits of this revenue–rent gap, it has often been pointed out, tended to be distributed over a rapidly increasing number of rentiers, through the subdivision of estates as well as an enormous proliferation of intermediate tenure-holders (the real socio-economic basis of the Bengali high-caste Hindu bhadralok). A large number of individual rentiers were therefore by no means particularly prosperous by the end of the nineteenth century and the beginning of the twentieth.

analysis of East Bengal sale and mortgage records from the statistics of the Registration Department. This seems to provide considerable evidence of some growth in peasant differentiation in the active delta zone too, as well as the spread there of new forms of sharecropping. His work questions, further, the tendency—occasionally evident in the Rays as well as in Bose—to make a possibly over-sharp distinction between the zamindar and the jotedar, the latter often assumed to have become by the twentieth century the principal source of exploitation of poor peasants, sharecroppers, and labourers. The files of the Court of Wards (where zamindari management records become accessible for estates administered temporarily by the government) suggest frequent combinations made by landlords of zamindar, intermediate-tenure, and even raiyati forms of holding. The zamindar, in other words, could also sometimes be a jotedar, and vice versa, and the older and the newer barga sharecropping forms of exploitation could intermesh in complicated ways. Nakazato's sophisticated brand of Marxism was able to combine a continued emphasis on the exploitative nature of both, conceptually distinct though interrelated, forms of surplus extraction—in his language, the more 'thickly feudal', 'colonial landlordism', and 'semi-feudal' barga—with a recognition that the result may not always have been uniformly immiserizing for cultivators. The sharp agrarian conflict in parts of East Bengal during the early years of the twentieth century over produce versus money rent was an attempt by the gentry to siphon off the 'embryonic profit' which some among the latter had started amassing under conditions of buoyant jute demand and high prices.[38]

Continuity theories have perhaps had a longer run in studies of the Madras Presidency. The first major study of the ryotwari system, by Nilmoni Mukherjee in 1962, had highlighted the importance of 'local influences' and 'traditional political processes' in its making. This stood in contrast to Eric Stokes's explanation of the move away from zamindari settlement in terms of a change of intellectual moods in England, in a pro-peasant, romantic-cum-paternalist direction. A few years later, Frykenberg's work on the early colonial administration

[38] Ray and Ray 1992: 215–37; Ray 1979; Chatterjee 1986; Nakazato 1994.

of Guntur district carried the continuity emphasis to an extreme by suggesting that Company authority had been superficial, and real power was wielded still by local networks of Indian officials and gentry. As for rural differentiation, Dharma Kumar followed up her effective demolition of the once widely-held assumption of a major rise in the proportion of landless labourers during British rule (through depeasantization and the decline of rural handicrafts) by questioning Washbrook's suggestion that in the dry areas the rich were getting richer. Patta registers of raiyat holdings seemed to show no evidence of such a concentration at higher levels across time. C.J. Baker's subsequent massive study of the Tamilnadu countryside between 1880 and 1955, possibly the most substantial overarching work on a single region thus far, raised some doubts about the reliability of patta statistics (courts often refused to accept them as evidence, and the same family could own more than one patta). But he too suggested a broad continuity and emphasized, rather, the stability of regional differences. The zones of abundant water resources (particularly the valleys of Kaveri, Periyar, and Tambraparni), not unexpectedly, revealed the greatest differentiation; the arid inland plains of Salem and Arcot the least.

An interesting effort to complicate this broad consensus has by a coincidence been by another Japanese historian. Basing himself on a statistical analysis of village settlement registers in one part of the wet zone (Lalgudi taluka in Tiruchirapalli, in the Kaveri basin), H. Yanagisawa suggests that the data might take on a slightly different complexion if its information about the caste composition of landholders is also taken into account. Statistical continuity with respect to distribution by acreage across bigger and smaller holdings might be the result of two significant, but contrary, social processes. A slow decline was taking place in the proportion of land held by Brahmins. (In 1865 this had been as high as 38.5 per cent of the cultivated area, even though they numbered no more than 10 per cent of the population of Lalgudi taluka.) The percentage of Depressed Caste (Dalit) landholders, conversely, went up from only 2 in 1865 to 36 in 1895 and 208 in 1925. Though their individual plots were usually tiny, they still held only 5 per cent of the total cultivated area at the end of the period. There was also a significant rise in land held by non-Brahmin, but fairly substantial, families. Yanagisawa relates these contrary trends to three processes: high castes moving away from villages towards urban professions and leasing out their lands; upward mobility, often through trade followed by investment in land, of the upper stratum among non-Brahmin castes; and some rise even among the lowest categories, in large part, he thinks, through the impact of large-scale labour migration from these regions to Sri Lanka and the South East Asian countries. This could have reduced the potential supply of labour, allowing for some bargaining, while many migrants, even among those who had gone abroad as plantation labourers, seem to have returned with some additional resources. A conjoint development was a slow shift in the form of agricultural labour from permanent, at times semi-servile, pannaiyal to more mobile day-labourer status. Yanagisawa's sample is very limited, but his findings do give rise to some interesting speculation about the possible material counterparts of non-Brahmin and Dalit movements in the South during the late-colonial era.[39]

The Forms of Labour

Post-Independence census returns and sample surveys have consistently indicated that landless or near-landless agricultural labourers constitute from between one-fifth to one-fourth of the rural labour force. As we have noticed already in passing, it is now well established that such a situation did not come about more or less *de novo* through colonial structures and policies. S.J. Patel's work, at first sight convincing, compares census figures for occupations between 1871 and 1931. Patel tried to establish a rising curve for agricultural labour. The effort ran aground—along with at least one main 'proof' of deindustrialization, as will be seen soon—in face of more nuanced and critical methods of using census statistics developed by scholars like Daniel and Alice Thorner.[40] Then in 1965 came Dharma Kumar's major study of land and caste in South India which emphasized the

[39] Mukherjee 1962; Frykenberg 1965; Kumar 1975: 229–61; Baker 1984; Yanagisawa 1996: chapters 2, 5, *et passim*.
[40] See, for instance, Daniel Thorner's elegantly titled 'Agrarian Revolution by Census Redefinition', reprinted in Thorner and Thorner 1962: 131–50.

very strong correlation between agricultural labour and the low-caste status of groups like the Cherumans of Malabar or the Paraiyans of Tamilnadu. This is evident from late-nineteenth-century data, and on the basis of more impressionistic information, from the earliest days of British penetration into South India. Castes like these had then been categorized as agrestic slaves, bound to toil on their high-caste master's lands on a permanent, hereditary basis. Though parts of Dharma Kumar's book had a polemically anti-Marxist slant, the country's leading Marxist historian, Irfan Habib, came to endorse her basic point about the continuity into colonial times of large numbers of landless labourers from the pre-colonial period, and even highlighted this as one of the specificities of pre-capitalist Indian rural society.[41]

But continuity in terms of a very broadly construed category is not a sufficient argument for assuming that the forms of landless labour in pre-colonial or early British times were identical with those seen a century or more later. In fact, what would at first sight seem a fairly basic rupture took place around mid-century through the British 'abolition of slavery'—though this, for obvious reasons, was not the kind of discontinuity that anti-colonial scholarship would be likely to emphasize. Extending belatedly to India, the prohibitions on the slave trade and then on slavery that had already been enforced in other parts of the British empire, Act V of 1843 denied to masters the use of courts to assert their claims on slaves. The more decisive change was the provision in the Indian Penal Code of 1860 which made the possession of slaves a legal offence.

A closer look quickly reveals, however, that both 'slavery' and its 'abolition' need be put within quotes, and complicated in at least two fundamental ways. Not only were there many kinds of 'slaves' in pre-colonial and early-colonial India: the application of that term itself is not free of ambiguities, as indeed in most situations other than the classic large-scale plantation slavery of ancient Rome, European colonies in the West Indies, and the US antebellum South. An in-between category, 'bonded labour' had been recognized as permissible by the Law Commission in 1841, while the 1843 and 1860 enactments did not specify who could be regarded as a slave and who, therefore,

[41] Kumar 1965.

needed to be freed. In practice, working relations were little affected, for 'most labouring arrangements could be construed as valid contracts between freely-consenting parties', above all, as we shall see, various forms of long-term, even hereditary-debt bondage. Moreover, 'labour in general was hardly ever entirely free' in colonial India (and not just there, one could add), for elements of extra-economic compulsion entered into all forms, from formal slave to factory worker.[42] The British, it is true, did try to draw a sharp legal distinction between slave labour and free labour in India from around the mid-nineteenth century, grounding the latter in the notion of a voluntary contract and emphasizing the unfettered right of anyone to sell his labour power. But many have argued that the dichotomy that was now instituted, condemning slave and valorizing free wage labour, was in large part an ideological construct which helped naturalize the modern power of the market and of money to bind people.[43]

The term 'slave' seems to have been used in early-colonial times in three rather different contexts. First, there was the purchase and use of slaves by town-centred Indian courts, aristocrats, and European elites associated with the trade in overseas (often African) slaves. The Dutch and then the English had encountered this trade as a flourishing Arab-run enterprise and enthusiastically participated in it for a long time. Slaves of this type were not employed in production, and the political importance they had sometimes enjoyed in earlier centuries seems to have ended: but they remained a badge of honour for their masters as well as a source of diverse kinds of entertainment. English journals in Calcutta in the late eighteenth century freely advertised slave auctions, carrying advertisements for 'Coffrees who can play well on the French horn', or even ' very handsome African ladies of the true sable hue'. This was the slavery that came under increasing attack through the

[42] Anderson 1993: 104; Sarkar 1985: 97–8.

[43] Gyan Prakash has been foremost among the historians making this point, occasionally coming close to suggesting that the 'abolition', through implicitly validating bonded labour, actually worsened conditions for many rural toilers. An excessive nervousness about possibly 'justifying the economic effects of colonialism as liberating', seems to make him sometimes rather chary about criticizing pre-colonial forms of servitude: Prakash 1992: 17; see also Prakash 1990.

spread of evangelical and abolitionist moods in Britain, and it seems to have disappeared quickly from the mid-nineteenth century. A second, more domestic service-related slavery was that which held sway across rural and urban areas within large and prosperous Muslim and Hindu households. This, like the first, was related to the master's sense of prestige and personal comfort or pleasure, but was a product of distress sales or 'voluntary' bondage rather than the overseas trafficking and public auctions. Here the boundary lines between slave, servant, mistress, and even wife become much less clear. It is significant, for instance, that in Bengali the same word, 'dasi', could mean woman slave, servant, and wife (usually in non-bhadralok households). Such domestic servitude could continue for generations without transfer or sale and does not seem to have been a purely lower-caste phenomenon. Late-nineteenth-century memoirs by the literati sometimes suggest warm, paternalistic relationships, though what these looked like from 'below' is difficult to guess. As for late-colonial changes, recent feminist scholarship has tended to emphasize retrogression rather than progress with regard to this category. The household 'chores' of women were detached more rigorously than ever from 'productive' labour in fields or factories, and constraints came to be imposed on certain elements of fluidity present earlier. Thus, a study based on the household-related papers of the nazims of Murshidabad has argued that a growing insistence on the purity of legitimate descent eroded the position of 'illegitimate' princely children and their slave-mothers.[44]

Agrestic servitude was most prominent, and harshest, in the South, notably in the wet rice areas of Malabar, Kanara, southern Tamilnadu, and parts of Andhra. Much more than the other two forms, it was connected to low-caste status. There is even a Kerala myth that Parashuram, after creating the land there from the sea, gave it to Brahmins and also provided slaves from forest tribes to till it for them. But there were also other determinants, which enabled not dissimilar relations of near-servile hereditary dependence to flourish even where caste structures were less rigid. The seasonal fluctuations in labour demand in agriculture made the maintenance of a reserve for peak times an important asset for the more prosperous landholders, and,

[44] Sarkar 1985; Chatterjee 1999.

as already mentioned, the close links between debt and bondage both before and after the mid-nineteenth-century 'abolition' could ensure such a supply. In Punjab, for instance, landowners were not averse to working in the fields—unlike the higher castes in most other parts of the country. But that region through late-colonial times also reveals the presence of a large number of labourers of various types: sepidar artisan castes who often worked in the fields while carrying out their traditional jajmani functions; siri permanent farm servants; migrant agricultural labour from other provinces (which would become very prominent with the mid-twentieth-century Green Revolution in that state); as well as peasant proletarians, those with land so inadequate as to necessitate labouring on other people's farms. For every category, credit-constituted dependence was often crucial, while the demand for agricultural labour varied with ecological conditions and types of crop. It was higher for wheat, and therefore in the more fertile tracts of Central Punjab and the Canal Colonies; it was less in the arid south-east subsisting on jowar and bajra, and much less commercialized in colonial times.[45]

While there may not have been much change in the proportion of landless labourers, indications are not lacking to suggest that late-colonial developments quite often worsened their conditions. Forest restrictions, processes of sedentarization, tightened conceptions of private property, and the decline in the military labour market all cut into earlier opportunities of additional income and spatial or social mobility for landless or near-landless groups, particularly in the drier parts of the subcontinent where caste structures had been fairly fluid. Washbrook develops the theme of a 'golden age of the Pariah' in South India during the decades of what in earlier historiography had been termed eighteenth-century anarchy, for the weakening of controls would have facilitated social mobility.[46] And both the Orientalizing and more modernistic dimensions of colonial law outlined earlier may have pulled in a similar direction. Colonial legal and administrative practices often linked up with, consolidated,

[45] Hjele 1967: 71–126; Saradamoni 1973: 371–85; Bhattacharya 1985: 105–52.
[46] Washbrook 1993: 68–86.

and utilized 'traditional' forms of labour control. Officials on tour continued princely or zamindari patterns of extracting unpaid labour or free provisions from villagers, and, once again carrying on earlier practice, 'statute labour' was sometimes deployed on early-colonial public works. But there was also as we have seen the importation of tightened bourgeois notions of the sanctity of contract through judicial practice, and then the Contract Act of 1872, as well as specific legislation controlling labour made in the interests primarily of British planters and businessmen. These diminished the position of debtors and labourers *vis-à-vis* creditors and employers, whether the latter happened to be Europeans or Indians—though the former, most notoriously the Assam tea planters, also enjoyed additional privileges. Thus the Apprentices Act of 1850 allowed the master to administer 'moderate chastisement . . . as may lawfully be given by a father to his child', while the pressure of Calcutta-based European businessmen led to the Workmen's Breach of Contract Act of 1859: under which a magistrate, on being approached by an employer, could sentence a labourer who was allegedly neglecting or refusing to work to three months' imprisonment with hard labour.[47]

Most notorious of all, of course, was the system of mobilizing in-dentured labour for work on plantations in South Asia and overseas. This took the place of slave labour in the British Caribbean (Trinidad, Guyana) and Mauritius after the abolition of slavery in 1834, and was extended later to parts of India, Fiji, and Natal. Indentured labour produced a series of what had become everyday consumer items in the West and then elsewhere: tea, principally in Assam and north Bengal; coffee (as well as the increasingly vital industrial raw material of rubber) in the Nilgiris, Malabar, and Coorg; sugar in Trinidad, Guyana, Mauritius, Fiji, and Natal. The magnitude of this export of labour demands some emphasis, for it was a key mode through which late-nineteenth-century India became central to the entire system of British and indeed world imperialism. Total Indian overseas labour migration amounted to around 6.5 million between 1834 and 1924, nearly 1.5 million of this under systems of indenture. Of the total flow of indentured labour to destinations within the British empire,

[47] Anderson 1993.

no less than 85 per cent came from India (around 1.25 million; no other country exported more than 100,000 labourers).[48]

The distinguishing feature of indenture was that the workers over the period stipulated by the contract could not renegotiate its terms or withdraw their services, while 'desertion' could invite criminal prosecution. Unlike the 1859 Act, by which employers at least had to approach magistrates and only civil charges were possible, the laws made principally for Assam tea plantations in 1863, 1865, and 1882 gave planters, initially overwhelmingly European, sweeping powers to arrest workers on their own, and have them charged under criminal law. And various kinds of extra-legal coercion continued, too, buttressed by the racial bond with the colonial state.

Assam represented perhaps the worst-case scenario. Here a low density of population allowed massive and virtually free grants of lands by the state to European planters, but also made labour availability a problem. The local labouring classes were soon condemned as unwilling, lazy, and sunk in opium-induced languor. They appear in fact to have been quite rational in showing no inclination to work in arduous conditions and at wages below those in their own localities. Wages had been fixed at Rs 5, 4, and 3 for men, women, and children, in 1865, and they were still that in 1900 despite a 100 per cent rise in food prices. 'Coolies' had therefore to be recruited from far-off regions, above all from Chhota Nagpur and other tribal regions of Central India. Recruitment happened through a chain of arkattis, operating via a combination of advances and sheer trickery, resulting in a situation exceptionally oppressive. The system was successful from the planters' point of view as it enabled British Indian tea to displace Chinese as the principal global variety in the 1880s; it also maintained a regime of very low wages in a naturally labour-scarce region, helping to keep profits high despite falling tea prices towards the end of the nineteenth century. But Assam became a byword for extremes of racist oppression, and in the 1880s turned into the first example of a degree of intervention in labour matters by emergent middle-class nationalism. Dwarkanath Ganguli, Assistant Secretary of the Indian Association, wrote a series of articles in 1886–7 in the Calcutta daily

[48] Northrup 1999: 89–91.

Bengalee based on first-hand material collected by a Brahmo preacher, and occasional resolutions were moved in early Congress sessions condemning the indenture system. More important perhaps was considerable, if inevitably sporadic, labour protest and occasional violence, and the paradox of 'high cost for cheap labour': costs of recruitment kept going up since much leaked its way to the arkattis. By the early twentieth century even Curzon was making occasional critical comments about planters, and the indenture system came to be phased out from 1915—after Gokhale had raised the matter in the Imperial Legislative Council in 1912, and C.F. Andrews had launched a powerful campaign focussed particularly upon conditions in Fiji. 'Free' labour did not of course end exploitation, or even migration, for that in the end had always been bound up with the need for advances and the consequent debt trap that went on operating at subordinated levels of rural society. As we shall see, labour catchment areas (LCAs) which supplied the bulk of Indian indentured labour remained also the key geographical regions for the 'free' workforce of capitalist industries—and that often even the methods of recruitment did not change very much.[49]

To many, probably in fact to most, commentators the conditions of indentured recruitment and labour have seemed atrocious enough to warrant the label given them by Hugh Tinker: 'a new system of slavery'.[50] But there have also been some recent revisionist interpretations, the more extreme among them likely to appeal only to the wilder advocates of neo-liberal economics. Indenture, it has been suggested, was after all a formal contract where labour power was exchanged for wages. Unlike slavery, it was not life-long or hereditary, but for a fixed number of years; and instances of protest or resistance were not particularly abundant in most plantation regions. Labourers may therefore have been exercising their free rational choice and moving from low to higher labour productivity areas. Arguments like these appear suspiciously similar to the words of a planters' representative defending Assam indenture in 1901 to the Central Legislative Council: 'When the coolie goes to a garden he

---

[49] Behal and Mohapatra 1992: 142–72; Dasgupta 1992: 173–98.
[50] Tinker 1974.

begins to receive a wage and begins to live, whereas in Chota Nagpur he only exists.'[51]

But, like 'forced' commercialization, the theme of indenture, or for that matter labour migration in general under colonial conditions, does have complexities, and here the more nuanced forms of revisionism can sometimes be helpful. There is little doubt, for instance, that there were considerable variations within the system. Recruitment conditions seem to have been somewhat less oppressive in South Indian catchment areas, where use was made of a pre-colonial kangani structure of labour contractors developed over centuries to supply migrant Tamil labour to Sri Lanka. The migrants here, when belonging to Dalit groups, could have been freed from agrestic slavery through a kangani advance, while many came from relatively higher-caste landholding strata like the Vellalars. The considerable return migration, as we have already seen, contributed to a degree of upward mobility. Indigenous merchants—the Nattukottai Chettiyars—were among the major financiers of the whole system of kangani recruitment and indeed even of the planters in Sri Lanka.[52] In all these respects conditions in the labour recruitment areas of the North (the tribal regions, and, the most important of all catchment areas, the Bhojpuri belt of the eastern United Provinces and north-west and north Bihar) were very different, and much worse. Here massive migration coincided with stagnation, if not decline. Nor can indentured recruitment be separated from local structures of exploitation in the catchment areas which were

[51] Behal and Mohapatra 1992: 143. Breman and Daniel have provided perhaps the most cogent and theoretically acute rebuttal of such arguments through a close reading of the term that became the ubiquitous word for all such labour—'coolie'. This shared with the proletariat of metropolitan capitalism only the first of its two basic characteristics: that of having become free of traditional customary obligations and relationships of dependence (possibly servile) on masters/patrons. But unlike the full-fledged proletarian, the coolie had not been allowed to attain the capacity of freely selling her/his labour power, and consequently signified 'the person who had been . . . cast adrift into a category of proto-proletarian individuals devoid of their personhood', a status, moreover, which became permanent rather than transitional. See Breman and Daniel 1992: 268–70.

[52] Mayer 2003: 55–88.

indigenous, or perhaps increasingly an amalgam of colonial and Indian: above all, there was the chronic debt trap which made arkatti advances initially attractive, or even indispensable. (We need to keep in mind also, particularly for the tribal areas, the links between both indentured and 'free' migration and the closing of access to forests, the erosion of community tenurial forms, and the loss of land to outsider moneylenders and peasant settlers.) And there do exist bits of concrete evidence showing some instances—usually involving women subjected to gross family oppression—where entry into plantation labour could have seemed like freedom: as when a young Gond girl married off to, and frequently beaten by, the son of the local rentier ran away with a tea garden recruiting agent. Crispin Bates and Marina Carter have teased out from the details of this early-twentieth-century case the important conclusion that 'migration could be both a conscious choice and yet one which derived from circumstances of oppression or deprivation.'[53]

The location of the main LCAs is an interesting problem, for they have remained more or less constant over generations, supplying both indentured labour to plantations in India and abroad, as well as 'free' labour to factories and other kinds of employment down to contemporary times. The puzzle is that while well populated, these are not the regions of maximum density. Bengal, notably, never became an LCA, and even Calcutta's jute mills increasingly drew their supply from far-off upcountry sources; nor, on the other hand, are they the poorest and most arid like western Rajasthan, or the dryest parts of interior Gujarat or Maharashtra. There seems no reason why these

[53] Bates and Carter 1993: 162–4. On the same theme of a necessary ambiguity, see also the exceptionally sensitive paper by Mohapatra (1996: 134–55) on the 'dilemma of return' among Indian labourers in the West Indies. There is much evidence of a passionate longing for Calcutta, the port from where they had been shipped to Trinidad: in December 1899 one of the shipped even plunged into the sea, hoping to swim his way back. Yet, for the many who did return after indenture was abolished, life back 'home' proved intolerable: they remained unemployed in the city and were treated as outcastes in the villages from where they had originally come and to which they could never really return. Some in the 1920s even agitated for repatriation to the Caribbean.

areas should have been worse affected than others by the general factors which nationalist analysis usually blamed for depeasantization, like excessive revenue or rent pressure, forced commercialization, deindustrialization. In a pathbreaking analysis way back in 1978, a decade before environmental questions began to attract serious historical attention in India, Lalita Chakrabarti drew attention to certain ecological specifics of the LCAs. She focused on north Bihar–East UP, and parts of interior Andhra and Tamilnadu, leaving out the tribal zones as they have very distinctive characteristics. Prior at least to more recent irrigation inputs, these LCAs were located at the margins of wet-rice zones, typically combined rice with inferior crops such as millets as subsistence for the poorer inhabitants, had patches of poor soil intermixed with fertile alluvium, and were regions where the margin of extensive cultivation was inelastic. In this intermediate belt, Chakrabarti argued, commercialization, which in both the richer and the poorer but sparsely populated areas could improve conditions for upwardly-mobile rural strata, tended to produce 'involution'—the poorer peasants were forced into less and less fertile land for their low-quality subsistence crops, and often obliged to migrate.[54]

Chakrabarti's paper was innovative also in a second way. Contrary to the well-established nationalist tendency to harp on the iniquities of European-dominated indentured migration to plantations in South Asia or across the seas alone, she emphasized the ways in which the emergence of the industrial labour force was 'a part of the story of so-called coolie migration.' Those from LCAs who migrated under overseas contract were 'exactly those who came as "free labourers" to factory gates'; and in both cases the migrants tended to be not so much peasants losing land as members of artisanal or service castes who had been more or less landless even earlier. Along with Breman's near-contemporaneous questioning of the distinction between 'formal' and 'informal' sectors, Chakrabarti's essay thus pointed to the fluidity of labour forms. In yet another of its many paradoxical consequences,

---

[54] Chakrabarti 1978: 249–327. Mohapatra subsequently extended Chakrabarti's ecology-oriented analysis, with some modifications, to tribal recruitment from South Bihar, to Assam plantations, as well as nearby mines: Mohapatra 1985: 13–42.

colonialism, which had tried to sedentarize populations and fix firm identities, simultaneously contributed to enhanced movement, promoting the growth of what Breman has termed 'footloose labour'. These themes will engage our attention again, when we turn to questions of industrial and urban entrepreneurship and labour.

For the moment it might be appropriate to end this section on rural life with the vivid testimony of Ramsukh, a young man from a rural weaver family of Ferozepur tehsil, Punjab, dated 1888:

> We did not work till 10 years old, or we used to bring in wood for fuel or herbs for food . . . When I was 11 or 12 I began to tend the goats of Tenti Gujar. I got only my food and clothing in return for labour. My father and elder brother used to weave. As my younger brothers got bigger they helped in weaving or with fuel and herbs. At 14 years of age we began to work for Zamindars in hoeing etc. and got one anna per day . . . We used to borrow some grain from different Zamindars for food, and work it off in labour. Two or three years matters thus went on. I became more intelligent and took to weaving work with father and brother, the younger ones worked still at odd jobs.[55]

The forms of labour go on changing, the categories into which historians or economists divide up the production and reproduction of social life run into each other: food-gathering, pastoralism, agricultural labour, artisanal work, maybe in other instances migration to distant plantations, factories, city slums. What remains constant are lives of endless toil and exploitation.

Famines and their Diagnosis

Life in the submerged and mobile world that we have been looking at was miserable enough in normal times. But the times were often far from normal, for the history of British-ruled India is interspersed by repeated and devastating famines in which rural landless labourers and artisans were invariably the worst affected.

Famines, it is true, were nothing new for many parts of a subcontinent like India, with an agriculture overwhelmingly dependent on notoriously uncertain monsoons and vast rain-shadow areas away from

---

[55] Cited in Bhattacharya 1985: 114.

rivers and without irrigation—the dry regions that have already figured prominently in our story. There is some evidence, though, that they became more frequent in the late eighteenth and nineteenth centuries. William Digby's *Prosperous British India* (1901) located fourteen major famines between the eleventh and seventeenth centuries, an average of one every fifty years or so. But there were twelve big ones between 1765 and 1858, and then a massive bunching together in the last three or four decades of the nineteenth century, with famine or scarcity scarring twenty out of the forty-nine years between 1860 and 1908. The famines during the late nineteenth century came in two major waves: between the mid-1860s and late 1870s (Orissa 1866, Bengal–Bihar 1873–4, the Maharashtra Deccan and much of the South 1876–8), and again in the late 1890s (the devastating famines of 1896–7 and 1899–1900, affecting an area with a total population of about 125 million). After 1908, in contrast, there were no big famines, only numerous scarcities in particular areas—with the very major exception of Bengal in 1943, when between 1.5 and 3 million died of famine followed by epidemics.[56] This shows an uneven distribution over time which we will look at subsequently.

The question of enhanced frequency will remain somewhat uncertain, for information about pre-colonial times is scanty. But one of the significantly new features of the late nineteenth century, which India shared with many other parts of the colonial or semi-colonial world, is a West/non-West divide which did not exist earlier. Famines had now become specific to 'backward' or underdeveloped countries alone, and went on happening despite vastly improved communications that should have enabled the quick transport of food, and despite new technologies for enhancing agricultural production—the benefits of which remained largely confined to the West. We are on the threshold of a distinctively modern world, where malnutrition, scarcity, and famine stalk the poor in many underdeveloped countries. In Europe and North America, by contrast, large numbers of affluent people try to cut down on their calories, and varied degrees of social security provisions help mitigate the considerable poverty that still survives.

The international dimensions of the Indian famines of the late nineteenth century have attracted some attention in recent years. The

[56] Bhatia 1963: chapter 1.

late 1870s saw big famines, triggered off everywhere by massive droughts not just in India, but also in China, large parts of South East Asia, Egypt and North Africa, and north-east Brazil. Most of these regions were affected also in the other big drought-cum-famine wave of the late 1890s. In the late 1960s the environmental scientist Jacob Bjerknes formulated a theory accounting for this periodicity of acute drought. Excessive warming of the eastern tropical Pacific waters lead to weak monsoons: the so-called El Nino effect. A converse effect, La Nina, has also been discovered, associated with excess rain and often floods, and the entire pattern has been termed El Nino-Southern-Oscillation (ENSO). But climatic fluctuations alone, while undoubtedly important, cannot provide a sufficient explanation of the scope and long-range impact of the late-nineteenth-century famine waves. El Nino had happened earlier, too, though data is scarce and the late-nineteenth-century droughts do seem to have been of unusual intensity; and there is little evidence that countries like China and India had fallen behind Western Europe in living standards through earlier manifestations. What is needed, in addition, is what Mike Davis, in an important overall survey, has called a 'political ecology' of famine, bringing together the findings of environmental science with analysis of the economic and other dimensions of imperialism as constitutive of Third World backwardness.[57] The late 1870s and late 1890s were also years of massive European expansion in Africa, Afghan wars, intrusions into large parts of China, the final defeat of American Indian resistance, the US conquest of the Philippines and establishment of their control over Cuba, the extinction of the Central Asian khanates by tsarist Russia—all years during which, to paraphrase Lenin, the division of the world between the imperialist powers was completed.[58]

What happened with famines in the course of the nineteenth century was not just or primarily their enhanced frequency, but significant changes in their nature, and important shifts in official policies and attitudes. A lieutenant governor of Bengal noted during a scarcity in that province in 1891 that there was food in the country, and 'anyone could feed himself for an anna a day', but 'the usual agricultural

[57] Davis 2001.
[58] Ibid.

labour by which landless labour earn wages is at a standstill, and they have to resort to relief works to earn that anna.'[59] In British official jargon this was called the shift from 'food' to 'work' famines: no longer usually an absolute absence of food, at least in some parts of the country, but inadequate purchasing power among the poor. Here lay the empirical kernel of what Amartya Sen developed a century later into a sophisticated theory of modern famine. There was no necessary correlation, he pointed out, between 'some people not having enough food to eat', and 'there not being enough to eat'. Through his categories, 'exchange entitlements' and 'capabilities', Sen simultaneously expanded the narrowly economistic or monetary notions of purchasing power to include questions of health, sanitation, education, and the entire 'quality of life'.[60] Shortfalls in food supplies through natural calamities like droughts, floods, or pests were still almost always the proximate reason for a famine, just as epidemics were its frequent accompaniment or sequel. But the precise impact was heavily mediated by social structure and human agency: differentials by class, caste, gender, or age, the degree and efficacy of state or private relief. The countryside suffered more than the cities,[61] the landless far more than those with land; the 'normal' family pattern—of women getting their food later, and often in shorter quantities than their menfolk—sharpened during scarcities, and children were the first to be sold off in times of acute distress. Sen informs us that his childhood memory of millions flocking into Calcutta from the countryside begging for a morsel in 1943–4, at a time when a middle-class family like his own never had any problem eating their normal meals, later provided the initial stimulus for his work on famine.[62]

The other major change related to the ways in which colonial rule tackled famine or scarcity, and the values underlying state policies. In South Asia, as in most other pre-capitalist societies, the giving of alms to beggars and the poor had been valorized as a form of individual

[59] *Famine Commission Report* (1898), cited in Bhatia 1963: 8.

[60] Sen 1981; for a helpful summary, Dreze and Sen 1989: Introduction.

[61] Metropolitan or urban populations could at times get special protection, as notably during the 1943–4 famine, when rationing was introduced in Calcutta.

[62] Sen 1981.

piety, and famine relief tended to come from individual rulers, zamin-dars, rich people, and the occasional religious establishment, rather than through well-defined state policies or philanthropic institutions. In specific situations there could also be occasional efforts by rulers to bring down prices through regulating markets (the instance of Alauddin is well known), though here, as well as with regard to organized charitable work by religious groups, things seem to have been less systematic and well developed *vis-à-vis* medieval Europe with its Church and its notions of a 'just price'. As the very different values embedded in classical political economy spread their wings over British rulers and sections of Indian elites, however, individual charity to the 'undeserving' poor came to be denigrated as conducive to indolence and parasitism, while the panacea for high food prices and famines was felt to lie basically in improved communications and free trade. Traders animated by considerations of profit and not charity, it was assumed, would use the new railways to quickly transport grain to famine-stricken areas and so bring down prices there, provided governments did not foolishly interfere in 'normal' market operations through de-hoarding or price controls. As famines became more devastating, a degree of state relief to the starving also came to be recognized as necessary, but this had to be strictly related to work done by them on public projects like roads or irrigation (what came to be called 'test relief'), with wages deliberately kept lower than market rates to inhibit 'indolence' and encourage the 'work ethic'.[63]

While such laissez-faire values, transplanted from Protestant and capitalist Britain, came to have an autonomous strength of their own, their connections with the material interests of the colonial state and business groups are quite obvious. Maintaining an export surplus in agricultural commodities from India even amidst scarcity had become necessary to Britain's overall balance of payments and for meeting the burden of Home Charges, besides being highly profitable for European exporting firms and shipping and insurance concerns. The values in play also dictated parsimony in government expenditure on famine relief. Material connections also go some distance towards

[63] See Sharma 2001 for an interesting discussion of the evolution of British Indian famine policies and values.

explaining the bunching of the worst instances of famine during the last decades of the nineteenth century. These were the years of a falling rupee kept pegged to silver when Britain and much of the developed capitalist world had moved to the gold standard, enhancing the financial burdens of the Indian government in its expenditures in Britain. Bagchi suggests that this distinction between the media of circulation in international payments was an obvious symbol during these decades of 'the consolidation of the capitalist centre and its separation from the colonial periphery', or, as he puts it, 'silver is for the East, gold is for the West.'[64] The boom in agricultural exports meant also the expansion of commercial or high-priced crop acreage at the expense of poor people's items like millets. Simultaneously, as we have seen, access to forests was drastically curtailed by colonial forest laws, depriving the rural poor of common property resources. These had been particularly important in times of scarcity even for the poorer peasants, alongside the landless. During the same decades, periodic Afghan problems and a real or alleged Russian bogey were also felt to necessitate increased expenditure on the army and on commercially unprofitable but strategically important railway construction, even while famines, started off by natural calamities but considerably worsened by government niggardliness, ravaged large swathes of the subcontinent.

Here, as always, it would be simplistic to present colonial famine policy as an unchanging monolith. In India, as for that matter in late-eighteenth and early-nineteenth-century Britain, laissez-faire did not establish its empire without internal fissures and debates. Ravi Ahuja has shown, in a paper on the Madras famine of 1780–3, how the Company administration had arranged food supplies from Bengal, tried to regulate prices, and attempted some de-hoarding of stocks. This could be, and sometimes was, justified by appeals to still common notions of the 'moral economy' kind in Britain. But material considerations seem to have been, once again, the main determinants. The Company in the South was fighting a major war, and it could not afford to let the supply of food for its army be disrupted. Unlike the situation a century later, labour resources still appeared scarce, and there were fears that migration to French or Mysore territories could

[64] Bagchi 2003: 155–79.

seriously weaken the British military position.[65] Later on, too, despite the growing influence of laissez-faire dogmas, local and provincial officials could be found advocating interventionist policies, though they were generally now overruled by their superiors. In 1817, for instance, a superintendent of police in the North West Provinces wanted to take penal action against hoarders, and even procured a fatwa justifying it from local Muslim law officers. His superiors vetoed his action, citing the 'principles of political economy'. A better-known instance is Lieutenant Governor Campbell, who was able to keep mortality figures down to only 23 during the Bengal–Bihar famine of 1873–4 despite a drought which had destroyed much of the winter crop, through government import of rice from Burma and the payment of normal wages at test relief centres. Such departures from market fundamentalism and parsimony were condemned as unaffordable by the Famine Commission of 1880, and the dominant official view remained the one conveyed by the Government of India to Bombay and Madras during the great famine of 1876–8: 'the task of saving life, irrespective of the cost is one which is beyond our power.' The note went on to assert that 'the indiscriminate charity of a Government is far worse' than even 'the evils of indiscriminate private charity.'[66]

Yet absolute laissez-fare, blindly relying on the panacea of free trade plus some organized private philanthropy (notably, the work of Christian missionaries), proved in the end, on grounds of humanity and prudence alike, impossible to maintain in the face of recurrent massive mortality. Famines were regularly accompanied by what officials came to term 'famine crimes': sharply rising curves of statistics of grain-looting, theft, burglary, and dacoity. Such signs of popular disaffection apart, the spate of late-nineteenth-century famines led to increasing public criticism of what seemed total callousness, from emerging Indian middle-class opinion as well as critics in England. Beginning with the North Indian famine of 1837–8 and culminating in the Famine Codes of the 1880s, a degree of state involvement came to be seen as necessary in the form of reductions in land revenue, the grant of loans, and test relief centres where the genuinely afflicted

[65] Ahuja 2002: 351–80.
[66] Sharma 2001: 54–5; Bhatia 1963: 83–6, 90–1.

would work in return for low wages on roads, embankments, and, increasingly, on canal irrigation projects.[67] The evolution of these structures, however hamstrung by financial parsimony, probably had something to do with what might otherwise appear a strange anomaly: there were numerous scarcities but no major famine in British India between 1908 and 1943. Yet these were decades, as we have already seen, when per capita agricultural production was stagnant or in decline in many parts of the country—with the major exception of the Punjab, which had massive irrigation canals—amidst a rapid growth in population after 1921. Here perhaps lay the beginnings of what Amartya Sen finds to be the dominant pattern also in post-colonial India: chronic hunger and undernourishment in many rural areas,[68] but acute starvation and large-scale mortality staved off by state intervention. The expansion of channels of expressions of popular protest against the iniquities that lie behind this has been an important factor in the provision of some state amelioration to distress. It was probably not an accident that the decline in big famines in British India roughly coincided with the growth of some forms of representative governance from *circa* 1909, while the temporary absence of such checks due to war and post-1942 repression allowed the Bengal governor to grossly neglect remedial measures during the Bengal famine of 1943.

The deep impact of famines on peasant life is well indicated by the ways in which they have lingered in folk memory. Famines often act as a folk calendar by which local time and the ages of people are calculated. Near Delhi, during the famine of 1860–1, an old man of 90 could still recall the chalisa of 1783–4 as the worst he had ever

---

[67] Sharma (2001) suggests that where such departures from strict laissez-faire through relief proved reasonably efficient, a quasi-'hegemonic' effect could manifest itself, with the desperately poor and starving becoming grateful for the little that was being done for them by benevolent officials. The undoubted popularity among the rural poor that Christian missions gained through relief work found expression at times in large-scale conversions. This happened for instance among Dalit Madigas and Malas of Andhra in 1876–8, when the number of Indian Christians in Nellore shot up from 3012 to 20,794 between 1871 and 1881: see Arnold 1984: 74–5.

[68] Kalahandi in Orissa springs to mind today, as well as reports of pockets of starvation and suicide from many other parts of India.

witnessed. Popular rebellions apart, famines constitute the other kind of moment when the state is compelled to gather masses of detailed information about the conditions and mentalities of people—which are otherwise rarely mentioned in official records. So, famines have attracted the attention of social historians who are eager to explore the hidden worlds of the subaltern.

What emerges from such work is a highly differentiated portrayal of both famine impact and of the responses to such calamities. Arnold's study of the Madras dry belt during the Great Famine of 1876–8 finds a sharp division in these respects along the faultline that separated what in official terminology was called 'ryot' (peasant proprietors, in this predominantly non-zamindari region) and 'coolie' (agricultural labourers). The first category usually suffered much less than the second, and at times had the resources (including a degree of literate or middle-class contacts) to draw up petitions to the authorities. Prominent in these were prayers for revenue remissions. The wholly or largely landless, mostly labourers or artisans, were the groups that poured into relief centres, which the more respectable peasant proprietor strata tended to avoid because such assistance entailed hard and socially demeaning physical labour. Even amongst the poorest, however, the serving of food in ways that ignored caste taboos was often an obstacle. In these and many other ways, the distinctions along lines of economic and social hierarchies were deepened by famine. However disruptive of the 'normal' order for a while, the net effect was to enhance peasant subordination to superiors (landlord, moneylender, trader, revenue official) and 'coolie' subordination to the 'ryot'. And this despite the fact that famine at times could be accompanied by unrest and protest. Here again the differentials stand out. Both Arnold and Sharma find the more collective forms of protest, like food riots at weekly markets in large villages or small towns where people normally congregated, to have been more common in the early phase of a famine, when prices rose sharply but misery and starvation had not yet sapped energies for survival. As village society disintegrated further through deepening misery, class and gender differences could become more obvious: those with no access to food at all preyed on the slightly better-off through petty theft or dacoity. Women were left behind with children to starve in villages while men could migrate to cities and look for some meagre chances of survival.

Sharma suggests an interesting link also with the harvest cycle. In the North Indian famine of 1837–8, the kharif (autumn) crop, linked to the basic subsistence needs of all types of peasants, was affected first, stimulating collective protests as prices of foodgrains soared. The rabi in this region was more related to cash crops, demanded access to irrigation and greater inputs, and therefore only the richer elements could sow it in a bad year—becoming in the process targets of the wrath and individual violence of the starving.

As the misery deepened, more and more had to take to the road, desperately seeking succour in cities or merely wandering around more or less aimlessly in search of a little food or charity. Every famine thus swelled the numbers of that footloose substratum of casual toilers or seekers for work that has been, and remains, a crucial but often forgotten dimension of South Asian society.

In sharp contrast, the better-off sections in the country and, particularly, the cities, suffered little or not at all from famines, since these were now characterized not by a total absence of supplies but by high prices that were not impossible for them to pay. The evident gap in ability to meet elementary needs could, however, at times bring about a degree of elite or middle-class guilt and some relief efforts. In political terms, the most important consequence was an undermining of the earlier faith of large sections of the middle-class literati in the supposedly providential nature of British rule. Imperial claims to bringing order and prosperity now sounded increasingly hollow. It was probably no coincidence that the decades from roughly 1870 to 1900 were marked also by the emergence of middle-class anti-colonial nationalism, embodied above all in the economic analysis that had its centrepiece in the theory of the 'drain of wealth'.

Bibliography

Ahuja, Ravi, 'State Formation and "Famine Policy" in Early Colonial South Asia', *Indian Economic and Social History Review*, 39 (4), 2002

Amin, Shahid, 'Small Peasant Commodity Production and Rural Indebtedness: The Culture of Sugarcane in Eastern U.P. *c.*1880–1920', in Ranajit Guha, ed., *Subaltern Studies I* (Delhi: Oxford University Press, 1982)

————, *Sugarcane and Sugar in Gorakhpur: An Inquiry into Peasant Production for Capitalist Enterprise in Colonial India* (Delhi: Oxford University Press, 1984)

————, 'Dimensions of Dependence', in David Ludden, ed., *Agricultural Production and Indian History* (Delhi: Oxford University Press, 1994)

Anderson, M.R., 'Work Construed: Ideological Origins of Labour Law in British India to 1918', in Peter Robb, ed., *Dalit Movements and the Meanings of Labour in India* (Delhi: Oxford University Press, 1993)

Arnold, David, 'Famine in Peasant Consciousness and Peasant Action: Madras, 1876–8', in Ranajit Guha, ed., *Subaltern Studies III* (Delhi: Oxford University Press, 1984)

Bagchi, Amiya, 'The Great Depression (1873–96) and the Third World: With Special Reference to India', in G. Balachandran, ed., *India and the World Economy, 1850–1950* (Delhi: Oxford University Press, 2003)

Baker, C.J., *An Indian Rural Economy 1880–1955: The Tamilnad Countryside* (Delhi: Oxford University Press, 1984)

Balachandran, G., ed., *India and the World Economy, 1850–1950* (Delhi: Oxford University Press, 2003)

Banaji, Jairus, 'Capitalist Domination and the Small Peasantry: Deccan Districts in the Late 19th Century', *Economic and Political Weekly*, Special Number (XII), 1977

Bates, Crispin, 'Regional Dependence and Rural Development in Central India: The Pivotal Role of Migrant Labour', *Modern Asian Studies*, 19 (3), 1985

————, and Marina Carter, 'Tribal and Indentured Migrants in Colonial India: Modes of Recruitment and Forms of Incorporation', in Peter Robb, ed., *Dalit Movements and the Meanings of Labour in India* (Delhi: Oxford University Press, 1993)

Behal, Rana, and Prabhu Mohapatra, 'Tea and Money Versus Human Life: The Rise and Fall of the Indenture System in the Assam Tea Plantations 1840–1908', in E. Valentine Daniel, Henry Bernstein, and Tom Brass, eds, *Plantations, Peasants and Proletarians in Colonial Asia* (London: Frank Cass, 1992)

Bhaduri, Amit, 'Forced Commerce and Agrarian Growth', in idem, *On the Border of Economic Theory and History* (Delhi: Oxford University Press, 1999)

Bharadwaj, Krishna, 'A Note on Commercialization in Agriculture', in K.N. Raj, Neeladri Bhattacharya, Sumit Guha, Sakti Padhi, eds, *Essays on the Commercialization of Indian Agriculture* (Delhi: Oxford University Press, 1985)

Bhatia, B.M., *Famines in India: A Study in Some Aspects of the Economic History of India, 1860–1965* (Bombay: Asia Publishing House, 1963)

Bhattacharya, Neeladri, 'The Logic of Tenancy Cultivation: Central and South-East Punjab, 1870–1935', *Indian Economic and Social History Review*, 20 (2), 1983

————, 'Agricultural Labour and Production: Central and South-East Punjab, 1870–1940', in K.N. Raj, *et al.*, *Essays on the Commercialization of Indian Agriculture* (Delhi: Oxford University Press, 1985)

————, 'Lenders and Debtors: The Punjab Countryside, 1880–1940', in Sugata Bose, ed., *Credit, Markets, and the Agrarian Economy of Colonial India* (Delhi: Oxford University Press, 1994)

————, 'Pastoralists in a Colonial World', in David Arnold and Ramachandra Guha, eds, *Nature, Culture, Imperialism* (Delhi: Oxford University Press, 1995)

Blyn, George, *Agricultural Trends in India 1861–1947: Output, Availability, and Productivity* (London: Oxford University Press, 1966)

Bose, Sugata, *Agrarian Bengal: Economy, Social Structure, and Politics, 1919–1947* (Cambridge: Cambridge University Press, 1986)

————, ed., *Credit, Markets, and the Agrarian Economy of Colonial India* (Delhi: Oxford University Press, 1994)

Breman, Jan, *Patronage and Exploitation* (Delhi: Manohar, 1979)

————, and E. Valentine Daniel, 'The Making of a Coolie', in E. Valentine Daniel, Henry Bernstein, and Tom Brass, eds, *Plantations, Peasants and Proletarians in Colonial Asia* (London: Frank Cass, 1992)

Chakrabarti, Lalita, 'Emergence of a Labour Force in a Dual Economy', *Indian Economic and Social History Review*, XV (3), 1978

Charlesworth, Neil, 'Rich Peasants and Poor Peasants in Late 19th Century Maharashtra', in Clive Dewey, ed., *Arrested Development in India: The Historical Dimension* (Delhi: Manohar, 1988)

Chatterjee, Indrani, *Gender, Slavery and Law in Colonial India* (Delhi: Oxford University Press, 1999)

Chatterjee, Partha, 'Agrarian Structure in pre-Partition Bengal', in Asok Sen, Partha Chatterjee, Saugata Mukherji, eds, *Perspectives in Social Sciences 2: Three Studies on the Agrarian Structure of Bengal, 1850–1947* (Calcutta: Oxford University Press, 1982)

Chaudhuri, Benoy, 'Agrarian Economy and Agrarian Relations in Bengal', in N.K. Sinha, ed., *The History of Bengal 1757–1905* (Calcutta: University of Calcutta, 1967)

Dasgupta, Ranajit, 'Plantation Labour in Colonial India', in E. Valentine Daniel, Henry Bernstein, and Tom Brass, eds, *Plantations, Peasants and Proletarians in Colonial Asia* (London: Frank Cass, 1992)

Davis, Mike, *Late Victorian Holocausts: El Nino Famines and the Making of the Third World* (London: Verso, 2001)

De, Barun, ed., *Perspectives in Social Science: Historical Dimension* (Calcutta: Oxford University Press, 1977)

Dewey, Clive, and A.G. Hopkins, eds, *The Imperial Impact: Studies in the Economic History of Africa and India* (London: Athlone Press, 1978)

Dhanagare, D.N., *Peasant Movements in India 1920–50* (Delhi: Oxford University Press 1983)

Digby, William, *Prosperous British India: A Revelation from Official Records* (London, 1901)

Dreze, Jean, and Amartya Sen, *Hunger and Public Action* (New Delhi: Oxford University Press, 1989)

Frykenberg, R.E., *Guntur District 1788–1848: A History of Local Influence and Central Authority in South India* (Oxford: Clarendon Press, 1965)

Guha, Ranajit, *Elementary Aspects of Peasant Insurgency in Colonial India* (Delhi: Oxford University Press, 1983)

Guha, Sumit, 'Some Aspects of the Rural Economy in the Deccan', in K.N. Raj, Neeladri Bhattacharya, Sumit Guha, Sakti Padhi, eds, *Essays on the Commercialization of Indian Agriculture* (Delhi: Oxford University Press, 1985)

———, ed., *Growth, Stagnation, or Decline? Agricultural Productivity in British India* (Delhi: Oxford University Press, 1992)

Habib, Irfan, 'Mughal India', in Tapan Raychaudhuri and Irfan Habib, eds, *The Cambridge Economic History of India, Volume I, c.1200–c.1750* (Cambridge: Cambridge University Press, 1982)

Hjele, Benedicte, 'Slavery and Agricultural Bondage in South India in the Nineteenth Century', *Scandinavian Economic History Review*, XV (1–2), 1967

K.N. Raj, 'Introduction', in K.N. Raj, Neeladri Bhattacharya, Sumit Guha, Sakti Padhi, eds, *Essays on the Commercialization of Indian Agriculture* (Delhi: Oxford University Press, 1985)

Kumar, Dharma, *Land and Caste in South India: Agricultural Labour in the Madras Presidency During the Nineteenth Century* (Cambridge: Cambridge University Press, 1965)

———, 'Landownership and Inequality in Madras Presidency, 1853–4 to 1946–7', *Indian Economic and Social History Review*, 12 (3), 1975

Ludden, David, ed., *Agricultural Production and Indian History* (Delhi: Oxford University Press, 1994)

Islam, M. Mufakharul, 'Trends in Crop Production in the Undivided Punjab: A Reassessment', in Clive Dewey, ed., *Arrested Development in India: The Historical Dimension* (Delhi: Manohar, 1988)

Markovits, Claude, Jacques Pouchepadass, and Sanjay Subrahmanyam, eds, *Society and Circulation* (Delhi: Permanent Black, 2003)

Mayer, Eric, 'Labour Circulation Between Sri Lanka and South India in Historical Perspective', in Claude Markovits, Jacques Pouchepadass, Sanjay Subrahmanyam, eds, *Society and Circulation* (Delhi: Permanent Black, 2003)

Mohapatra, Prabhu, 'Coolies and Colliers: A Study of the Agrarian Context for Labour Migration from Chota Nagpur, 1880–1920', in *Studies in History*, I (2), 1985

————, 'Longing and Belonging: The Dilemma of Return Among Indian Immigrants in the West Indies, 1850–1950', *International Institute for Asian Studies Yearbook 1995* (Leiden, 1996)

Mukherjee, Nilmoni, *Ryotwari System in Madras 1792–1827* (Calcutta: Firma K.L. Mukhopadhyay, 1962)

Mukherji, Saugata, 'Some Aspects of Commercialization of Agriculture in Eastern India', in Asok Sen, Partha Chatterjee, and Saugata Mukherji, *Perspectives in Social Sciences 2: Three Studies on the Agrarian Structure of Bengal, 1850–1947* (Calcutta: Oxford University Press, 1982)

Nakazato, Nariaki, *Agrarian System in Eastern Bengal, c.1870–1910* (Calcutta: K.P. Bagchi, 1994)

Narain, Dharm, *The Impact of Price Movements on Selected Crops in India, 1900–39* (Cambridge: Cambridge University Press, 1965)

Northrup, David, 'Migration from Africa, Asia, and the South Pacific', in Andrew Porter, ed., *The Oxford History of the British Empire, Volume III: The Nineteenth Century* (Oxford: Oxford University Press, 1999)

Parthasarathi, Prasanna, *The Transition to a Colonial Economy: Weavers, Merchants and Kings in South India, 1720–1800* (Cambridge: Cambridge University Press, 2001)

Patnaik, Utsa, ed., *Agrarian Relations and Accumulation: The 'Mode of Production' Debate in India* (Bombay: Oxford University Press, 1990)

————, 'The Agrarian Question and Development of Capitalism in India', in Alice Thorner, ed., *Daniel Thorner Memorial Lectures: Land, Labour and Rights* (New Delhi: Tulika, 2001)

————, and Manjari Dingwaney, eds, *Chains of Servitude: Bondage and Slavery in India* (Madras: Sangam Books, 1985)

Pouchepadass, Jacques, *Champaran and Gandhi: Planters, Peasants and Gandhian Politics* (Delhi: Oxford University Press, 1999)

Prakash, Gyan, *Bonded Histories: Genealogies of Labor Servitude in Colonial India* (Cambridge: Cambridge University Press, 1990)

————, ed., *The World of the Rural Labourer in Colonial India* (Delhi: Oxford University Press, 1992)

Raghavan, T.C.A., 'Malguzars and Peasants: The Narmada Valley, 1860–1920', in Sabyasachi Bhattacharya, ed., *Essays in Agrarian History: India 1850–1940* (Special Number) *Studies in History*, 1 (2), 1985

Raj, K.N., Neeladri Bhattacharya, Sumit Guha, Sakti Padhi, eds, *Essays on the Commercialization of Indian Agriculture* (Delhi: Oxford University Press, 1985)

Ray, Rajat, and Ratnalekha Ray, 'Zamindars and Jotedars: A Study of Rural Politics in Bengal', in Burton Stein, ed., *The Making of Agrarian Policy in British India, 1770–1900* (Delhi: Oxford University Press, 1992)

Ray, Ratnalekha, *Change in Bengal Agrarian Society, c.1760–1850* (Delhi: Manohar, 1979)

Raychaudhuri, Tapan, and Irfan Habib, eds, *The Cambridge Economic History of India, Volume I, c.1200–c.1750* (Cambridge: Cambridge University Press, 1982)

Robb, Peter, ed., *Dalit Movements and the Meanings of Labour in India* (Delhi: Oxford University Press, 1993)

Roy, Tirthankar, *The Economic History of India, 1857–1947* (New Delhi: Oxford University Press, 2000)

Saradamoni, K., 'Agrestic Slavery in Kerala in the Nineteenth Century', *Indian Economic and Social History Review*, 10 (4), 1973

Sarkar, Tanika, 'Bondage in the Colonial Context', in Utsa Patnaik and Manjari Dingwaney, eds, *Chains of Servitude: Bondage and Slavery in India* (Madras: Sangam Books, 1985)

Sen, Amartya, *Poverty and Famines: An Essay on Entitlement and Deprivation* (Oxford: Clarendon, 1981)

Sen, Asok, 'Agrarian Structure and Tenancy Laws in Bengal, 1850–1900', in Asok Sen, Partha Chatterjee, and Saugata Mukherji, *Perspectives in Social Sciences 2: Three Studies on the Agrarian Structure of Bengal, 1850–1947* (Calcutta: Oxford University Press, 1982)

———, Partha Chatterjee, and Saugata Mukherji, *Perspectives in Social Sciences 2: Three Studies on the Agrarian Structure of Bengal, 1850–1947* (Calcutta: Oxford University Press, 1982)

Sharma, Sanjay, *Famine, Philanthropy, and the Colonial State: North India in the Early Nineteenth Century* (New Delhi: Oxford University Press, 2001)

Thorner, Alice, *Daniel Thorner Memorial Lectures: Land, Labour and Rights* (New Delhi: Tulika, 2001)

Thorner, Daniel, 'Agrarian Revolution by Census Redefinition', in Daniel Thorner and Alice Thorner, *Land and Labour in India* (Bombay: Asia Publishing House, 1962)

———, *The Agrarian Prospect in India* (Delhi: Allied Publishers, 1976)

————, and Alice Thorner, *Land and Labour in India* (Bombay: Asia Publishing House, 1962)

Tinker, Hugh, *A New System of Slavery: The Export of Indian Labour Overseas 1830–1920* (London: Oxford University Press, 1974)

Tomlinson, B.R., *The Economy of Modern India, 1860–1970* (Cambridge: Cambridge University Press, 1993)

Washbrook, David, *The Emergence of Provincial Politics: Madras Presidency, 1870–1920* (Cambridge: Cambridge University Press, 1976)

————, 'Economic Development and Social Stratification in Rural Madras: The "Dry Region", 1878–1929', in Clive Dewey and A.G. Hopkins, eds, *The Imperial Impact: Studies in the Economic History of Africa and India* (London: Athlone Press, 1978)

————, 'Land and Labour in Late Eighteenth Century South India: The Golden Age of the Pariah?', in Peter Robb, ed., *Dalit Movements and the Meanings of Labour in India* (Delhi: Oxford University Press, 1993)

Yanagisawa, H., *A Century of Change: Caste and Irrigated Lands in Tamilnadu, 1860s–1970s* (Delhi: Manohar, 1996)

4

Trade, Industry, and the Political Economy of Empire

As we move now from the primary to the secondary and tertiary sectors of late-colonial Indian economic life, a partial change in the order of presentation seems advisable. So far, the argument has proceeded from the bottom up: from food-gathering-nomadic to settled agriculture; from agricultural production, as conditioned in part by long-term ecological determinants, to the contradictory implications of late-colonial intensified commercialization. Colonial structures and policies affected all these levels, but their salience becomes more obvious as we enter the domains of commerce, industry, and finance. And correspondingly, the debates set off by nationalist criticism around issues such as the drain of wealth, deindustrialization, and barriers to indigenous industrial development acquire greater relevance, even though many try to ignore or dismiss such issues.[1] However, even as we emphasize the validity of older history-writing on these areas, albeit with considerable modifications, we also need to go beyond them. This will involve the incorporation of some research that is sometimes dismissed too quickly as neo-colonial revisionism. I refer, in particular, to recent studies of a number of themes that diverge from older nationalist parameters. Some of them reveal the survival, and even sometimes a development through adaptations, of 'traditional' forms of trade, business life, and handicrafts.

[1] The best known of such efforts, in the opinion of many scholars, has been Kumar 1983, where drain of wealth and deindustrialization do not figure even in the index.

The preceding chapters have ranged fairly freely across the entire late-colonial era. As our themes move closer towards imperialist–nationalist conflict, chronological divisions become more relevant. Though not necessarily always, a rough watershed will be seen as having been formed by the First World War and the beginnings of Gandhian nationalism. Economic developments and mounting nationalist pressures during the post-1919 era necessitated significant changes in the political economy of colonialism.

OF DRAINS AND TRAINS

Drain Inspectors? Ideas on the 'Drain of Wealth' and Beyond

It is convenient to begin with some basic data. I take this, deliberately, from an author whom it is difficult to suspect of any anti-colonial nationalist bias: B.R. Tomlinson. Like most other countries of Asia, Africa, Latin America, and Australasia, India by the late nineteenth century had been slotted into the capitalist world economy as a supplier of foodstuff and raw materials to the industrialized West (most notably Britain), and as a market for the export of Western manufactures. Britain was far and away the largest supplier of Indian imports—over 60 per cent in 1913. The subcontinent was quite crucial in providing a captive market (safeguarded by the absence of any protective tariffs till the 1920s), particularly for cotton textiles, iron and steel, and engineering products. In 1913, for instance, the quantum of imported Lancashire piecegoods went beyond 3000 million yards for the first time (and, as it transpired, the last as well), and India that year took in 43 per cent of the total British exports of that item by volume. This was important particularly because, by the late nineteenth century, British textiles, metal goods, and engineering exports to Europe and North America were severely restricted by increases in domestic protection against foreign competition, notably in Germany and the USA.

British dominance appeared less marked so far as Indian foodgrains and raw material exports were concerned. Continental Europe, as a whole, bought more rice, raw jute, raw cotton, oilseeds, and hides and skins between 1900 and 1913. Yet even this worked significantly to imperial advantage, because of a vital balance of payments dimension. India maintained a balance of payments surplus with North America and Europe by not importing much from them. These were precisely the parts of the world where British deficits were increasing. Conversely, India had a deficit balance with Britain, but this was more than made up by its surplus in relation to other parts of the world. The net result was that 'Britain's visible and invisible payments surplus with India enabled her to make good between two-fifths and one-third of her deficit with the other industrialized nations, and to continue to perform as an economy with a world-wide balance of payments surplus long after her trading position had declined.'[2]

Despite the prominence given to the export of capital in many theories of imperialism, this was possibly a less significant dimension of the Indo-British colonial connection. British capital investments in Latin America, the USA, and Canada were considerably higher—51 per cent of total portfolio investments between 1865 and 1914 went to the Americas, as against only 14 per cent to Asia. The bulk of the investments in India went to government loans, railways, and export-oriented plantations, mines, and jute mills. Funds seem to have come mainly from ploughed-back profits and capital raised from European residents in India. There was thus very little real transfer of resources from Britain to India, and foreign capital investment was important primarily as feeder to the dominant structures of commerce and finance.[3]

Still, late-colonial India had apparently a very favourable balance of trade. Agricultural exports in particular expanded through much of the late-nineteenth and early-twentieth century, even during the world economic downturn from 1873 to 1896. There were also visible signs of 'development', notably an impressive and rapidly expanding network of railway lines and a number of modern industries using up-to-date technology. In terms of conventional economic analysis and assumptions of automatic market-driven or export-led growth,

---

[2] Tomlinson 1979: chapter 1. The quote (from p. 6) sums up the findings, regarding the balance of payments question, of Saul 1960: chapters III and VIII.

[3] Bagchi 1972: chapter 6 (158–62).

these should have represented major plus factors. Yet there was ample evidence of massive, and quite possibly growing, Indian poverty. Terrible famines broke out in many parts of the subcontinent during the 1870s and again in the 1890s, and even the obviously tendentious estimate of national income made by Lord Curzon during the budget debate of 1901–2 amounted to no more than Rs 30 (two pounds sterling) per head per year. The corresponding estimate for Britain in 1901 was GBP 52—twenty-six times greater. It was this paradox that became the provocation and starting point of the classic nationalist theory of the 'drain of wealth'.[4] The theory famously argued that the export surplus in goods was continually drained away by the flow of a whole range of invisible items, in the shape of official and unofficial remittances, to Britain.

This remittance question had been central to Indo-British relations from as far back as the mid-eighteenth century. The drain had been critically discussed by a host of observers, both British and Indian, two early examples being Edmund Burke and Rammohan Roy. A brief historical sketch of its changing forms should be helpful. Down to 1757, European traders were obliged to bring bullion into India, in the teeth of much criticism at home. The dominant mercantilist wisdom at this time asserted that gold and silver should be exported as little as possible. Indian cotton and silk goods then had flourishing markets in the West, which, however, could offer little in return in terms of goods. British woollens, at that time the principal manufacture, obviously had a negligible market in South Asia.

The problem was solved dramatically by Plassey. Now the plunder from Bengal, profits made from duty-free inland trade, and the 'surplus' from diwani revenues (after the Company had obtained revenue-collecting rights from the Mughal emperor in 1765) sufficed for what were still euphemistically termed 'investments' in India. A strange investment, indeed, for, in effect, the profits of military conquest were used to purchase goods for export from India. By the turn of the eighteenth century into the nineteenth, however, the decline

[4] The paradox is aptly summed up by the opening sentence in Bagchi 1972: 1—'In 1900, India, "the brightest jewel in the British Crown", was one of the poorest nations in the world.' I take the national income estimates for India and Britain from the same section.

in the traditional exports of cotton and silk manufactures in the face of Manchester competition raised acute remittance problems for the EIC, its servants, and private European traders alike. This was tackled, initially, by the development of indigo and the export of Indian opium to China for tea purchases; and then, on a much more stable and successful basis, through the rapid expansion of the export of foodgrains and agricultural raw materials or semi-processed goods—wheat, rice, raw cotton, raw and finished jute, tea, oilseeds, hides and skins, etc. What remained constant, through these many changes in form, was the need for a unilateral transfer of funds to Britain. After 1858, the burden of the EIC's London establishment and of dividends to its shareholders was replaced by the costs of maintaining the secretary of state's India Office, and the interests on the India Debt in Britain. The latter, already considerable thanks to the Company's military adventures and the expenses of suppressing the 1857 rebellion, was further enhanced when, after the takeover of the Company by the Crown, compensation to the EIC shareholders were also paid out of it. These 'Home Charges' additionally included pensions to British Indian civilian and army officers, military and other stores purchased in Britain, the costs of army training, transport, and campaigns incurred outside India (but charged to Indian finances), and the guaranteed interest on railways. In 1901–2, for instance, the Home Charges came to £17.3 million. The major items that year were 6.4 million for the railway interest, 3 million interest on the India Debt, 4.3 million for army expenses, 1.9 million for stores purchases in Britain, and 1.3 million towards pensions. To this official account must be added the less easily quantifiable private items: remittances made by British officials while still serving in India, and the transfer of profits made in India by British business houses.

Nationalist polemic concentrated mainly on what could be estimated or guessed to be the total amount of the drain, which was sometimes crudely equated with the surplus of exports over imports. This was accompanied with criticism of official policies responsible for the drain. Such accounts dwelt less on the precise mechanisms of the drain through which profits made in rupees in India could be transformed into British sterling. Yet these were possibly the more crucial factors, since they reveal the complex interlocking of government and business interests, of official structures with what, by the late nineteenth century, had become a massive chain of British-controlled banks, and of export-import, shipping, and insurance firms as well as managing agency houses. In 1888 a diehard imperialist, Sir John Strachey, explained the mechanism of the drain with clarity and frankness: 'The Secretary of State draws bills on the Government Treasury in India, and it is mainly though these bills, which are paid in India out of the public revenues, that the merchant obtains the money that he requires in India, and the Secretary of State the money that he requires in England.'[5] To explicate: would-be purchasers of Indian exports in Britain paid in sterling to buy Council Bills from the secretary of state. The latter used this sterling to meet the Home Charges. The Council Bills were then dispatched by the British purchasers to India and exchanged for rupees from the Government of India's revenues.

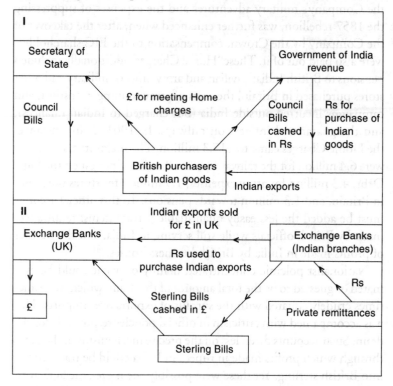

[5] Strachey 1888. These were lectures addressed to Cambridge undergraduates.

These rupees were used to buy Indian goods for export. Conversely, British officials and businessmen in India remitted their savings and profits in rupees through the purchase of sterling bills from British-owned exchange banks. The London branches of these banks paid in pounds for such bills. The money for that came from Indian exports that had been purchased with the rupees obtained through the sale of sterling bills. The diagram above may be helpful.

Both Home Charges and private remittances were thus funnelled through Indian exports. So the drain of wealth, as nationalist economists repeatedly pointed out from Dadabhai Naoroji onwards, found its visible expression through India's growing export surplus. The drain, originally 'mercantilist' in its link with the trade monopoly of the EIC, had in course of time become closely associated with the newer processes of exploitation through free trade and with the structures of British Indian finance capital. A neat three-stage periodization of British colonialism in India had been suggested by R.P. Dutt in the 1940s, mercantilist/free trade capitalism/finance capital.[6] He elaborated some of the insights and stray suggestions of Marx which need to be complicated through a concept of overlapping phases. The precise mechanisms of the drain of wealth can provide an entry point into this story of earlier forms of colonial extraction. They never entirely died out, but they were continuously transformed and integrated into newer patterns.

Things were complicated and, on the whole, worsened for India by the rapid depreciation of silver in terms of gold in the late nineteenth century. At a time when the bulk of the developed world, above all Britain, made something like a fetish about a gold-pegged currency, the Indian rupee was maintained on the silver standard, with the free coinage of silver into coins at very low rates. British bankers and merchants were eager to export America's new production and Europe's demonetized stock of silver. The consequent influx of silver into India led to a decline of the rupee–gold sterling exchange rate from 1s 10d in 1874 to 1s 2d in 1892.

An important consequence was that while world agricultural prices declined during the 1873–96 depression, the export prices of Indian goods remained stable since the fall was counteracted by the

[6] Dutt 1947/1970.

depreciation of the silver rupee. Agricultural exports boomed in this situation. Dietmar Rothermund has argued that the consequences were anything but beneficial for most Indian peasants, even though nationalist economists on the whole favoured the low exchange rate since it gave some unwitting protection to the infant Indian textile industry by pushing up the price of Lancashire imports. The benefits of the agricultural boom went largely to British export and shipping firms, along with their Indian subordinates. This was because crops were often hypothecated to usurer-traders, now increasingly connected through a hierarchy of advances to the big foreign concerns located in the ports and cities. In Rothermund's words, 'The depreciation of the currency and the pre-emption of the productive capacity of vast parts of the country combined so as to achieve the miracle that India could export produce at "stable" export prices even at a time when severe famines tormented the country. By absorbing silver and exporting wheat at the lowest price India served as the buffer at the base of the world economy of the late nineteenth century.'[7]

The point can be generalized further, as Amiya Bagchi has suggested. It was hardly a coincidence that by the late nineteenth century, when gold had become the standard of currency in all West European countries, the USA, and Japan, silver remained the standard in the two biggest colonized regions, the Indian colony and the Chinese semi-colony. This, Bagchi argues, was 'in some ways the most obvious symbol of the consolidation of the capitalist centre and its separation from the colonial periphery . . .'[8] There was, however, one major point of weakness in this whole structure from the British point of view. The low rupee–sterling ratio meant a growing burden on the finances of the Government of India, since more had to be paid in rupees to meet the Home Charges. Ultimately, the mints had to be closed to free silver coinage in 1893, pushing up the rupee to 1s 4d in 1898, and India moved to a kind of gold exchange standard.[9]

The drain theory has always had its severe critics, ranging from blatant apologists of colonialism to more serious commentators who

[7] Rothermund 1970: 1–23.
[8] Bagchi 2003: 155–79.
[9] The currency issue would remain vital, in changing forms, and we will encounter it again in our discussion of post-1914 developments.

were doubtful about many nationalist formulations, excesses, and silences.[10] Three broad lines of debate may be distinguished. First, the quantum and significance of the drain, it has been suggested, was greatly exaggerated by nationalist economists. Tacitly equating drain with the easily quantifiable Home Charges, K.N. Chaudhuri calculated in 1968 that the amount involved in it ranged from between 1.8 per cent to 0.8 per cent of estimated national income between 1898 and 1914.[11] More generally, it has been suggested that too much should not be made of the export–import imbalance since external commerce as a whole, whether for better or for worse, still affected only a small (though growing) part of the economy. Not everything within the Home Charges, again, could be condemned as purely exploitative, since the stores purchased and loans raised in Britain would have either required payment at higher rates or not been available at all. There was thus also a 'productive' element in it. Nonetheless, all but the crudest of apologists did admit that 'the existence of some "drain" can hardly be disputed': most notably perhaps 'the use of the Indian army without paying for it' in numerous expeditions, far away from Indian borders, entirely in British interests but funded by Indian revenues.[12]

The private remittances dimension has been much more difficult to estimate, but evidently adding it would substantially enhance the amount of the drain. Once again, an argument of productivity or development has been deployed in relation to this, since it is obvious that some visible signs of a more modern capitalist economic life did emerge in the late-colonial era, initiated primarily through British investments in communications, mines, and some industries. The argument shifts at this point to questions about the basic nature of such development or modernization. More precisely, as we shall see in

[10] An appropriate instance of criticism of the first kind would be, once again, Sir John Strachey, who followed up his lucid exposition of the mechanism of the 'drain' with the blunt assertion that 'England receives nothing from India except in return for English services rendered or English capital expended.' Strachey 1888: 115.

[11] Chaudhuri 1968: 31–50.

[12] The two quotes are taken from Charlesworth 1982: 52, and Tomlinson 1975: 337–80. Tomlinson then went on to state that such maintenance and deployment of the British Indian army was 'the only irreplaceable advantage derived by India.'

greater detail during our discussion of the railways and industries, the relevant issues concern the extent of the backward or forward linkages of these new sectors: how far, if at all, they contributed to overall growth. Bagchi has explored the precise ways in which the weight of the British political and economic presence (above all in eastern India) constituted the greatest inhibition against indigenous capitalist development. His work updates the traditional nationalist thesis.

Critics of the drain theory, and more generally of what was allegedly an exaggerated estimate of the harmful and exploitative dimensions of British rule, have had recourse recently to a third kind of argument. They emphasize the somewhat superficial nature of empire, the ways in which it had to function through, and perhaps be dependent on, Indian groups and structures. In 1982 Charlesworth approvingly mentioned a new tendency 'to emphasize the weakness and limitations of imperialism, [which] would suggest that India's problem was that foreign modernizing impulses were not strong or intrusive enough, rather than that they were devastatingly destructive.' Tomlinson argued similarly: 'where large-scale "exploitation" of the producer occurred it can best be ascribed to the strength of the hold maintained by traditional marketing and credit-supplying agencies and to the inability of the forces of the world economy to break down existing institutional barriers to widespread economic development.'[13] Not everyone is likely to share this confidence in the beneficial effects with which the imperialist world economy would have blessed mankind if only it had had unfettered sway. Arguments of the kind deployed by Tomlinson underestimate the extent to which 'traditional' agencies will have been modified by the British presence, as well as the likely impact of and gains from colonial control over the commanding heights of external commerce, banking, and finance. But it needs to be added that the debates have sometimes highlighted the inadequacies and silences of the old positions, and in that sense have helped deepen understanding. A blanket rejection of this strand of research, animated by an excess of nationalist zeal, does not help.

We need to underline some important limits to the traditional nationalist critique. The Naoroji tradition tended to concentrate

[13] Charlesworth 1982: 69; Tomlinson 1975: 7–8.

overwhelmingly on the official, Home Charges dimension of the drain, both because this was easily measurable and out of a desire to bring about specific changes in government policies. More 'structural' dimensions, notably the negative implications of private foreign control and exploitation of key sectors of the economy, were mentioned at times, but more or less in passing: their elaboration had to wait for a later Left-nationalist-cum-Marxist mode of analysis.[14] Nationalist criticism focussed almost entirely on the Indo-British connection, largely ignoring India's overall situation within a world economy dominated by a group of Western countries.[15] Most significantly, perhaps, was the strong tendency to slur over the ways in which both British rule and British capital functioned—crucially through Indian structures of control and exploitation. Indians were anything but an undifferentiated mass equally impoverished by foreign domination; substantial gains were made by significant groups among them. Out of the desire to build a common anti-colonial platform, and also out of less laudable material connections relating to their own elitist locations, nationalist leaders tended to play down this second aspect.

A brief glance at Dadabhai Naoroji's classic text, *Poverty of India* (1876), may help to illustrate the power, as well as the limits, of the nationalist economic critique. Naoroji followed up his pioneering (and for his time quite impressive) attempt to calculate the per capita income of Indians with the pertinent observation that 'the mass of

[14] There were, it is true, occasional striking exceptions. Thus, G.V. Joshi (Joshi 1880) described the growing domination by British commercial firms, banks, and plantations as a kind of 'absentee landlordism, taking away not only the rent of the land, but also the profits of enterprise. . . . They represent so much adverse possession of our total industrial field—of work and profitable enterprise': cited in Ganguli 1977: 119.

[15] A point forcefully argued by G. Balachandran, who suggests that the resultant lacuna has helped some recent 'revisionist' historians to argue that by the inter-War years India was no longer a source of significant gain for metropolitan interests. For the neglected themes include 'India's involuntary role in advancing Britain's efforts to regain its financial pre-eminence, and its contribution to the stability and functioning of the world economy and its recovery in the Depression . . .': Balachandran 2003: Introduction (24–5).

the people could not get this Rs 20, as the upper classes had a larger share than the average.' On occasion he also showed an awareness of a possible 'internal drain . . . as between classes and regions within the country'. But a nationalist closure commonly follows, as in the following passage: 'In reality there are two Indias—one the prosperous, the other poverty-stricken. The prosperous India is the India of the British and other foreigners. The second India is the India of the Indians.' The logical structure of *Poverty of India* consequently takes on the form of a series of slippages, in a progressively narrowing social direction. The text begins with the theme of mass poverty, moves on to the 'the source of evil being the official drain', and ends with the call for more jobs being made available to educated Indians.

Imperial Steam: The Railways and their Far-reaching Consequences

With their far-reaching material presence and manifold consequences, the railways constitute the most impressive and enduring monument to British rule in India. They began operations in 1853 with the 35-mile-long Bombay–Thana line. By 1900 they extended over 23,672 route miles, constituting the fourth biggest in the world and the largest in Asia outside Russia. By 1947 the miles of lines laid had risen to 44,722. The largest single site of British capital investment in India,[16] around the 1880s the railways employed around 200,000 men, women, and children annually for construction and maintenance work alone, while its operating line workers numbered 380,000 in 1901 and over a million in 1947. The railways, in fact, seem to have stood at the organizational and technological core of those of the economic, political, social, and ecological transformations that produced modern India. This, however, has had a paradoxical consequence. Entering into the histories of so many dimensions of colonial modernity, the railways have tended to figure as background rather than becoming a subject for full-scale specific research.[17]

---

[16] Around 236 million pounds sterling by 1902, the great bulk of it of British origin. See Thorner 1955: 201–6; also available in Kerr 2001: 93.

[17] This lag is emphasized in Kerr 2001: Introduction (1–5).

Like so much else in colonial rule, and perhaps in capitalist modernity in general, the consequences of the building of this massive and ever-expanding network of railways have been highly debatable. To pose a counterfactual, there can be little doubt that some of the diverse and contradictory implications would have become manifest even had the railways been built in an India not conquered by the British. The demand for wooden sleepers would have adversely affected forest resources regardless, and it is likely that the pattern of uneven development, with some regions and groups benefiting and others being disadvantaged, is connected not with those who ordered the construction but with the very nature of the construction. On the other hand it cannot be gainsaid that the benefits of the vastly enhanced speed and lower costs of transport brought about by the railwys meant a decline of livelihood capacity for those in the business of earlier forms of transport: in the South Asian case, pack oxen, bullock carts, river boats, and coastal shipping. Given the contradictions and their susceptibility to debate, the basic fact that must be asserted is that railway constructions and operations were for a century inseparable from colonialism, binding the subject inextricably with the long general debate between more and less pessimistic assessments of the overall economic consequences of British rule in India, nationalist criticism, and meliorist rebuttals. In a controversial prediction made in 1853, Marx had thought that the railways would be 'the forerunner of modern industry' in India. By 1881 he had revised that assessment, stating in a letter that the 'railways were useless to the Hindus' and formed part of 'a bleeding process with a vengeance'.[18] Marx's second assessment is much less known than the first. Together they draw attention to the basic ambiguities which must accompany any assessment of the significance of colonial railway construction. A cautious and balanced conclusion—of undoubted advances side by side with possibilities shot through with retardation—was drawn by Daniel Thorner in 1955, at the end of his pioneering study of the railways in India, and represents possibly the best summary: 'It would appear

---

[18] Marx n.d.: 87, 337. It is interesting that the 1881 letter was written to a well-known Russian Narodnik intellectual, and that it used the same 'bleeding' metaphor which was a favourite of Dadabhai Naoroji's.

that the very economic changes which the railways made possible in India were retarded by the way in which the railways were built and the way they were run.'[19]

As we have already seen in passing, the railways became an important part of the nationalist critique of British rule, above all because of the very peculiar way in which they were financed. Under pressure from British investors, the EIC reluctantly accepted (and the post-1858 Crown government continued) a system of guaranteed dividend of 5 per cent to railway company shareholders, paying the difference out of Indian revenues if profits fell below that amount. In 1901–2 this came to one-third or more of the annual Home Charges. The consequences in terms of construction were even more harmful, for this strange system of private investment at public risk was tailor-made for extravagance and waste. Railway companies, for instance, opted for an unnecessarily broad track gauge. When the state began to construct some lines on its own by fits and starts from around the 1870s, it tried by contrast to save money by going instead for the metre gauge, thus leaving a major problem of incompatibility for post-Independence successor regimes. Recklessly constructed railway embankments often disrupted natural drainage channels, causing waterlogging. This was widely held to be partly responsible for the ravages of 'Burdwan fever' (malaria) in many parts of eastern India.

The inefficiency and waste apart, the more structural aspects of colonial railway construction and management also show problematic features frequently attacked by nationalists.[20] Decisions about track placements were governed by the strategic and economic priorities of British rule and British business groups. Late-nineteenth-century imperial paranoia about a possible Russian invasion of India led to the construction of a thick cluster of economically unremunerative lines in the north-western part of the country, the burden of which, of course, had to be borne by Indian taxpayers. Otherwise, the major trunk lines ran out from the main ports (Bombay, Calcutta, Madras) to the hinterlands, transporting raw materials and foodgrains for export and

---

[19] Thorner, in Kerr 2001: 96.

[20] The latter often argued that investing similar resources in irrigation would have boosted agricultural production and been a much more effective way of preventing famines.

taking in British imported manufactures. Interconnections between inland regions, by contrast, were often neglected. Freight rates, again, were managed in the interests of British exporters and importers. Railway companies charged lower rates to and from ports than for comparable inland distances. It was often cheaper, for instance, for Bombay manufacturers to purchase British rather than Bihar coal: production costs of the latter were naturally lower, but railway freight charges hiked its price enormously. Much money was spent on running luxurious first class compartments, in practice a virtual European monopoly, while 'natives' had to travel in atrociously overcrowded third class bogeys. The railways became, in fact, a favoured locus for racist incidents of the kind that Gandhi made famous in the context of South Africa.

Most far-reaching of all, perhaps, were the ways in which the feedback effects of railways—the principal ground for Marx's 1853 prediction about the railway system becoming the forerunner of modern industry—came to be falsified, or at least greatly retarded, by the logic of colonialism. Financial capital, management, and most of the equipment and skilled labour came overwhelmingly from Britain. This severely hindered the creation and diffusion of new skills among Indians and blocked the possibility of their forming links with the rest of the Indian economy. Rails, points, fishplates, machinery, locomotives, even sleepers were almost entirely built outside India. Only 700 locomotives had been produced within India till 1941, though the railway workshops set up by the various companies for repair and maintenance work were actually quite capable of manufacturing many more. This was especially true of the big units at Ajmer and Jamalpur. That this did not happen was directly related to the interests of British locomotive firms which had become heavily dependent on the captive Indian market as, over time, the European countries and the USA developed big railway industries of their own. In 1898, for instance, Secretary of State Hamilton was successfully pressurized by the North British Locomotive Company to impose a standard engine design on all Indian railways, which effectively blocked the further manufacture of other types that had been developed in workshops like the one at Jamalpur.[21]

[21] Hurd 1983, in Kerr 2001: 159–60; Lehmann 1965: 297–306.

The long-term implications of the coming of the railways are wider than their indisputable entanglements with imperial exploitation. The most obvious economic fallout was a quickening of mobility and a lowering of transport costs. This strengthened tendencies towards a greater uniformity of prices across a single subcontinental market. Some efforts have been made to quantify the impact of the railways in this regard. Hurd has estimated that the fall in transport costs through railways, as compared with the available data regarding the expenses incurred in transporting goods by pack bullocks, bullock carts, or boats, meant a saving of about 9 per cent of the national income in 1900. The leakage or 'drain' through the system of guaranteed dividends, by contrast, was minimal, according to Hurd: not more than 0.3 per cent of the national income. The shift towards the railways did involve, of course, significant losses for those engaged in earlier forms of transport, but the balance between gains and disadvantages varied greatly according to regional conditions. Thus, cheap transport by water would have been common in the lower reaches of the great river valleys (notably eastern India), as well as in some coastal stretches, but much less elsewhere. River boats, for instance, had been extremely important for inter-regional trade down the Ganges and its tributaries to the east of Allahabad in pre-rail times. They diminished in importance further upstream. Ian Derbyshire's careful study of the impact of the railways on this region finds that the new mode helped to bring about an important long-term shift in economic balance, with a relative stagnation or decline of eastern UP districts as against growth in the western part of the province. In the former, boatmen and weavers (hit by Lancashire imports brought in by the railways) suffered, while the rail link with Calcutta helped only to make the region a major catchment area for the export of indentured and other forms of 'surplus' labour. A dense network of railways and the construction of canals, by contrast, made the western Doab a 'minor Punjab' in the late nineteenth century, and it could specialize in wheat and sugarcane production. A regional survey of Bengal by Mukul Mukherjee found that even in a terrain that favoured river transport and made railway construction difficult, ultimately the 'marginal advantage' came to rest with the latter. River transport tended to be seasonal, subject to natural calamities, and highly variable in time.

The shift towards railways reduced the extent of price differentials—between markets and across seasons.[22]

The railways have been generally looked at in terms of their impact, and of course they constitute an indispensable background to an enormous range of late-nineteenth- and early-twentieth-century developments: the intensification of commercialization, real or alleged deindustrialization, and the growth or decline of towns, to mention only some of the more obvious ones. In 1995 Ian Kerr introduced an interesting new focus in his appropriately titled *Building the Railways of the Raj*. He concentrated on the everyday details of the highly varied labour processes that were required for railway construction and maintenance as ongoing processes. The railways necessarily involved the bringing together of labour processes and forms of organization of the most diverse kind. These traversed the most simple as well as the most complex kinds of work, ranging from consulting engineers in Britain who were armed with the latest in technological expertise, to the coolie moving earth in Assam with methods and tools that may not have changed for centuries. Railway workers were hierarchized into relatively well-paid and skilled engineers and drivers (mainly European or Eurasian for a long time), through an intermediary stratum of white collar station-masters and clerks, down to a mass of unskilled manual labourers hired by contractors on a casual basis.[23]

This multiplicity of forms and levels had interesting implications for early railway labour movements and organizations.[24] The

[22] Hurd 1983; Derbyshire 1987: 521–45; Mukherjee 1980: 191–209; all three are available in Kerr 2001.

[23] Kerr draws out an interesting theoretical inference from this long-term reproduction and coexistence within railways of 'advanced' and 'backward', 'formal', and 'informal' kinds of labour and management forms. Going back to Marx's distinction of 'formal' and 'real' subsumption of labour to capital (which Jairus Banaji deploys in an agrarian context: see the previous chapter), he suggests that here assumptions of linear progression need to be abandoned. Historians of capitalist industrial development and of labour in many countries are in fact increasingly questioning such linearities, in ways not unrelated to contemporary situations where big factories seem often to be giving way to revived forms of dispersed 'putting-out' or 'domestic' production.

[24] As documented in Kerr 1985.

privileged European or Anglo-Indian segment contributed to racist tensions, but it also brought into India techniques of trade union organizations which were later emulated by Indian employees and workers. European or Anglo-Indian drivers and skilled mechanics, for instance, organized an Amalgamated Society of Railway Servants as early as 1874, just three years after a similarly named union had been founded in England. In 1897–9 a successful strike by European and Eurasian guards on the Great Indian Peninsular (GIP) railway acted as a catalyst to union formation and strikes by Indian signallers on the same line. At a very different level, the occasional consolidation of a very large mass of building workers at particularly difficult construction sites could produce moments of violent confrontation, as at Bhore Ghat in 1859 where over 40,000 were at work. There were, moreover, numerous incidents of dacoity and train-wrecking for which disgruntled or discharged coolies were often blamed.[25]

The implications of the railways, both far-reaching and ambiguous, extended far beyond the economy. Along with improved roads, steamships, and the post and telegraph services (and, in the twentieth century, telephones and the radio), the late-colonial revolution in communications was motivated in large part by, and contributed enormously to, the tightening of British politico-material controls.[26] It was equally indispensable for the development of anti-colonial nationalism across a vast subcontinent. Gandhi, as is well known, trenchantly condemned the railways in his *Hind Swaraj* (1909–10) as one of the worst features of the modern civilization that the British had brought to India. At the same time, on his return from South Africa, he spent a year deliberately travelling third class across the country to experience at first hand the woes of ordinary Indians. The railways were always vital for the countrywide movements that he inspired and organized, in significant part through his own incessant railway journeys. But the railways stimulated not some singular 'Indian' identity; rather, they helped in the construction of many and often mutually conflicting solidarities, including those centred around

[25] Ibid.: PE34–PE40; Chakrabarty 1976: 523–50.

[26] Deep Kanta Lahiri Choudhury's nicely titled book *Telegraphic Imperialism* (Lahiri Choudhury 2010) argues this point in detail.

region, language, class, caste, and religion, as *Hind Swaraj* percept-ively noted.[27] In conventionally social terms, they made the strict adherence to certain kinds of caste and gender barriers more difficult (with regard to interdining, for instance), and occasionally aroused conservative ire at the spectre of intermingling. But they also helped enormously in the consolidation of brahmanical Hindu and Islamic orthodoxies of ritual and belief, notably by making pilgrimages much easier as well as enabling their commercialization—approximating, more and more, to modern tourism.[28] As in so much else, what appears indisputably traditional was, quite often, invented, or at least greatly transformed, by the modern.

In keeping with the current academic focus on cultural meanings, research has started to explore the production and appropriation of representations or images of the railways in India.[29] Railway archi-tecture, for instance, often expressed the varied and changing moods of British builders. Lahore Station, built five years after the climacteric of 1857, was fortress-like in appearance. Victoria Terminus in Bombay (1887), in sharp contrast, adopted the luxuriant Indo-Saracenic style, mingling self-confidence with the desire to appear Oriental—a characteristic of that era of imperial durbars. Lines built to carry European passengers to hill resorts tried to evoke an atmosphere of home away from home. The railway stations at altitudes had mod-est English-style buildings and were given names like Runny-meade, Wellington, and Lovedale. A literature of railway travel quickly

[27] By accelerating and intensifying communications to an 'unnatural' ex-tent, Gandhi argued, railways have made people much more aware 'of differ-ent natures, different religions', and of 'distinctions' in general: specifically, he attributed to it part of the responsibility for the growth of Hindu–Muslim tensions: Parel 1997: 49–51.

[28] H.H. Risley, an exceptionally acute official observer, noted in 1891 how railways were stimulating pilgrimages to high-Hindu sacred places, and 'Cooks' steamers' swelling the number of Muslims going to Mecca and Medina. 'Both Benares and Manchester have been brought nearer to their customers, and have profited by the increased demand for their characteristic wares. Siva and Krishna drive out the tribal gods as surely as grey shirtings replace the more durable handwoven cloth.' Risley 1891: Introductory Essay, xxix–xxx.

[29] Kerr 2003.

developed, both among the English, for whom travel in luxurious first class compartments came to represent an attractive combination of the exotic with the comfortable, and soon among Indians as well. Among early instances of the latter there is Bholanath Chunder's *Travels of a Hindoo* (London, 1874), and another, part travel guide part farce, in which the Hindu gods come down to visit British India, travel by train, and get thrown out of a first class waiting-room by Europeans. One of them buys a watch: a reminder that the railways played a crucial part in the spread of disciplinary clock-time and the manufacture of watches which became particularly vital for office-going commuters on suburban trains.[30] Indian representations quickly spread to all cultural levels, from folk songs, popular woodcuts and prints, and decorations on women's garments, to a multitude of stories, poems, novels, and films. The predominant signification seems to be of modernity, which is at times celebrated but more often shot through with ambiguity. In R.K. Narayan's *Malgudi Days*, newcomers regularly arrive by train to disrupt the placid contentment of that small town. The railway is a recurrent symbol also in Satyajit Ray's *Apu* trilogy, signifying for the film's hero the need to venture forth into the new—in ways which are exciting but also painful, at times cruel.

Indian and European Commerce, Finance, and Entrepreneurship

Bazaars, Townsmen, Rulers, and Enclaves

An interlocked structure of government-backed Presidency banks, exchange banks with their headquarters abroad, and foreign (mostly British) business firms had over time come to constitute the most prominent component of the worlds of Indian commerce and finance in late-colonial India. This world controlled the bulk of the export–import trade (and was in that sense responsible for the 'drain of wealth', with which such trade was intimately related), shipping, modern forms of banking and insurance, plantations, mines, and a significant part of the emerging factory industries. Not unnaturally, this modern, or European, or generally Western, segment of British

[30] Roy 1887.

Indian economic life has, for a long time, attracted much scholarly and political interest. Apologists for colonial modernity and nationalist as well as Left critics have all explored these commanding heights of the late-colonial economy. A significant, if sometimes controversial, shift downwards has been taking place, however: and here economic history rejoins and contributes to some of the overall shifting of parameters of analysis that we have already encountered. Residues of old assumptions regarding a relatively self-sufficient pre-colonial Indian village—consequently a somewhat marginal and static commercial life—and then a sharp rupture through the colonial impact, or in other words a traditional/modern dichotomy, have come to be challenged by various kinds of 'returns of the repressed'. These have sometimes taken the form of continuity arguments, stressing the survival and vibrancy of indigenous forms of trade, finance, and even the handicrafts once so easily deployed to buttress the notion of near-total deindustrialization. There has also been the 'invention of tradition' variant which looks upon the 'unchanging' village as a nineteenth-century product of colonial discourse and/or 'peasantization'. But more complex patterns come out of some of the relatively recent research which has focused on the theme of circulation: questioning the frameworks of pre-colonial immobility, mere continuity, and colonial immobilization alike.[31] The progress of research thus justifies an arrangement of data about commercial life and finance that moves upwards from below, even as it simultaneously emphasizes interconnections and the ultimate subordination of such 'levels' to imperial politico-economic control by the more obviously modern sectors.

For quite some time now, research on medieval, and more particularly Mughal, India has come to recognize the fairly high level of commodity production in many parts of the subcontinent. It also acknowledges the existence of sophisticated merchant groups, well-developed systems of hundi (bills of exchange) that were crucial for both trade and revenue collection, and the existence of far-flung networks of oceanic, river, and overland commerce. Controversies continue about whether this was followed by a marked

[31] Markovits, Pouchepadass, and Subrahmanyam 2003: Introduction, *et passim.*

eighteenth-century hiatus or decline which would have been due, in varying proportions, to the breakdown of the Mughal peace or to the harmful consequences of early Company rule. In 1983, a major work by C.A. Bayly argued a case for substantial continuity in levels of Indian business life across the upper and middle Ganga plains: the decline in some areas associated with political disintegration being balanced, on the whole, by growth in adjacent regions. The disruption in the North Indian economy, Bayly suggested, came considerably later, in the second quarter of the nineteenth century. The Company's pacification efforts, aimed at establishing a monopoly over the legitimate use of force, had by then eliminated or reduced earlier forms of court and upper-class patronage, and disrupted the old military labour market by demobilizing many Indian martial formations. The resultant decline of demand for manufacture led to a long depression in northern India from around the mid-1820s to the 1840s. However, this did not mean a permanent collapse of indigenous commerce, for it was succeeded, on the whole, by renewed growth. Bayly's thesis said relatively little about the regions of early and direct Company domination, notably Bengal. Here the older nationalist-cum-Left argument of significant decline through British exploitation still appears fairly cogent.[32]

Soon after the publication of Bayly's seminal work, Rajat Ray tried to extend into the late-colonial era the argument of a flourishing bazaar economy of Indian bankers, merchants, and inland exchanges that operated through well-established traditional forms of arhat (commission agencies) and hundis. This, he suggested, always remained an important intermediate level, located between the European-dominated highest tier of exchange banks, international export-import firms, and managing agencies on the one hand, and on the other a bottom layer of peasant-artisan-peddler subsistence economy dominated by rural moneylenders. The colonial enclave was thus 'not the only "organized" sector in the economy', as is often assumed. Ray went on to suggest that the weakening of imperial domination after the First World War led to an increasingly successful penetration of the higher reaches of the Indian economy by the intermediate, indigenous

[32] Bayly 1983.

bazaar sector, typified by the rise of business houses, such as those of the Birlas and the Ispahanis, which were connected, respectively, with Gandhi and Jinnah. Post-colonial Indian capitalist groups thus have a long pedigree.[33]

Newer work along these lines continues the effort to explore continuities and interruptions across long stretches of time and space. But it has become more suspicious of excessively neat patterns and disjunctions of the kind implied by Ray's model of 'three distinct conglomerations': European enclave, bazaar, and rural. A glance at two essays might convey something of the flavour of this new line of research.

Claude Markovits explores an apparent paradox. Many of the pan-Indian merchant communities that dominated modern Indian business life were migrants from the drier, semi-pastoral north-west of the subcontinent: Khatris, Aroras, Multanis, Marwaris, Bhatias, Khojas, Lohanas, Bohras, Memons, Parsis, Gujarati Vanis. All came from various parts of Punjab, Rajasthan, Sindh, and Gujarat. The flow (circulatory rather than one-way, for connections with origins have seldom been disrupted) from drier areas towards zones of wet or riverine settled agriculture seems natural enough. What demands explanation, however, is the striking capacity of such merchants, most notably the Marwaris, to dominate commercial life in the regions they have moved into over the past two or three centuries. The internal diversity of the dry zone, with pockets of irrigated or rain-fed agriculture alternating with vast tracts of semi-nomadic pastoralism, may have necessitated the early development of commercial expertise and of credit instruments like hundis. North-west India lay astride the main sea and land routes that connected Central Asia and the Middle East with the river valleys of the Ganga and the Deccan: a situational advantage that enabled the accumulation of merchant capital. But political factors, Markovits suggests, were probably more crucial. Merchants from the dry zone, who had developed close links with

---

[33] Ray 1988: 263–318. A similar, broadly three-tier, model of the economy was subsequently worked out for a particular region: see Yang 1998. It should be mentioned that a longue durée history of Indian capitalist groups had been suggested many years back by D.R. Gadgil (Gadgil 1959), but this was not followed up for several decades. See also the essays in Tripathi 1984.

Rajput ruling clans through mediating their revenue transactions, used these to develop connections with the expanding Mughal state in the sixteenth and seventeenth centuries. This state itself operated to a significant extent through Rajput officials, greatly facilitating the penetration of much of northern India, notably by merchants from Jaipur, Bikaner, and Marwar (who have come to be generically called Marwaris). Early-twentieth-century merchant houses in Banaras, for instance, believed that they were descended from Rajasthani merchants who had come in the sixteenth century as commissary officers to Rajput units serving in the Mughal army. Similar connections re-emerged on an enhanced scale under British rule, initially with the opportunities that were opened up for provisioning colonial armies: setting up 'regimental bazaars' and serving as military contractors, and then through discharging vital intermediary roles in the distribution of imported British goods and the purchase of agricultural commodities for export. British presence and expansion on a more global scale were utilized profitably by a number of other trading groups, like the Chettiars of the Madras Presidency who established or expanded their circulatory networks spanning Burma, Malaya, and Ceylon; and Sindhi merchants from Shikarpur and Hyderabad who seem to have established outposts in the most unexpected parts of the world.[34]

'Bazaar' and 'enclave' thus interpenetrated each other in a number of ways, and the connections extended down to much more humble levels, too. Neeladri Bhattacharya's essay explores the world of the peddler. Rejecting models of a unilinear transition towards modernity, he emphasizes 'the combined existence of a various universe of traders, itinerants, merchants and companies, and . . . their mutual struggle for control and survival.'[35] Virtually anyone with a donkey, a bullock, or a cart could be a small-scale peddler in this peripatetic world of interpenetrating groups—which included itinerant artisans and entertainers meeting the cultural and ritual needs of villagers. Above this level of localized peddling there were traders who covered much longer distances, often in big groups or caravans: cattle-dealers

[34] See the essay by Claude Markovits, 'Merchant Circulation in South Asia . . .' in Markovits, Pouchepadass, and Subrahmanyam 2003. See also, for the Marwaris, Timberg 1978; and for Sind merchants, the pioneering work of Claude Markovits (Markovits 2000).

[35] Bhattacharya 2003: 165.

who became progressively more vital as arable farming expanded, for instance; or, notably, a trans-Himalayan commerce of impressive extent and antiquity linking South Asia with the Central Asian lands, Tibet, and China. Staggering numbers could be involved in such long-distance transhumance and trading: in 1877–8, for instance, 78,000 powindahs crossed the passes into Afghanistan. Relationships between such traditional commerce and the transformative pressures of the capitalist world market have been marked both by hostility— efforts at surveillance and control—and necessary, if hierarchized, co-ordination. The British, as we have seen with regard to food-gatherers and pastoralists, were extremely suspicious of mobile groups, and often sought to subject them to regimes of repressive and disciplinary regulation. They were generaı ' perceived as threats to both political and moral order.

Such attitudes towards relations between the sedentary and the itinerant were not entirely novel. Bhattacharya notes that these have been shot through with ambiguities that have found expression in folk tales and songs. The wanderer is a figure both attractive and alarming for settled people. Women peddlers were suspected of promiscuous living; the men of theft, kidnapping, or brigandage. Still, the interdependence remained vital, for the reach of the small town or village bazaar or fair had its limits, and the world market could not have penetrated the rural hinterland without operating through chains of intermediaries extending down to the humblest of peddlers. The Marwari cloth houses of Delhi distributed Lancashire, and then, increasingly, Indian mill-made piecegoods. They penetrated village markets through peripatetic Khoja traders. Readers of Tagore's novel *Ghare-Baire* (translated as *The Home and the World*) will recall the figure of Panchu, a near-landless villager surviving by bartering cheap imported cloth and trinkets in return for grain from women of lower-caste households—till his humble trade is disrupted by a nationalist landlord and student activists who impose a boycott on foreign goods.

Noteworthy: Banking and Currency

Relations between traditional and modern, indigenous and European business life in late-colonial India were marked by both interconnections and varying degrees of mutually beneficial adjustments, as well as by a basic and growing subordination of the traditional-indigenous. The latter produced conflicts, but did not rule out collaboration. In fact, it seems appropriate to think in terms of not two but three levels, for below the world of the bazaar—of traditional merchants, bankers (shroffs), and commission agents (arhatiyas) operating through hundis—there lay a subsistence economy of poorer peasants and artisans where monetization was low or negligible and among whom loans and payments were often still made in kind. As late as the 1950s, a National Sample Survey estimated the share of the non-monetized sector at 43 per cent for rural and 8–11 per cent for urban areas.[36] In purely quantitative terms the non-monetized and traditional sectors combined may even be said to have been predominant: a point that has been occasionally used to suggest that colonial domination and exploitation were, after all, somewhat superficial. Such arguments elide, usually for the purposes of an apologia, the crucial fact of British control over the commanding heights of the economy. This crucial fact meant that the subordinate levels had to modify and adjust themselves to fit in with the overall world economy of imperialist colonialism. As Rajat Ray points out, the late-nineteenth-century bazaar was in most ways 'a completely reshaped fragment of the country's indigenous commercial traditions: the shape of the fragment being determined by the contours of the colonial economy into which they were pressed by the imperial regime.'[37]

It is convenient to subdivide the ensuing account of the highest level of late-nineteenth- and early-twentieth-century business life under two broad headings: banking and currency; and the more modern forms of European and indigenous entrepreneurship.

The historian of the State Bank of India has reminded us that the gradual and uneven insertion of modern financial institutions and

[36] Chandavarkar 1983: chapter IX, 764.

[37] Thus the hundi channels now followed the new railway routes, moving inland from Bombay and Calcutta, while that multi-purpose credit instrument had been confined into being a pure bill of exchange for inland commerce. Indigenous bankers no longer had the functions of money-changing and serving as remittance agents and treasurers to governments and European companies which had made the Jagat Seths, for instance, so influential in the early eighteenth century; Ray 1992: 13–14.

practices in British India did not emerge from any abstract or homo-genized drive for capitalist modernity, but 'were called forth either by the compulsions of imperial finance or by the felt needs of local European commerce.'[38] Company and Crown officials could not but be heavily influenced by the institutions and ideas they tended to bring over from Britain with their cultural baggage. And yet the significant gaps and differences remained quite noticeable. Nor can British business interests ever be assumed to have been a uniform monolith bereft of internal fissures or shifts over time.

One obvious instance of a colonial difference was the long time lag in setting up a central bank for British India. The idea was occasional-ly mooted, even as early as the 1770s when Warren Hastings had made such a suggestion. But a central body functioning as government banker and banker to other banks, and regulating note issue and foreign exchange transactions, did not come into existence prior to the Reserve Bank of India, which was set up in 1935. In Britain, the highly prestigious Bank of England had been discharging such functions since 1696. But it was a purely private body, with considerable autonomy *vis-à-vis* the government. Neither the Company nor its post-1858 successor probably wanted to grant an umbrella bank such independence. The nearest equivalents, which, however, manifested far greater official involvement, were the three Presidency banks: Bank of Calcutta, 1806 (which, renamed the Bank of Bengal in 1809, remained the most important), Bank of Bombay (1840), and Bank of Madras (1843). All three were brought together to form the Imperial Bank in 1921, the predecessor of today's State Bank of India. In all three major centres of EIC authority, there was a simultaneous growth of private European banks, fostered primarily by the need felt by Company servants and the growing number of private traders alike to have secure channels for the remittance of profits to England. From this emerged the early-nineteenth-century agency houses, many of which set up banks or carried on banking functions themselves. This was a rickety structure, over-dependent for profits and remittances on indigo plantations and export. The interpenetration of manifold forms of commerce with private banking functions continued in more

---

[38] Bagchi 1987: 3.

effective ways after better organized European business firms and managing agencies replaced the older agency houses following the financial disasters of the early-1830s and late-1840s in Bengal.

Till the 1840s there was a fair degree of somewhat equal collaboration between Indians and Europeans in the working of the Presidency and other 'modern' banks in Calcutta, Bombay, and Madras. This fitted in with the general pattern of early-colonial business life. European banks and agency houses, quite often set up by adventurers who had come over with paltry initial funds, had to depend on Indian banians, dubashes, or guarantee-brokers for part of their working capital. The data unearthed by Bagchi from the records of the Bank of Bengal indicate even an apparent predominance of Indian over European. The former received from two-thirds to four-fifths of the loans that were advanced between 1809 and 1832. The figures are perhaps somewhat deceptive, since discounts on salary and private bills were excluded, and some of the Indians were agents of foreign firms. Nonetheless, they remain rather significant.

This early importance was reflected in the fairly crucial role played in the day-to-day functioning of the Bank of Bengal by the top Indian official, the khazanchee (cash keeper). Till the mid-1840s this was a prestigious post, though, characteristically, the incumbent's salary was much less than that of similarly placed British officials. The post was held between 1832 and 1844 by someone as prominent in Calcutta's elite literary life as Ramkamal Sen.[39] All this changed with the rapid decline of Indian enterprise in Calcutta after the collapse of the Union Bank in 1847. The Bank of Bengal came to have dealings almost entirely with European firms, and the khazanchee was relegated to lowly clerical functions.

---

[39] Among major borrowers from the Bank of Bengal in its early years were Rusomoy Dutt, an ancestor of R.C. Dutt, and Dwarkanath Tagore who in the 1830s and early 1840s became the leading Bengali entrepreneur. Ramkamal Sen was associated with the founding of Hindu College, had connections with the Asiatic Society, and was the grandfather of the Brahmo religious reformer Keshabchandra Sen. Ramkamal was involved in an acrimonious dispute with his British boss Udney in the Bank of Bengal, where he seems to have held his ground with dignity and some success: Bagchi 1987: 118–21, 239–44.

From the 1850s, the Presidency and other European banks occupied what amounted to an intermediate level in the overall modern banking structure. Above them rose the London-based exchange banks, financing the most decisive sectors of India's export–import trade and related operations. The agency houses, though not the Presidency banks, had had exchange dealings earlier, as had the Parsi magnate of Bombay Jamsetjee Jeejeebhoy. But by the second half of the century the domination in such matters of the London money market (the 'City', the equivalent of today's Wall Street) was complete. We must remember that even the British Indian government had little power over the London exchange banks, which combined far-flung international operations with freedom from the discipline which central banks in advanced capitalist countries were beginning to exercise over commercial banks within their territories. In effect, Bagchi suggests, foreign exchange banks operating in colonial countries were the 'true precursors of today's transnational banks'.[40]

Indian banks of the modern kind perforce had to occupy the lowest, and usually struggling, level of the late-colonial banking structure. Till the Company Act of 1850 (made more effective in 1857 through making registration compulsory), the domain of proper joint-stock enterprises was confined in India to the Presidency banks. A royal charter was needed for the vital privilege of shareholders to have only limited liability in case of insolvency. In effect, this hit Indian businessmen who ventured into the modern sector harder than Europeans, and made inter-racial collaboration, however profitable, always a risky proposition. British partners could always cut and run home, leaving their Indian counterparts with the entire burden of debt. This happened both in the 1830–4 agency house crisis set off by the collapse of Palmer & Co. in 1830, and with the fall of the Union Bank in 1847. But even after the recognition of limited liability in 1850, the progress of Indian joint-stock banking remained slow and marked by very sharp ups and downs. As with Indian business enterprises in general, the crucial financial decisions and channels of power had passed into tight, interlocked European control. There was spectacular growth,

[40] Bagchi 2003: 177.

with 25 flotations during the cotton boom of 1863–5, followed by precipitous decline. There were only 2 Indian joint stock banks in 1870, and the total rose slowly to 9 by 1900.

A fresh impetus came with the Swadeshi Movement, but that too ended with the collapse of Lala Harkishen Lal's Peoples Bank in 1913, which brought down with it no less than fifty-five Indian banks. As with Indian enterprise in general, a more stable growth in modern Indian banking became possible only in the qualitatively changed economic and political situation after the First World War. Failures continued numerous, but by 1936 the share of joint stock banks registered in India in total deposits had risen to 40 per cent, while the exchange banks' proportion had declined, notably after *c.* 1920, to 29 per cent. The Imperial Bank, however, remained by far the largest single unit, with 29 per cent of deposits. This remained a private, largely British-dominated concern, till it was nationalized and made into the State Bank of India in 1955.[41]

The colonial drive towards centralized governance and exploitation obviously demanded a uniform and stable medium of exchange across the country. This was not easy to achieve. Like pre-capitalist economies virtually everywhere, the Company had to begin with a situation of enormous variation in coinage systems in different regions, as well as a great diversity of currencies—gold (like the 'Madras pagoda'), silver, copper, as well as cowries (sea shells imported from the Maldives). The diversities were a source of considerable profit for shroffs, who charged commissions (batta) for every money-changing transaction. Initially, Company rule even added to the diversities, for the Presidency banks and some of the agency houses issued paper notes. These, however, proved affordable for only the richest of Indians, apart from European salary-earners and businessmen. The first major step towards uniformity came only in 1835, coincidentally the same year as the Macaulay Minute which established English as the medium for higher education. In this year, the silver rupee was declared legal tender for the whole country, with a 15:1 parity with gold coins, which were subsequently demonetized in 1853. There was initially a problem about the availability of sufficient silver. This

[41] Chandavarkar 1983: 779–82.

led to the institution of a centralized paper currency in 1862. Its control was taken over entirely by the government and this ended the Presidency banks' power to issue notes. The notes would have a metallic reserve, while the coinage of silver remained unrestricted for the public, entailing only a small fee.

India had thus been moved to a silver standard, precisely around the time when gold was displacing silver rapidly in the developed parts of the world: a situation of 'silver is for the East, Gold is for the West', as an anonymous 'Indian Official' would sum up the matter in 1878. What made the silver standard increasingly unstable, and eventually untenable, was the basic fact of a rapid decline of silver in terms of gold from the early 1870s as more and more countries in the West shifted from silver to gold, at a time when silver production from new mines was booming. The silver rupee, which could be exchanged for 2s in terms of the gold pound sterling, was worth only 1s 2d in 1892. Some of the consequences of this decline have been noted already, in connection with Home Charges and agricultural export prices: several other dimensions need to be mentioned now, in particular a series of internal tensions within British governing and business circles alike. Marcello de Cecco's careful analysis notes that British Indian monetary policy during these decades became subject to contradictory pulls from three directions. The British Indian government wanted to push up the exchange rate in favour of the rupee, and repeatedly suggested closing the mints to free silver coinage, as well as moving towards a gold standard. Its budgetary problems were made acute by the continually depreciating rupee. Army costs had grown on account of the military adventures of Lytton and subsequently Dufferin, while Lancashire continued to insist on the abolition of import duties on cotton manufactures. Government officials were also hit by the depreciation, for it reduced their pensions in terms of sterling. But expatriate British business interests pulled the other way very strongly, as exports of agricultural products boomed, despite the worldwide depression, due to the falling silver rupee. The India Office in London had to mediate between these opposite pressures. On the whole, for two decades business interests won out over Indian officialdom, probably because both the Home Government as a whole and the City thought that maintaining the Indian export surplus was vital to the entire structure of British balance of payments. The reasons for this have been explained earlier.[42]

By the 1890s, however, the pressures on Government of India finances had become acute enough to necessitate a change in policy. In 1893, mints were closed to private silver coinage, and official coinage was also reduced, forcing up the rupee–sterling exchange to 1s 4d by 1898. A compromise 'gold exchange standard' functioned from 1898–9, under which the rupee, still in silver, would be backed by a Gold Standard Reserve. In the context of the disruption of world gold supplies due to the Boer War, the latter, so far held mainly in India, was shifted to London in 1902 and was invested in British government securities: a move, de Cecco emphasizes, that signalled the tightening of London control over Indian financial policy management. But the vicissitudes of the Indian rupee did not end with this. Indeed, they entered a more acute phase of crisis and debate in the 1920s and 1930s.[43]

European and Indian Entrepreneurship: Regional Variations

In our survey of business life so far, continuities have on the whole outweighed change. The focus has been on a countrywide vertical

[42] Certain interesting anomalies may be briefly mentioned here, as another reminder that neither 'British' nor 'Indian' interests were homogeneous, and that occasional cross-cutting affinities were possible. We have already mentioned that Indian nationalist opinion on the whole seems to have been happy with the falling exchange, even though it was obviously enhancing the burden of their bête noir, the Home Charges. They took surprisingly little interest in the whole currency issue in this period, in very sharp contrast to what would happen in the 1920s, as we shall see. This was also a matter where the particular interests of 'Manchester' did *not* determine British policy, for the depreciating rupee in effect afforded an indirect protection to the rising Indian-owned textile mills of Bombay. City finance, in combination with expatriate business pressure and imperial considerations as a whole (maintaining British balance of payments) proved more powerful, presaging a pattern that would become increasingly prominent in the twentieth century.

[43] The account of currency policy in the preceding two paragraphs is based on de Cecco 2003: 223–44. This is an extract from de Cecco 1974. See also Chandavarkar 1983.

hierarchy, with British firms controlling the commanding heights but Indian merchant groups still playing vital and, indeed, indispensable roles. The late-colonial era, however, saw fundamental innovations. These were manifest in the development of a distinctly modern sector that ran on firmly capitalist lines: plantations, mines, and big factories operated by steam or electrical power. The striking fact, however, was a significant, and in many ways growing, lag or backwardness in the levels of industrialization. The Indian economy had been closely tied to that of the country that had pioneered industrialization. But in relation to India the British displayed little or no interest in investing in cotton textiles, steel, or engineering—precisely the areas in which they led the world till late in the nineteenth century. They chose to concentrate, instead, on tea plantations, coal mines, and jute mills. The colonial era would end with an India that was still without a heavy engineering, chemicals, or machine-tools industry. The railways ran on imported engines, and even textiles were dependent on imports of its mill machinery. Backwardness was accompanied by British predominance in the bulk of the modern enterprises that did emerge: an imbalance which was probably more striking than that manifested in internal commerce and finance. The third crucial feature was a regional distinction: British enterprise was overwhelmingly preponderant in and around Calcutta, eastern India in general, as well as in the much less industrially developed North and South. But in Bombay and Ahmedabad, Indian cotton manufacturers were clearly dominant, and British–Indian relations were significantly less unequal.

Discussions about industrial development in colonial India long remained focussed on the possible explanations of the evident lag. A debate raged between internal and external stresses. Indian failure was attributed to general features like allegedly immutable caste occupations, and/or an otherworldly outlook on life in general. Parsis, so prominent among the pioneers of industrialization in Bombay, were thought to be the exception proving the rule, for a reasonable case could be made out for something like a 'Protestant ethic' to explain their success. The Bombay/Calcutta contrast regarding Indian success or failure could then be interpreted in terms of deficiencies among the Bengali middle-class bhadralok, their supposed aversion to risk-taking business activity, and their preference for safe rentier incomes. There were some more materialist variants of such cultural interpretations, made popular by Max Weber: the permanent zamindari settlement introduced in eastern India by Cornwallis diverted capital from trade or industry to land, for instance, in contrast to raiyatwari forms elsewhere, inhibiting such investments; or the presence of higher and easier profit rates in commerce, finance, or usury as compared to industrial returns. The alternative nationalist approach predictably sought to shift the blame squarely in the direction of colonial policies. It highlighted numerous discriminatory practices, most commonly an unfair tariff structure which for long debarred the infant indigenous cotton textile industry from any protective duties and imposed a free trade regime which was of evident benefit to Lancashire's textiles. The point seemed clinched when in 1896 an import duty on cotton goods imports, necessitated by the sorry state of British Indian revenues, was sought to be counterbalanced by a countervailing excise on Indian textile production. The argument is strong, but, as we have seen with regard to the drain of wealth discourse, it is limited to specific policies, as distinct from any deeper and detailed exploration of structures.

Amiya Bagchi offered an elegant alternative model that rebutted the culturalist and internalist arguments, while simultaneously deepening and extending the nationalist critique.[44] Otherworldliness or caste had long been discredited as explanations for backwardness, since they were, at best, over-generalizations grounded in Orientalist stereotypes. They took no account of the data concerning considerable flexibility in caste occupations over time, revealed, for instance, by census returns. The nineteenth-century Bengali bhadralok repeatedly urged the need for business enterprise, and numerous abortive efforts were in fact made in that direction in the late-nineteenth and early-twentieth century, though with little success.[45] The Brahmos

[44] Bagchi 1972.

[45] This failure contrasted sharply with the prominence of figures like Dwarkanath Tagore in the early nineteenth century, who were fully the equals, if not more, of the European entrepreneurs of their time. Dwarkanath's grandson Jyotirindranath's efforts in the same direction, however, could be no more than pathetic, serio-comic failures, as his younger brother Rabindranath affectionately recalled in his *Jivan-smriti*. The difference clearly related to the much greater weight by then of the British economic presence in Bengal, for

were probably as 'modernist' and 'Protestant' as the Parsis, while the business communities that eventually came to dominate Indian capitalism, notably the Marwaris, were quite traditional in their values. The consequences on the ground of the zamindari and raiyatwari settlements were, as we have seen, not too different, as both came to be characterized by considerable absentee landholding. As for the greater profitability of trade, British firms effectively straddled the worlds of commerce, finance, and industrial enterprise alike.

Bagchi opted for a simpler and more 'tangible' explanation, in terms of the sheer weight of British economic and political presence that combined with strong elements of racial solidarity-cum-discrimination. This was much more evident and had a longer existence in eastern as compared to western India. In so far as industrial development was geared primarily to exports, British control over exchange banks and shipping lines was a marked advantage that became clear from the mid-nineteenth century. Giant firms like Peninsular & Oriental (P&O) and British Indian Steam Navigation organized 'conferences' to exclude competitors through rate wars. These came to be interlocked with the higher reaches of the world of banking, also British-dominated, and British railway companies and managing agencies. Interlocking, between British business interests as well as between businessmen and government officials, followed both formal and informal channels, for at whites-only clubs such people would meet and strike deals tilted against potential Indian competitors. As late as 1944, an organization of Indian manufacturers complained of a competition 'on more than equal terms' in which Europeans procure 'from the mystic bond of racial affinity with the rulers of the land . . . invisible, but not the less effective, advantage . . .'[46] The purchases of and patronage to civil engineering by government and military stores were heavily oriented towards imports, in other words European firms, till things began to change a little from the early twentieth century. The possibility of a major European war began to make wholesale reliance on expatriate

---

it was European competition that ruined Jyotirindranath's abortive shipping and other ventures.

[46] All India Manufacturers Association, November 1944, cited in Bagchi 1972: 166.

connections less advisable. This was, incidentally, one reason why Curzon decided to support the Tata effort to start India's first successful steel mill—in what became Jamshedpur—in the early years of the twentieth century. Curzon even ordered a railway line of fifty-five miles to help the supply of iron ore; also, at this point Belgian imports of steel had become a threat to British interests.

Bagchi thus extended the interpretive frame much beyond the old nationalist emphasis on specific, reversible policies such as tariffs and rupee–sterling exchange rates. He worked out a structural dimension. The tilt in favour of British interests operated countrywide. But critical to Bagchi's argument, and central particularly to the proof he suggested for it, was also the eastern/western and Calcutta/Bombay contrast. British rule came much earlier to Bengal and was more total there in the sense that few significant princely states survived in that region, this being in sharp contrast with western India. Calcutta became and remained the heart of British enterprise in India and indeed, in some ways, in the entire East for the British dominated tea plantations, coal and other mines, and jute mills. There was a remarkable degree of European interlocking of interests and oligopolistic control, manifest above all in the ramifications of the managing agencies. Around 1916, for instance, Jardine & Skinner were managing 8 tea, 3 coal, 2 jute, 1 timber, and 1 trading company. The same organization also served as agents to several insurance companies, ran shipping lines in collaboration with British India Steam Navigation, imported Manchester piecegoods, and exported jute goods and tea. In 1911, 7 managing agencies (Andrew Yule, Bird, Begg-Dunlop, Shaw Wallace, Williamson-Magor, Duncan, Octavius Steel) controlled 55 per cent of the jute, 61 per cent of the tea, and 46 per cent of the coal companies. The control of the managing agencies extended to the supply of labour: Bird, for instance, had started as labour contractors for the East Indian Railways.[47] The racial predominance of white men was clear from the fact that there were virtually no Indian members in the Bengal Chamber of Commerce prior to 1914.

British control was almost as tight over the much less industrially developed North and South of the country. The first centre of factory

[47] Bagchi 1972: 163, 176, *et passim*.

industry in the United Provinces, Cawnpore (Kanpur), grew with the supply of harness and saddlery, boots, and woollen and cotton cloth for the British Indian army—for all of which British businessmen were invariably preferred. The small number of coffee plantations and cotton mills in Madras Presidency were likewise controlled by British managing agency firms, notably Binny and Parry.

The Bombay Presidency presented a very different picture. Major cotton textile centres emerged in Bombay city, followed shortly afterwards by Ahmedabad from the 1850s, owned mostly by Parsi and Gujarati businessmen. The Maratha presence had delayed the establishment of full British political authority in western India for a couple of generations after Plassey, and large chunks of territory had to be left even afterwards to princely states. These were, no doubt, dependent ultimately on Company or Crown, but they still constituted some sort of hindrance at times to a complete uniformity of control. The delay enabled the development of a significant Indian presence in business life: in shipbuilding for a while, then in opium dealing with China, and cotton traders. Much of the opium was grown in the princely states, where Indians had a little more say in political and economic matters than in formally British territory. Not that discrimination was not also evident here: Marika Vicziany, for instance, has argued that the turn by Indians to cotton manufactures had a significant connection with their progressive ouster from the world of overseas commerce and shipping by the 1860s, when British shipping monopolies tightened controls. In 1893 an effort by the Tatas to break into the British monopoly of overseas steam navigation, in collaboration with a Japanese rival to the latter, was foiled by a ruthless rate war waged by P&O, which at one stage even offered to transport cotton free to Japan.

But the British had little interest in starting cotton mills in Bombay: a curious anomaly in strictly economic terms which Amartya Sen tried to explain in terms of a predominant 'social ethos' in Britain through which Lancashire was widely recognized not just as a major pressure group but as a national cause.[48] The same inhibition did not operate

[48] In his budget speech of 28 March 1877, for instance, John Strachey declared that 'The interests of Manchester, at which foolish people sneer, are the

in jute mills, even though Dundee already had a jute industry: this was not a national cause in the same way, and in any case the Scots quickly came to occupy a very prominent position in the ownership and management of the Bengal mills. Indian prominence in the premier modern industry of western India came to be reflected via a significant presence within the Bombay Chamber of Commerce, as well as through considerable collaboration in business and other matters between European and, particularly, Parsi businessmen.

How far, then, was there a fundamental conflict between Indian and British capitalist interests in late-colonial India, of the kind often assumed in nationalist and much Left nationalist and Marxist writing? Bagchi helps to complicate such assumptions through a formula of short-term collaboration and long-term conflict. Till the early twentieth century, and indeed in some ways prior to about 1919, there was really little hard economic reason that could push Bombay mill-owners to anti-British nationalism, even though there were specific issues of dissension such as low-duty or duty-free Lancashire piecegoods imports and the countervailing excise. Bombay in the late nineteenth century concentrated on manufacturing low- or medium-count grades of yarn for the domestic handloom weavers' market. It also opened up a flourishing market for these in China. Lancashire imports, in contrast, consisted of the finer kinds of yarn as well as cotton piecegoods: lines of manufacture into which Bombay did not and often could not enter. In addition, there was a substantial minority of European capitalists in the Bombay industry and the Bombay Millowners Association; many managers of the Indian-owned mills were Europeans, and the entire industry remained totally dependent on Britain for its machinery.

Ahmedabad did go somewhat more into cotton cloth, and from around 1905 things began to change even for Bombay. The China yarn market came to be flooded by Japanese mills, making a move towards home consumers advisable for them. This was bound ultimately to intensify competition and sharpen the conflict with Lancashire. It was only after the First World War, and even then primarily in

---

interests . . . of millions of Englishmen': cited in Sen 1992: 109–26. See Ray 1992: Introduction, for an excellent overview of the entire subject.

Ahmedabad, that sections of Indian capitalists felt it both beneficial and advisable to extend strong support to Indian nationalism. In the late nineteenth century the traditional business communities had retreated into their bazaar domain, carrying on the compradore activity of supplying European business houses with raw materials and distributing their imports. By contrast, after the First War they began to enter and succeed within the world of modern capitalist industry—and in a big way. As for the Tatas, the importance and availability of state support—indispensable for their steel production (the railways provided the main market)—ensured a generally loyalist stance right down to 1947.

One might even speculate, keeping in mind the immense internal variations among different groups of emergent Indian capitalists, whether Amiya Bagchi's formulation should not be reversed for many sectors to emphasize, rather, the collaborative element. As we shall see, in so far as Indian capitalists were visibly becoming aware of collective class interests, this was more often directed not against the British but their own workers. Police and state help would soon become indispensable in face of growing labour solidarity and militancy in the early twentieth century. The assumption of the coming into being of a self-conscious, unified 'national bourgeoisie' is then not really very helpful. Even in the countries of classic bourgeois revolution, England and France, research increasingly indicates that groups clearly identifiable as bourgeois had been remarkably thin on the ground at moments of militant political action. There seems little reason to assume, a priori, that the Indian case was much different.[49]

Deindustrialization and the Traditional Industries

Along with the drain of wealth, the charge of deindustrialization was, as we have seen, frequently flung at colonial rule: the idea that British domination deliberately shattered the traditional and world-famous handicrafts of India, the handspun and hand-woven yarn and cloth in which India had led the world for many centuries. This

[49] See particularly the 'revisionist' attack on the orthodox Marxist readings of the French Revolution associated with Alfred Cobban and François Furet, which certainly dominate the historiographical field at present. For a helpful, if controversial overview, see Comninel 1987.

view, we have equally seen, was central to the thought of nationalist and many Marxist critiques of British rule. Its exponents ranged from Marx, whose much-quoted remarks were about Manchester imports uprooting a village self-sufficiency based on the 'union' of agriculture and handicrafts; through Naoroji, who asserted the notion of decline through a parade of export–import statistics; down to Gandhi, whose call for Ram Rajya was based on reviving the spinning wheel. And yet the subject remains controversial, indeed peculiarly difficult to clinch in either direction. With regard to the decisive decades—starting with the opening of Indian markets to Lancashire from 1813 down to the third quarter of the nineteenth century—all-India statistics are simply not available. Reliable census data were compiled only from 1881.

The only hard figures Naoroji could offer were trade returns. These were damaging enough, for they indicate plummeting cotton and silk cloth exports, and rapidly rising yarn and piecegoods imports as secular trends from the second decade of the nineteenth century. In addition, Naoroji could point to numerous instances of grossly unfair British tariff policies of 'one-way free trade', protective duties against Indian manufactures and very low or non-existent import duties in relation to British goods. On this basis he asserted that a 'natural' and inevitable decline of handicrafts confronting machinery was not what had happened, but instead that the decline was in significant part the result of deliberate policies which a hypothetically independent India could have prevented or at least reduced. What remained uncertain, however, was the possibility of an expansion of internal demand for cloth or other commodities, which theoretically could have been sufficient to cover the losses incurred by the collapse of exports (unlikely ever to have been more than a small part of the aggregate consumption) as well as the loss of a part of the home market to British goods. There was quite a lot of scattered data about the ruin of a number of famous centres of artisanal production—the internationally reputed cottons and silks of Dacca and Murshidabad, for instance—and an evident decline in courtly demand. There are ample references, many of them in British sources, to the retreat of a large number of Indian handicrafts before foreign competition.

But there is still sufficient room for debate, for such a large country, about the overall macro-economic trends. The impressionistic case for decline was strongest for cotton spinning, once the occupation for large numbers of village women, particularly widows. The charkha, Gandhi wrote in his autobiography, had become virtually unknown in Gujarat's villages when he launched his campaign for its revival, and the differential impact on women's employment probably deserves greater attention than paid to it so far. Yet, from the vantage point of the twentieth century, it was also indisputable that artisanal occupations, most notably handlooms, had far from vanished, and were in some cases even expanding.

For many years there did appear to be one bit of macro-economic proof of deindustrialization. Census statistics for variations in occupational figures between 1881 and 1931 seemed to indicate a substantial rise (+28.5 per cent) in the number of workers in agriculture, and a decline in those employed in manufacture (-8.2 per cent). However, in a closely-argued essay of 1960—which inaugurated the more recent debates over the issue—Daniel and Alice Thorner, themselves lifelong critics of imperialism who had no quarrel at all with the general view that India's traditional handicrafts had declined from their pristine glory—pointed out that the statistics, looked at more carefully, could not bear the burden that had been imposed on them.[50] The key problem, as in all pre-industrial societies, was the coexistence of different kinds of occupations—agriculture, handicrafts, trade—within many households. This made for uncertainties and the adoption of shifting definitions of terms in census classification over time. Another essay by the Thorners about agrarian categories was aptly termed 'Agrarian Revolution by Census Classification'. They pointed out that many census reports contained a residual category termed 'general labour', which fluctuated wildly over different census enumerations and varied inversely with the percentages of those returned as employed in agriculture. Statistics for female labour were also extremely uncertain. Their analysis of the data seemed to indicate a rough stability in proportions over the half century. But then, as they pointed out, this was no evidence either way of what may have happened in earlier, pre-census decades.

The controversy attained a previously unknown level of acrimony in the late 1960s when a somewhat provocative essay by Morris David Morris rejected deindustrialization and claimed a significant economic

[50] Thorner and Thorner 1962: 70–81.

advance under colonial rule in the nineteenth century. Cheap factory yarn may have adversely affected cotton spinning, but Morris argued that it simultaneously benefited Indian weavers by reducing their costs. Lower prices, he postulated, enhanced demand—a move down the demand curve—while there was also 'a shift to the right of the demand curve' due to 'changes in custom' (tribals moving from jute to cotton cloth, women learning to cover their breasts). So British textile imports may have 'at worst . . . skimmed off the expanding demand' without harming Indian handloom weaving. Similar arguments could be suggested for other crafts that had figured in the nationalist narrative of decline.

Among the many rejoinders to Morris, the most effective was one made by Toru Matsui. He pointed out that the nineteenth-century fall in cloth prices had two components—related to yarn, and to woven cloth. Both were revolutionized by the new technologies. Indian handloom weavers could have benefited only from the first, not the second, for there seemed to be no indication of improved technology or organization in traditional crafts.[51] The crafts, therefore, still faced major problems in competing with both Lancashire and, increasingly, Indian mill cloth. Matsui questioned Morris' argument of a sufficiently large expansion of Indian demand: demand rose because prices fell, not vice versa, so there was no indication of a really massive autonomous surge in demand even in Morris' framework. Matsui, along with other critics, went on to point out that Morris' arguments remained entirely hypothetical, with no firm statistical backing whatsoever, and the debate had not been advanced much by his intervention.[52]

Matsui suggested a disaggregation of the discussion in terms of specific areas, since the obvious variations across regions and times would probably preclude any conclusive resolution of the debate on an all-Indian plane. A decade after the Morris controversy, Bagchi attempted such a specific study, aiming to clinch the more general

[51] We shall see, though, that Tirthankar Roy has since argued an opposite case on this point: Roy 2000a, discussed below.

[52] Morris 1968: 1–15; the rejoinders by Toru Matsui and several leading Indian historians (notably Tapan Raychaudhuri and Bipan Chandra) were brought together in the *Indian Economic and Social History Review*, 5 (1), 1968.

question. He returned to the attempt to test deindustrialization by the proportion of people engaged in, and/or dependent on, industry, in relation to the total population—which had been common before the intervention of the Thorners. He sought to compare the data collected by Buchanan over 1809–13 from four north Bihar districts with the 1901 census figures for occupations in the same region. His findings did seem to indicate a significant decline in the number of people dependent on rural or small-town industrial employment, most notably in cotton spinning and weaving. Depending on the alternative criteria of average family size which he adopted, the percentage of population dependent on industry had apparently gone down from 14.2 per cent to 20.2 per cent in 1809–13, and from 5.5 per cent to 11.6 per cent in 1901. Once again, this provoked an acrimonious controversy. Marika Vicziany questioned the reliability of Buchanan's estimates and reminded Bagchi of Thorner's warning about the mixed nature of primary/secondary/tertiary occupations in traditional households. Bagchi vigorously defended his position and suggested that the pre-modern absence of differentiation was, perhaps, exaggerated: weavers in many areas do seem to have been specialized artisans not pursuing other occupations. Like numerous similar debates, in the end the controversy generated more heat than light.[53]

The latest entrant in this long series of arguments has been Tirthankar Roy.[54] While brushing aside the Morris arguments, Roy argued, on the basis of his considerable and impressive research on textiles and other small industries, that most indigenous manufactures (above all, cotton cloth), and imports of similar but not identical commodities, related to 'segmented markets': so, handlooms could survive and even advance despite Lancashire piecegoods. The tone of his argument was often unnecessarily aggressive, and his evident admiration for the dubious values of liberalization and globalization seemed intended to provoke. Nor could Roy, any more than the others, suggest any way of testing what might have happened in the pre-census era. In that sense, his argument hardly demolished the whole concept

[53] Bagchi 1978. For the subsequent controversy with Vicziany, see Vicziany 1979: 105–43.
[54] Roy 2000a: 1442–7.

of deindustrialization. That said, his research on small industries is innovative and impressive, and it would be a pity if his polemical zeal were to encourage dismissals of his perspective.

A Vexed Question: Did Handicrafts Decline?

Till the early 1990s historical discussion about handicrafts—reports and occasional studies of particular small industries apart—had concentrated overwhelmingly on their decline or the reverse. Handicrafts, in other words, were implicitly taken as a kind of residue, without internal change in technology or organization. Their study related almost entirely to the question of European competition. Lines of interpretation that were not interested in the deindustrialization debate could simply pass them by, as was largely the case with the *Cambridge Economic History of India* edited by Dharma Kumar. Since then, historical perspectives have been transformed as attention has come to be focussed upon the possibility of changes within traditional small-scale industries. This may help to explain the survival of many of these into the twentieth century: even a fairly significant growth, after a possible period of decline.

About that survival, and slow growth, there is really little dis- agreement, as indicated by the data put forward by the two pre-eminent economic historians, Tirthankar Roy and Amiya Bagchi—ideo- logically poles apart—whose views we have discussed in some detail. Roy's estimate of relative shares in total cotton cloth output, based on Bombay Millowners' Association Reports, found handlooms still ahead of mill production in 1905–9. But both were far behind imported textiles (51.8 per cent). From the First World War on, Indian mills forged ahead, and by 1930–4 they had gone up to 51.5 per cent, with handlooms 31.7 per cent and imports a poor third at 16.8 per cent. The share of handlooms, it should be noted, did not go down, for both had expanded at the cost of imports. Bagchi's statistics, derived from the *Fact-finding Committee (Handlooms and Mills)*, 1942, and a series of Tariff Board reports, indicate a broadly similar pattern.[55]

The most striking work on this novel theme of 'the strategies and consequences of survival' of handicrafts has been by Tirthankar Roy,

[55] Roy 1993: 28; Bagchi 1972: 226–7.

and consequently it deserves to be discussed in detail.[56] As remarked earlier, there is in Roy's debunking of the idea of deindustrialization a celebratory note which plays down industry's exploitative aspects and largely ignores the possibility that both survival and growth may have been related to worsening conditions among many producers.[57] Roy's assumptions and framework are not shared by many scholars who otherwise work on similar lines. The shift in attention towards the potential dynamism of small industries is also part of a historiographical trend that had manifested itself in the classic lands of capitalist industrialization, including Britain: here too artisanal production seems to have been far more significant, and persistent for a much longer time, than had been noticed earlier. The fascination and horror inspired by the Industrial Revolution—or, in Marx, the hope that workers massed in big factories would become the grave-diggers of capitalism—may to an extent have distorted the perspective.[58] Current trends have evidently been stimulated by the contemporary tendencies towards post-Fordist 'flexible accumulation', when big factories are going out of vogue in many parts of the world. Contrary to both classical economic and orthodox Marxist teleologies, the phase of large factories now appears to be contingent rather than the inevitable and highest product of capitalism.

As earlier, studies of cotton textiles have been central to the new revisionism. Roy's analysis begins with drawing attention to a 'virtually endless scope for differentiating . . . in textiles.' These distinctions enable the coexistence of decline in some sectors and regions with survival and growth in others, and operate in relation to two variables: types of products, and kinds of weaving processes and production relations.

Lancashire competition in the late-nineteenth and early-twentieth

[56] Roy 1996: Introduction, 13.

[57] Two instances: 'stricter control on work processes'; greater weight of 'controllers of capital and information': see Roy 1993: 3.

[58] Sabel and Zeitlin 1985: 133–76; Berg 1985. It might be noted, though, that artisans had figured much more prominently than Lancashire factory workers even in E.P. Thompson's classic study of the growth of labour class consciousness: Thompson 1963. And the Communards of Paris of 1871, whom Marx hailed, had not been employed, in the main, in factories.

century was mainly in 'coarse-medium' textiles, woven from yarn of 20–26 counts. Indian mills initially concentrated on spinning yarn and coarser cloth for both the home market and exports to China and Japan. Then they gradually superseded British imports in the coarse-medium category. Handlooms operated in relation to demand below, and above, these levels. Rural weavers could have an advantage with village consumers on account of the cheap and durable cloth they made, but theirs remained a stagnant or declining occupation. Weavers of this kind were regularly mentioned in official reports as among the principal victims of famines. Roy's recent research, and that of others, however, indicates that urban weavers in some parts of the country came to represent a very different type. They successfully adjusted to foreign competition by concentrating on fine cottons and silks, on multicoloured and bordered textile products and finished garments, rather than on piecegoods that had to be stitched after purchase.

The second distinction, therefore, relates to the types of weavers and their differential distribution. To understand this we need to go back to pre-colonial times. Bengal—and eastern India generally—was marked by the location of relatively immobile weavers within village society, apart from a string of towns in what is now eastern Uttar Pradesh, and some famous centres like Dacca and Murshidabad which were connected to court demand—which declined rapidly in the early-colonial era. This region was hit earliest and hardest by post-1757 Company monopoly control, followed by Manchester imports, and here even Roy has little quarrel with a theory of decline. The products tended to be somewhat less developed kinds. Colour, for instance, was less prominent than in the South. This, Roy suggests, was a weaver situation defined by tight merchant-usurer control over relatively stagnant village artisan production. Many parts of southern and western India, however, presented a very different picture both in the twentieth century and, probably, going back to pre-colonial times. The weavers, or at least the more prosperous among them, were located more in towns, and their own traditions, as well as other data, indicate a quite remarkable mobility. Weaver migration, Roy and Douglas Haynes have argued, happened in response to shifting court and/or temple demands in pre-colonial times, while from the nineteenth century it often became an effective strategy for countering foreign competition. Thus, a weaver community calling themselves Sourashtras, today based mainly in Madurai, claim in their legends to have moved from the Gujarat–Maharashtra region (allegedly after the fall of Somnath) to Devagiri, and then to the Vijayanagar capital of Hampi, before arriving at their present location. Migration in more recent times has often been to small towns that sprang up or persisted near the big industrial cities. Housing costs would have been lower there, while the other advantages of quasi-urban locations would have remained the same. Thus, the Padmasali have moved from Telangana, with its highly oppressive nizam rule, to small towns in western Maharashtra. Considerable numbers of Muslim weavers (Momins, Ansaris, Jolahas) from eastern UP moved to similar towns north and north-east of Bombay. By 1940, coastal Andhra, south Andhra, and Tamilnadu had 15, 10, and 25 weaving towns respectively, while in 1982 the four southern states had 42 per cent of all looms in India.[59]

But the broad regional distinction has also gone along with differentiation within particular areas. Poverty-stricken Bengal village weavers and central Indian Mahar weavers of coarse cloth were, for example, often forced to combine their traditional occupations with agricultural or casual labour. So did the skilled artisans of the Kanpur–Banaras–Mau belt, or, even more, the developed karkhanas of centres like Sholapur, Nagpur, and Salem. Differentiation among artisans, Roy suggests, has been most marked in the South and the West. Here, alongside the control exercised over many producers by merchants, there also developed the phenomenon of some small producers who rose 'from below' to become manufacturers and merchants: what Marx characterized as the 'really revolutionary road' to capitalism. Correspondingly, other weavers became dependent, virtually wage labourers.

'Traditional' handlooms, Roy goes on to emphasize, have also been quite capable of modernizing their technologies, moving to fly-shuttle looms and, as electricity availability improved in small towns from around the 1920s, to power-looms. He stresses the connections between these shifts and the rise of small weaving masters

[59] Haynes and Roy 1999: 35–67.

who became manufacturers. The other kind of development in more recent times—the way owners of big mills have increasingly turned to small production units or domestic putting-out forms—reverses long-standing assumptions about the normal pattern of transition to full-scale capitalism. Roy does not overly attend to this pattern; one is tempted to suggest that evidence of the human costs of such contemporary 'deindustrialization' in the inner cities of major industrial centres like Bombay, Ahmedabad, and Kanpur would have been difficult to accommodate within his overall view of the subject.[60]

Roy's more recent research has unearthed an impressive amount of data about other traditional small industries which also managed to survive through adaptations often associated with a move towards towns. He does not discuss other crafts, like spinning, pottery, and iron-smelting, which almost certainly declined. Thus, brassware survived because of high transport costs that blocked foreign competition, while enhanced commercialization led to its concentration in some urban centres, as in today's Moradabad. Leather is another striking instance of progress. Chamars (Jatavs) began to shift in a big way towards cities like Kanpur. India developed a flourishing export trade and became, by the 1890s, the biggest world exporter of tanned hides, even as European boots and shoe imports went on expanding.[61] This was probably associated with the emergence of an upwardly mobile stratum among this section of Dalits who, in the twentieth century, were prominent in a series of struggles for empowerment: the Ad Dharm of interwar Punjab, Ambedkarites, the Bahujan Samaj party of recent years.

As noted, the centrally troubling feature of Roy's work has been a near refusal to acknowledge that survival, even growth, could often be related to the immiserization of substantial numbers of artisans. Roy may have realized, even if belatedly, that immiserization is inescapable as an issue in this broad area of research: his work on labour in small

---

[60] See, for instance, Roy 2001, which explicitly omits discussion of the 'modern' small industries constituted in large part by the process just mentioned.

[61] Roy 1999.

industries moves a little in the direction of such a recognition. It indicates how the undoubted growth of carpet manufacturing in response to international demand went along with a transition from the somewhat intimate relationship between traditional skilled masters and apprentices (ustad–shagird), to more impersonal and openly oppressive wage-labour relationships with the growth of big karkhanas in North Indian cities like Amritsar, Agra, and Srinagar during the interwar years. Child labour, in particular, became a scandal by the 1930s. It remained confined to big units in the post-Independence years because restrictions on child labour were enhanced, and also because North Indian urban centres declined because of large-scale migrations of Muslim weavers after 1947. But problems of this nature persisted with the reincarnation of small units in eastern Uttar Pradesh. One of Roy's papers, about continuity and change in the production of wool, vividly describes the ways in which a gradual shift has taken place from migrant pastoral communities which combined the keeping of herds, weaving, and trade, towards separating these occupations alongside the growth of an urban woollen garments industry. Environmental dimensions are skilfully woven into the narrative. Roy relates the evident decline of shepherds to the growing pressures on grazing lands as forest laws began to restrict access, and as the spread of settled agriculture and tighter notions of private property reduced the availability of such 'wastes'.[62]

But exploitation and conflict have been highlighted much more, and within more suggestive frameworks, by several other historians, sometimes equally 'revisionist' in their approaches even if not disagreeing with Roy's basic thesis of the survival and adaptive capacities of small industries. The additional element in the work of such historians is an emphasis on conflictual relations within crafts, an aspect largely missing in Roy despite his focus on internal changes. Two instances must suffice for present purposes. The first relates to the early-colonial era, but indicates some processes which continued in different forms into later times. A number of studies of the late eighteenth century have highlighted a deterioration in artisanal conditions because of changes in artisans' relations with merchants. The Company, through

---

[62] Roy 2003: 257–86.

its combination of state power and monopoly over purchases, was able to drastically curtail their bargaining power *vis-à-vis* merchants. Earlier, there was little impediment to weavers taking advances from a particular trading group and then repaying the debt by selling to another at a higher price. There were dramatic instances of weaver protests in the Carnatic against what Arasaratnam has defined as a transition from 'price worker' to 'wage worker'. In addition, Prasanna Parthasarathi's study of eighteenth-century South India has highlighted the part played by rigorous notions of contract imported from Britain, which vastly strengthened the position not just of the Company but also of Indian merchants. This led to a corresponding decline in the income, status, and conditions of artisans, which, Parthasarathi suggests, was the principal reason why indigenous merchants in many parts of the country collaborated actively with the British.[63]

In an essay that attempts a longue durée study of Surat weavers and jari producers, Douglas Haynes blends Roy's emphasis on the dynamism of small manufacturers with what amounts to a recuperation of a Marxian focus on class relations and conflict. Attention should shift, he suggests, from the question of artisanal survival in the face of imports, towards 'considering the nature of their relations with dominant Indian classes.' Surat weaving and jari concerns moved from a preponderance of small units towards larger workshops during the interwar and immediate post-war years. Then they shifted back again to scattered sites of production. The shift was dictated not so much by technological changes but by the logic of class tensions. A rough balance between employers and artisans had characterized the decades before Independence. Most weavers came from nearby places and were united by caste ties, both among themselves and with

---

[63] The theme of the subordination of artisans through the Company blending of monopoly trade with state power had been already explored by N.K. Sinha and Hameeda Khan for Bengal, and S. Arasaratnam for Madras. Parthasarathi's particular combination is this conjoining of Indian with British legal history, pointing out that the subordination of labourers which had begun in England from the fourteenth century was being speeded up, precisely at the time when Company rule was expanding in India, through erosion of customary rights via redefining laws of property and criminality. Sinha 1967; Arasaratnam 1996: 85–114; Parthasarathi 2001.

many of their employers. This reduced conflict, despite the atrocious working conditions. The situation began to change after 1947: the hopes of labourers soared, fuelled by the promise of more progressive labour laws. The Congress, and then the Socialists, led major strikes in jari and art silk manufactories between 1947 and the early 1950s. The employers, however, hit back effectively with a return to loose, decentralized manufactures, as well as by higher recruitment from migrants who did not enjoy caste and regional unities. This was an early manifestation of the pattern that has marked so much recent labour history, in India and elsewhere. The centrality of shifting relations between the worlds of formal and informal, urban and footloose, labour will be foregrounded again during our discussion of capital and labour in 'modern' enterprises.

Capital and Labour: Plantations, Mines, and Factories

The railways apart, factory chimneys soaring above congested industrial cities became the most obvious embodiments of change in late-colonial India, signs of modernity to admirers and critics alike. The indisputable novelty of machines—running on steam or electricity and owned by capitalist industrialists who employed a factory proletariat—led to the conceptualizing of industrial and labour history in terms of a series of dichotomies. The dualisms consisted in stark contrasts of rural with urban; feudal, traditional, or pre-modern with modern capitalist; traders with industrialists; small artisanal manufactures with big factories; and casual or migrant labourers with a stable urbanized industrial workforce. In an associated polarity, the workplace was contrasted with the neighbourhood where workers lived. The latter was often seen as the location where retrogressive ties of caste, kinship, religious community, and village were reproduced, all of which blocked the full flowering of a committed labour force— a scenario regretted by managers and management-oriented scholars; or of a truly revolutionary proletariat, this absence being bemoaned by labour organizers and Marxists. The dichotomies found their clearest manifestation in law. A series of Factory Acts starting from 1881 made a pervasive disjunction between the 'formal' and 'informal' sectors of industry and labour.[64] The first would be progressively subjected to state regulations which fixed working hours and minimum wages, and provided for a degree of welfare facilities; the second was almost entirely unregulated. The legal distinction was based on a combination of size of production unit and use or non-use of mechanical power. The informal or 'unorganized' sector has always remained very much the dominant form of labour. Nonetheless, the formal sector has, until recently, been the site of most labour organization as well as for research on industrial and labour history. The reasons are obvious: the 'formal' was far more open to bureaucratic styles of management, and of trade union and political mobilization alike; and both necessarily generate documentation, leave behind a paper trail. Any survey of that research has to begin with this set of polarities.[65]

Dualistic approaches were further stimulated by the prolonged separation between on the one hand historical studies of modern industry and labour which focussed on class and interest groups, and which had a political-cum-economic orientation; and on the other social-anthropological work which had little to do with history or political economy, and which focussed on the countryside, 'traditional' tribal and peasant societies, and affinities of caste, kinship, and family.[66] Early research of the first kind could develop a managerial slant, investigating questions of entrepreneurial and labour efficiency, degrees of motivation, and mechanisms of labour control and discipline. Equally, it could be oriented towards labour. The latter concerns have often been an important component of writings by labour activists, present or past. Both, however, were broadly unilinear and teleological. Both accepted the pattern of Western capitalist development as the norm. In the radical variant, there was the added expectation of the ultimate growth of revolutionary socialist consciousness among the

[64] For a study of early factory laws, see Sarkar 2009: 247–79.

[65] In 1950, India had fewer than 10 million industrial workers, among whom considerably less than half (*c.* 2.5 million, according to one estimate) were employed in what the law recognized as factories. Even the larger figure amounted to *c.* 6 per cent of the total labour force, and only 17 per cent of non-agricultural employment: Breman 1999: 1–42. For a brief overall survey of recent Indian labour history, see Sarkar 2004: 285–313.

[66] Parry 1999: Introduction.

working classes. Both, therefore, faced the problem of evident lags or retardations in the Indian situation. Explanations, as we have already seen in the context of entrepreneurial history, could be in terms of either colonial constraints or the persistence of indigenous structures and values.

In an older form of radical politics that oriented research on labour, the focus was on strikes, the rise and fall of trade unions, debates on Communist or other leadership strategies. Explanations for the ebb and flow of labour movements and organizations were made in terms of a combination of economic conjunctures and 'correct' or 'incorrect' styles of leadership. These kinds of writings were later criticized as economistic and/or written 'from above', from the vantage point of leadership and organization; blind towards key questions of culture and autonomy of workers themselves.[67]

After the pathbreaking work of E.P. Thompson altered the terms of radical labour studies, two major interventions helped to transform Indian labour history. They, however, pointed in somewhat opposed directions. In 1989, Dipesh Chakrabarty, the lone member of the Subaltern Studies group to write about urban workers, introduced the turn towards questions of culture associated both with the Subaltern Studies project and with Thompson.[68] He differed, however, from both these models in one crucial way. The basic optimism of Thompson and early Subaltern Studies about the radical potentialities of labour or peasant culture gave way in Chakrabarty to an elegant study of the reproduction of feudal, pre-capitalist, deeply hierarchized values within colonial factories as well as in workers' organizations. These were no longer seen as unfortunate lags, likely to be overcome sooner or later through the assertion of a basically unilinear trajectory, similar to that of the advanced capitalist West. They were reconfigured, rather, as structural features of a colonial situation inimical both to

---

[67] The best work of the management-oriented kind is probably Morris 1965. E.P. Thompson's *Making of the English Working Class* was published in 1963 but began to have an impact on Indian labour history only from the 1970s. Samples of earlier work could include Karnik 1967, Sen 1970, and the impressive research on Bengal labour history of scholar-activist, Ranajit Dasgupta, later brought together in Dasgupta 1994.

[68] Chakrabarty 1989.

any hegemonic bourgeois culture of factory management and work, and to class consciousness in the full Marxist sense. Even sincere and dedicated trade union and often Communist organizers—who came inevitably from the educated and 'respectable' (in Bengal, Chakrabarty's research area, 'bhadralok') stratum, could not escape the pulls of this semi-feudal and paternalist culture. This made their relations with the workers hierarchical and undemocratic. Workers' attitudes towards employers and overseers similarly varied between 'deference' and 'defiance'. Militant moments were not rare, but such internalized weaknesses blocked the growth of stable and long-lasting trade union structures.

No serious South Asian labour historian after Chakrabarty has been able to ignore the intersections of community ties of caste and religion with class, or assume a simple, inevitable progression towards higher forms of class consciousness. But the prioritization of the 'backward linkages' of labour perhaps contributed to the marked neglect of labour history for a number of years after Chakrabarty's book. If culture was the decisive dimension, and if that culture needed to be explored in terms of its roots in the countryside, it involved a shift in focus towards peasants and away from workers. Meanwhile, industrial labour itself, along with the militancy long associated with it, appeared as a defunct idea, for India as well as for advanced capitalist countries in the new era of post-Fordist 'flexible accumulation'. Big factories, contrary to all expectations, began giving way to a revival of small production units of the putting-out and domestic kind. These were free alike of formal state regulation and strong trade unions. The early 1990s, after the collapse of 'actually existing socialist' regimes, seemed to confirm the conviction about the demise of the role of the worker. The era marked a real nadir in Indian labour history.

What is striking, indeed paradoxical, is the very significant and impressive revival in labour studies since then—despite, or in face of, the new situation. This was inaugurated by a second major historiographical landmark for labour studies: two books by Raj Chandavarkar.[69] Their overall context was set precisely by the changes in recent years. They broke down most of the polarities which had

---

[69] Chandavarkar 1994; Chandavarkar 1998.

underpinned earlier work. A major significance of Chandavarkar's studies lay in his systematic and powerful deconstruction of these opposites, starting with that between the formal and informal sectors. Work along such lines had already started, most notably by Jan Breman.[70] Chandavarkar, however, brought the new approaches together in his detailed study of Bombay textiles. The assumption of an inevitable linear evolution—from artisanal forms through putting-out and manufacture to big factories—had already come under interrogation even for the era of the 'classic' industrial revolution in the West by the 1980s.[71] Now Chandavarkar was able to show the pervasive combination of large factories with putting-out units, small workshops, and petty or artisanal forms of production even in Bombay, the point of origin and for long the heart of Indian capitalist development. 'Independent' industrial investment in factories could be made by the same businessman who also engaged in putting-out, commercial activities, and 'compradore' trading in British piecegoods imports. The conventional Marxist distinctions of trader/industrialist and compradore/national now appeared far more fluid and tenuous. A major part of even second- and third-generation industrial workers retained strong links with their village homes. Clearly, migration was not generally a one-way journey from village to city, but much more of a circular movement—a point made earlier by Breman. Chandavarkar went on to argue that one should abandon the perennial search for explanations of such flexible and non-linear forms of capital and labour in terms of their assumed backwardness or colonial difference. Instead, one should explore whether these could not have been reasonably successful adaptations by both capitalists and workers to specific, material circumstances. Nor were the supposed 'peculiarities' of Indian labour always all that specific to colonial conditions. The 'jobber' who recruited and largely managed millworkers as an intermediary between the capitalist and the labour force was not really an Indian peculiarity: the name itself was actually borrowed from Manchester.

[70] Breman 1976: 1870–6; Breman 1996.
[71] See, for instance, Berg 1985, emphasizing the predominance of non-factory forms throughout the era of the major innovations in cotton textile technology.

Frequent short-term fluctuations in the price of raw materials, and in the demand for yarn and cloth, made multiple and flexible investments quite logical. The retention of links with villages by workers, most of whom left their wives and children there, saved housing costs and higher wages which mill-owners might otherwise have had to meet. On the other hand the oppressive conditions of factory work, the uncertainties of employment, and the atrocious housing facilities made urban workers who still had some land in villages prefer circular movements between village and city, invest their savings in land, and look forward to returning permanently upon retirement. Nor were such features necessarily inimical to labour militancy; rather, workers with links with land could afford to go on long-term strikes more than the completely proletarianized, who would be more prone to strike-breaking.

The thrust of Chandavarkar's work is thus clearly opposed to Chakrabarty's 'cultural' emphasis. Chandavarkar argues that many of the apparent specificities which the latter had highlighted could be explained more simply as rational responses to material conditions and pressures. The sporadic nature of labour militancy, the failure to develop stable organizations, the dependence on middle-class leaders who were outsiders—all this was rooted much more in the extent and efficacy of capitalist-cum-colonial state repression. Actual workers in leadership positions would normally face instant dismissal or worse, while the low level of literacy made dependence on educated people with some knowledge of the law quite indispensable The colonial/indigenous binary which ran through Chakrabarty's arguments was questioned as well. Chandavarkar goes so far as to suggest that colonialism was also a process by which labour was cheapened and more fully subordinated to capital, Indian as much as foreign.

In an essay of 1981 (reprinted in Chandavarkar 1998), as well as an introduction to a work on oral history (based on interviews with Bombay workers, activists, and others), Chandavarkar made another significant departure from the general run of labour history studies. He drew attention to the importance of worker neighbourhoods, mohallas or chawls: the highly concentrated residence areas of millworkers in what was known as Girangaon, the 'mill village' in Central Bombay before the ravages and reconstructions of today's deindustrialization.

The lines of authority in factory and neighbourhood often coalesced, as the 'jobber' also doubled up as house agent, usurer, shopkeeper, or petty trader. Yet power relations could sometimes be reversed through effective neighbourhood pressures during big strikes, for the authority of the capitalist was necessarily weaker here than it was within the factory. The shop floor, as is conventionally assumed, was not, therefore, the sole site of labour consciousness, nor was the neighbourhood a locus of backward pulls towards caste, religious, and rural affiliations. At times the latter could also be a source of or sustenance for labour militancy. However, this was not necessarily always so. There were many incidents of communal and other kinds of sectarian strife. Above all, Girangaon was able to develop, for an entire historical era, a vivid street culture and life of its own, as documented by oral history. Adarkar and Menon's collection fills up to a considerable extent the gap left by earlier work on Bombay, including Chandavarkar.[72]

A similar broadening of the scope of labour history has in fact been a crucial characteristic of the rich corpus of recent research. This has been helped by a belated coming together of historical and anthropological approaches, a larger use of vernacular material (including the occasional writings of workers themselves that are now being unearthed), collections of oral testimony, and a belated but very significant gendering of labour history in the work of historians like Janaki Nair, Samita Sen, and Chitra Joshi. Our account here is largely confined to the late-colonial era and to the decades prior to the First World War climacteric. It needs to be emphasized, however, that no account of labour history today can, or should, remain unaffected by contemporary processes of the 'informalizing' of industrial labour and the accompanying loss of worker rights. These processes have produced a greater concern with the modes of constructing memory, vital for assessing the value of oral sources. This is also another way in which history and anthropology may come together. A sense of loss regarding earlier livelihood and labour patterns animates much of the recent work, which leads to a fresh assessment of the worth of

[72] Chandavarkar 1981: 630–47; Chandavarkar 2004: 121–90. See also Adarkar and Menon 2004.

the fast-declining 'formal' sector of today. This sector was never more than a small part of non-agricultural labour, but it was the section which made significant gains in the direction of somewhat more human conditions of life and dignity—in very large part through its own heroic endeavour.[73]

The theme links with theoretical work arguing that the very notion of legally free labour being a constituent part of the capitalist order may be in need of revision. Free labour was a product of political and legal intervention by the state and not an inevitable product of capitalism. Its precise meanings have fluctuated with the strength or decline of labour militancy.[74] It is paradoxical that now, when conventional Marxist wisdom stands challenged, the centrality of class struggle in the evolution of capitalism still remains unassailable. Histories of capital and labour are, indeed, inseparable, and worker protests and organizations will figure prominently at many points later, starting with brief references to specific kinds of plantations, mines, and industries.[75]

The theoretical emphasis on the contingent nature of labour rights under capitalism has led on to the questioning of yet another binary, that of slave and free labour. Except under labour pressure, the

[73] Even a brief and therefore incomplete checklist of the major works on labour history over the last decade would include the already mentioned study of railway construction workers by Ian Kerr (Kerr 1995); the coming together of historical and anthropological approaches in Parry, Breman, and Kapadia 1991; Simeon 1995; Nair 1998; Samita Sen's highlighting of gender dimensions, still somewhat rare in labour studies, in Sen 1999; and two finely crafted longue durée studies of the rise and fall of specific centres of factories and labour movements, Joshi 2003 and Breman 2004.

[74] A pioneering work in this context has been Steinfeld 2001.

[75] A note on arrangement might be helpful at this point. Peasant and labour movements were obviously bound up with the many tensions of agrarian and urban industrial life which this and the preceding chapter have been surveying, but they were also inflected by relationships of caste, religion, and gender, and would come to develop complicated articulations with nationalist and communal currents in course of time. It seems more convenient, therefore, to postpone their more detailed consideration till after discussions of society and culture, though such a part-separation of structure from self-conscious activity is of course quite problematic.

'normal' situation under capitalism seems to be of legally voluntary contracts between workers and employers which include grossly un-equal penal clauses for violation: civil damages like fines, at most, for masters; criminal punishments involving imprisonment, forced labour, forfeiture of wages, and corporal punishment for employees. All this has made working conditions semi-servile. Nor has this inequality been a product merely of the whims of capitalists, or a consequence of great helplessness among workers. This situation has been based on the massive state intervention that gave legal sanction to such penal contracts. The classic British method that prevailed for almost five hundred years, till the late-nineteenth-century abolition of slavery, was the proliferating genre of 'master and servant' legislation which extended in England from the fourteenth century and later throughout the British empire. Indian applications began with the Madras Police Regulations of 1811 and culminated in the Workman's Breach of Contract Act of 1859. In labour contracts that involved an advance which the master gave to the worker, breach of contract for non-performance of the contracted work by the latter was punishable by imprisonment for up to three months. The employer had only to approach a local magistrate to set the law in motion. The 1859 Act was repealed only in 1925, fifty years after its prototype had been abolished in Britain. The British master and servant law, however, was abolished in 1875 under trade union pressure. An even more brutal version was soon developed for tea plantations with Act VI of 1865.[76]

Unedenic Gardens: Tea, Indigo, and Plantation Labour

The term 'plantation' in the colonial Indian context contains considerable ambiguity. It was used to describe rather different kinds of production relations with respect to two of its most prominent forms, indigo and tea. Indigo plantation was a bit of a misnomer. It stood not for any large-scale estate farming managed directly by planters—the more common usage of the word, as notably in the antebellum South in the USA and the West Indies—but it represented external forms

[76] Anderson 2004: 422–54. See also the Introduction to this work by Hay and Craven.

of exploitation that battened on small peasant production. Under the system in Bengal, European indigo planters more or less forced peasants to take usurious advances, in return for which they had to cultivate indigo and sell it to the planters at quite unremunerative prices. Such extremes of oppression saw to it that indigo farming was abandoned in Bengal after the 'Blue Mutiny' of 1859–60. The system had not been able to establish working relationships with an agrarian structure dominated by permanently settled zamindars. Peasant protests aroused the sympathy of some landlords, a major section of the literati, European missionaries, and even some colonial high-ups. In north Bihar, by contrast, for some two generations planters were able to insert themselves with more success into the existing land hierarchy as intermediaries between zamindars and peasants, ensuring regular rents as thikadars for the former. They made cultivators grow indigo on a part of the land, usually on three kathas in a bigha, in the tinkathia system common in Champaran. Sometimes, as in Darbhanga, hired labourers were used to cultivate indigo on lands which planters controlled directly. As the first asami-wari system remained predominant, indigo plantations did not become a separate enclave: rather, the planters made every effort 'to fit as closely as possible into the local economic organization', which remained of a 'quasi-feudal' sort. Declining indigo prices from around 1897 sharpened the animus of planters against an upper stratum of dominant-caste peasants who were eager to get into the increasingly profitable market of foodgrains. Indigo, in other words, had become a barrier to the growth of indigenous commercial agriculture. This led to conflicts which, after a preliminary round *circa* 1907–8, eventually provided the occasion for Gandhi's entry into rural mass politics in 1917.[77]

The classic Indian plantations were the Assam tea gardens, owned for long principally by British planters and cultivated on large estates by paid labour. There were also smaller tea, coffee, and rubber estates in the South Indian hills.[78] Particularly in Assam, this was a wage

[77] Pouchepadass 1999: 129, and chapters 5, 6.
[78] A marginal Indian presence also emerged by the late nineteenth century among tea planters, notably some Bengali-owned gardens in the Jalpaiguri

labour regime which was anything but free: as Jayeeta Sharma puts it, 'the state created a legal apparatus to import plantation workers on indentured and penal contracts. The entry of over a million labouring migrants irrevocably changed Assam's social landscape and nurtured new notions of racial and cultural alterity. The consequences reached beyond an imperial labour regime to create intricate interplays between cultural constructions of race, social histories of resistance, and local imaginings of modernity and nationhood.'[79] The indenture system under which workers were recruited was described by Hugh Tinker as a 'new system of slavery'. Tea plantations began in Assam in 1838–9, coinciding precisely with the beginnings of the export of indentured Indian labourers to sugar plantations in the West Indies—where they became the preferred substitute for African slaves emancipated in 1833. Labourers of both kinds were recruited from Chhota Nagpur and the west Bihar–east UP regions, which also provided the bulk of the labour force for a number of other tropical colonies of Britain and France. Indenture proved to be a device, both effective and inhuman, to immobilize labour after it had been mobilized over long distances.[80] A much larger workforce, however, was sent to Assam than to the West Indies: at its peak in 1919 at least 900,000 were taken to Assam, whereas the corresponding number for the West Indies never exceeded 110,000. Also, a much higher proportion of women labourers was sent into Assam.

After some initial hiccups, when a speculative 'tea mania' in the early 1860s was followed by a major slump in 1865, the indenture system was stabilized through Act VI of the latter year. This tightened the 1859 breach of contract law for the special case of Assam:

---

region of north Bengal, and there were some investments in tea by the small Assamese middle class. Indian entrepreneurship in tea faced difficulties from their much more powerful and influential European planters of the same kind as seen in other sectors of commerce and industry: Dasgupta 1992: chapter 4.

[79] Sharma 2012: 5.

[80] The standard official and planter justification for using indentured labour in Assam was scanty population and the 'laziness' of the local Assamese, often stereotyped as immersed in opium. The more important point was that indenture immobilized labour and kept wages down.

planters no longer had even to approach magistrates to enforce the penal contract but were given the power of summary arrest—without a warrant—of absconders. The importance of such extra-judicial powers is indicated by the much lower figure of formal prosecutions in Assam as compared to the West Indies—planters could depend on more informal methods of coercion. Workers were prisoners in these 'gardens', a word cruelly ironic in view of the terrible reality. Once brought in from their far-off homes, often by deceit, they were made to live in virtual isolation from the world beyond their work areas. The conditions of transport of 'coolies' from hinterland catchment areas were reminiscent of the notorious 'Middle Passage' of Africans kidnapped by Europeans and enslaved aboard 'slaver' ships for sale across the Atlantic.[81]

Massive labour mortality en route in the early 1860s necessitated a few 'welfare' provisions in the 1865 Act. These included a degree of state inspection of the arkattis who organized recruitment in the catchment areas in a hierarchized system dominated ultimately by big British managing agencies. They also fixed a nine-hour day and a minimum wage of Rs 5 a month. But operationally the minimum wage rate soon became the maximum, and, remarkably, remained constant for half a century amidst a 100 per cent rise in foodgrain prices after 1875. Further powers were given to the planters in 1882, reducing inspection levels and extending the indenture period from three years to five in the context of falling tea prices from 1878. Planters countered the decline in prices by pushing up the volume of tea production—from 6 million lb in 1872 to 75 million lb in 1900. A good indication of the truly barbaric conditions in Assam is provided by the mortality rate of 5.4 per cent among labourers recruited under the 1882 rules, as compared to the general Assam figure of 2.4 per cent. Labour mortality consistently outstripped the birth rate, necessitating a continual and increasing dependence on indenture inflows, which were steadily accelerated. A group of Santal headmen who, in a public relations exercise, had been taken to Assam in 1894 by the Indian Tea Association (the organization of the European planters),

[81] A passage often represented in works of fiction, and with special poignance in recent times by Barry Unsworth's Booker Prize-winning novel, *Sacred Hunger* (1992).

reported that conditions in most gardens were intolerable: flogging was frequent, sick leave was refused, and maternity leave granted for only five days.

Such extremes of exploitation in the end proved counterproductive. Internal contradictions led to the eventual repeal of the 1865 Act in 1908. Planters had faced a paradox: the 'high cost of cheap labour', because the many-tiered and corrupt arkatti system was plagued by leakages. Despite the incredibly repressive nature of the gardens, labour disaffection and resistance were not rare. They found expression in desertion (about 5 per cent annually over 1882–1901 of those governed by the 1882 Act), an average of 272 prosecutions per year for 'rioting' and 'unlawful assembly' by around 1900, and mass outbreaks and assaults on European managers, as at Rowmari in Lakhimpur in 1903. By this time an increasingly vocal Indian criticism of Assam 'slavery' was joined by some top British officials: Henry Cotton, ex-commissioner of Assam, and, even two figures generally notorious for their anti-Indian views, Bampfyld Fuller and Curzon. The arkatti system was gradually replaced by sirdari recruitment, where sardars were equivalent to jobbers. By then, this had also become standard practice in mines and mills. Planters lost their powers of private arrest in 1908, and penal contracts finally ended with the repeal of the Breach of Contract Act in 1925.[82]

Trouble Underground: Mines and Mine-workers

A second major field of predominantly British investment was mines. Investment began with the opening up of the rich mineral resources of what is now south Bihar, Jharkhand, and north Orissa. It started with with coal: the Raniganj fields began to be mined as early as 1814. Growth in the production of coal was soon greatly stimulated by the increasing demand for steamships and railway engines. A second major spurt came with the discovery of the very rich and near-the-surface coalfield of Jharia in the 1890s, which sent production shooting up from 4.7 million tons in 1896–1900 to 19.3 million tons in 1916–20. The late nineteenth century was also marked by

---

[82] The above paragraphs are based on Behal and Mohapatra 1992: 142–72; and Mohapatra 2004: 455–80. See also Behal 1985: PE19-PE26.

the development in adjacent regions of mica, iron ore, copper, and manganese mines. But coal always dominated the mining sector, employing 81 per cent of mining labour in 1921, comprising over 100,000 men, women, and children.

The patterns of organization and exploitation were significantly different in coal as compared to tea. However, there was the same tie-up at the apex with Calcutta-based British managing agencies, the state, and—particularly vital for coal mining—British railway companies. Mines came up in the same region as one of the two major LCAs in India, along with a local population of adivasis and lower castes who were pauperized by curtailed access to forests and loss of land to outsiders. Unlike far-off, under-populated north Assam, again, there was a developed zamindari system in this permanently settled region. There was no need, therefore, for long-distance recruitment of workers through indenture. Big collieries acquired zamindari rights and leased out small plots in return for a stipulated number of days of work in the mines. This introduced a semi-serf system reminiscent of Scottish mines in the eighteenth century. Local Indian zamindars also came to mutually beneficial arrangements with mine-owners. They used their power as landlords to send their tenants to the mines in lieu of payments that mine owners made to them. The resultant structures represented a close, though unequal, symbiosis of colonial capitalism with indigenous quasi-feudal patterns of domination. By the inter-war years, however, recruitment methods began to shift to ticcadars and sirdars, the local forms of the jobber system. Mine owners were spared spending money on payments to zamindars or on purchases of estates. They now had access to a more controlled labour force. The bulk of the miners, however, still came from nearby districts. Even in the late 1960s, almost half of the Jharia labour force came from the districts of Dhanbad, Hazaribagh, and Gaya.

Another special feature of coal was the considerable, though fluctuating, presence of Indian—at first, Bengali—entrepreneurship. Dwarkanath Tagore was one of the pioneers. His Carr-Tagore firm purchased the Raniganj mine from the bankrupt Alexander agency house in 1835 and set up the Bengal Coal Company (BCC) which, in its initial phase, was predominantly in Bengali hands. But this was taken over by Englishmen after the Tagore enterprises crashed in

1847. The BCC, however, henceforth a British concern, remained for a long time the biggest name in coal mining. More unusually, there was a second wave of bhadralok enterprise in coal, from the 1890s till the mid-1920s, there being sixty-two Bengali mines in 1897. Bengalis, moreover, led in opening up the close-to-surface coal of Jharia. Leading firms included Laik-Banerji, a collaborative venture of the petty zamindar of Dishergarh with a former clerk of the BCC. To an extent, the importance of local zamindars in coal mining helped Indian enterprise. Another Bengali magnate, N.C. Sircar, came to be known as the coal prince. Bengali entrepreneurs in the early 1920s set up an Indian Mining Federation as a rival to the British Indian Mining Association. But because it found access to funds difficult, Indian enterprise remained a subsidiary affair in this area. This necessitated the mining of low-cost, near-surface, poor-quality coal. Indian enterprises suffered, moreover, from an unfair allocation of railway wagons and purchases: the white 'collective monopoly' that Bagchi has analysed operated in coal as well. By the 1920s the Bengali presence was challenged by upcountry, mainly Marwari, businessmen. They advanced often in collaboration rather than through confrontation with European firms, trying to take them over gradually from within. By the late 1920s Seth Sukhlal Karnani was able to push out N.C. Sircar from his premier Baraboni colliery. This entry-ist strategy paid off handsomely after 1947, when local entrepreneurs were able to capture most of the old British managing agency firms handling coal.

Common to mining and the tea plantations was the atrocious exploitation and misery of the workforce. For a long time, underground illumination facilities were kept in a primitive state to save costs. There was little electrification, which meant dependence on highly inflammable kerosene lamps. The workers were overwhelmingly illiterate and untrained. Mining disasters, consequently, were a continual possibility and happened often. There were health hazards too. Till the late 1920s, prior to a ban on underground work by women, they formed a high proportion of the miners, as much as 37.5 per cent in 1920. Quite often, they were accompanied by their children. Adivasi communities were more used to men and women working together than caste Hindus, and women helped in the carrying of coal underground to the pithead, as well as—before the spread of steam-powered winding engines—in the arduous task of turning the windlasses to bring up the coal buckets. At every level, then, the deployment of technology already widely in use elsewhere was here delayed by the greed for profit and callous disregard for the lives and conditions of 'native coolies'. Labour organization emerged late in the mines—not before the 1930s, in fact. Apart from the obvious hindrances to unionization on account of the extent and brutality of management control, proximity to their village homes often meant that workers would quietly slip away when conditions appeared intolerable, rather than engage in the much more dangerous endeavour of collective action.[83]

If we now move a thousand miles south, to the gold mines of Kolar in the princely state of Mysore, a situation similar and yet different confronts us. British exploitation of Kolar began in 1873, peaking in 1905 when 35,000 miners were put to work in some of the deepest mines in the world, at times 8000 feet below surface. Their work was comparable to the atrocious conditions of work among Africans around the same time in Johannesburg. Decline began early, though, from the 1920s, because the greed for quick profits began to exhaust the reserves. This eventually made Kolar virtually a ghost town, and so it remains today. There was no airconditioning before the 1930s, and mine temperatures could touch 115°F. It being impossible for European supervisors to venture below at such temperatures, a rigorous police surveillance and search machinery had to be instituted to prevent workers leaving the mines from thieving the gold. Recruitment, as in Chhota Nagpur, was from the nearby districts (particularly North Arcot and Salem in Madras Presidency), and was organized through labour contractors. As has been and remains the general pattern in India, workers in such highly oppressive sectors were very largely lower castes and Dalits who, in this part of the South, began to call themselves Adi-Dravidas.

Janaki Nair's work on Kolar highlights a paradoxical situation, one that contrasts sharply with what can be inferred about labour attitudes in the eastern Indian mines. Despite conditions of work that were

[83] Simmons 1976a: 189–217; Simmons 1976b: 455–85; Simeon 1995: chapter I, 6–8; Simeon 1999: 43–76.

every bit as bad, if not worse, as in the eastern Indian mines, Kolar's miners did not seem to have felt any nostalgia for the village life that they had left behind. It seems that the day-to-day personalized discrimination, oppression, and violence of untouchable life in the Karnataka villages—significantly different, one would guess, from the somewhat more egalitarian conditions among adivasis—made at least some of the more vocal Kolar miners refrain from romanticizing their past rural lives. Rather, they celebrated their new life as miners.[84] Unlike in the Transvaal or in eastern India, Kolar had little problem maintaining a stable labour force. Wages were considerably higher than the rates of nearby agricultural labour, and the novel access to ready money afforded some access to urban pleasures, particularly perhaps for the women, who did not work underground and could thus dress relatively well. Miners' songs reproduced in some Tamil journals contrasted the 'little gruel' and 'tatters' in the 'wild countryside' with the 'mutton and rice' of Kolar. Social hierarchies were difficult to reproduce so vigorously in the new environment, and Kolar became a major centre of upward mobility aspirations among the Adi-Dravidas. They were inspired by ideologies of social reform, rationalist critiques of caste ideology, and a Buddhist revival led by Iothee Thass. But such idealization did not extend to any illusions about the possibility of reducing management exploitation. Open organization was impossible for very long, for the early-twentieth-century Mysore state combined a precocious statist developmental ideology with extreme labour repression. Trade unions remained illegal till 1942, sixteen years after they had been legalized in British India. Still, there were numerous assaults on surveillance agents, as in December 1907 after a woman

---

[84] Not a totally rare phenomenon, it needs to be added. To take an example from a very different time and mileu, Christopher Pinney's fieldwork at Nagda, Madhya Pradesh, where a big rayon factory owned by the Birlas is located, reveals an interesting diversity of attitudes to changing times today. Neighbouring village upper castes complain about worsening times, Kaliyuga, with urbanization spreading immorality and agricultural workers leaving off as soon as they hear the distant factory siren. Managerial staff at the factory combined a developmental ideology with an occasional neo-Gandhian romanticism of the lost rural past. Factory workers, in sharp contrast, have no such nostalgia, and welcome the better paid, if also more risky, factory work as good for the poor. See Pinney 1999: 76–105.

worker had been molested by some watchmen. Anonymous notices also appeared condemning management practices. One of these, scrawled on a rock to denounce a new system of checking attendance by taking thumb impressions, sparked off a twenty-one-day strike in 1930. Interestingly, the strike had no visible leaders.[85]

An Old Yarn: Jute Mills and Markets

A thick cluster of jute mills developed from the 1850s along the banks of the Hooghly river to the north and south of Calcutta. These were marked by two striking features, one of them apparently anomalous. Bengal jute was able to surpass and eventually marginalize an earlier Scottish (Dundee-based) industry which did not get much political backing from the British government or Parliament. Dundee, however, was the pioneer, having shifted from coarse linen, made from flax and hemp, to jute from the 1830s and particularly in the 1850s, when the Crimean War blocked the import of Russian flax. The colonial attitude to Bengal jute was different from that towards Indian cotton, concern having been often expressed at the rise of a competitor to Manchester textiles in Bombay. In sharp contrast to Bombay again, both raw jute exports and the production of jute manufactures were almost exclusively a British domain till at least the 1920s.

This was largely due to the mills' proximity to the world's principal centre of cultivation of the jute fibre ('paat'): the small peasant economy of eastern Bengal was well connected by rivers with Calcutta. Already in pre-colonial times the region had some handlooms, producing rough garments from jute as well as matting and bags. These were sometimes exported to nearby regions through country shipping. But both jute manufactures and markets were utterly transformed by the commercial revolution of the nineteenth century. International demand for packaging material soared spectacularly. Once the transition was made to machine-based production, jute hessian and gunny sacks largely satisfied the demand for a century.

Early Bengal jute mills (the first was set up by Ackworth in Rishra in 1855) had a rather chequered history. They served the old handloom

[85] Nair 1998.

markets within the country and in nearby areas of South East Asia. The first attempt to export to Britain in 1868 proved a disaster. Things began to change when four medium-level Dundee entrepreneurs of the mid-1870s woke up to the fact that moving the centre of manufacture so much closer to the raw material source would probably pay off handsomely. They set up very successful mills at Shyamnagar and Titagarh. The coming together of the millowners in the Indian Jute Mills Association (IJMA, 1884) enabled periodic restrictions on production through short-time work, which were set in accordance with market fluctuations. This made jute production something like a collective monopoly. From the 1880s Dundee was progressively driven out of its once-wide international markets by Bengal, notably from markets in Australia, the USA, South America, and South Africa. Jute now entered upon an era of uninterrupted and growing prosperity till the mid-1920s. Dundee did make a few protests. However, so many of the Calcutta jute millowners and managers were themselves from Scotland that Dundee remained the source of jute machinery and retained entrepôt functions.

The jute lobby within Britain was much weaker than Manchester cotton, which is generally assumed to have been a major national interest. Perhaps even more important was the fact that the massive export of raw jute and jute manufactures from British India was vital for maintaining Britain's threatened balance of payments and the world supremacy of gold sterling. As for British (often Scottish) predominance over jute, that is easily explained by the existing British controls over the external commerce, shipping, railway, and financial structures of Calcutta and eastern India in general. This control was much more absolute than it ever became in Bombay. The higher levels of the trade in raw jute from the Bengal countryside to the mills on the Hooghly were also controlled by British firms, while jute cultivators themselves were small peasants with no organization of their own—helpless underdogs with little or no knowledge of changing conditions in a world trade that might bring them relative prosperity or utter disaster (as during the 1930s Depression) in utterly unpredictable ways.

The extent of British predominance is indicated by the fact that there was only one Indian director in the entire jute industry in

1911—and that in the smallest firm. On the other hand the four biggest managing agencies (Bird, Duff, Andrew Yule, Jardine & Skinner) controlled 41 per cent of the total number of looms in 1912, and as much as 55 per cent in 1936. Marwari businessmen slowly began to establish a toehold. This happened initially in internal trade (about half of the jute balers were Marwaris by 1900), where they began the direct shipping of raw jute overseas from 1907 and accumulated funds through speculation in jute futures ('fatka') during the First World War. They started their first mills just after this: Birla and Hukumchand in 1918–19. Dipesh Chakrabarty has suggested, though, that the sustained high profits made by British jute firms proved in the long run somewhat counterproductive as they bred a great deal of complacence. That, in turn, led to a neglect of technological and managerial innovation. Amazingly low amounts, for instance, were kept aside as depreciation of industrial machinery. The mentality was 'mercantilist': making quick, virtually speculative, profits through low-quality products with few signs of long-term capitalist 'rationality'.[86] The absence of technological improvement made the industry eventually helpless when packaging methods and materials began changing. A period of secular stagnation or decline set in from the time of the Depression, from which Bengal jute has never really recovered.[87]

Jute mills in their heyday constituted late-colonial India's biggest factory industry: 90 mills employed a total of 300,000 workers in 1929 before the Depression set in.[88] The figures, however, fluctuated enormously, and cannot be taken too literally. There was a

[86] But such rationality, whether in the Marxist or the Weberian schema, was perhaps more of an abstract model for initiating analysis rather than depictions of ground-level realities of capitalism in most of its manifestations, even in metropolitan countries. The passage from the abstract to the concrete in Chakrabarty's reading of Marx's *Capital* is possibly somewhat unmediated, enabling an overdrawn contrast between the industrialized West and colonial capitalism.

[87] Bagchi 1972: chapter 8; Chakrabarty 1989: Introduction and chapter 2; Sen 1999: chapter 1.

[88] The corresponding peak figures for the interwar years in Bombay cotton textiles were *c.* 80–90 and 150,000 or less. Jute mills on an average tended to be considerably bigger than cotton mills in Bombay.

predominance of migratory or casual badli workers, and the mill documents available are either inadequate or scrappy. This provides an important point about 'conditions of knowledge of working class conditions'—one of the planks for Chakrabarty's argument about the backward nature of colonial capitalism. All commentators on jute labour have noted its circulatory character. Clearly, the findings of Breman and Chandavarkar regarding cotton textiles of the Bombay region are as applicable to the Calcutta industrial area.

From the point of view of jute mill-owners, Calcutta was blessed in its location. It was the lynchpin of the eastern Indian railway and shipping system, at the junction of three migrant labour flows: indentured labour recruited by arkattis (many of those brought in were not eventually employed); the seasonal flow at harvest time of agricultural labourers from UP, Bihar, and Jharkhand tribal areas to the richer agricultural districts of Eastern Bengal where wages would be higher at that time; and the natural attraction of a growing metropolis for casual labourers of all kinds. There was thus a reservoir of floating labour at most times, which enabled employers to expand or contract production in accordance with market fluctuations. They could keep a large proportion as badli or casual labour, which gave them an obvious advantage. Such a labour-surplus situation allowed the jute magnates to keep wages down (though jute wages were slightly higher than in tea plantations and mines), as well as avoid the costs of a separate recruitment system—unlike the tea planters of a distant province like Assam. Nor did mill sardars (jobbers) have much by way of recruiting functions. Along with the babus (clerks), they managed the point of entry to the mill and discharged a rather chaotic and often corrupt discipline on the shop-floor. Workers, however, came in 'personally', using the backward linkages of the already employed to their villages along family, kinship, caste, and religious networks. Initially, a significant proportion of men and women workers came from the nearby Bengali-speaking districts. From the 1890s there was a major change as upcountry labour came in growing numbers from eastern UP and western Bihar, already the principal LCAs for plantations in Assam and overseas. Mill-owners considered them more docile. A circulatory pattern, where wives and children remained behind in the villages, would necessarily become more the norm as distances from hinterland to place of work increased. Thus emerged a major, long-term contrast between the working class of the Calcutta region and that of Bombay and Ahmedabad. Jute labour in the suburbs of Calcutta was increasingly non-Bengali in composition, adding ethnicity to class as a barrier to social or political interaction with the bhadralok in the city. Bombay textile labour, largely Marathi-speaking for a long time, would be less ghettoized and maintain deeper connections with city life.

Research on jute labour history is important for two kinds of theoretical contributions, innovative as well as highly controversial. One, by Dipesh Chakrabarty, we have noted above and will again below. The other, by Samita Sen, achieved a gendering of many of the key themes in labour history. For a start, Sen makes the point that the neglect of the informal sector has contributed towards making women's work invisible: obvious, really, but seldom noted before fieldwork-based studies of contemporary processes of informalization. The presence of a significant but steadily diminishing proportion of women in the jute mill labour force, again, was seldom noted before Sen. Women constituted about 20 per cent of jute workers before the 1890s, during the early phase, before the flow of upcountry labour. This went down to between 12 per cent and 17 per cent over the next fifty years, and became a negligible 2 per cent in the 1970s. The fairly low proportion of women even in the early phase stood in sharp contrast to late-nineteenth-century Dundee and Manchester, which used the cheap labour of women and children before the era of effective factory legislation and transformed technologies. The initial contrast with Dundee, puzzling at first sight in the context of the fairly unskilled nature of much mill work, may have been related to the significantly higher age of marriage in Western Europe, a long-term feature which historians of the family like Jack Goody have traced back to the early centuries of the Christian era. This allowed large numbers of unmarried women to work in factories. More significant, however, is the progressive marginalization of women in jute mills. Sen distinguishes among three facets. The decline in the proportion of women was accompanied by a stereotyping of female labour as 'naturally' unskilled and therefore poorly paid: this, despite the fact that jute mill technology remained fairly stagnant and did not require very long training. At the same time, women's work was branded socially and morally disreputable. These features, Sen stresses, represent not a mere continuation or reproduction of 'traditional' patriarchal values which relegated women to domestic work alone. The were more a strategic coming together of evolving forms of capitalism and Indian patriarchy. A labour force that was circulatory rather than permanently urbanized, which involved work in mills by male family heads while women and children stayed on in villages and sought supplementary earnings, saved mill-owners the expenses of housing or an effective 'family' wage, while they simultaneously satisfied patriarchal notions of respectability and avoided the perils of women's work in unfamiliar environments. For women driven to such work because of poverty, there was a related loss of status. Jute mill women tended to be those who were detached or driven out from rural society, as well some occasional rebels: disobedient widows, women living independently or in temporary liaisons with menfolk, prostitutes.

Sen emphasizes such 'cultural' dimensions, even as she highlights their changing historical contexts. Thus, the decline of some traditional kinds of women's work in the countryside, notably spinning and the husking of rice by hand, pushed more women of poorer families towards casual rural employment or factory work, at the same time as the more fortunate or successful sought to climb up the social hierarchy by adopting brahmanical norms of seclusion for 'their' womenfolk. Institutions like purdah or the seclusion of women, Sen suggests, may have been strengthened by the fact that so many more men had to live far away in cities. It was strengthened also because the small proportion of women who worked in mills lived in a predominantly male environment that proved often to be dangerous for them. There could have been some links, too, between the widespread shift from bride-price to dowry and the consequent devaluation of women's work outside the home.

Meanwhile, the norms themselves were changing. New notions of respectability and decorum evolved among sections of the upper castes who composed an amalgam of elements appropriated from Victorian morality and traditional Indian standards of right and wrong behaviour. Such norms did slowly percolate downwards, through processes of appropriation in which caste mobility or sanskritizing movements played a significant part. The spectacle of women who moved away from the legitimate familial domain to work in factories—which were perceived as dens of immorality—consequently produced elements of a moral panic. It consolidated the deep gulf between the bhadralok gentry and largely non-Bengali workers, but it also stimulated occasional philanthropic, and eventually political, interventions by middle-class people.

Chakrabarty's focus on the cultural dimensions of mill management, labour, and labour protest has been interrogated and complicated by later research. The starkness of the contrast between his approach, and what he rejected as economistic and teleological forms of Marxist interpretation, has been partially resolved by other historians who recognize that pre-capitalist traditions or forms of community consciousness—religious, caste, family—were not just reproduced but were modified through specific and changing circumstances. Two central points of debate were initiated by Chakrabarty's work. One was the long-term oscillation between class conflicts and religious or communal strife which provided little or no indication of any linear trend towards greater 'maturity'. The other was the paradoxical combination of 'deference' with occasional 'defiance' in labour attitudes towards managements, an alleged general acceptance of the owner as 'ma-baap' though punctuated by moments of extreme militancy. As attempts began to float labour organizations from the 1920s, this second anomaly took the form of coexistence of some very powerful strikes, including industry-wide stoppages in 1929 and 1937. This, however, went along with the very limited reach and instability of labour organization. As late as 1945, an official enquiry found that only 18 per cent of jute workers were union members.

Details about the second kind of paradox would be best studied when we come to the post-1918 era: the first demands some attention now. The locus of debate, notably between Ranajit Dasgupta and Chakrabarty, related to the evident oscillation between class and religious community identities in the mill areas during the 1890s. That decade, as we have seen, was marked by a large shift towards recruiting migrant upcountry labour. At the same time, the long-term boom in jute from 1895 led to efforts to extend a working day that was already stretched across 12 hours or so, and which was quite free of legal restrictions on the hours of work of an increasingly male labour force. In addition, electric lights were introduced into mills from 1894 which enabled working nights under a system of shifts. There were clashes between workers and their sardar jobbers, protests over wage cuts, and much resentment at the widespread practice of holding back a week's wage to prevent workers from going off to a nearby mill which might offer more. This was competition which the IJMA could not really prevent. The consequences in terms of labour protests were, however, quite contradictory: a spate of strikes in 1895–6, several of the largest involving only one specific religious community. The immediate provocation was a refusal by managers to grant holidays over Bakr Id and Muharram for Muslims and over the Rath Jatra for Hindus. More striking was an outbreak of Hindu–Muslim communal violence in some mill areas around the same time, mainly over the issue of cow-protection. This again was followed by violence basically directed against the police and Europeans. Militant workers came more from informal or small enterprises rather than from the mills. They were agitated by the municipal destruction of what they claimed was a small mosque. The demolition led to the Tala riots of 1897.[89]

The riot can be partly explained by a sort of a carry-over of political sentiments from east UP and west Bihar. The region had witnessed acute Hindu–Muslim tensions in the early 1890s over cow-protection movements. Chakrabarty suggested that such apparently diverse and contradictory outbreaks were linked to deep-seated notions of community 'honour' (izzat), which, workers thought, was violated at different times by members of another community or by policemen, or mill managers. More economy-oriented historians have sought to relate these highly charged notions of honour and dishonour to the new tensions of industrial and urban life. For those who came from afar, reliance or claims on community or kinship bonds, real or part-invented, was vital for getting or retaining employment,

---

[89] The first comprehensive survey of early labour conditions and protests remains Dasgupta 1994: esp. 315–405. The article was initially published as a separate paper in 1979. See also Chakrabarty 1989: chapter 6; and Basu 2004: chapter 4. The relative spaces given to class- and community-related disturbances in these works differ sharply in line with the authors' varying emphases.

credit, accommodation. It was necessary for basic survival. A sudden uprooting from rural life could also foster nostalgia for past ties, this contrasting with the situation in the Kolar mines, where the sheer weight of rural caste oppression felt by Dalits apparently led to a different sensibility.[90]

Chandavarkar's stress on the importance of working-class neighbourhoods was followed by Subho Basu's in his study of the Calcutta suburban towns. These were abruptly transformed in the late nineteenth century by the coming of jute mills. Bhatpara provides a striking instance: an old centre of brahmanical learning, as its name indicates, it was transformed by the massive inflow of upcountry labourers from the 1890s. Its population went from 21,000 to 85,000 between 1901 and 1931. Mill managers took over much of the administration of these transformed mill towns. Appointed as municipal commissioners, they wanted a cleaner environment for their spacious residences and were alarmed by frequent epidemics of cholera, smallpox, and plague. The combination of shop floor and local political authority in the hands of these foreigners naturally bred tensions in an era of emergent nationalism. Local zamindars were disgruntled because of threats to their rents, which they derived from insanitary overcrowded bazaars and slums and which the municipality sought to curb. Workers and casual labourers were much more seriously affected by threats of eviction on grounds of urban sanitation and beautification. At the same time, a significant section of the local bhadralok was also attracted by the planned 'improvement', which would be carried out mainly at the cost of the poor: the poor, moreover, were recent migrants in these towns who spoke a different language. They were therefore an alien species. A poem by a Bhatpara Brahman described the immigrant workers as 'buying and selling in their strange Hindi . . . Singing songs that sound like the howl of dogs.'[91]

[90] Ranajit Dasgupta (1994: 316) cites a poignant Bhojpuri folk song:
  The watching of cows is gone,
  The bath in the Ganges is gone,
  The gathering under the pakari tree is gone,
  God has taken away all the three
[91] Basu 2004: chapter 3; Chakrabarty 1989: 148. As for continuities down to today, one can mention the massive destruction of slums in Mumbai in

Late-nineteenth-century bhadralok attitudes towards the new phenomenon of factory labour did occasionally include a more philanthropic-reformist component. Sasipada Banerji, a Brahmo social reformer, worked in the Baranagar mill area over 1866–75. He set up a night school, a working men's club, a savings bank. He propagated notions of temperance among workers and even started a journal, perhaps the first of its kind in India, *Bharat Sramajibi* (1874). This too was a middle-class effort at 'improvement', though of a more caring kind, even if the tone was morally self-righteous and the message was to inculcate habits of thrift, industry, and discipline among the poor. Banerjee's biographer, a fellow Brahmo, quite unselfconsciously cited a commendation by a British mill manager who said that men trained by Sasipada proved 'the most careful and painstaking in their work'.[92]

The Bengali middle class seemed to be indifferent to the mid-1890s wave of jute labour unrest. A few lawyers, most of them Muslims, though, did come forward to defend some of the Tala riot accused. A decade later, however, one such lawyer, A.C. Banerji, led a group of nationalist activists who were associated with strikes among printers, railway clerks, and jute-mill workers. They tried to organize trade unions, none of which proved long-lasting. Their contacts were almost entirely with Bengali employees and workers.

Spinning Stories: Cotton Mills in Western India and Elsewhere

The cotton mills which developed in western India—in Bombay from 1855, at Ahmedabad from 1861—and which grew to become late-colonial India's biggest factory industry, present a striking contrast to eastern Indian plantations, mines, and jute. They formed the bastions of Indian entrepreneurship. Parsis were the most prominent among their owners, particularly in the early decades. There was, however, also a substantial component of Gujarati Hindus, a number of Muslims, and some Marwaris and Jews. Indian capital accounted for nearly half

---

early 2005, rendering some 80,000 homeless, to make the city 'world class'. Those affected would have included a large proportion of immigrants coming from outside Maharashtra.

[92] Chakrabarty 1989: 146; Tattvabhushan 1904.

of the total value of private capital investment in Bombay Presidency in 1914, and the province then accounted for as much of 87 per cent of the total value of Indian capital investment in modern industry. Not that the 'normal' colonial constraints were absent here: a free-trade regime geared to the interests of Lancashire yarn and piecegoods imports prevailed till the mid-1920s, British control over railways, shipping, insurance, overseas trade, and over financial structures in general. In addition, in the absence of an Indian machine-tools industry, Indian textile mills were entirely dependent on British engineering firms and import agencies for their machinery till Independence: the first Indian ring-frame was manufactured only in 1946. We have already seen one element that helps to explain the success of Indian enterprise in western India despite the handicaps. Company mastery, which was definitively established only around 1820, came relatively late in this region, two generations after it came to Bengal. The map of western India contained a patchwork of princely states which were interspersed by chunks of directly ruled British territory. This was very different in appearance from the Bengal Presidency. It allowed a higher degree of autonomy to Indian commercial enterprise and enabled a considerable accumulation of indigenous mercantile capital: particularly with the export of raw cotton, shipping (till the early nineteenth century) and the very profitable opium trade with China, which was also vital for some decades for Company remittances of profits. Such accumulation became a principal base for investment in the cotton mills from the mid-1850s. The first mill, which began production in 1856, was set up by C.N. Davar, a wealthy Parsi merchant who had participated for many years in the China and Asian trade in collaboration with English commercial firms.[93]

The other key explanation for the success of the Bombay entrepreneurs lay in the specific patterns of Indian enterprise in the Bombay

[93] Morris 1965: chapter 3. The contrast between eastern and western India, we have seen, was central to Bagchi's explanation for the slow and uneven growth of Indian capitalism under colonial rule. His basic argument was strengthened by Vicziany's subsequent data relating the beginning of the shift of indigenous merchants in Bombay from raw cotton and opium exports to cotton mills to tightening British control over external trade and shipping from the 1850s: Vicziany 1976: 163–96.

mills, best analysed by Chandavarkar. These were neither marked by the kind of total subordination to British capital which happened in Bengal, nor were they plagued by continual conflict. Their survival and growth depended on adjustments within overall constraints. This was facilitated by the fact that Indian, especially Parsi, business elites had already acquired prominence in Bombay city life in the early nineteenth century. This enabled considerable social interaction between European and Indian men of wealth and privilege in that most cosmopolitan of British Indian cities. In Bengal, such social intercourse largely disappeared after the generation of Dwarkanath Tagore and Rammohan Roy. Some of the favoured Indian magnates, for instance, entered Bombay municipal government through appointment as justices of the peace as early as 1834. They went on to become members of the Governor's Executive Council from 1862, and gained dominance over the city administration through the municipal reforms of 1872 and 1888.[94]

This inter-racial collaboration extended to Bombay mill ownership and management. British engineering firms had a clear stake in the growing demand for mill machinery from Indian mills. The emergence of a substantial (though never dominant) number of European-owned mills, as well as of a large group of European managers and technicians in Indian enterprises, happened together to further consolidate the mixed social life. This contradicts the widespread notion that there was a homogeneous or universal British desire to throttle Indian textiles. The import of machinery for Indian mills was highly profitable, and some British firms moved from that to setting up mills in Bombay—as when Greaves Cotton diversified in the early twentieth century from being suppliers of textile machinery to managing the largest group of mills. British and Indian mill-owners sat together in the Bombay Millowners Association, set up in 1875, with Indians predominant. The absence of major British investment in an industry that was

[94] A further small indicator of the special position of the indigenous elite in Bombay: art schools were set up in the 1850s in Calcutta and Madras, entirely under official auspices and funding, but the equivalent institution in Bombay was established in 1856 through a donation made by the Indian business magnate Jamshetji Jeejebhoy.

emerging as a challenge to Lancashire was clearly a favourable factor for the growth of Indian enterprise.[95]

As we have seen, Chandavarkar has analysed the apparent peculiarities or elements of backwardness in Bombay textiles as fairly rational adjustments on the part of managements as well as by workers to objective constraints, rather than as specificities of culture or as the persistence of pre-capitalist or mercantile mentalities. 'Flexible' investments, simultaneously and in varying proportions in factories, putting-out or small manufacture, trade (including the import of Lancashire textiles), or other forms of business made sense, given the many uncertainties of textile production—notably the vagaries of raw cotton production and prices, and of the market demand for manufactured yarn and cloth. Flexibility was also ensured by the fact that as much as a third of the labour force of the Bombay textiles was made to work on a casual basis. On the whole, a migratory or circulatory movement was preferred, where workers kept their wives and families in the villages and returned to the countryside periodically and after retirement. We have seen that such mobility could suit the immediate interests of workers, too, given the atrocious housing and other conditions of life in urban slums (chawls), since employers generally refused to invest money on housing and sanitation. A further consequence was that the distinction between the formal and informal, or organized and unorganized sectors, which was constituted through law (particularly, as we shall see, the series of Factory Acts from 1881 on, made primarily in the context of Bombay textiles), always remained tenuous. Workers, except for the particularly skilled minority, could or had to frequently move from the one to the other. The official maintenance of that distinction, however, has become a permanent feature of the Indian labour scene: it was profitable for capitalists, big or small, as it kept the informal—much the bigger—sector of the labour force open to unregulated exploitation. Restricting the scope for inspection and regulation also reduced administrative burdens. From

---

[95] In 1911, 92 textile mills in Bombay Presidency had only Indian directors, as against 12 solely European or Anglo-Indian and 25 with both racial communities: the corresponding figures for Bengal jute mills were 0 and 49. Bagchi 1972: 183 (Table 6.7).

the inter-war years, as workers in the formal sector won better living standards through trade union pressures, it was also in their interest to restrict entry into their relatively privileged world. The degree of difference between formal and informal has thus varied over time, a point made powerfully by Chandavarkar.[96] Above all, the adjustments made by Indian textile entrepreneurs related to what precisely they decided to manufacture. In the early decades, there was an evident desire to avoid excessive competition with Lancashire imports of certain varieties of yarn and piecegoods. As Bagchi showed statistically with official documents related to the excise duty controversy of the 1890s, Lancashire imports had come to dominate the market for better-quality (higher count) yarn, while only 6 per cent of Indian yarn was of counts over 24. Conversely, less than 18 per cent of yarn imported into Bombay was of counts of 24 and under. Indian textile mills, therefore, concentrated in the last quarter of the nineteenth century on manufacturing yarn of lower counts for supply to Indian handlooms, and to the Chinese and Japanese markets. After some initial years of not very successful experimentation with combined spinning and weaving mills—when the early growth of the late 1850s was interrupted by the boom in Indian raw cotton exports and prices during the 'cotton famine' in Lancashire due to the American Civil War—spindles grew much faster than power-looms in the Bombay textile industry during a period of virtually uninterrupted growth, from the 1870s till the 1890s. No less than 42 mills were constructed in Bombay between 1875 and 1895, 12 of them between July 1873 and December 1874. There was a fivefold rise in Indian export of yarn in the 1880s, and in 1883 Indian mills, for the first time, outstripped Lancashire in yarn sales to China.

An additional advantage during these decades was the falling value of the silver rupee, which made Lancashire imports more expensive and kept Indian yarn prices low. Piecegoods production was more of a challenge due to Lancashire's dominance in a wide range of medium qualities: handlooms survived, as we have seen, at levels lower and higher than this big intermediate zone. There was also a lack of

[96] See his Introduction to the volume on Bombay oral history: Adarkar and Menon 2004.

bleaching facilities and dyeing and printing capacities in Indian mills. Bombay (unlike Ahmedabad) turned more towards weaving for the home market only from around the turn of the century, as spinning mills grew in China and Japan. It was then that the competition with Lancashire sharpened, inspired briefly by the politics of the Swadeshi Movement around 1905. This was followed by a state of much enhanced strength after the First World War. Bleaching and dyeing facilities were introduced after about 1900, while yarn exports to China declined permanently from after 1906.[97]

The avoidance of excessive confrontation, however, did not obviate periodic panics in Lancashire about the rise of a formidable rival in Bombay. Lancashire's powerful Parliamentary lobby ensured great publicity for such alarms, which led occasionally to intervention by the British government. This took two main forms: total opposition to even very low import duties on Lancashire cotton goods, and efforts to regulate Indian mills through Factory Acts.

Even the very low tariff which had been imposed in the 1870s on account of the financial needs of the British Indian government (Home Charges were going up as the rupee depreciated) was abolished in 1882. When these charges came back in a very stringent currency and financial situation during the 1890s, a countervailing excise was imposed on Indian textiles. This provoked a wave of Indian newspaper and middle-class protest, particularly in Bombay. A boycott of British goods was suggested for the first time.

Meanwhile the spurt in the development of the Bombay mills in 1874–5 stimulated speeches in Parliament and British newspaper campaigns about the long hours and inhuman conditions of work in Indian-owned mills: perfectly valid criticisms in themselves, even though often obviously motivated, and seldom mentioning equivalent conditions in the Assam plantations or the Calcutta jute mills. Indian nationalist opinion tended to be equally tendentious, but in the opposite direction: the *Amrita Bazar Patrika* of 2 September 1875 declared, in the context of the campaign over labour conditions in Bombay, that 'a higher death-rate amongst our operatives is far more preferable to the collapse of this rising industry.'[98] But neither British nor Indian

[97] Ibid.: 229–34; Chandavarkar 1994: 244–51.
[98] Chandra 1966: 336.

standpoints concerning factory legislation can be taken as monoliths. Despite Lancashire pressures, it took six years after the first Factory Commission of 1875 for a law to be made in 1881. It was applicable only to units that employed more than a hundred workers and used mechanical power. The law was extended to the whole country at the insistence of Bombay manufacturers, though the debate on the issue had been largely confined to the Bombay mills. Only the hours and age of child labourers were restricted, and 'child' was defined as between 7 and 12. The maximum hours of work for that age group were restricted to nine. A further Act, in 1891, extended the scope of applicability to factories with more than fifty workers, and for the first time imposed a limit on the hours of work for women. Occasional pleas for regulating working hours for adult male labourers were repeatedly rejected. A weekly holiday was introduced only in 1891, and there was no question of fixing minimum wages. The 1885 Factory Commission justified the omission of male workers from the scope of factory laws on the grounds of English experience, where restricting hours of work for women and children had allegedly made long hours unprofitable for owners. There was a note of dissent from two philanthropically minded members. An English doctor and a prominent Bombay citizen, S.S. Bengalee, pointed out that women and children were only 25 per cent of the Bombay labour force whereas they constituted as much as 74 per cent of the workforce in Lancashire. The weakness of labour reformism was apparent in the composition of this commission, which included three Parsi and one British mill-owner, and only a single official member. The dissent note indicates, however, the presence of a philanthropic initiative, once again cutting across racial lines. Apart from Bengalee—businessman, journalist, social reformer, and member of the Governor's Council as well as of the Factory Commissions of 1885 and 1890 who repeatedly urged regulating hours of work for children—the other prominent Indian member was N.M. Lokhande, a radical anti-Brahman activist associated with Jyotiba Phule's Satyashodhak Samaj. A contemporary of Sasipada Banerji, he was far more determined than his Bengali contemporary to promote labour welfare. He shifted the reformist focus from the educational and moral uplift of workers towards an attempt to change their work conditions. Apart from writing frequently about the sufferings of mill labourers in the journal *Din*

Bandhu (Friend of the Poor) which he edited, Lokhande set up a Bombay Millhands Association. This was somewhat shadowy, and hardly a full-on trade union, but still an organization that organized a meeting of 5500 workers in October 1884—to endorse a memorial to the Factory Commission, pleading for holidays on Sunday and the restriction of working hours for adult males from 6.30 a.m. to sunset.

Conditions worsened for male workers with the gradual introduction of electric lights in mills from 1893 onwards. This enabled, as the Factory Commission of 1908 pointed out, some Bombay mills to work 'for 14 and a half hours daily with one set of hands', as the earlier natural limit of sunrise-to-sunset could now be overcome. The 1911 Act, passed under a Liberal administration in Britain that was more hospitable to labour demands, fixed for the first time the adult male working day at 12 hours. Women would work for a maximum of 11 hours and children for 6. But minimum wages still were not fixed.[99]

Despite frequent complaints by mill-owners that were reported in several official enquiry reports, there was seldom any actual problem about labour recruitment, as Morris David Morris established in his study of the Bombay textile industry. Chronic labour shortages should have pushed up wages, especially since labour costs were only a small proportion of the outlay by mill-owners. Profit expectations were high, and there was no shift to more capital-intensive techniques. Yet this never happened, except during the one real spell of shortage during the plague panic in Bombay in the late 1890s, at which time wages did rise.[100]

Morris' study set a certain pattern for research on Bombay labour that can be traced down to Chandavarkar. It has a slant that is different from the work on Bengal. The persistent emphasis, in sharp contrast to Chakrabarty's, was on a kind of 'rational choice', a desire to seek 'hard' connections with material conditions and motives without probing too many possible cultural or traditional dimensions. As already suggested, though this is often convincing, it can lead to

[99] *Report of Bombay Factory Commission, 1885*; Punekar and Vanickayil 1990: pt IV.
[100] Morris 1965: 199, *et passim*.

some neglect of less tangible, but not necessarily less important, aspects of the life of entrepreneurs and workers. For earlier decades in Bombay, there is nothing comparable to Samita Sen's work on the gender dimensions.[101] There is, moreover, a certain noticeable disregard of questions of caste and religion. We are often left with hard statistics. Women's employment in mills rose sharply in the 1880s amidst large-scale distress migration from Deccan districts because of the famines of the previous decade. The figure then declines, predictably, with the fixing of maximum working hours for women in 1891. It was still about one-fifth of the total workforce, however, in the 1920s, but then it went down to one-tenth by the 1940s. As for caste and religious loyalties, Morris warned against exaggerating their influence, and explained their persistence with other factors: jobbers recruiting from kinspeople or particular groups of workers trying to establish 'corners' for relatives in workplaces and slums. Both Morris and Chandavarkar found systematic discrimination only against Dalits, who were generally confined to the lowest-paid jobs in ring-spinning departments, while intermediate-caste workers, as well as Muslim men, were predominant among weavers. Significantly, the Kunbi-Maratha caste cluster, the principal base of Phule's movement, mustered in strength within the workforce of Bombay mills. This makes Lokhande's interest understandable, even though he repeatedly urged an extension of the Maratha category to include all non-Brahman groups in order to create something like a broad alliance of toilers.[102] Conversely, the presence of a Dalit (particularly Mahar) underclass within the labour force caused problems when a militant trade union movement developed from the 1920s. It was confined predominantly to weavers.

The Bombay industrial labour force had two distinctive features that distinguished it from jute mill labour in Bengal. These related

---

[101] For gender aspects in later years, see Kumar 1989: 133–62.

[102] Morris 1965, *passim*; Chandavarkar 1994: chapters 3–5. For Lokhande, the best account is O'Hanlon 1985: chapter 6. We get more data on such aspects, and particularly about women workers, for the later decades of Bombay labour history, through, notably, the research of Radha Kumar and the oral history volume compiled by Adarkar and Menon. This will be taken up in later sections, dealing with Bombay labour in the post-1918 era.

to workers' places of origin, and the degree of their articulation with larger city life. Till well into the twentieth century, the recruitment areas for Bombay mills were certain relatively depressed rural areas of the Bombay Presidency itself. Foremost among these was Konkan, particularly its Ratnagiri district, which suffered from mountainous, relatively poor soil, long traditions of out-migration, and diminishing prospects due to the fall of the Maratha state (which had employed large numbers as soldiers and officials). The Gujarat districts of the Presidency had a long history of commercial prosperity, and the substantial development of an independent peasant stratum in some areas. They were close to the other developing industrial centre of Ahmedabad. These districts supplied large numbers of migrant business elites to Bombay but relatively few industrial workers. The decline and then end of indentured migration abroad did turn part of the outflow from eastern UP and western Bihar, those perennial LCAs, towards Bombay. But that happened at a later date than upcountry migration towards Calcutta. The Bombay labour force was, for a long time, largely Marathi-speaking. Though this diminished over time, the linguistic tie initially permitted easier contact with sections of the largely Marathi intelligentsia of the city. Unlike the jute industry, again, mills in Bombay came to be concentrated in the north-central part of the city, not in its outlying suburbs. Given the difficulties of transport, workers lived as close as possible to their place of work. By 1933, 90 per cent of the millworkers lived within fifteen minutes' walking distance from their place of work. Thus there emerged the 'Girangaon mill village', as workers called it, right in the heart of the city, particularly in the municipal wards of Parel, Byculla, and Worli. This bestowed upon industrial labour a kind of visibility in city life which never happened in Calcutta. It lasted till the industry itself was virtually destroyed in the wake of the defeat of the 1982 strike.

Workplace and neighbourhood were thus tightly bound together in Bombay. Structures of domination, exercised primarily through the ubiquitous but by no means homogeneous or always all-powerful jobber, extended to both. We have already noted the key features of the grossly unequal and power-laden, yet occasionally reversible, relationships bound up with housing, credit, and employment. Conditions in the chawls were always terrible. Even in the 1930s, for

30–40 per cent of the people in the mill districts, chawl life meant sharing a single room among more than six persons. In one case, six families shared a single room. Protests also began early, as well as efforts to build an autonomous everyday social and cultural life in Girangaon. This was helped by the fact that such gross overcrowding meant that much of the workers' spare time was necessarily spent on the street. This stimulated a collectivity in leisure hours, though it also meant frequent brawls. The rich cultural life of Girangaon, setting a particular tone to the entire life of Bombay for a whole epoch from the late 1920s down to the early post-Independence decades, will engage us in more detail later.

Lokhande was able to organize at least two big meetings of mill-workers, in 1884 and 1890. He drew up memorials for Factory Commissions: the second of these meetings reportedly attracted 10,000, and the speakers included, remarkably, two women operatives. Labour historians have also unearthed a number of 'spontaneous' protests, independent of middle-class interventions: notably a rash of strikes in the early and mid-1890s, directed against the brutal extension of working hours following upon the new electric lights, as well as against arbitrary fines. These, however, were confined to particular factories or departments alone, unlike the impressive general strikes of the inter-war years. They have not yet been traced to formal or stable labour organizations. They were also different from the protest strike of 1908 against the trial of Tilak.[103]

The mills of Ahmedabad differed from those of Calcutta and Bombay, in that they were located in a region famous for many centuries for its handlooms, exports of woven cloth to far-flung places, and well-developed traditional merchant groups. Ahmedabad was founded as early as 1411. Its history, therefore, had an element of continuity—entirely absent in Calcutta and Bombay—with pre-colonial times as

[103] Sen 1970; Punekar and Vanickayil 1990. As with Bengal, it is more convenient to take up the Swadeshi years of labour history in a later section on nationalism.

well as with artisanal traditions that had declined before Lancashire in the nineteenth century but had not entirely been wiped out. The economic—and, to some extent, the political— presence of colonial power was also less prominent here than in the metropolitan cities founded by the British, for much of Gujarat consisted of princely states.

The first cotton mill was initiated by a prominent Ahmedabad Nagar Brahman, Ranchodlal Chhotalal, in 1861, with financial support from a number of Gujarati Bania businessmen. After a slow start, Ahmedabad's mills grew rapidly from the closing decades of the nineteenth century, their number rising from 12 in 1894 to 26 in 1899 and 49 in 1914. Unlike Bombay, there was always a greater emphasis on the domestic market. Mills supplied yarn to handloom weavers as well as coarse and finer piecegoods. By the early 1900s Ahmedabad was growing faster than Bombay. It had a far higher proportion of looms to spindles. It also manufactured yarn of higher counts. There was thus a greater potential for conflict with Lancashire, a fact which may partly explain the closer relations of Ahmedabad's textile magnates with Gandhian nationalism from the 1920s. This did not happen with Bombay mill-owners.

Ahmedabad was somewhat special, too, because the bulk of its workers came from adjoining areas. As late as 1929, 80 per cent were from a fifty-mile radius of the city. Many more settled within Ahmedabad, making only infrequent visits to their village homes. Groups with spinning and weaving traditions were very prominent, Muslims and Kanbis among the weavers (the Kanbi-Patidars whom we will meet again as central to inter-war Gandhian nationalism), and untouchable Dheds and Vankars among the spinners. As elsewhere, Dalits were excluded from the more privileged and better-paid weaving departments, in significant part because of pollution taboos: spinners had to touch the thread with their hands and suck yarn onto the shuttle while replacing a bobbin. Thus, caste barriers were prominent, both between workers and their employers (overwhelmingly Gujarati high caste) and among workers themselves. They were continually consolidated as recruitment was organized by muqaddams (jobbers) from among their kin groups. A caste- and community-based segment-ation of labour became the dominant pattern. This was also true of other industrial centres, though studies of Ahmedabad seem to have devoted more attention to this phenomenon.

Labour conditions in Ahmedabad were as wretched as elsewhere. The sunrise-to-sunset work pattern meant a working day of as long as 13 hours in summer. As electric lights were introduced around 1905, this could become 15 hours for adult men. There was the usual decline of women and children labourers after the factory laws. Some women workers even organized a petition in 1891 against fixing maximum hours, since they were afraid, with good reason, that they would no longer be considered employable. Restrictions on the hours of work for children, however, were often evaded by the device of half-time work in more than one mill, and the proportion of women and children remained higher in Ahmedabad than elsewhere (15 per cent and 13 per cent, respectively, in 1921). This was possibly because the more stable urbanization of labour meant that more workers came with their families to settle here. Workers first lived in squalid self-erected hutments (wadas), divided along caste and religious community lines. They then moved into management or municipality erected one- or two-room tenements, set out along narrow alleys—hardly better than their counterparts, the chawls of Bombay. Despite the harsh conditions, however, there was never any problem with labour supplies. Wages were higher than those of agricultural labourers in the countryside. They were also better than the uncertain income that could be expected from the bazaar economy of urban 'informal' work.

There are scattered references to sporadic protests from the early days of the industry. There were occasional strikes over specific grievances in particular mills which developed a tradition of meetings beside the 'Chandola' tank. Workers would be informed about the meetings through the distribution of a metal disc or token. Packets of long hair and bangles would be sent to non-strikers as symbols of their 'feminine' cowardice: a gender stereotyping that workers deployed. There was a bigger strike in 1895, involving 8000, against the new practice of paying wages fortnightly rather than weekly. Dalit labourers apparently acted as strike-breakers, lured by the prospect of getting better places in the mills. The foundation of the Ahmedabad Millowners Association in 1891 was partly in response to the felt need for joint action against labour protests.

Ameliorative initiatives from 'above' came to acquire much greater and more permanent importance in Ahmedabad than elsewhere. A clear link can be established with the distinctive style of Gandhian trade unionism starting with the 1918 strike. As in Bombay, but more decisively so in Ahmedabad, the linguistic-cultural affinity between the Gujarati intelligentsia and the overwhelmingly Gujarati workers helped the process. A Swadeshi Mitra Mandal began philanthropic work among millworkers from 1905. A few years later there emerged the key figure of Anasuyabehn Sarabhai, sister of the leading textile magnate Ambalal. She came under Fabian Socialist influence as a student at the London School of Economics, and, on her return, she set up a school for children in a chawl which was owned by her brother in 1914. Two years later, she organized with Shankarlal Banker a Majoor Mitra Mandal which ran evening classes for adults and tried to improve healthcare and home hygiene of workers and their families. Such efforts helped to create a base for Gandhi's intervention in Ahmedabad in 1918.[104]

Cotton mills would eventually proliferate across a large number of cities and towns in many parts of India, but that happened only in the inter-war years. Early centres outside western India, among which we will briefly glance at Kanpur and Madras, were distinguished by a very strong European presence which conformed to the ubiquitous domination of British business in the late nineteenth and early twentieth century outside Bombay Presidency.

The lead of British business till the early twentieth century in what they spelt 'Cawnpore' (Kanpur) is easily explained by the connection of the two industries that developed there, leather and cotton, with the needs of the British Indian army. Kanpur had grown from the early nineteenth century as trading centre and cantonment town. Military needs for leather lay behind British efforts to modernize production in the 1860s and shift its centre from villages to the city. Two ex-indigo planters set up Cooper & Allen to supply boots and shoes to the army.

---

[104] The above account is based mainly on Breman 2004.

Cotton mills also came up from around the 1860s at British initiative (there were no Indian-owned mills before the 1920s), though their numbers were much less than in Bombay and Ahmedabad: only seven mills even in the early twentieth century. To some extent, though, this was balanced by the size of the mills, which were often bigger than in western India. None of the Kanpur units in 1905 had less than 40,000 spindles and 500 looms. The army demand was central here as well, and Kanpur enjoyed a major boom during 1914–18 supplying tents, jeans, and drills for the British Indian army that had been vastly expanded to fight in Mesopotamia and on the Western Front. As in jute, entrepreneurship in India at times involved an element of upward mobility for Englishmen not from privileged backgrounds. Several early mill-owners were ex-workers from Lancashire. Like Ahmedabad, Kanpur drew on traditional weaving castes for a significant part of its workforce in the early years; Koris and, in particular, Muslim Julahas were particularly prominent. There were never too many women and children among Kanpur's workers, and the large Muslim presence perhaps contributed to a greater reluctance in relation to women's work outside homes. Most workers came from districts in UP, but in such a large province this still could involve considerable distances, and the Bengal and Bombay pattern of circular mobility seems to have been the rule in Kanpur too. Migration patterns and experiences could vary widely, and Chitra Joshi's fine account conveys unusually rich detail culled from memoirs, and the accounts of workers who lived in what she calls an 'in-between world', neither fully rural peasant nor urban labour, marked by a continual movement across spaces and social categories, and constituting the poignant experience of 'lost worlds'.[105]

British domination over the external trade and financial structures of Madras Presidency was as complete as it was of Bengal. The Bank of Madras, for instance, one of the three Presidency banks located at the apex of the country's banking hierarchy, did not have a single

[105] Joshi 2003. See also Bagchi 1972: 185–8.

Indian director from its foundation in 1876 till its merger with the Imperial Bank in 1921. Modern industries were thin on the ground in the South, though it would become a major growth area of textiles by the inter-war years. What little there was in the late nineteenth century was overwhelmingly controlled by the British. The biggest textile mill was the Buckingham & Carnatic complex in Madras city. Set up in the mid-1870s by Binny & Co., it was a very large general merchant concern with numerous cargo boats, steamers, and docks which a decade later set up a woollen mill in Bangalore too. Buckingham & Carnatic became one of the biggest units of textile production in the country, as they made massive profits with wartime supplies of khaki to the army. They had also a rather special labour policy, within which elements of paternalism went along with a firmly authoritarian structure not entirely free of racism. The company did provide unusually good housing and some medical facilities for its workers. This did not prevent occasional clashes, and as early as 1878 a strike took place, demanding time off on Sunday afternoons. There was a riot in 1902 against the supply of poor quality yarn which had made it difficult for workers to meet their weaving quota. Buckingham & Carnatic, as we shall see, also became the centre of early trade union activity from about 1918, which culminated in one of the biggest and most prolonged post-world war strikes, in 1920–1. The strike, however, eventually collapsed amidst a bitter caste riot. Untouchable Adi-Dravida workers, who, for obvious reasons, had less staying power, broke the strike and faced violence from higher-caste co-workers. Caste divisions in the South were notoriously more rigid than elsewhere, and, clearly, industrial conditions helped to reproduce and possibly aggravate them within the factories.[106]

British commercial firms often diversified into industries. This happened in the cotton-exporting firm of Harvey & Co., which set up textile mills in Tinnevelli, Tuticorin, and Madurai between 1884 and 1892. The third major British trading firm in the South, Parry & Co., came to specialize in sugar, spirits, and later fertilizers. It will be more convenient to take up in a later section the growth of modern sugar factories, along with the other industries that developed mostly after 1914—notably, light engineering, cement, and paper.

[106] Bagchi 1972: 188–91; Murphy 1977: 291–321.

Beyond Blacksmiths: Iron and Steel

With its abundant iron resources, the subcontinent had an old iron-manufacturing tradition. This was based on the use of charcoal from timber for smelting rather than coal, and it was quite adequate for pre-colonial firearms and the work of village blacksmiths who prepared or repaired agricultural tools. Some early efforts by British entrepreneurs—notably the ex-Company servant Heath in the 1820s who started iron manufacture at Porto Novo (South Arcot) with some backing from his old employers—continued charcoal and initiated only minor improvements in technology. This provided no real alternative to traditional manufactures and had to be wound up by the 1870s. By this time much of the home market had been captured by imports of iron and steel from Britain, which used modern coke-based technology and badly affected the old rural industry. The Bengal Iron Works of the British managing agency firm Martin & Co. started manufacturing iron by modern methods near Asansol in 1874. It too had a chequered career and did not venture into steel production till much later.

The real breakthrough came from the Tatas, the most striking late-colonial Indian instance of daring capitalist entrepreneurship. The Tata family had built its fortune on opium and raw cotton exports, and then on cotton mills in Bombay and Nagpur. It combined this with a large-scale import trade in iron and steel. This enabled it to master local market conditions. Tata Sons' efforts at pioneering steel manufacture in India in the early twentieth century encountered some of the usual colonial obstacles: private British railway and engineering companies preferred to rely on what they assumed to be much better quality British steel, while the London money market from where funds were initially sought refused to risk capital in a venture that was started entirely by an Indian firm.

There were two new favourable factors, both of which were skilfully used by the Tatas. Swadeshi enthusiasm was at a high peak in the years immediately following Curzon's Partition of Bengal in 1905, and in August 1907 the entire amount of Rs 23 million that the Tatas asked for was subscribed in three weeks by 8000 Indian investors in a wave of enthusiasm. Patriotic fervour was strengthened by public confidence in a firm already well known for its business acumen—in sharp contrast to most instances of Swadeshi enterprise. At the same time, British authorities, both in London and Calcutta, had come to feel that a centre of steel production within India would be a major asset. Belgian steel imports were in any case capturing much of the Indian market from British firms, and, in the event of a European war, which seemed increasingly likely, a source for steel within the colony would be a major strategic asset. The Tatas effectively played on this second string. They first obtained the goodwill of the secretary of state (Lord Crewe visited the fledgling plant in 1911), and then they remained demonstratively loyal to the empire in the subsequent decades of anti-colonial nationalism. It may be noted, then, that the Tatas, the one truly modern and innovative group among Indian capitalists, hardly fit with the stereotype of a 'national' rather than 'compradore' bourgeoisie in political, or for that matter economic, terms.

The site for the steel plant was chosen carefully and after much geological and other research. Sakchi (soon to be renamed Jamshedpur, or Tatanagar) was on the Bengal–Nagpur railway line to Calcutta, *c.* 150 miles away from the city. There were enormous reserves of iron at Gurumaishini and Noamundi, and in the rich Jharia coalfield, all located within 50–115 miles of the site. The British Indian government helped out by constructing a railway line between Gurumaishini and Sakchi, and agreed to buy 20,000 tons of steel annually for ten years for the state-owned railways. Steel would also be one of the first industries to be given tariff protection under the new policy of 'Discriminating Protection' adopted in 1921. The technology, however, had to be entirely imported, and there was initially a large staff of European and American technicians, as many as 325 foreigners among the initial workforce of about 4000. The plant grew fast, and steel production climbed up from 3000 tons in 1911 to 429,000 tons in 1928. The labour force touched a peak of 30,000 in 1923–4.

Alone among the industries of that time in India, steel required large numbers of skilled workers who were recruited from all over the country. They were well paid, given company housing in what grew as a real company town, the local municipal administration being managed and tightly controlled by the firm. But there was also a big underclass of unskilled 'coolies' and 'rezas' (women workers), drawn from neighbouring adivasis and lower castes, in contrast to skilled workers who were multi-provincial and mostly upper castes (Brahmins, Rajputs, Kayasths), plus a fair number of Muslims. Unskilled and casual workers were, as usual, housed in makeshift slums. Thus, ethnic-cum-caste hierarchies came to be reproduced even in this most modern of Indian industrial centres, and there was also an obvious link of the composition of skilled workers with the caste linkages of the late-colonial educated elite. But controls, relatively better conditions for a substantial section, and hierarchical divisions did not prevent occasional powerful labour protests in Jamshedpur from the 1920s—as we shall see.[107]

Labour in the Informal Sector

Research on labour conditions and movements in the 'informal' sector is still relatively new. It runs into major difficulties except for the most recent years, since the methods of fieldwork and oral testimony—vital for an area which has little by way of written sources—cannot be taken too far into the past. The more recent historians of labour have repeatedly stressed the interconnections and permeability of the formal/informal divide, and sought to present something like a total picture of the urban environment within which their specific area of study is embedded: Raj Chandavarkar, Samita Sen, Chitra Joshi, and Jan Breman. Their principal focus has, however, inevitably been the industrial labour force. An important full-length study of the urban poor of UP deliberately integrated within that category both factory workers and labour in the informal sector, though it does not really venture into the decades prior to the First World War.[108] Whole areas of such work, therefore, remain to be explored. Research on domestic service, for instance, is just beginning,[109] though a glance at the rich literature of middle-class memoirs and biographies, or for that matter imaginative literature, immediately reveals the virtually ubiquitous presence of a very considerable number of household servants, both men and women, in upper-, middle-, and even often lower-middle-

[107] Morris 1983: chapter VII, 583–92; Bagchi 1972: 291–303; Simeon 1995: chapter 1.

[108] Gooptu 2001.

[109] Ray and Qayum 2009.

class families. Prostitution has so far been studied almost entirely in terms of its implications for gender and sexuality, leaving the terms and structure of sex work, its interconnections with poor people and toilers in general, relatively underexplored.

However, even for this underexplored field, some rather conventional sources or secondary work sometimes provide illuminating insights. Two instances will have to suffice. Factory Commissions at times reported particularly terrible labour conditions in small and/ or seasonal concerns which were unregulated. The report of 1885, for example, went into great detail about a cotton-ginning unit in Khandesh, where, during the peak season of March–April, labourers, mostly women, were made to work day and night for eight days continuously. They were then thrown out and replaced by another batch. A list compiled about early strikes in Calcutta mentions protests by palanquin bearers (1823), river porters (1853), bullock-cart drivers (1862), and Howrah Station porters: the last, remarkably, seem to have demanded an eight-hour day as early as 1862. Bombay municipal meat-sellers went on strike in 1866, Ahmedabad tailors and brick-field labourers in 1873.

But these were before the era of factories had begun on a large scale, and, once that started, the Marxist compiler passes on with evident relief from such actions by 'toilers' to the working class 'proper'. There is no reason at all to think that protests by informal sector labour ever stopped, or were necessarily less important or effective.[110] One of the most detailed accounts of a nineteenth-century strike that has been reconstructed by a historian is that of Bombay municipal sweepers, in July–August 1889.[111] Wages were reduced from initial relatively high levels (not very much less than those of most millhands), and there were many grievances against the muqaddam intermediaries who functioned as the immediate bosses. There were actually two strikes in quick succession. Both were smashed by the municipality which evicted sweepers from the chawls that it controlled amidst the fury of a Bombay monsoon. The strikes were followed by a Municipal

[110] Sen 1970: chapter 6.
[111] Masselos 1982: 101–39.

Servants' Act (1890) which made refusal of duty punishable by fines and/or three months' imprisonment. But municipal sweepers in many Indian cities remained a restive lot; as we shall see, there were strikes by them in Bombay and Calcutta during the inter-war years, several of them led by Left-nationalist or Communist activists, sometimes by women.[112] A substantial part of informal labour was carried on under official auspices for road and house construction, forest clearing, various forms of unpaid (begar) services for officials on tour, as punishment for convicts, and in the course of military operations. Documentation becomes more available for this, even far back into the past. It is not surprising that labour historians have now turned to such material.[113]

A last, interesting, if also speculative point: strikes, or the collective withdrawal of work or services, have a long genealogy going back much before the first factories. This is indicated by the fact that words for such events exist in a number of Indian languages. Most terms that figure in today's lexicon of labour or socialist movements are clearly translations or straight loans from English (e.g. 'sreni' for class, 'samajvad' for socialism). Not so, though, for 'strike': here we have a well-established, indisputably indigenous, battery of related terms—'dharmaghat', 'hartal', 'bandh'. The first, Bengali, word, is particularly interesting, for it points presumably to some kind of ritual by which those going on a strike would take a pledge before a symbol of Dharmathakur, a folk deity in parts of Bengal that some scholars think is a remnant of ancient Buddhism. The rite itself has disappeared, but the word survives, an indicator of a long, largely forgotten, history of movements of working people.

---

[112] Sweepers working in private houses seem also to have been assertive, developing at times what one anthropologist has termed a kind of jajmani system from below, asserting a right to be the sole and permanent service provider to a particular household. If a sweeper were to be dismissed, replacing him was made impossible as no other sweeper would agree to do his work resulting, in a kind of primitive trade unionism using traditional caste sanctions. See Mayer 1993: 357–95.

[113] For instance, Chitra Joshi has started work on the deployment of convict labour, and Radhika Singha on the Mesopotamian Labour Corps raised in the First World War.

Colonial Economic Policies

Many specific aspects of government policies have already figured in our narrative: forest, revenue, rent laws, irrigation, Home Charges, currency, railways, tariffs, labour regulations—to mention only some among many. We still need to discuss theoretical assumptions that undergird policies, as well as certain macro-aspects of government revenue and expenditure.[114]

A prominent theme in earlier discussions has been whether or not the British Indian administration was guided basically by laissez-faire notions and was therefore no more than a 'night-watchman state'. Did it live up to the stereotypical image of nineteenth-century British governance and economic theory once the remnants of mercantilist interventionism had been swept away? This assumption was deployed in quite different ways. The colonial government refused to give fiscal protection to infant Indian industries. Its apologists cited laissez-faire as justification, and claimed that that was the only rational basis for economic policy. Early nationalist critics broadly shared the assumptions of neo-classical, pre-Keynesian, economic theory. They, however, pointed to its unfair or tendentious applications in India: for instance, obvious favours shown to British commercial and industrial interests by the state at many points. Some nationalists, notably Ranade, were aware however of alternative economic notions that were already widespread in Germany, notably Friedrich List's justification of protection for infant industries. From the 1920s and 1930s on, laissez-faire itself came under attack, and the British Indian state was strongly criticized for its adherence to it.

In the 1960s and 1970s historians like Sabyasachi Bhattacharya showed that no such assumption of laissez-faire actually guided nineteenth- or early-twentieth-century British Indian governance. Old stereotypes regarding Victorian Britain had by then been discredited, for it had become clear that moves towards greater state intervention had been already under way both in theory and in practice. Both John

[114] As throughout this chapter, the survey of state economic policies will be from about the 1870s till 1914, after which the succession of War, Depression, and War, the development of mass nationalist movements, and the growing strength and assertiveness of Indian capitalist groups would necessitate numerous significant shifts.

Stuart Mill and late-nineteenth-century Utilitarians like Strachey and Fitzjames Stephens—from different, part-radical, or conservative-paternalist perspectives—had moved away from the defence of a minimalist state. Meanwhile the German Historical School developed an alternative perspective of economic development more suited to the needs of late starters in industrialization. But much more important than theory, however, in Bhattacharya's assessment, were pragmatic considerations and responses to specific pressures, particularly from British business interests. Such considerations, in fact, had led to a whole range of interventionist initiatives: granting land virtually free of cost to Assam tea planters; indenture; forms of labour disciplining directly under state auspices; the construction of railways under the guaranteed interest system; the construction of railways by the state for strategic reasons that were often commercially unremunerative—to mention only some of many instances. During the 'cotton famine' of the 1860s, which was brought about by the American Civil War, Manchester lobbies—otherwise the greatest advocates of laissez-faire—demanded that the British Indian state should actively promote irrigation and take other measures to encourage cotton cultivation in India. An MP from Lancashire went so far as to declare that the 'principle of political economy . . . was true as regards most countries but it did not apply to India.'[115] James Wilson, Finance Member of the Indian Government, seemed to agree. In a letter to Walter Bagehot in July 1860 he declared that 'public works and roads, with a view to increasing production of cotton, flax, wool, and European raw materials', should be a prime governmental duty in India.[116] At the same time, laissez-faire was a phrase frequently used by British administrators and their apologists for the obviously ideological purpose of blocking nationalist pleas for the protection of Indian handicrafts and emerging factory industries. Bhattacharya consequently summed up the underlying logic of British Indian state policy as 'discriminatory interventionism', not laissez-faire.[117]

[115] J.B. Smith in the Commons, 5 August 1869, Parliamentary Debates, House of Commons, National Archives of India.

[116] Wilson to Bagehot, July 1860, Parliamentary Debates, House of Commons, National Archives of India.

[117] Bhattacharya 1965: 1–22; Bhattacharya 1971. See also Stokes 1959.

There were signs of some changes, however, in the early decades of the twentieth century, even before the major changes of the post-1914 decades. One of the strands went back several decades, and was manifested in an admiration for the disappearing skilled handicrafts of India. Officials like Birdwood and E.B. Havell brought over to India some of the romantic anti-industrialism of Ruskin, William Morris, and the Pre-Raphaelite group of artists and thinkers. For them, the destruction of Indian crafts under the rampant commercialism of their own country represented a contemporary equivalent of the devastation wrought by industrialism on the supposed medieval unity of art and life and artisanal values which they had come to admire. The significance of these dissidents, however, lay in the field of art, where they became a major inspiration and support for the 'Orientalist' movement typified by the Bengal School of Art. A connection also developed between these ideas and Gandhian values. Men like Havell helped introduce more sympathetic attitudes among a section of British Indian officials towards artisanal production in general, notably handloom weaving. Around 1905, Havell was trying to encourage the use of Kay's late-eighteenth-century invention of the fly-shuttle in Bengal to enable handlooms to survive or grow. There was a favourable reference to that initiative in an official survey of Bengal industries by J.G. Cumming in 1908.

A more significant influence on senior administrators were the efforts of Alfred Chatterton. In 1906 he was given charge of what amounted to a new Department of Industries in Madras Presidency. He made a series of efforts to introduce new technology in India, notably aluminium manufacture. The government set up a pilot factory which was then handed over to a European barrister. It also invested in improved methods of chrome tanning and lift irrigation. Such initiatives, like similar moves in the United Provinces, were, however, rudely cut short in July 1910. Secretary of State John Morley blocked all attempts to start pioneering factories by officials. Morley was something of a laissez-faire ideologue. But times were against him, since strategic considerations were increasingly in favour of making India a little more self-sufficient in key manufactures, given the increasing likelihood of a European war. We have already seen this factor at work behind the very unusual support given to the Tatas to start a steel plant in Jamshedpur.[118]

We now turn briefly to the financial structure of the Raj. It embodied a highly centralized system, controlled by the secretary of state and the central government. It had developed particularly in the wake of the Crown takeover, but was gradually modified on considerations of practical, bureaucratic convenience. Beginning with 1870 (under the viceroyalty of Mayo), certain items of revenue and expenditure were handed over to provincial administrations, and even (under Ripon) to local bodies—to a minor extent. Such financial devolution became in course of time a key element in the gradual transition towards provincial autonomy. As for the overall budgetary situation, this was fairly centralized down to the late 1890s, as enormous costs of suppressing the Mutiny were followed by the depreciation of the silver rupee, and by expenditure on famine relief and military campaigns. The situation improved after that, as the mints were closed to free silver coinage, and with the shift to a gold exchange standard. But the government added to the difficulties by its rigid adherence to financial orthodoxy. This was evident in its rejection of any kind of deficit financing. A number of interest groups also had to be kept happy, or at least prevented from being too restive—principally British officials and businessmen, but also to some extent the more privileged or wealthy Indians.

The fiscal system consequently remained highly regressive. The major burden fell on peasants and the poor in general. 'It was no part of the functions of public finance', declared Finance Member James Wilson in the Legislative Council on 14 April 1860, 'to equalize the conditions of men'.[119] Land revenue was the biggest item, but its centrality as percentage of total revenue diminished slowly. It declined further in real terms on account of rising agricultural prices. Revenue payers were the upper stratum of peasants, at times in effect petty landlords, and their large numbers made the British hesitate

---

[118] Bagchi 1972: chapter 2. For Havell and the fly-shuttle, see ibid.: 222, and Sarkar 1973/2010: chapter 3.

[119] Quoted in Bhattacharya 1965.

to enhance the burden overmuch. This set a long-term trend which has continued into post-colonial times. The other main items of income were the opium monopoly, the extremely regressive salt tax (the addition to its price being negligible for the well-off but very oppressive for the really poor), and customs duties. The last was kept low under pressures that we have already touched on. Despite financial stringency, income tax, introduced briefly by Wilson in 1860 under pressure of Mutiny debts, and then permanently from 1886, remained ridiculously low: less than 2 per cent for incomes between Rs 500 and Rs 2000 per annum, at a time when the per capita income of Indians was calculated by Curzon at Rs 30 p.a. Income-tax payers were British officials, many of them enjoying astronomical salaries, businessmen, both British and increasingly Indian, and the more successful of professional men. These were groups that the colonial administration had no desire to hurt.

Public expenditure, consequently, constituted a low percentage of the national income in India. This continued from the late nineteenth century on, at a time when it rose rapidly in the Western countries as well as in Japan. It was spent, too, in predictably regressive ways. The army always absorbed 25–30 per cent of state expenditure. It was, after all, about half the military strength of the entire British empire. Indian soldiers were deployed more than a dozen times abroad in the nineteenth century, the costs being passed on to Indian taxpayers. Together with civil administration, this accounted for about half the total expenditure, while Home Charges amounted to another 16 per cent or so in the late nineteenth century. Big amounts went also to the railways, both under the guaranteed interests system and from the hands of the state. By contrast, expenditure on socially productive items, indisputably beneficial for the empire's subjects, was negligible: 2–4 per cent on education before 1914. This jumped to around 7 per cent by 1931, being the fruit of the 1919 constitutional reforms under which elected Indians were put in charge of the subject in the provinces. Another 2 per cent was spent on health. Literacy, for those above ten years, received a miserable 6 per cent in the late nineteenth century. Dharma Kumar calculated education expenditure as being around 0.2 per cent of the national income at that time, rising to 0.5 per cent in the early twentieth century. Much of it went to higher education rather than to primary: abysmally low, even in comparison to the most adequate state investment in education in post-1947 India.[120]

Demography and the National Income

Before the institution of the decennial census in 1871, population estimates, while not infrequent, dealt only with particular regions, most often towns.[121] They varied very widely in their degree of reliability. Two broad conclusions seem to emerge from Leela and Pravin Visaria's careful summary of the extant knowledge. There was a fairly large population already in the 1750s, and there was a slow growth rate due to high mortality rates, periodically aggravated by famines and epidemics. Historians of Mughal India speak of a 100 to 150 million range, which appears very high in comparison with about 20 million in France at the end of the seventeenth century, or to figures of less than 10 million in Britain prior to the Industrial Revolution. We are speaking, of course, of a subcontinent, and one that was marked by sub-tropical conditions where survival, if often on very low living standards, must have been easier than in cold climates before the coming of modern technology.

Census returns also reveal numerous problems. We have already seen how apparently dramatic changes in occupational figures, at one time thought to prove deindustrialization, revealed on closer scrutiny to be a product of changing definitions of census categories. Aggregate figures, however, become progressively more reliable, particularly as they were corrected by demographic scholars like Kingsley Davis. They indicate a broad continuation of the old pattern till the early 1920s. The average annual growth rate remained no more than 0.6 per cent, and then, in a much-written-about departure, doubled

[120] This and the preceding paragraph are based mainly on Dharma Kumar, 'The Fiscal System', in Kumar 1983: chapter 12, alongside Bagchi 1972: chapter 2.

[121] Population and national income estimates become increasingly uncertain and controversial as we go further back in time, and both subjects bristle with technicalities about which I have no expertise whatsoever. What follows will therefore be a very brief and general account.

to 1.2 per cent per annum between 1921 and 1941. But this was still far below the rates of the late twentieth century both in India and in the underdeveloped countries generally; it hardly justified the explanations of poverty on account of overpopulation which had already become common in some official circles by the late colonial decades. Demographic growth rates, in fact, were still considerably below those manifested in many Western countries, including Britain, in the initial phase of industrialization. Correlations seem fairly obvious between slow growth and periods or regions of famine and/or epidemics.

In aggregate terms, the population rose from 255 million to only 257 million between 1871 and 1881, a decade that saw widespread famines. There was some increase in the next decade, which was relatively free of such calamities; the population went up to 282 million in 1891. Then came another disastrous decade, leaving India with a population of 285 million in 1901. Ten years later this had grown to 303 million, but then the war decade again cut the growth down drastically. In 1921 the population stood at 305 million. The correlation with famines can be established also by a look at the regional variations in population figures. A contrast has been seen between areas of particularly slow growth across much of western and northern India, which were prone to repeated droughts; and the eastern parts of the country where rainfall was usually much more adequate—the wet/dry belts dichotomy that we have noted.

Along with famines came epidemics, quite often killing off millions. Malaria was endemic, particularly in the eastern and northern parts of the country. Cholera and related diseases like diarrhoea and dysentery were devastating in the absence of a filtered water supply to most of the 'native' quarters of cities. Smallpox was another major killer, diminishing only slowly with the spread of vaccination from about 1900. Most dreaded of all was the plague, which hit Bombay and western India from 1896, causing enormous panic and carrying political consequences in the context of the rise of extremist nationalism. It spread to Punjab and the North a few years later, killing some two million in the single year of 1907. There was also a deadly influenza epidemic immediately after the end of the war, over 1918–20.

Two other features stand out from the census statistics, one of which is still a part of Indian life. The sex ratio was consistently tilted against women, varying from 1037 and 1056 males to 1000 females between 1881 and 1921. This was partly explainable by the tendency towards undercounting women: a limited explanation. Disparity was greatest in the northern provinces: as much as 1135 men to 1000 women in 1921. The South, by contrast, was the only region where women outnumbered men, a difference which some have attributed to the prevalence in regions like Kerala of matrilineal practices. The Punjab–Kerala contrast has persisted into the twenty-first century. The other striking feature was the very high rate of infant mortality. There were 278–295 live births per thousand between 1871 and 1921. Census figures, with all their problems, still convey a vivid picture, then, of the basic features of late-colonial Indian society: mass poverty and undernourishment; utterly inadequate provisions for elementary medical care, hygiene, and education; and a deeply unjust gender hierarchy where girl children were (and are) grossly neglected, if not deliberately killed off soon after birth.[122]

National income estimates are even more uncertain, controversial, and abstruse. There is the additional question of degree of relevance—how much do figures of gross national product or per capita income really convey about the everyday conditions and quality of life of most people in a still predominantly rural, and significantly non-monetized, society (as large parts of India were till well into the twentieth century)? Our discussion of the question for the pre-1914 era must remain extremely brief.

Despite the obvious difficulties of calculation, attempts at estimating national income began early in late-colonial India, starting with Naoroji way back in the 1870s. The reasons were clearly political. It was important for emergent nationalism to assert not just that India was an extremely poor country, which no one could seriously doubt, but that poverty was growing, and that British policies were primarily responsible for both poverty and its growth. National income therefore came to occupy a central place in debates between officials and patriotic critics around the turn of the century. Curzon sought to

[122] Visaria and Visaria 1983: 463–532.

refute William Digby's sarcastically entitled, *Prosperous British India* (1901). The book, by an Indophile Englishman who drew upon Naoroji's estimates, was a powerful indictment.

What is interesting and revealing about this debate today is that the opposed estimates, all in significant part more or less intelligent guesses, were not really all that different from one another. No one could deny either the fact of massive poverty, or the yawning gap between India in this respect and Western industrialized countries like Britain. Curzon estimated per capita income at Rs 30 per annum; Atkinson, more optimistically, put it at Rs 39.5. At the exchange rates current then, this came to between £2 and 3, at a time when the income per head in Britain has been estimated at £52 annually. The debate really turned around whether such abysmal poverty was growing, or whether a slow improvement was taking place; and whether the responsibility lay with colonial structures and policies, or with Indian climate, customs, the habits of its peoples, its overpopulation, etc. Such arguments have a habit of recurring even in today's discussions and debates, as we have had occasion to see at various points.

As for estimated per capita national income across time, this seems to have varied roughly in inverse proportion to population growth rates, indicating that changes either way tended to be somewhat marginal. There was some slight increase in per capita income for the decades 1870–1920, when population growth was minimal: Heston puts it at *c.* 0.5 per cent per annum. After the demographic turn from 1921 onwards, this fell to 0.1 per cent: operationally, close to zero. What was pulling growth down was clearly agricultural stagnation over the major part of the country, notably in the Bengal region, with the exception of Punjab (as Blyn had shown). For 66 per cent of the national income came from the primary sector, at the beginning of the century, and, even in the mid-1940s, it was 53.3 per cent. Such a negligible growth in per capita income becomes more revealing if one recalls that Britain's real national product had grown at well over 2 per cent per annum in the nineteenth century, and much higher growth rates had become common in many parts of the world by the early twentieth century. Japan, for instance, whose living standards seem to have been similar to India's in the mid-nineteenth century, grew at a rate 5–10 times that of India from the Meiji Restoration till 1945.

Not only was India under British rule backward, then: the lag in world terms was growing over time from the early twentieth century.[123]

Bibliography

Anderson, Michael, 'India 1858–1930: The Illusion of Free Labour', in Douglas Hay and Paul Craven, eds, *Masters, Servants, and Magistrates in Britain and the Empire, 1562–1955* (Chapel Hill: University of North Carolina Press, 2004)

Arasaratnam, S., 'Weavers, Merchants, and Company: The Handloom Industry in South-eastern India, 1750–90', in Tirthankar Roy, ed., *Clothes and Commerce: Textiles in Colonial India* (New Delhi: Sage, 1996)

Bagchi, Amiya Kumar, *Private Investment in India 1900–1939* (Cambridge: Cambridge University Press, 1972)

———, 'Deindustrialization in Gangetic Bihar, 1809–1901', in Barun De, ed., *Essays in Honour of Professor S.C. Sarkar* (New Delhi: People's Publishing House, 1978)

———, *The Evolution of the State Bank of India—The Roots, 1806–1876: Part I, The Early Years, 1806–1860* (Bombay: Oxford University Press, 1987)

———, 'The Great Depression (1873–96) and the Third World: With Special Reference to India', in G. Balachandran, ed., *India and the World Economy, 1850–1950* (Delhi: Oxford University Press, 2003)

Basu, Subho, *Does Class Matter? Colonial Capital and Workers' Resistance in Bengal, 1890–1937* (Delhi: Oxford University Press, 2004)

Bayly, C.A., *Rulers, Townsmen and Bazaars: North Indian Society in the Age of British Expansion, 1770–1870* (Cambridge: Cambridge University Press, 1983)

Behal, Rana, 'Forms of Labour Protest in Assam Valley Tea Plantations, 1900–1932', *Economic and Political Review*, 20 (4), 1985

———, and Prabhu Mohapatra, 'Tea and Money Versus Human Life: The Rise and Fall of the Indenture System in the Assam Tea Plantations 1840–1908', in E. Valentine Daniel, Henry Bernstein, and Tom Brass, eds, *Plantations, Peasants and Proletarians in Colonial Asia* (London: Frank Cass, 1992)

Berg, Maxine, *Age of Manufactures 1700–1820: Industry, Innovation, and Work in Britain* (Oxford: B. Blackwell in Association with Fontana Press, 1985)

---

[123] Heston 1983: chapter 1; Roy 2000b: chapter 7. For a more detailed analysis, Sivasubramonian 1977: 427–89.

Bhattacharya, Neeladri, 'Predicaments of Mobility: Peddlers and Itinerants in Nineteenth-century Northwestern India', in Claude Marcovits, Jacques Pouchepadass, Sanjay Subrahmanyam, eds, *Society and Circulation: Mobile People and Itinerant Cultures in South Asia, 1750–1950* (New Delhi: Permanent Black, 2003)

Bhattacharya, Sabyasachi, 'Laissez Faire in India', *Indian Economic and Social History Review*, 2 (1), 1965

———, *Financial Foundations of the British Raj: Men and Ideas in the Post-Mutiny Period of Reconstruction of Indian Public Finance, 1858–1872* (Simla: Indian Institute of Advanced Study, 1971)

Breman, Jan, 'A Dualistic Labour System? A Critique of the "Informal Sector" Concept, I: The Informal Sector', *Economic and Political Weekly*, 11 (48), 1976

———, *Footloose Labour: Working in India's Informal Economy* (Cambridge: Cambridge University Press, 1996)

———, 'The Study of Industrial Labour in Postcolonial India—The Formal Sector: An Introductory Review', in Jonathan Parry, Jan Breman, Karin Kapadia, eds, *The Worlds of Indian Industrial Labourers in India* (New Delhi: Sage, 1999)

———, *The Making and Unmaking of an Industrial Working Class: Sliding Down the Labour Hierarchy in Ahmedabad, India* (Delhi: Oxford University Press, 2004)

Chakrabarty, Dipesh, 'Early Railwaymen in India: "Dacoity" and "Train-wrecking" c.1860–1900', in Barun De, ed, *Essays in Honour of Professor S.C. Sarkar* (Delhi: People's Publishing House, 1976)

———, *Rethinking Working-Class History: Bengal 1890–1940* (Delhi: Oxford University Press, 1989)

Chandavarkar, A.G., 'Money and Credit (1858–1947)', in Dharma Kumar, ed., *The Cambridge Economic History of India, Volume 2: c.1750–c.1970* (Cambridge: Cambridge University Press, 1983)

Chandavarkar, Rajnarayan, 'Workers' Politics and the Mill Districts in Bombay between the Wars', *Modern Asian Studies* 15 (3), 1981

———, *The Origins of Industrial Capitalism in India: Business Strategies and the Working Classes in Bombay: 1900–1940* (Cambridge: Cambridge University Press, 1994)

———, *Imperial Power and Popular Politics: Class, Resistance and the State in India, c.1850–1950* (Cambridge: Cambridge University Press, 1998)

———, 'From Neighbourhood to Nation', in Neera Adarkar and Meena Menon, eds, *One Hundred Years, One Hundred Voices: The Millworkers of Girangaon: An Oral History* (Calcutta: Seagull Books, 2004)

Chandra, Bipan, *The Rise and Growth of Economic Nationalism in India* (New Delhi: People's Publishing House, 1966)

——, 'Reinterpretation of Nineteenth Century Indian Economic History', *Indian Economic & Social History Review*, 5, March 1968

Charlesworth, Neil, *British Rule and the Indian Economy, 1800–1914* (London: Macmillan, 1982)

Chaudhuri, K.N., 'India's International Economy in the Nineteenth Century: A Historical Survey', *Modern Asian Studies*, II (I), 1968

Comninel, George C., *Rethinking the French Revolution: Marxism and the Revisionist Challenge* (London: Verso, 1987)

Dasgupta, Ranajit, *Economy, Society, and Politics in Bengal: Jalpaiguri, 1860–1947* (Delhi: Oxford University Press, 1992)

——, 'Poverty and Protest: A Study of Calcutta's Industrial Workers and Labouring Poor, 1875–1899', *Labour and Working Class in Eastern India: Studies in Colonial History* (Calcutta: K.P. Bagchi, 1994)

de Cecco, Marcello, *Money and Empire: The International Gold Standard, 1890–1914* (Oxford: Wiley-Blackwell, 1974)

——, 'Indian Monetary Vicissitudes: An Interlude', in G. Balachandran, ed., *India and the World Economy, 1850–1950* (Delhi: Oxford University Press, 2003)

Derbyshire, Ian, 'Economic Change and the Railways in North India, 1860–1914', *Modern Asian Studies*, 21 (3), 1987

Dutt, R.P., *India Today* (Bombay: People's Publishing House, 1947; revised edn, Calcutta: Manisha, 1970)

Gadgil, D.R., *Origins of the Modern Indian Business Class: An Interim Report* (New York: International Secretariat, Institute of Pacific Relations, 1959)

Ganguli, B.N., *Indian Economic Thought: Nineteenth Century Perspectives* (New Delhi: Tata-McGraw Hill, 1977)

Gooptu, Nandini, *The Politics of the Urban Poor in Early Twentieth-Century India* (Cambridge: Cambridge University Press, 2001)

Haynes, Douglas and Tirthankar Roy, 'Conceiving Mobility: Weavers' Migrations in Pre-colonial and Colonial India', *Indian Economic and Social History Review*, 36 (1), 1999

Heston, A., 'National Income', in Dharma Kumar, ed., *The Cambridge Economic History of India, Volume 2: c. 1750–c. 1970* (Cambridge: Cambridge University Press, 1983)

Hurd, John, 'Railways', in Dharma Kumar, ed., *The Cambridge Economic History of India, Volume 2, c. 1750–c. 1970* (Cambridge: Cambridge University Press 1983)

Joshi, Chitra, *Lost Worlds: Indian Labour and its Forgotten Histories* (Delhi: Permanent Black, 2003)

Joshi, G.V., 'The Economic Situation in India', *Quarterly Journal of the Poona Sarvajanik Sabha*, 1880

Karnik, V.B., *Strikes in India* (Bombay: Mankatalas, 1967)

Kerr, Ian, 'Working-class Protest in Nineteenth-Century India: Example of Railways Workers', *Economic and Political Weekly*, Review of Political Economy, 20 (4), 1985

———, ed., *Railways in Modern India* (Delhi : Oxford University Press, 2001)

———, 'Representation and Representations of the Railways of Colonial and Postcolonial India', *Modern Asian Studies*, 37 (2), 2003

Kumar, Dharma, ed., *The Cambridge Economic History of India, Volume 2: c.1750–c.1970* (Cambridge: Cambridge University Press, 1983)

Kumar, Radha, 'Family and Factory: Women in the Bombay Cotton Textile Industry, *c.* 1919–1939', in J. Krishnamurty, ed., *Women in Colonial India: Essays on Survival, Work and the State* (Delhi: Oxford University Press, 1989)

Lahiri Choudhury, Deep Kanta, *Telegraphic Imperialism: Crisis and Panic in the Indian Empire, c.1830–1920* (London: Palgrave Macmillan, 2010)

Lehmann, Frederick, 'Great Britain and the Supply of Railway Locomotives of India: A Case-Study of "Economic Imperialism"', *Indian Economic and Social History Review*, 2 (4), 1965

Markovits, Claude, *The Global World of Indian Merchants, 1750–1947: Traders of Sind from Bukhara to Panama* (Cambridge: Cambridge University Press, 2000)

———, Jacques Pouchepadass, and Sanjay Subrahmanyam, eds, *Society and Circulation: Mobile People and Itinerant Cultures in South Asia, 1750–1950* (New Delhi: Permanent Black, 2003)

Marx, Karl, 'The Future Results of the British Rule in India', *New York Daily Tribune*, 8 August 1853, and letter to N.F. Danielson, 19 February 1881, in K. Marx and F. Engels, *On Colonialism* (Moscow: Foreign Languages Publishing House, n.d.)

Masselos, Jim, 'Jobs and Jobbery: The Sweeper in Bombay under the Raj', *Indian Economic and Social History Review*, 19 (2), 1982

Matsui, Toru, 'On the Nineteenth-Century Indian Economic History—A Review of a "Reinterpretation"', *Indian Economic & Social History Review*, 5 (1), 1968

Mayer, Peter, 'Inventing Village Traditions: The Late 19th Century Origins of the North Indian "Jajmani System"', *Modern Asian Studies*, 27 (2), 1993

Mohapatra, Prabhu, 'Assam and the West Indies, 1860–1920: Immobilizing Plantation Labour', in Douglas Hay and Paul Craven, eds, *Masters, Servants, and Magistrates in Britain and the Empire, 1562–1955* (Chapel Hill: University of North Carolina Press, 2004)

Morris, David Morris, *The Emergence of an Industrial Labour Force: A Study of the Bombay Cotton Mills, 1854–1947* (Berkeley: University of California Press, 1965)

———, 'Towards a Reinterpretation of Nineteenth-Century Indian Economic History', *Indian Economic & Social History Review*, 5 (1), 1968

———, 'The Growth of Large-Scale Industry to 1947', in Dharma Kumar, ed., *The Cambridge Economic History of India, Volume 2: c. 1750–c. 1970* (Cambridge: Cambridge University Press, 1983)

Mukherjee, Mukul, 'Railways and Their Impact on Bengal's Economy, 1870–1920', *Indian Economic and Social History Review*, 17 (2), 1980

Murphy, E.D., 'Cotton and Community in India: The Madras Labour Union, 1918–21', *Indian Economic & Social History Review*, 14 (3), 1977

Nair, Janaki, *Miners and Millhands: Work, Culture and Politics in Princely Mysore* (New Delhi: Sage, 1998)

O'Hanlon, Rosalind, *Caste, Conflict and Ideology: Mahatma Jyotirao Phule and Low-Caste Protest in Nineteenth Century Western India* (Cambridge: Cambridge University Press, 1985)

Parel, Antony J., *Hind Swaraj and Other Writings* (Cambridge: Cambridge University Press, 1997)

Parry, Jonathan, Jan Breman, and Karin Kapadia, eds, *The Worlds of Indian Industrial Labourers in India* (New Delhi: Sage, 1999)

Parthasarathi, Prasanna, *The Transition to a Colonial Economy: Weavers, Merchants and Kings in South India, 1720–1800* (Cambridge: Cambridge University Press, 2001)

Pinney, Christopher, 'On Living in the *Kal(i)yug*: Notes from Nagda, Madhya Pradesh', in Jonathan Parry, Jan Breman, and Karin Kapadia, eds, *The Worlds of Indian Industrial Labourers in India* (New Delhi: Sage, 1999)

Pouchepadass, Jacques, *Champaran and Gandhi: Planters, Peasants and Gandhian Politics* (Delhi: Oxford University Press, 1999)

Punekar, S.D., and R. Varickayil, eds, *Labour Movement in India Documents: 1891–1917, Volume 2* (Indian Council of Historical Research/Bombay: Popular Prakashan, 1990)

Ray, Durgacharan, and Dwarakanath Bidyabhushan, eds, *Debganer Marte Agaman* (Calcutta: Gurudas Chattopadhyay and Sons, 1887)

Ray, Rajat Kanta, 'The Bazaar: Changing Structural Characteristics of the Indigenous Section of the Indian Economy Before and After the Great Depression', *Indian Economic and Social History Review*, 25 (3), 1988

————, 'Introduction', in Rajat Ray, ed., *Entrepreneurship and Industry in India, 1800–1947* (Delhi: Oxford University Press, 1992)

Ray, Raka, and Seemin Qayum, *Cultures of Servitude: Modernity, Domesticity, and Class in India* (Palo Alto: Stanford University Press, 2009)

Raychaudhuri, T., 'A Re-interpretation of Nineteenth Century Indian Economic History?', *Indian Economic & Social History Review*, 5, March 1968

Report of Bombay Factory Commission, 1885 (no publisher, n.d.)

Risley, H.H., *Tribes and Castes of Bengal: Ethnographic Glossary* (Calcutta: Bengal Secretariat Press, 1891)

Rothermund, Dietmar, 'The Monetary Policy of British Imperialism', *Indian Economic and Social History Review*, 7 (1), 1970

Roy, Tirthankar, *Artisans and Industrialization: Indian Weaving in the Twentieth Century* (Delhi: Oxford University Press, 1993)

————, ed., *Clothes and Commerce: Textiles in Colonial India* (New Delhi: Sage, 1996)

————, *Traditional Industry in the Economy of Colonial India* (Cambridge: Cambridge University Press, 1999)

————, 'Deindustrialization: Alternative View', *Economic and Political Weekly*, 35 (17), 2000a

————, *The Economic History of India 1857–1947* (New Delhi: Oxford University Press, 2000b)

————, *Outline of a History of Labour in Traditional Small-scale Industry in India* (Noida: V.V. Giri National Labour Institute, Research Studies Series 015, 2001)

————, 'Changes in Wool Production and Usage in Colonial India', *Modern Asian Studies*, 3 (2), 2003

Sabel, Charles, and J. Zeitlin, 'Historical Alternatives to Mass Production: Politics, Markets and Technology in Nineteenth-Century Industrialization', *Past and Present*, 108, 1985

Sarkar, Aditya, 'The Work of Law: Three Factory Narratives from Bombay Presidency, 1881–1884', in Marcel van der Linden and Prabhu Mohapatra, eds, *Labour Matters: Towards Global Histories* (New Delhi: Tulika, 2009)

Sarkar, Sumit, *The Swadeshi Movement in Bengal, 1903–1908* (New Delhi: People's Publishing House, 1973; second edn, Ranikhet: Permanent Black, 2010)

————, 'The Return of Labour to South Asian History', *Historical Materialism*, 12 (3), 2004

Saul, S.B., *Studies in British Overseas Trade 1870–1914* (Liverpool: Liverpool University Press, 1960)

Sen, Amartya, 'The Pattern of British Enterprise in India, 1854—1914: A Causal Analysis', in Rajat Kanta Ray, ed., *Entrepreneurship and Industry in India, 1800–1947* (Delhi: Oxford University Press, 1992)

Sen, Samita, *Women and Labour in Late Colonial India: The Bengal Jute Industry* (Cambridge: Cambridge University Press, 1999)

Sen, Sukomal, *Working Class of India: History of Emergence and Struggle, 1830–1970* (Calcutta: K.P. Bagchi, 1970)

Sharma, Jayeeta, *Empire's Garden: Assam and the Making of India* (Ranikhet: Permanent Black, 2012)

Simeon, Dilip, *The Politics of Labour under Late Colonialism: Workers, Unions, and the State in Chota Nagpur* (Delhi: Manohar, 1995)

———, 'Work and Resistance in the Jharia Coalfield', in Jonathan Parry, Jan Breman, and Karin Kapadia, eds, *The Worlds of Indian Industrial Labourers in India* (New Delhi: Sage, 1999)

Simmons, C.P., 'Indigenous Enterprise in the Indian Coal Mining Industry, *c.* 1835–1939', *Indian Economic and Social History Review*, 23 (3), 1976a

———, 'Recruiting and Organizing an Industrial Force in Colonial India: The Case of the Coal Mining Industry, *c.*1880–1939', *Indian Economic and Social History Review*, 23 (4) 1976b

Sinha, N.K., ed., *The History of Bengal 1757–1905* (Calcutta: University of Calcutta, 1967)

Sivasubramonian, S., 'Revised Estimates of the National Income of India, 1900–01 to 1946–7', *Indian Economic and Social History Review*, 14 (4), 1977

Steinfeld, Robert J., *Coercion, Contract, and Free Labour in the Nineteenth Century* (Cambridge: Cambridge University Press, 2001)

Stokes, Eric, *The English Utilitarians and India* (Oxford: Clarendon Press, 1959)

Strachey, Sir John, *India* (London: Kegan Paul, 1888)

Tattvabhushan, Sitanath, *Social Reform in Bengal: A Side Sketch* (Calcutta: City Book Society, 1904)

Thompson, E.P., *The Making of the English Working Class* (New York: Vintage Books, 1963)

Thorner, Daniel, 'The Pattern of Railway Development in India', *Far Eastern Quarterly*, 14 (2), 1955; rpnt in Ian Kerr, ed., *Railways in Modern India* (Delhi: Oxford University Press, 2001)

————, and Alice Thorner, '"Deindustrialization" in India, 1881–1931', in Daniel Thorner and Alice Thorner, *Land and Labour in India* (Bombay: Asia Publishing House, 1962)

Timberg, Thomas A., *The Marwaris: From Traders to Industrialists* (Delhi: Vikas, 1978)

Tomlinson, B.R., 'India and the British Empire, 1880–1935', *Indian Economic & Social History Review*, 12 (4), 1975

————, *The Political Economy of the Raj 1914–1947: The Economics of Decolonization in India* (London: Macmillan, 1979)

Tripathi, Dwijendra, ed., *Business Communities of India: A Historical Perspective* (Delhi: Manohar, 1984)

Vicziany, Marika, 'Bombay Merchants and Structural Changes in the Export Community, 1850–80', in K.N. Chaudhuri and C.J. Dewey, eds, *Economy and Society: Essays in Indian Economic and Social History* (Delhi, 1976)

————, 'The Deindustrialization of India in the Nineteenth Century: A Methodological Critique of Amiya Kumar Bagchi', *Indian Economic & Social History Review*, 16 (2), 1979

Visaria, Leela, and Pravin Visaria, 'Population (1757–1947)', in Dharma Kumar, ed, *The Cambridge Economic History of India, Volume 2: c. 1750– c. 1970* (Cambridge: Cambridge University Press, 1983)

Yang, Anand A., *Bazaar India: Markets, Society and the Colonial State in Gangetic Bihar* (California: University of California Press, 1998)

5

Society and Culture

The Country, the City, and the New Middle Class

Picturing India: The Country and the City

Sometime in the early twentieth century, a British soldier sent back home a picture postcard of a 'ploughman' silhouetted against the setting sun. Scrawled beneath it was the assertion: 'This picture *is* India.' The message essentializes an eternally rural India and makes the villager the authentic Indian. The postcard, however, would in all probability have been prepared in a studio in a city or a small town. A local person would have been hired and dressed as a peasant so that the studio could make a profit.[1]

Stereotypical contrasts between village and town have been among the most pervasive cultural constructs known to all corners of the world. They go far back in time, acquiring great prominence with the simultaneous birth of industrial civilization and anti-industrial romanticism in the West. Colonial times in India are replete with such contrasts, in the written and visual imagery of British and Indians alike. They have been associated with other binary oppositions: changelessness and change, purity and corruption, stagnation and progress, decline and advance. A major expression of 'Orientalism'—of modern Western images of the non-West—the terms of contrast perpetually oscillate between the contemptuous and the romantic in such constructions of the Other. The essentializations can be of the country (or the Oriental city) as a whole, like that made by our

[1] Pinney 1997: 9.

British soldier, or broken up into sub-types, each in its turn converted into a stereotype. The eight-volume *People of India* (1868–75), which Canning had ordered before leaving India, for instance, contained photographs of 'Goojur landholder', 'Brinjara and Wife', 'Bunnea', and so on. Each social type was portrayed with clothes and signs of occupations assumed to be typical, and had captions confidently ascribing invariant character traits.

But such stereotyping was no monopoly of the colonials, nor was it necessarily the product of Western domination. The papers of Census Commissioner H.H. Risley contain a section comprising translations of vernacular proverbs current among particular castes about other castes superior or inferior to them.[2] As for village and town, the binary oppositions here run right through modern Indian culture. An early Bengali text about Calcutta, Bhabanicharan Bandyopadhyay's *Kalikata Kamalalay* (1823), counterposed the language and values of a rustic visitor to those of city people. The opposition between traditional village purity and modern urban corruption that attained classic form in Gandhi has remained a standard trope of poetry, stories, and novels for almost two centuries now,[3] and Satyajit Ray's depiction in *Jalsaghar* (1958) of a declining, music-loving landlord at the point of losing his property to the brash nouveau riche urban upstart has had abundant counterparts in Indian literature, theatre, and films.[4] Left-wing variants of the same trope include K.A. Abbas's *Dharti ke Lal* (1946) and Bimal Roy's *Do Bigha Zameen* (1953), in both of which sharecroppers or poor peasants have to move to the city, losing their ancestral land to crooked zamindars or moneylenders. The spatial shift is often associated with moral degeneration.[5]

[2] Ibid.: 9, 34–42; 'Proverbs Illustrating the Peculiarities of Castes', in 'Printed circulars, notes and memoranda on caste and religion in Bengal, July 1900–June 1901', Risley Collection, MSS EUR.E. 295/11, British Library.

[3] Among the celebrated critical works to examine this theme as represented in English literature is Williams 1973.

[4] The central theme of the parvenu's upward thrust simultaneous with the aristocracy's downward slide has several Western literary counterparts as well, the best known being Chekhov's *The Cherry Orchard* and Lampedusa's *The Leopard*.

[5] A fine recent treatment of this theme of loss of land to villainous zamindars within the Telugu cinema can be found in Srinivas 2013.

Our survey (in Chapter 3) of late-colonial rural life has indicated the simplifications embodied in most such representations. In particular, the assumption of the village as more or less uniform on a subcontinental scale, unchanging prior to British rule and then disintegrating—common to observers as different in their perspectives and values as Marx, Maine, and Gandhi—has to be wholly rethought. It is extremely implausible to suggest that the village was egalitarian, as assumed by many—though not by Marx, who noted that its apparently simple and idyllic life had been shot through with caste distinctions. Irfan Habib's classic study of the agrarian system of Mughals drew attention to the shifting frontiers between the settled and the unsettled, between stable village-centred peasant societies and part-migratory food-gathering and pastoral communities with looser habitational structures.[6] In colonial times conjoint processes of revenue enhancement, communicational integration, commercialization, and the interest of the state in enhancing profit and control stimulated a more one-way expansion of settled agriculture. The post-1920s demographic leap accelerated the retreat of forest and pasture before arable. But sedentarization went alongside contrary tendencies, enhancing mobility. Tribals, dispossessed by forest laws and the lower ranks of increasingly differentiated peasant communities, were dragged away into colonial plantations in India and abroad, while increasing numbers moved towards mines, factories, and cities in patterns of cyclical, footloose labour flows.

Contradictory tendencies towards stabilization and movement, upward and downward mobility, reproduced themselves in rural social life. The advance of the settled village meant also the consolidation of stronger caste hierarchies, as well as the spread of brahmanical and orthodox Islamic structures and values. Caste hierarchies have generally been embodied in settlement patterns in villages, with separate quarters for different castes, and certainly for Dalits, accompanied quite often by separate water wells. Such tendencies were greatly strengthened by the new forms of communication, which revolutionized the movements of both human beings and their ideas and images. Mechanical print, in nineteenth-century India, could strengthen orthodoxies through wide dissemination of texts of power,

[6] Habib 1963/2013.

both colonial and indigenous. New techniques for the mechanical reproduction of visual artifacts also facilitated the spread of uniform images of gods and goddesses in their 'classical', high-Hindu forms. H.H. Risley noted in 1891 that not just 'Manchester', but also 'Banaras', had benefited from the communicational leap: 'Siva and Krishna drive out the tribal gods as surely as grey shirtings displace the more durable handwoven cloth. Pilgrimages become more pleasant and popular.' Cook's steamers had swollen the numbers going to Mecca, and the 'influence of Mahomedan missionaries and returned pilgrims has made itself felt in a quiet but steady revival of orthodox usage . . .'[7] Risley did not comment on the obverse, namely that the very same processes could potentially undermine conservative structures as well, old or new. The possibilities of communication between broadly similar subordinated strata, so long little connected or aware of each other, had now increased, enabling solidarities and collective action among subordinate castes and Dalits on scales previously impossible, as well as the gradual percolation of unorthodox notions and practices. If modern transport networks enhanced colonial power, their links with nationalist consolidations against British domination is at least as evident. Despite his well-known strictures against the railways, are is difficult to imagine the countrywide reach attained by Gandhi without that most visible form of industrial modernity.

Most such contradictory impulses originated largely in cities or small towns. Given the very uneven spread of literacy and print, our sources of information also have an urban slant. Villages and towns, though, were not all that rigidly separate from each other, for the new middle class had a foot in both. It typically combined urban service and professional or clerical occupations with rentier income drawn from the countryside. A large proportion retained their ancestral homes in villages or small towns, kept wives, children, and kinsfolk there, and long retained the habit of calling the village house by a more intimate name. In Bengal, this was the contrast between 'bari', as distinct from the less intimate 'basa' (accommodation, usually rented), in the city where they were employed. Primary and secondary education, too, was sometimes available in small towns or even big villages, for the middle

[7] Risley 1891: Introductory Essay, xxix–xxx.

class invested considerably in starting schools, mostly for children of their social group, in the countryside. Rural areas like Bikrampur in East Bengal, for instance, or some pockets near Pune and in coastal Andhra, where the gentry held a disproportionately large number of ancestral homes, became exceptionally rich in schools by the early twentieth century. This was made possible by the policy of grants-in-aid for schools and colleges introduced by Wood's Despatch in 1854. But the higher levels of education were located in the big cities, which became therefore the point of entry, and often residence, of service and professional groups. Cities were becoming the centre of gravity. We need to turn, then, to the patterns of urban living in colonial times as the principal seedbed of the colonial middle class, as well as of an ambiguous modernity.

The Road to Urban Spaces: Refashioning Colonial Cities

Two contrary images have dominated written accounts and visual representations of the colonial or 'Oriental' city. Densely crowded bazaars and narrow twisting lanes; hovels occasionally interspersed with mansions and the palaces of the rich and powerful; temples and mosques surrounded by shops; and all combining to reveal a world dirty, unhygienic, the breeding ground of disease—yet often with a romantic and exotic charm. In total contrast, there also emerged European enclaves which would gradually be penetrated and taken over by upwardly mobile sections of Indian society. These would be islands of quiet (till the proliferation of motor cars), showing broad avenues lined with trees, bungalows surrounded by gardens and lawns, and numerous other signs of the growing affluence and up-to-date modern amenities of civilized living. The bustling street life and culture of the 'native' areas, which served as outdoor havens from miserable and overcrowded dwellings, gradually lost their sway. Instead, diverse patterns of privatized domesticity blossomed, confirmed and extended by the proliferation of new communication technologies and urban amenities. The first set of images has a timeless quality, the second clearly indicates change. They point towards the perennial historical problem of changelessness and change, the jostling of contrasting approaches emphasizing either ruptures brought about by colonialism, or basic continuities.

The broad consensus among historians had at one time been that the eighteenth century was an era of general decline. Centralized Mughal rule disintegrated, leading to political turmoil and a wholesale deindustrialization from the early nineteenth century and a significant fall in levels of urbanization. Certainly, imperial cities like Delhi, Agra, and Lahore, as well as centres of courts and/or skilled handicrafts (Dacca, Murshidabad, and Patna were prominent eastern Indian instances in early British times) lost much of their older lustre.[8] Laments for lost splendour became a standard theme in North Indian Urdu literature, produced by a declining literati bereft of courtly patronage, one such being the famous dirge composed by Wajid Ali Shah, the dispossessed nawab of Awadh: '*jab chhor chale Lucknao nagari . . .*' In Urdu poetry, it has been suggested, the slow extinction of the Mughal aristocracy contributed to the post-1857 vogue for the marsia, a form of elegy, as against the earlier favouring of the qasida (panegyric).[9]

C.A. Bayly's argument of an important compensatory dimension has, however, come to be fairly widely accepted now, the idea being that the decline of one centre or region was often accompanied by the rise of another. This was because political authority, revenue and trade flows, the expenditure on armies and upper-class consumption, and religious life and organization all moved in interrelated ways into the new area of growth.[10] There was a significant expansion of small towns in the mid-Ganga region from around the 1720s. Mughal officials, no longer transferred frequently as centralized control declined, came to acquire a more stable control over land in that region and fostered the growth of towns with a distinct qasba culture. And the nineteenth-century growth of new urban centres associated with British rule—the

---

[8] Surat, premier port of the Mughal empire and the place where the English EIC had set up its first factory, was another city which declined (till its late-twentieth-century revival and growth). For this the devastating Maratha raids under Shivaji in the 1660s seem to have been largely responsible. See Yagnik and Seth 2005.

[9] Das 1991: 92–3.

[10] Bayly 1983: chapter 1, *et passim*.

spectacular rise of Calcutta, Bombay, and Madras, the spread of railway towns, mercantile centres, and eventually industrial townships—is undeniable. Such a horizontal expansion certainly counterbalanced whatever quantitative decline may have occurred in the aggregate size of the urban population in the interregnum between Mughal and British imperial regimes. But quantitative continuity can go hand in hand with significant change, as we saw with agricultural labour and artisanal life. Certainly, the new shape of the colonial city or town did come to possess many novel features in terms of spatial organization, physical appearance, and forms of sociability.

Key changes related to the constitution, or the sharpening, of two kinds of distinctions. The contrast between European and 'native' living spaces, amounting at times to something like segregation, was the most obvious feature of colonial urban development. Over time, there was also a progressive demarcation between rich or middle class, and the poor within the Indian areas.[11] At the same time, successful Indians moved into European enclaves and gradually purchased or built similar houses with modern civic amenities. Multifarious physical manifestations of urban modernity spread slowly into such domains, always with a time lag as compared to the West, even though the gap was not too large—at least not for the European inhabitants. New technological innovations appeared thick and fast from the 1870s. The summer capital of Simla was the first to receive electric lighting. In Calcutta, underground water pipes and drains began to be constructed from the 1870s, a pontoon bridge spanned the Hooghly river in 1874, horse-drawn trams came in 1880, and the gas lights that had been introduced around 1856–7 began to be gradually replaced by electric street lamps from 1891.[12] The first telephone was installed in 1882, a

[11] There had been considerable economic and status differences, of course, within pre-colonial Indian cities, but on the whole a less rigid spatial segregation. The political and military elite associated with the court might live within the walls of the citadel, but otherwise the havelis of the rich would be located in the same narrow twisting lanes as the homes of the wretchedly poor. This is still noticeable in the old quarters of cities with pre-colonial histories, such as Old Delhi and Lucknow.

[12] Electric street-lighting had begun in the West only about a decade earlier, with Edison's invention of the incandescent lamp enabling a public electric

few motorcars appeared on the streets in 1894, by about 1900 there were electric lights and fans in a handful of houses, and electric trams began to replace horse-drawn vehicles. The cinema came with even less of a time gap, with a showing of Louis Lumière's *Arrival of a Train* and *Leaving the Lumière Factory* in a Bombay hotel on 7 July 1896, only six months after the very first cinematographic show in Paris on 28 December 1895. Appurtenances of modernity were introduced primarily for the comfort and pleasure of Europeans, but the spillover among Indian residents was unavoidable. Bombay cinema shows, for instance, arranged 'reserved boxes for Purdah ladies and their families' and offered a broad range of prices, extending from 4 annas to Rs 2.[13] Despite shared urban comforts, the contrast persisted between the spacious houses and wide streets of the European areas and the squalid and congested native quarters. Plague panics at the turn of the nineteenth century led to sporadic efforts through 'improvement trusts' to raise standards of hygiene in the Indian quarters of big cities.

The most obvious contrast between European and indigenous urban space lay in the pattern of urban architecture. British Indian public buildings till the last quarter of the nineteenth century tended to be straightforward imports of contemporary European forms. These were at first predominantly neo-classical, suggesting the hope, embodied in stone and brick, that the British empire would be as long-lasting as the Roman. But there were echoes, too, of the Romantic rediscovery of the Gothic. Neo-classicism ruled over the early Government Houses at Madras (1798–1803) and Calcutta (built under Wellesley around

---

system in the Pearl Street district of New York in 1881. Among the best accounts of city planning in relation to Calcutta is Datta 2012.

[13] Roy 1902: chapter 10, included in *Census of Bengal, 1901, Part I, Volume VII* (Calcutta, 1902); Ghosh 1991; Barnouw and Krishnaswamy 1963. Ghosh makes the important point that concentration on the purely destructive dimensions of colonial modernity has often led to a certain underestimation of the role of some Indian artisans and engineers in the spread of such amenities. There was also some conservative resentment, though. Water pipes and taps, for instance, aroused fears of a weakening of caste barriers, and a poem published in a Calcutta journal in 1870 even expressed alarm that common water supply would eliminate the distinctions between high and low.

the same years), while churches tended to follow Gothic patterns. The latter style became dominant in Bombay's public buildings, typified by the vast Victoria Terminal (1878–87) modelled on London's St Pancras. Bombay was distinctive also in the much greater role of elite Indian funders and designers. Gothic buildings like Cowasjee Jahangir's University Hall and Premchand Roychand's Clock Tower are visible reminders of the far closer relationships between British and Indian (particularly Parsi) businessmen in Bombay than anywhere else.

Around the 1870s, public architecture began to acquire an indigenous (usually Islamic) colour as more appropriate for an empire that claimed to be both modern and Oriental. This was a counterpart of the durbar-style imperial assemblage with which Lytton had ushered Victoria in as Empress of India in 1877. Architects like Chisholm and Major Mount developed the Indo-Saracenic style, manifest notably in Madras' public buildings, Ajmer's Mayo College for sons of princes, and Aligarh Muslim University. Efforts at Indianization—choosing eclectically from 'Hindu' and, more often, 'Muslim' elements—culminated in the vast Victoria Memorial at Calcutta, constructed under Curzon. Self-conscious echoes of Fatehpur Sikri and the Taj were combined there with a strong element of the European classical. This was in part because a classical revival had meanwhile begun during the high noon of empire. In the decades immediately preceding the war of 1914–18, the colonial architecture of post-Boer War South Africa came to influence British Indian styles through the work of Edward Baker.[14]

European private housing followed a different pattern, not borrowed from Britain, except in the eighty-odd hill stations where altitude and climate allowed English-style cottages to flourish. These were often adorned with names derived from the Lake Districts.[15] Barracks constituted the standard housing of the bulk of the European soldiers. Their numbers had been enhanced after 1857 to comprise

[14] For a helpful survey of British Indian public architecture, see Metcalf 1989.
[15] A good account of these hill stations is Kennedy 1996. For Simla as a kind of 'little England', see Kanwar 1990.

114 cantonments, located either in fortified areas within cities, or outside but next to native towns (Secunderabad next to Hyderabad, for instance). As crucial bases of British power, these were protected with open spaces that surrounded them and allowed free range to artillery fire: the reason why the Maidan in Calcutta was placed next to Fort William after the shock of Siraj-ud-doulah's capture of Calcutta. After 1857 the space contiguous with Delhi's Red Fort was also ruthlessly cleared of streets and houses of Indians to enable guns to be trained on Chandni Chowk.

Outside hill stations and cantonment barracks, however, the classic British Indian housing form was the bungalow-compound complex, in the Civil Lines of British officialdom and other elites: secluded areas into which successful Indians penetrated over time. Such buildings also housed district officials in small towns, and they were spread over the countryside in the form of the inspection and forest bungalows that still survive in considerable numbers to provide resting places for tourists. In contrast with the indigenous manzil or haveli, which had an inner courtyard enclosed by rooms on all sides to ensure women's segregation, the bungalow was a single-storey, low-density, horizontal structure. It had high ceilings to keep temperatures down, verandahs running outside the rooms, and lawns or gardens separating the sahib's house from the compound walls. The bungalow permitted privacy for the entire European (or Westernized Indian) conjugal unit. The sahib would meet natives on the verandah, while the entire area would be marked by broad, tree-lined roads, and new civic amenities.[16]

But we need to disaggregate now: there were considerable variations in the histories of different cities under colonial rule, and the contrasts have been highlighted in recent decades by historical research focussed on specific urban centres.

At one extreme we may place the old imperial and nawabi capitals of Delhi and Lucknow, major points of the 1857 Rebellion. After its suppression, British efforts at social control were at their most visible and brutal in these two cities. A real sense of shock was palpable because, before the Rebellion, personal relations between resident Englishmen and Indians in these cities had been fairly friendly, typified

[16] King 1976.

by Henry Lawrence's closeness to Urdu culture and to elite nawabi families in Lucknow.[17] In pre-1857 Delhi, too, despite a cantonment on the Ridge, Europeans had lived mostly within the walled city in houses rented from Indians. After the 1857 panic Indians were driven out of both cities for a number of months, literally into the cold, for they were forced to live in the open through the winter months. Muslims were kept out longer than Hindus as rulers believed that they were more responsible than Hindus for the uprising. Both in Delhi and Lucknow, Hindus suffered less than Muslims in the aftermath of 1857, and some Hindu traders even benefited from the general reshuffle of property that accompanied the restoration of British power. Houses and places of worship were extensively destroyed on the pretext of military necessity, though a more plausible reason was the sheer thirst for revenge: there was even a suggestion that the Jama Masjid be destroyed. A much enlarged British garrison was located for some fifty years in the old residential area of Daryaganj, inside the walls of Shahjahanabad, contributing to congestion in the old city. The problem was aggravated by the refusal of the British army to widen the entrances through the city walls. British civilians moved out of the old city (except for a pocket immediately south of Kashmiri Gate) into the Civil Lines to the north of the city walls. Military logic led similarly to the construction of several straight avenues cutting through the twisting lanes of Lucknow—as Baron Haussmann had done for the reconstruction of Paris after the Revolution of 1848—enabling the army to quickly move into action against possible insurgents. Soldiers occupied the Imambara and many palaces until 1877, and, once again as a deliberate insult, the cantonment was relocated east of the city, in the Dilkusha Gardens, which was previously an area of aristocratic country residences.

Post-1857 British policies of control and intrusive intervention have been highlighted in Veena Oldenburg's study of Lucknow.[18] The

[17] See also Dalrymple 2004 for a touching short essay on James Achilles Kirkpatrick's closeness to local Muslim elites in early-nineteenth-century Hyderabad.

[18] Oldenburg 1984. This remains the most detailed account of, among other things, urban spatial rearrangements in Lucknow. For related aspects of urban architectural history, see Llewellyn-Jones 1983.

objectives were to ensure 'safety, sanitation, and loyalty'. Numerous by-laws tried to regulate types of housing, standards of hygiene, and the everyday life of the city's indigenous inhabitants. The punitive nature of post-1857 British policies in Delhi and Lucknow was reflected in the relatively slow growth of municipal autonomy and the late introduction of civic amenities. Underground water, sewage, and electric lights came to Delhi only around the time of the Imperial Durbar of 1902, a decade after they had reached Lahore. The fortunes of Delhi and Lucknow, however, eventually came to differ. Before 1857, Lucknow had been possibly the biggest Indian city after Calcutta, Bombay, and Madras. Afterwards it never recovered its old splendour, in large part because the central railway line connecting North India with Calcutta bypassed it, moving through Allahabad and Kanpur instead. Delhi, however, quickly recovered from a brief demographic dip after 1857. It became a key railway junction in 1867 and soon developed into a major commercial centre. By the 1890s textile mills had begun appearing as part of its urban regeneration.[19]

Oldenburg's occasional efforts to make Lucknow a 'paradigm' for post-1857 colonial urbanization, however, runs against considerable evidence of enormous variations. The United Provinces, for instance, saw the development of two types of slightly different small towns. After the eighteenth century, as the high-Mughal practice of frequent bureaucratic transfers broke down, the Muslim service gentry became more rooted in specific areas. This fostered the growth of qasbas—centres of Islamic learning and artisanal crafts—where Sufi eclecticism initially enabled considerable interaction with Hindu literati groups which, in turn, were equally well versed in Urdu culture. The closeness gradually declined, while the late nineteenth century saw the growth of an alternative kind of small trading town (ganj), predominantly Hindu and located near the new railway centres. Business activities in the ganj were closely integrated with Hindu piety, as C.A. Bayly's work has emphasized, and the preferred script was emphatically Devanagari, not Persian. Here lay the social roots of what would become a deep and growing linguistic and communal division.

[19] Gupta 1971: 61–77; Gupta 1981; Oldenburg 1984.

Allahabad's growth from the late nineteenth century at the expense of Lucknow indicates yet another pattern. The new hotspot attracted service groups and professionals with an English-medium education, in significant contrast to the reduced dynamism of Lucknow with its western UP Muslim elite. Allahabad seemed to combine a blend of the new with the age-old, for it was also the centre of the Kumbh Mela at intervals of twelve years. Even the agnostic Nehru, in his *Discovery of India*, thought this mela had originated in 'unknown antiquity'. Recent research indicates that this was far from being so. The first definite reference to the Kumbh—as distinct from the annual and much smaller Magh Mela—comes from as late as 1868, and the twelve-year festival seems to have been a deliberate 'invention of tradition' initiated by the local river 'pandas', who utilized the Orientalizing assumptions and sentiments of British officials.

There were many old temple towns, usually based on an intricate mingling of piety and trade, such as Banaras in the North and Madurai in the South. Banaras provides the most striking instance of this combination. Despite its reputation as age-old, there was much growth and significant change in the city over the course of the eighteenth century. The strategic location of the city on the Ganga, astride the meeting point of the riverine and land trade between Bengal and the Maratha lands, made it the inland commercial capital of the subcontinent in the latter part of the eighteenth century, its population then being around 200,000.[20] In the eighteenth century it was also the major centre for Maratha investments in commerce and piety alike, and most of the extant temples there were built around that time. So the image of a city of hoary and changeless antiquity as the premier Hindu religious centre was not exactly a myth, but it still demands considerable historicization.

The striking new feature under British suzerainty was a triumvirate: Bhumihar rajas; prosperous 'mendicant' Gossain managers of temples; traders, moneylenders, soldiers (prior to the British assertion of monopoly over military power), and merchant-banker families. The

---

[20] There was subsequently a slow decline, or at least stagnation, as river trade declined, and the trunk railway lines connecting Calcutta with the North and the West passed through Mughalsarai but avoided crossing the river.

raja, bereft of independent political power, sought compensation through religious patronage: above all, of the Ramkatha tradition, the *Ramcharitmanas* scholarship, and the celebrated Ramlila of Ramnagar across the river. Banaras became by the late nineteenth century the chief centre of a revival of conjoint, increasingly aggressive, Hinduism, and of Hindi in the Devanagari script. But the city also had a big Muslim population, considerable multi-religious exchange—Hindus enthusiastically participated in the Muharram, for instance, at least before the start of twentieth-century communalism, and to some extent despite it—and a rich urban, popular, and mainly artisanal culture that has been the subject of significant research.[21]

Direct British remoulding was not much in evidence in the other major temple cities, most prominent in the South. In many of them, like Madurai, only the appearance of factories in the inter-war years disrupted the picture of continuity. It is significant that though the British-constructed port city of Madras surpassed all the southern urban centres in size, the twelve towns that came next in size in 1871 had all been important urban centres for centuries. Towns in the South were marked by a sharp and very visible segregation between the Brahmin residential area close to the temple complex (the agraharam), and the non-Brahmin and Dalit quarters. This lay at the root of deep tensions which would explode in the early twentieth century.[22]

The three large metropolitan port cities of Calcutta, Madras, and Bombay were distinctive in their growth around English settlements that went back to the first century of the Company's presence in India. Initial military problems (notably Siraj-ud-doulah's capture of Fort William in 1756) had become a distant memory, and none of the three were affected by 1857. Beyond that, differences began, manifest in the distinct spatial demographic patterns that emerged from local conditions and histories.

British nostalgic accounts of Calcutta began to proliferate from 1900. Life became less and less comfortable for Europeans with the

---

[21] Freitag 1989; Kumar 1988.

[22] Bayly 1983: chapters 8, 9; Maclean 2003: 873–906; Gupta 1987: 121–48. Two noted works of fiction worth reading on this conflictual context are Anantha Murthy 1979, and Sarma 2007.

growth of nationalism. These accounts focused particularly on the 'saheb para', comprising the European business-cum-administrative centre of Dalhousie Square, crowded by day but deserted at night, as well as on European residential areas. Long immunity from military danger had encouraged European residences to proliferate southward along Chowringhee to Park Street and beyond, with an extension to the south-west into fashionable Alipore. There was, therefore, no very rigid racial barrier to segregate spaces. The Maidan, originally constructed as protection for Fort William, had become, and remains, the much-loved recreation ground for all kinds of city inhabitants. The saheb para was still very different from the Indian areas in appearance, with wide streets, impressive façades, glittering shops, and massive neo-classical public buildings (with the occasional Victorian Gothic thrown in, as in the High Court and New Market). Old British Calcutta hands boasted that their metropolis being a city of palaces, the second city of the British empire was surpassed only by London. The European population, however, was only about 10,000 in 1901, out of a total of 577,000. Beyond this privileged belt lay a heterogeneous intermediate zone of poor whites, Eurasians or Anglo-Indians of mixed white and non-white parentage, Muslim service and domestic groups, and small communities of Jews, Armenians, and Chinese. Beyond that again, to the north of the European business area, was Burra Bazaar, the centre of highly diverse indigenous business communities among whom Marwari immigrants came to predominate by the late nineteenth century. Bengali middle-class areas lay further north and east, with another pocket around Bhowanipur and Kalighat in the vicinity of the temple of the city's principal deity, Kali.

In physical appearance, Indian areas presented a sharp contrast to the European. Mansions of the rich lay cheek by jowl with slums or 'bustees' and brothels (from which the former often drew rental income), student hostels and colleges, and the 'messes' where clerks and students from similar parts of Bengal tended to live together. The city was extremely diverse, and the bulk of the Indian businessmen and large numbers of the labouring poor came from outside Bengal. Yet its dominant literary image was, and remains, primarily as the abode of Bengalis, and of middle-class Bengalis at that. In interesting contrast to the nostalgia about a 'renaissance' that was commonplace from the 1940s, negative perceptions about the city predominated among middle-class groups in the nineteenth century. There was much play on the verbal similarity of the name of the city with the time of 'Koli-yuga': the era of evil and degeneration in the high-Hindu notion of cyclical time.[23]

In contrast with Calcutta (and, even more, with Bombay), Madras was far less hybrid in character as far as its Indian inhabitants were concerned. A big section of its migrants came from nearby Tamil districts. Whole families came to the city, producing a less skewed sex ratio than in the other two metropolises. Distant cyclical migration was kept down by the slow growth of modern industry, though students, clerks, and professionals did come from many parts of the South. Communications with the North, however, were difficult, for the direct railway line from Calcutta, running through Orissa, was completed only in the late 1890s. Madras had the only university in the Presidency till well into the twentieth century. As elsewhere, the city began with distinct 'white' and 'black' towns. The former lay to the south of the latter and was at first clustered around Fort St George. But the absence of military threat, and a larger space for expansion than in Calcutta and Bombay, gradually blurred the distinction. European houses spread northwards and westwards beyond the original black town, and garden suburbs like Mylapore, Egmore, and Nungambakkam attracted prosperous Indians. The availability of space enabled horizontal rather than vertical construction. Many parts of Madras retained a rather rural appearance till fairly recently, reproducing the sharp distinction between different caste localities typical of villages.[24]

Bombay, a Company possession from 1661, grew rather slowly till the late eighteenth century. Unlike Madras and Calcutta, it had come up on a string of narrow islands running parallel to a thin coastal strip between the sea and the Western Ghats. But then, with the decline

[23] Sinha 1978; Mukherjee 1993; Chaudhuri 1990; Evenson 1989; Sarkar, 'The City Imagined: Calcutta of the Nineteenth and Early Twentieth Centuries', in Sarkar 1997: 159–85.

[24] Evenson 1989; Lewandowski 1975: 341–60. For the belated railway linkages of Madras, see Ahuja 2004.

of Surat, it grew rapidly, thanks to its superb natural harbour, the construction in the 1860s of railway lines across the Ghats, and the opening of the Suez Canal which made it the key entry point for overseas trade with the West. In the 1920s it was, by far, the biggest Indian port (controlling 40 per cent of the country's external trade), the largest cotton market in Asia, a major commercial hub, as well as the subcontinent's premier industrial centre.

What distinguished Bombay from Madras and even Calcutta—with its very diverse but more spatially segregated population, and the growing predominance of Bengali upper castes—was its remarkably polyglot, multi-religious, and cosmopolitan nature. From the 1930s such features helped make it the all-India centre of the film industry. Even a century earlier, an English visitor had described how 'in twenty minutes' walk through the bazaar of Bombay, my ear has been struck by the sounds of every language that I have heard in any part of the world, uttered . . . in a tone and manner which implied that the speakers felt quite at home . . .' He was struck, too, by the medley of temples, mosques, churches, pagodas, and Parsi places of worship, which showed few signs of the separation of religious zones.[25]

As elsewhere, there was an initial defensive separation of the English Fort area near the southern tip of the main island, and the non-white, polyglot but mainly Gujarati-speaking Parsi, Hindu, and Muslim mercantile settlements pushing northwards. The sense of security, in contrast to Delhi and Lucknow, was indicated by the decision to demolish the Fort walls just five years after the Mutiny. The Fort had been separated at first from civilian residential areas by a sprawling Bombay Green. After the walls were destroyed this was reduced in size to the Elphinstone (now Shivaji) Circle. Indigenous elites in Bombay also developed, and long retained, a much greater and more equal relationship with their British counterparts than in any other city. This was embodied in the extent of Indian investment in public buildings, the early nomination of Indians as justices of the peace from the 1830s, and increasing local control over the municipality from the 1870s.

---

[25] B. Hall, *Fragments of Voyages and Travels* (Edinburgh, 1832), cited in Kosambi 1980.

With this went, too, a growing stratification among Indians, manifest particularly in the spectacular growth of textile mills and other factories (138 of them by 1901) in what was now geographically the heart of the city, the Parel-Byculla area. Beyond the mills, rich or respectable residential areas spread west and northwards across what had once been sparsely populated or open spaces—into Worli, Mahim, Dadar, Bandra, Andheri, and beyond. The location of the working class near the centre of the urban complex gave Bombay, prior to the recent deindustrialization, a character very distinct from Calcutta where the jute and engineering works developed in suburban towns, or Madras with its late industrial growth. Labour acquired a visibility and weight in city affairs missing elsewhere. If the business community was largely Parsi and Gujarati Bania, the bulk of the industrial workers, as we have seen, were Marathi-speaking immigrants from the Konkan and the Deccan. They retained linguistic and cultural links with the growing Marathi component of the city's inhabitants, mustering strong among the intelligentsia and clerical strata. Here was another contrast with Calcutta, with its heavily non-Bengali workers pushed into the suburbs, and its bhadralok predominance in the city's cultural and political life.

But efforts at drawing sharper distinctions between the respectable and the labouring poor also began early in Bombay. European and Indian elites collaborated sporadically in the Back Bay project of reclaiming backwaters for the residences of the rich. This began in the 1860s, and culminated, much later, in the spectacular skyscrapers of Colaba. The plague panic of the 1890s also stimulated efforts at deepening segregation, slum clearance, and some attempts to improve sanitation through an autonomous improvement trust. As elsewhere, desire and plans regularly outstripped achievements. Bombay remained a city of great but not neatly separable contrasts, at least not before the recent moves to hand over vacant mill lands to estate developers.[26]

Ahmedabad, the last of the cities in this necessarily restricted sample, differed from most other modern urban centres in a number of ways.

---

[26] Chandavarkar 1994: chapter 2, *et passim*; Dossal 1991; Dossal 1996; Patel and Thorner 1996; Kosambi 1980.

Its continuous history goes back to the early fifteenth century, while the other cities that I have discussed had been founded in Company times, or were transformed, like Delhi and Lucknow, under British presence and control. Indian initiatives directed urban change here, not colonial imposition. It possessed a well-developed pre-colonial mercantile elite which had developed an unusual autonomous guild-type organization which we do not find elsewhere. This occasionally protested against policies of the rulers, and at times could get them reversed. Traditional forms of urban protest were interesting: closing down business centres (hartal), sitting in peaceful protest before officials (dharna), holding out threats of collective migration (hijrat). These could extend into the countryside, and would be deployed and elaborated effectively in twentieth-century Gandhian movements. Ahmedabad's (and other parts of Gujarat's) era of relative decline happened before colonial conquests, in the late-seventeenth and eighteenth centuries, primarily with Maratha incursions. In contrast, British rule at first brought renewed prosperity, and, eventually, the development of a modern textile industry. That shared considerable continuities with pre-colonial manufacturers and business elites. As compared to Calcutta, and to some degree Bombay, industrial development at Ahmedabad was almost entirely independent of British capitalists, even if the textile machinery had to be imported from Lancashire and elsewhere. British presence in Ahmedabad was relatively light, with a cantonment outside the old city walls but no significant European business community resided within the city itself. The case of Ahmedabad throws some doubt over the idea that colonial restructurings of physical and social urban environments were, always and everywhere, a one-way process of impositions and control. Culturally, too, continuities persisted with precolonial times. The Western-educated intelligentsia was not very prominent, and educational and social reform, while not absent, had, on the whole, a conservative appearance. It is significant that unlike many of the Anglicized Parsi businessmen who pioneered the Bombay textile industry, the first mill in Ahmedabad was set up by Ranchodlal Chhotalal, who never wore Western clothes.

The walled city on the eastern bank of the Sabarmati was the traditional centre of business life and also the area where the first mills came up. It long retained an old-world appearance, with its maze of narrow, crooked lanes and streets, and houses resembling havelis. Most colonial cities, as we noticed, comprised on the one hand neglected older areas, and European-dominated urban spaces where the amenities of modern city life came early. In Ahmedabad, however, it was the old city which first saw electric lights, underground water, and proper drainage, at the instance of Ranchodlal, in the 1880s. Such innovations were accepted by urban conservatives, though there was some opposition to piped water on the grounds that it ignored caste distinctions. Efforts at bureaucratic improvement in the 1910s, when the elected municipality had been briefly superseded by officials, ran up against the opposition of emergent nationalist groups who were often connected to industrialists. Nationalists, however, did not oppose modern innovations, they demanded an autonomous municipal development. Stronger modernizing changes were pushed through in the next decade by the new Congress-controlled municipality headed by Vallabhbhai Patel. In effect the nationalists, once in positions of local power, 'appropriated some of the policies of the colonial governments to their advantage.'[27] They, however, did not opt for democratization; in fact Patel even set up a General Ward for property-holders and the salaried middle classes: these could also vote in the residential wards, thus giving double votes to Patel's base. A class-based demarcation of urban space was also encouraged. Mills moved out from the walled city, eastwards across the railway line, while the modern residential zone of the rich developed to the west of the Sabarmati, on the other side of Ellis Bridge. Surprisingly, even Gandhi's Sabarmati Ashram came up on the west bank of the river.

Spatial restructuring, segregating rich from poor, came more easily to Ahmedabad than Bombay, for Ahmedabad workers, who shared community ties with most owners, were on the whole relatively compliant, even before the industry was largely destroyed from the 1980s. The old city, increasingly neglected, became the home of a diminishing part of the population, comprising only 5.5 sq. km of space in 1961, as against to 87 sq. km outside the walls. It primarily housed

[27] Raychaudhuri 2001. For Ahmedabad generally, see Gillion 1968; Spodek 1965: 438–90; Breman 2004; Yagnik and Seth 2005. Spodek also provides a historical account of the city over the twentieth century in Spodek 2011.

the poor, above all Muslims. The old/new contrast thus did ultimately emerge, but as a form of nationalist and post-colonial, rather than colonial, difference.

Hail Fellow Well Met: Urban Sociabilities from the Late Nineteenth Century

The colonial city spawned partially new, hybrid forms of sociability, a theme that demands much greater historical attention than it has received so far.[28] Social gatherings among expatriate Europeans generally tried to imitate practices at home, once the early colonial tendencies of turning native—mingling with prominent Indians, wearing Indian clothes, and consorting with Indian mistresses—had come to be frowned upon by the severe standards of Victorian morality.[29] The inevitable distance between original and imitation could not have been great, perhaps, in the major centres of European living, such as in the saheb para of Calcutta, or during the summer exodus of officials and their families to Simla, Darjeeling, and other salubrious places. Officials, businessmen, and missionaries might also leave their families in hill stations—for instance, at Landour above Mussoorie—while carrying on their work in the hot plains. With significant numbers of resident and privileged whites, these stations saw flourishing nineteenth-century British upper-class leisure activities: a racially exclusive club culture (generally male monopolies), parties and dances—including those for the serious business of 'coming out' for debutantes—English-language theatres imported from metropolitan cities, tennis, horse racing, football, and, above all, cricket from the latter part of the nineteenth century.[30] Life was much more lonely, though, for British people who were posted far away from the big cities, to outposts in small towns where their forced proximity

---

[28] The major exception here is Chakrabarty 2000: chapter 7. Elsewhere the theme generally emerges in connection with broader discussions, e.g. of the networks that developed around journals and publications. There would be considerable relevant material, though, in vernacular writings, e.g. in Bengali: Das 1990.

[29] For a vivid account of the earlier phase, see Dalrymple 2002.

[30] See Guha 2002.

to Indians often meant frequent clashes. In such places 'the European station . . . chattered and quarrelled, quarrelled and chattered'; and, in a novel written by an Englishman with criticism and irony about his compatriots, a bored memsahib boasted that she had once amused herself by hitting with a catapult-bolt a servant carrying boiling stew. The younger Englishmen, meanwhile, looked for postings nearer forests, where there would be 'that *sine qua non* of British bliss, things to kill.'[31] Women, while allowed greater, if highly formalized, access to forms of sociability than their Indian counterparts, lived lonely, bored lives.[32] One source depicts English women in Kanpur anxiously awaiting the arrival of their 'boxes' from home, carrying reassuringly familiar English goods which were difficult or impossible to get in these parts.[33] Racial tensions sometimes exploded over some small incident, real or imagined, of the kind which lay at the heart of Forster's *A Passage to India* (1924), where a young memsahib has a hallucinatory experience which deludes her into imagining she has been molested by a Muslim doctor. Racist exploitation was most obvious, as we have seen, in the plantation districts, specially the Assam tea gardens, where planters often behaved with a barbarity similar to that which was routinely practised by settlers in the African colonies.

Not all Europeans enjoyed equal privileges of rule. There were subtle distinctions even within the elite, a pecking order where officials claiming an aristocratic origin would tend to look down upon mere businessmen, and both were rather contemptuous of missionaries, particularly of those belonging to realtively plebeian nonconformist groups. And there was also the little-explored world of the poor whites: the betwixt-and-between life of Eurasians and Anglo-Indians—perpetually striving for recognition as proper whites but never quite succeeding—as well as the 'guttersnipe' elements of

[31] Thompson 1927: 8, 11, 22–3.

[32] The range of 'Anglo-Indian' fiction centring on these themes is very large. E.M. Forster's *A Passage to India* (1924) and J.G. Farrell's *The Siege of Krishnapur* (1973) are widely regarded as two classic works effectively dramatizing sahibs and memsahibs *vis-à-vis* 'natives'. An entertaining anthology on the theme of colonial life and social foibles is Vernède 1995; a wide-ranging academic study of the topic is Mukherjee 1994.

[33] Joshi 2003: 16 (quoting Yalland 1994: 112).

supposedly pure British origin who had dropped off or run away from ships and somehow eked out a living in the port cities. Some of these, surviving as paupers, beggars, and vagrants, became a source of great embarrassment to the colonizers.

Forms of urban sociability were very different among Indians, even those moulded by colonial education. A selective regional focus becomes unavoidable, the default choice having again to be Bengal, more specifically Calcutta.[34] In his case study of the Bengali adda— the form of regular yet entirely informal and unstructured conversation among friends that developed in the late nineteenth century and flourished through much of the twentieth—Dipesh Chakrabarty deploys this difference to build his argument about a partly alternative modernity. He thinks that the colonized tried to evolve such alternatives as a way of making themselves at home in a world defamiliarized by colonial capitalism. Adda was different from, though not unrelated to, majlis or 'baithak-khana' gatherings in the houses of patrons, zamindars, and the city nouveau riche around whom 'dals' (factions) coalesced in early-nineteenth-century Calcutta. It was also different from traditional village gatherings and gossip sessions in 'chandimandaps' (village shrines), those being much more obviously caste- and community-bound. But addas had their own boundaries. Wives prepared tea and refreshments but, till well into the twentieth century, seldom joined the discussions, and lower-caste servants, serving food, were entirely excluded from the discussions. Earlier forms of gathering around patrons were marked by a clear internal hierarchy among the participants themselves, between patrons and performers, singers, and dancers ranging from the illustrious to the disreputable. Adda in contrast had nothing of the courtly about it, being a much more middle-class social form with an element of democratic speech, even though there would be a well-known figure or two—often novelists, poets, or editors of a journal—around whom it constituted itself. One can trace a kind of sequence of such key

[34] I am all too aware of the growing strength of feeling among historians of areas other than Bengal that this region ought not to be a metonym of India, as it sometimes seems in the writings of Bengali historians. The heartening increase over the past decade and more of regional histories focussed on other Indian regions has begun eliminating this problem.

addas in Calcutta, connected with particular journals but meeting for informal, undirected talk rather than any goal-oriented planning of the next issue.[35]

But forms of sociability, old or new, were not the monopoly of such relatively exalted levels of bhadralok society. There is in fact an influential view that suggests a marked decline in 'popular' urban culture, in which women had played a significant part, in course of the nineteenth century. Victorian notions of respectability and puritanism, enforced by official censorship and elite bhadralok pressure, largely destroyed this rich plebeian culture, and condemned it as obscene and licentious. Simultaneously, strict controls were imposed on the public behaviour of women. Oldenburg developed this argument for the courtesan culture of nawabi Lucknow, revealing the processes that had denigrated courtesans—for long associated with a rich culture of music, song, and dance—and caused them to be seen as mere prostitutes.[36] Several scholars in Bengal—notably Sumanta Banerjee—elaborated this thesis of colonial subordination and the conquest of popular culture. Rich in ethnographic and historical material, these approaches still have a problem—an overuse of binary oppositions, in this case of a sharp, insufficiently demarcated distinction between

[35] The sequence would include gatherings connected with Bankimchandra and *Banga Darshan* in the 1870s and 1880s, several circles associated with Rabindranath, Pramatha Chaudhuri, and *Sabuj Patra* in the 1910s, the circles around *Kallol* and *Shanibarer Chithi* in the 1920s and 1930s, Benoy Sarkar's long-lived circle, the *Parichay Adda* which began around the poet Sudhindranath Datta in the 1930s and later became associated with the Marxist Left, and the addas around two other major poets, Buddhadev Bose and *Kabita*, and Bishnu De's *Sahitya Patra*. Some interesting material about the rough counterparts of such gatherings around journals, and the book trade, as well as the more traditional poetry gatherings (mushaira, kavi sammelan) can be teased out from the rich material in Orsini 2002. The study of late-nineteenth-century Banaras by Vasudha Dalmia depicts sociabilities of a slightly more traditional kind, centred around a key patron, Bharatendu Harishchandra: Dalmia 1997/2010. A.R. Venkatachalapathy's discussion of quasi-theological and subsequently commercial networks of patronage for the learned and their debates throws light on the specificities of the situation in late-nineteenth- and early-twentieth-century Tamilnadu: Venkatachalapathy 2012.

[36] Oldenburg 1991.

elite and popular culture. Such distinctions, at one time common in studies of the early modern European popular, are now abandoned because of their oversimplifications. It is more helpful to think in terms of varied or multiple appropriations by different social groups of texts and traditions that were not entirely dissimilar. In Indian urban culture, for instance, forms that are eulogized as popular or plebeian were frequently dependent on traditional patrons. Nor was there ever a total collapse of most such forms. Jatra or folk theatre still flourishes in Calcutta and elsewhere, albeit in modified forms. Lower-middle-class as well as elite forms of sociability did not disappear, even if changes with the coming of print and new forms of visual representation altered them considerably.

Other kinds of centres for informal gatherings and conversations were student hostels, where young men from the hinterland who had come to study in metropolitan cities resided. Those in UP towns were often suspected as dens of homosexual practices in pulp literature. Calcutta's counterparts, 'messes', comprised rooms rented by groups of students and young men, all usually from a particular district. From the interwar years, tea shops became a common sight, followed by coffee houses, two of which became famous: College Street, loved by generations of students, and Central (now Chittaranjan) Avenue, where Satyajit Ray and others who later became famous film directors would meet to discuss their art. As political life became more turbulent and engrossing, political addas combined stormy debates with relaxed chats.

At a more plebeian level were 'rowak' gatherings. These were of young men who sat together on verandahs adjoining their houses in the evenings for desultory gossip and animated discussion about the latest sports event or film star. When girls began to venture out in public spaces they greeted them with rude comments, particularly if they were from another area. About the women of their own 'para', however, the same young men could be fiercely protective and possessive, leading to clashes with their counterparts from elsewhere. At the same time, romances, often doomed, also bloomed from such encounters which contemporary fiction described.

Below this predominantly lower middle class, the urban poor, workers, and the casually employed would not have proper verandahs to sit and relax in, but the sheer misery of their slums and lack of domestic space (the chawls of mill districts like Parel in Bombay would be one example) compelled them to spend leisure hours in the open, collectively, in narrow lanes running next to hovels and tenements. Here men would gather, gossip, sometimes organize for collective action, while the women were kept busy with household chores and looking after the children. There was a busy and colourful street life in these areas.

Our survey has emphasized distinctions in sociability corresponding to different social levels. In the latter half of the nineteenth century certain new spheres of modern city life emerged where men and occasionally women (except the abysmally poor) could come together briefly as participants or, much oftener, as spectators. These included the theatre, the cinema from the turn to the twentieth century, and sport—mainly football and cricket. Chronologically, public theatres with their newly introduced proscenium stage, arrived first, made popular by tours of Parsi theatre groups from Bombay, and followed by broadly similar institutions in Calcutta and other cities from the 1870s.[37] In contrast to private theatrical shows staged at the homes of wealthy patrons and open to select invitees, the new theatre was open to all who bought tickets and the prices were reasonably low. The cinema followed a generation later, and, like the theatre, reached out to a far more variegated and part-plebeian public than the literate and cultured world in which writers and their readers moved and where the addas were located.

The reach and power of organized sports can be gauged from the ways in which they quickly became associated with emergent identities—anti-colonial nationalist, communal, regional, or caste. Tensions along racial lines were not uncommon, given that Europeans also had their own teams and had in fact introduced cricket, as well as the modern form of football, to India in the course of the nineteenth century. Football was the particular darling of Calcutta and Bengali middle-class men. Their rivalry with European teams acquired a sharp and at times brutal edge because of the Indian practice of playing barefoot while the English wore boots. The victory of Mohan Bagan

[37] See Hansen 2011.

over the East Yorkshire Regiment in the final of the IFA Shield Final of 1911 came to be remembered as a major landmark in the history of nationalism in Bengal.[38] Hindu–Muslim rivalry over football began somewhat later, as clubs like Mohammadan Sporting emerged in the early 1930s, while a regional element was introduced by the rise of East Bengal as principal rival to Mohan Bagan in the early post-colonial decades.

Cricket, while played everywhere, attained its first and greatest popularity among Indians in Bombay. A special note was introduced to Bombay cricket by the cosmopolitan, multi-elite nature of that city. Europeans introduced the game on the Maidan outside the Fort from the early nineteenth century, but by the 1870s there were as many as thirty Parsi clubs in the city.[39] A similar pattern of imitation-cum-rivalry characterized the conjoint rise of Hindu (in effect, upper-caste), and a little later Muslim, cricket clubs which produced the peculiar Bombay institution of the Triangular: tournaments among English, Parsi, and Hindu teams from 1907. The form became Quadrangular with the entry of a Muslim team in 1911. Playing games with each other did not eliminate conflict; rather, it often sharpened the clashes. There was a memorable fight over space in the 1880s, when the army took over parts of the Maidan for polo—quite a bit of it had already been appropriated by the European Gymkhana Club—thus ruining it for Indian cricketers. Petitions to the Bombay authorities by aggrieved Parsis and Hindus used a language which was very similar to what was used at the same time by the emergent Moderate Congress nationalists: in fact, Dadabhai Naoroji came out in support of the demands of the cricketers. This was the context in which the Parsi victory in January 1890 over the English team led by Lord Hawke came to be wildly celebrated by 12,000 Indian spectators, and indeed by the entire city, while European journalists wrote darkly about the 'surging . . . multi-coloured throng . . . gibbering, chattering and muttering . . .' Even more memorable was the rise, amidst great difficulties and discrimination, of the first important Dalit cricketer, Palwankar Baloo, a Chamar from a Deccan village. Beginning as a sweeper and

[38] See 'The Socialism of Soccer', in Guha 2001: 266.
[39] For a full history of cricket in India, see Guha 2002.

pitch-roller in a Parsi cricket club in Poona, he went on to become a world-class spinner.[40]

Women were non-existent, at best marginal, in these new public spaces and urban spectatorship. This is not to underestimate the impact and significance of the very new discourse of the 'freeing of women' (*stri-swadhinata*) that was the central feature of nineteenth-century middle-class social reform; nor of the legislations banning widow immolation, permitting widow marriage, raising the 'age of consent' (and eventually the age of marriage). But advances were normally accompanied by restraints, even among progressive communities or groups, notably the Parsis of Bombay and the Brahmos of Bengal. Middle-class women pioneered an interesting sartorial development suitable for public mobility—the sari worn in a new way, accompanied by blouse and chemise, and combining greater freedom of movement with more rigid notions of decency and decorum. The strong accent on modesty had not been necessary for earlier generations of women of the 'respectable' classes, who stayed inside the home and interacted only with close relatives. Trips outside the home were made in closed carriages. Despite the relative freedom enabled by the modern sari, well into the twentieth century very few bhadralok women could be seen walking on the streets without a male escort. The unpublished diary of a Marxist historian with Brahmo roots, recording his student days in Calcutta (*c.* 1917–23), mentions many instances when he accompanied his smart, highly educated unmarried cousins to visit relatives who lived very close. These and other constraints did not prevent—they may even have stimulated—a markedly romantic atmosphere evolving among these select groups of young men and women. Pre-marital love drew its self-expression from Tagore's poetry and songs, as is very evident from this diary.[41]

Early theatres had to hire their actresses from red light areas as social taboos forbade respectable women from joining the profession.

---

[40] The history of sports as an important part of social history, well developed elsewhere in the world, has begun to arouse scholarly interest in India, though there are a fair number of accounts of particular games and clubs. My paragraph is based primarily on Guha 2002. This was preceded by Nandy 1989 and followed by Majumdar 2004.

[41] Susobhan Sarkar, Unpublished Diary.

A few of them transcended their social origins to become reputed and respectable—perhaps most famously the actress Binodini in the Calcutta of the 1870s and 1880s.[42]

Literature, in Bengali as well as the other vernaculars, contributed significantly to the slow changes in social and emotional mores. Starting with Bankimchandra Chattopadhyay's novels from the late 1860s, the theme of transgressive love became prominent, drawing upon English literature as well as from indigenous traditions of Vaishnava lyricism that portrayed the illicit but holy love between Radha and Krishna. The novelty of novels lay in their locations which were, increasingly, the contemporary world and not the never-never mythological land of Brindaban. They were obliged to end with socially conformist resolutions and messages, but the readers—at least some of them—would have responded to the more audacious and unconventional aspects of the narrative.

Coeducation in colleges slowly developed and spread in major cities. Still, as late as the 1930s, girl students were escorted from their common room to the class by their professor, and there they would sit on benches firmly separated from the boys. Rabindranath Tagore was a daring innovator in this respect. His university at Santiniketan was not only coeducational but co-residential from the early 1920s. Daringly, university culture was saturated by his poems, drama, and songs celebrating love. Young men and women moved freely together and dress codes encouraged beauty and colour. Tagore also encouraged bhadralok women to come out on the public stage to act and dance in his plays, a big change from the boycott of the public stage in the late nineteenth century by the more conservative members of his own community, the Brahmos. In various cities of Bombay Presidency, women from reformist circles formed their own reading and writing groups from the late nineteenth century, and, later, women's associations for legal and social change. As a handful of women graduated from universities in the major cities at the end of the century—decades before their counterparts were allowed to receive degrees in Britain—some of them went abroad to train as doctors. Others were trained as nurses under the Dufferin Fund schemes.

[42] Bhattacharya 1998.

Gender changes were confined for long only to small, educated, middle-class groups. Much greater numbers of women would be affected, in contradictory ways, by diverse strands of nationalist politics—revolutionary terrorism (in its last phase), Gandhian, and Communist. And in the aftermath of Independence a flood of refugees forced many displaced women to take up jobs outside their homes, contributing to domestic tensions so sensitively portrayed in films like Satyajit Ray's *Mahanagar* and Ritwik Ghatak's *Meghe Dhaka Tara*. Steno typists included very large numbers of refugee women.

Forever Rising, Forever New: The Middle Class

The 'educated middle class' has been disproportionately prominent in the urban life of the late-colonial era as well as in history-writing.[43] There can be little doubt about the growing number or significance of this stratum as the nineteenth century neared its end. By the 1880s the number of English-educated Indians was approaching the 50,000 mark, if one takes the total of those with matriculation degrees as the indicator (the figure for those with BA degrees was still only about 5000). The number studying in the English medium went up fairly rapidly, from 298,000 in 1887 to 505,000 twenty years later, while the circulation of English-language papers grew from 90,000 in 1885 to 276,000 in 1905. It was still numerically a 'microscopic minority', as Viceroy Dufferin had termed it in 1888, and even in 1911 literacy in English was only 1 per cent. At the same time, the so-called unrepresentative character of the social group has been exaggerated by an unjustified conflation with the English-literate. The vernacular public sphere expanded much more rapidly. By 1905–7 the number of vernacular newspapers was 1107 as against 309 in English, with a circulation that had grown to 817,000 by 1905.[44] It needs to be added that tracts and newspapers could be read out to much larger numbers, as happened in times of political excitement, while mechanical reproduction enabled much wider and quicker dissemination of visual images than had been possible in the pre-print

[43] A 'reader' on the subject covering this and related aspects is Joshi 2010.

[44] I take these figures from McLane 1977: 4.

era. Print culture could thus touch the lives of many more beyond the well-educated or formally literate. English education, together with new modes of communication like the railways and postal services, gave its beneficiaries new capacities to establish contacts on a countrywide scale. English-educated government officials, lawyers, teachers, journalists, and doctors, as well as clerks with vernacular plus a smattering of English, worked fairly often outside their home areas. By the 1870s, colonies of educated Bengalis in many North Indian towns enabled Surendranath Banerjea to make several successful political tours and the Indian Association to set up a large number of branches outside Calcutta. The new education brought with it an awareness of the world events and global ideologies without which it would have been difficult to formulate conscious theories of nationalism.

The limits are equally evident. Higher education through a foreign medium had effects both alienating and divisive: features which had, simultaneously, economic, caste, and religious dimensions. In 1883–4 only 9 per cent of college students in Bengal came from families with annual incomes of less than Rs 200, understandable, given that the tuition fees in Calcutta's Hindu College had already been Rs 5 per month by the 1820s, rising to Rs 12 in its successor, Presidency College, by the last quarter of the nineteenth century. Fees, though, tended to be lower in most private colleges, as for instance in Ripon, Bangabasi, or City in Calcutta. But differential access was not related only to economic position. A basic fact of late-colonial South Asian history, to which we will repeatedly return, consisted of the ways in which cross-cutting factors of region, religious community, and caste led to highly differentiated access to education and the opportunities it held out.

Areas close to the early centres of British penetration and impact— Calcutta, Bombay, and to an extent Madras—gained an obvious head start over provinces in the interior, and these also happened to be regions where Hindus heavily outnumbered Muslims; or, as in Bengal, constituted the bulk of the gentry. For a time, the western United Provinces constituted an exception. The Muslim ashraf gentry, with its rich Urdu culture, constituted the cultural elite here, till things changed drastically in the aftermath of 1857. The British had so far attempted to work in co-operation with them as well as with the Urdu-educated Hindus in institutions like Delhi College, where science was imparted through Urdu translations and not in English. Members of that elite, consequently, saw no need to switch over to English for their higher studies. Things changed after the suppression of the Rebellion, as the British came to favour Hindu elites. Eventually in the 1890s, on account of Hindu communal pressure, Urdu in the Persian script was displaced as the language of law courts by Hindi in the Devanagari script. From the turn of the century a strong sense of Muslim political identity acquired its principal base in the region. A third obvious kind of distinction related to caste: the new middle class was not only generally Hindu, it was also overwhelmingly high caste. A small number of subordinated castes began to gain a toehold only from the last quarter of the nineteenth century, in significant measure thanks to missionary schools, creating the basis for another kind of identity formation.

Education, particularly its higher levels, required considerable cultural resources acquired over generations. Very rich sons of princes, big landlords, and successful businessmen, however, could make the leap to higher education immediately, with all the help that money could buy. Higher education came to be considered both possible and indispensable at middling social levels, for it was the gateway to respectable and comfortable jobs of the new kinds which were often combined with rentier income from land. This encouraged self-perceptions of the educated as a 'middle class' formation, located below the princes or zamindars but above those condemned to manual toil.

Such self-perceptions were both extremely common and at odds with social realities, and it is with this tension that it seems convenient to begin a deeper probe of the colonial middle class. Already, by the late 1820s, journals run by the first generation of the Calcutta Bengali literati touched by Western education described themselves as a *madhyabitta sreni* (middle class), and applied to the term characteristics commonly associated with the English or West European middle class. In the Western context, this implied entrepreneurship, or more generally, trade and industry, which gave it a leading role in bourgeoisie social transformations. Though Indian middle classes tried to appropriate this image, paradoxically, few among them had real-life connections with business: least of all, as the nineteenth century wore on, in Bengal, which was the earliest and major seedbed of the new literati activity.[45] There was some plausibility in the ascribed linkage within the 1820s and 1830s because of figures like Dwarkanath Tagore, the innovative entrepreneur who could deal with English traders in Calcutta on equal terms and who was also a friend of Rammohan Roy—the first intellectual described as 'modern'. The paradox deepened over the decades, where indigenous Bengali commercial enterprise collapsed after the late 1840s and business life became primarily the domain of European and then upcountry Marwari traders, financiers, and industrialists. The Bengali middle class became dependent on rentier incomes, big or (more commonly) small, derived from niches in the vast and ever-proliferating Permanent Settlement hierarchy of intermediate tenures, combined with professional or service incomes, for both of which some amount of English education had become a prerequisite.[46] 'Madhyabitta', then, was aspiration rather than reality, but aspiration can also be crucially important in the making of historical processes. Nor, it must be added, was the anomaly all that unique. The Indian colonial middle class of literati, aspiring but generally failing to achieve a class status not their own—at times 'substituting' for the missing or dormant class—would have a growing number of parallels in the less developed and/or colonial parts of the world.

This began with the phenomenon of the Russian intelligentsia. The absence of rootedness in a definitively formed social class has

---

[45] The dualism of aspiration and reality was vividly expressed by the *Amrita Bazar Patrika* of 9 December 1869: '*Madhyabitta* people are always considered the most useful group in any society. Our country's welfare depends to a large extent on this class. If there is ever to be a social or any other revolution in this country, it will be by the middle class. All the beneficial institutions or activities that we see in our country today have been started by this class. . . . The livelihood of *madhyabitta* people comes from landed property or the services . . . *Madhyabitta* people are often *gantidars* [holders of a form of intermediate tenures common in the Jessore-Nadia region of Bengal, from where the newspaper was then being published].'

[46] Bhattacharya 2005: 56, 59.

often been considered a source of weakness and inconsistency. But lack of such organicity has also enabled a degree of flexibility in attitudes, values, and aspirations in many parts of the world: educated sons and daughters of landed-gentry origin have advocated and sometimes tried to initiate industrial capitalist development; they have attempted to mobilize peasants and, with industrial growth, workers, in the cause of socialist revolution; and they have pioneered national movements against foreign rule which sought to and needed a multi-class appeal. Nineteenth-century Russia provides the prototype for such phenomena, and the original Russian category for its agents, the intelligentsia, is perhaps a more appropriate term for the new literati of late-colonial (and post-colonial) South Asia as well.[47] The connections of the nationalist 'middle class' of early-twentieth-century Bengal with zamindari or intermediate-tenure holding, as we shall see, clearly inhibited the pursuit of anti-landlord agrarian reform programmes even by the radical members of this class. Tagore, sensitive to peasant problems, tried to initiate welfare measures on his own estates but he avoided the questions of structural change in class relations. At the same time, Marxists, especially from present-day Kerala, Andhra Pradesh, Bombay, and Bengal, who came from identical class backgrounds, did turn to radical social and agrarian change from the 1920s.

In social composition, the new middle class was not always entire-ly different from its pre-colonial predecessors. Kayastha professional and clerical groups and the Muslim ashraf gentry of the North Indian qasbas had, for example, helped to man the Mughal bureaucracy. Their counterparts in some southern regions were the Niyogi Brahmans of Tamilnadu, who had held administrative posts for centuries at a succession of courts, and who moved to Madras in the later part of the eighteenth century to become the principal 'native informants' of the Company in matters of Orientalist scholarship and revenue expertise. First generations of the English-educated originated everywhere from the high castes or the Muslim elites. But self-perceptions were, once again, at odds with material reality, for the dominant discursive

---

[47] It implies a group that did not necessarily emerge from the ranks of a formed capitalist class but which still advocated a modern bourgeois culture.

emphasis of this new middle class was precisely on their novelty and break with the past, which could be alternately glorified or deplored. Here lay the key element of their modernity—consisting in self-image rather than empirically verifiable fact, and expressed in celebrations of the allegedly new, or in nostalgia for a lost world. What the two opposed images had in common was the assumption of a sharp, even total, break with the immediate past. This idea was strengthened by the replacement of Persian by English as the medium of higher education and in the upper layers of administration, the rise in stature and importance of vernacular print, and a shift in most parts of British India towards upper-caste Hindu dominance in administration and the professions. Additionally, for all upwardly mobile groups without very substantial landed or business incomes, education had acquired a new centrality as virtually the only path to a respectable life free of the burdens and taints of manual labour. Other roads, such as carving out a petty kingdom through force of arms, had been eliminated under Pax Britannica.

In the first century of their significant political presence in South Asia, the British were suspicious of Muslim recruits to their services because of their possible association with dispossessed Muslim rulers. Such suspicion rose to a crescendo for some years after the 1857 Rebellion, to be replaced from around the 1870s by an increasing effort to shift towards Muslim (and to some extent, lower-caste) Indians when a largely upper-caste Hindu-led nationalist movement emerged. The colonial policy change produced political effects among Indians as competition sharpened between privileged Hindus and Muslims. The new Hindu literati constructed an alleged historical era of 'Muslim tyranny' which had disappeared under the new dispensation which gave them better job opportunities. Once again, then, a break or rupture with the immediate past was eulogized, now in a way that did little justice to pre-colonial history and which seemed to anticipate later communal stereotyping. Here lay some of the problematic roots of the mid-twentieth-century historiographical model of a nineteenth-century 'renaissance', in contrast to an inferiorized 'medieval' past.

So far, we have been looking at the colonial middle class as a largely homogeneous phenomenon. But certain important variations become evident from a closer view, and they are of three kinds: regional differences, changes over time, and a possible distinction among layers within the middle class.

The frequently noted gap between the service-cum-professions-based middle class and business groups had a regional dimension. The standard historiographical model is principally derived from Bengal, where the British economic presence came first and penetrated deepest, leaving the literati groups few options after about 1850, except a combination of small tenurial rentier incomes, administrative jobs, and professions related to educational skills—occupations characteristic of what became the lifestyle of the bhadralok. As a mid-nineteenth-century Bengali couplet designed to encourage education put it, *lekha para kore je, gari ghora chare she:* he who learns to write and read will be able to ride on carriage and horse. Aspirations were frequently directed towards proper bourgeois entrepreneurial activities, but desire far outran performance—given the weight of British capital in key sectors and the development below them of immigrant, mainly Marwari, business groups. This model had often been extended to cover the whole country, and it did have numerous counterparts, as notably in the upper-caste literati formation based in Poona, in the interior of Maharashtra, and in a belated middle-class development in Bihar, where the middle class combined professions with rentier incomes derived from Permanent Settlement hierarchies and not from business activities. C.A. Bayly, in a seminal work, has however pointed to important differences that emerge as one moves up the Ganga valley. Significant European presence began here later than in Bengal, and it was much less overpowering, functioning often through collaborative networks with already established indigenous business groups. Bayly's micro studies of Allahabad were able to trace important connections of emergent professional groups, notably lawyers, with city business families.[48] Such links were important also for the centres of modern capitalism—Bombay and Ahmedabad. Successful business families and very rich landlords had little incentive to opt for service or professional occupations, and indeed even for modern education: in that sense, the Bengal or Poona model does retain a certain wider salience for understanding the colonial literati. In 1884–5, for

[48] Bayly 1983.

example, 53 per cent of Bombay's city college students came from families of government officials, professionals, and clerks, as against only 16.5 per cent from mercantile families. Their social composition thus did not differ all that much from that of the Bengali bhadralok, and both shared a markedly high-caste (and in Bombay, distinctively Brahmin: 43 per cent in 1885) slant, even when many students came from poorly paid clerical families.[49]

But high-caste origin could coexist with some differences across regions in relation to middle-class literati attitudes about subordinate castes. Caste was not much of a subject of discussion and debate among the Bengal bhadralok, for there was little sense that lower castes could pose a potential or actual threat to literati privileges till the end of the nineteenth century. In Bombay, by contrast, threat perceptions developed early, for a powerful critique of brahmanical privilege was already in place by the 1870s in the writings and activities of Jyotiba Phule, followed some decades later by Dalit affirmations inspired by Ambedkar. Tamil areas of Madras Presidency were the other locus of early anti-Brahmin protests, for here high-caste predominance was extremely crude and blatant: Brahmins, 3 per cent of the total Presidency population, provided 70 per cent of Madras University graduates. The narrowness of the caste elite in both regions also meant that a significant proportion of men of some wealth and influence came from non-Brahmin groups, providing favourable conditions for counter-elite formations. The sense of class superiority over those condemned to physical toil was cross-regional, but it could be shot through by a paternalist concerns for peasants, and more strongly for those sections (like the Bengal indigo cultivators in the 1850s and Assam tea labourers) who were directly exploited by Europeans.

The second kind of variation relates to time, and important work has been done by Tithi Bhattacharya for Bengal and by Veena Naregal for Bombay–Maharashtra. Bhattacharya's study brings together two lines of analysis which had so far been pursued in unconnected ways. That there was a significant mid-century change has been a historical truism for long, symbolized by the collapse of the Union Bank that

[49] McDonald 1966: 453–70.

Dwarkanath Tagore had founded in 1847, and the withering away of early indigenous Bengali enterprise with a tightening of British controls over the commanding heights of the Bengal economy (Dwarkanath's son and grandson, Debendranath and Rabindranath, were, economically speaking, pure rentiers). Also well known, and indeed obvious to anyone delving into the rich vernacular material left by the literati of that era, was the rejection and contempt the post-1850s bhadralok developed for what came to be termed the 'babu' culture of the Calcutta elite of the previous generation. Bhattacharya links the two processes to problematize what had been taken for granted: the centrality of education and culture in constituting the world of the bhadralok gentry after about 1850. The early-colonial urban babu was, in contrast to that prevalent image, not marked out essentially by education or modern cultural attainment: symbolic capital had then depended on lavish expenditure upon traditional kinds of ceremonies and entertainments, a 'language of splendour'. This was also in some ways a more open elite, for the continuing importance of business connections meant a certain mobility, so that many of the early-nineteenth-century Calcutta noveau riche came from castes fairly low down the social hierarchy: for these, social mobility demanded adherence to strict outward orthodoxy and demonstrative ways of registering loyalty to conservative norms. That Calcutta and its suburbs reported growing numbers of widow immolation (sati) in the decades immediately preceding its ban by Bentinck in 1829 was probably not unconnected to such upward mobility moves. The bhadralok literati of the second half of the century, however, rejected such ostentatious consumption, and, particularly among the Brahmo reformers, cultivated a somewhat puritanical and sanitized lifestyle. Debendranath's mood of renunciation after the death of his grandmother, vividly chronicled in his autobiography, can be read as an indicator of this significant shift in values. What had happened, Bhattacharya suggests, was a shift from part-independent 'byabsha' (business) to dependent 'chakri' (jobs, often clerical) in government and mercantile offices, along with the opening up of professions for which higher levels of education were now a prerequisite.[50] 'Vidya'

[50] The lower ranks of British administrative and commercial offices had been initially staffed by men of mixed white and Indian origin (termed Eurasians,

(learning) and its associated cultural patterns now became the hallmark of superior status: it still required a significant degree of economic resources, but a demonstrative display of the latter was no longer valued. The change, she suggests, is indicated by the shifts in social categories in some contemporary vernacular texts. Bhabanicharan Bandopadhyay's *Kalikata Kamalalay* (1823) had distinguished between three categories of Calcutta city-dwellers: banians and dewans (compradore agents of European businessmen and Company officials), the middling category of madhyabitta, and 'poor but bhadra'—the respectable poor. By 1861, however, the first category had disappeared, for Kaliprasanna Sinha's social skit *Hootum Pyanchar Naksha* had only two levels: the relatively better-off madhyabitta employed in the professions and services, and the world of the clerk (kerani).[51]

Bhattacharya's work thus adds new dimensions to what has been for long the standard way—i.e. a reformist/orthodox and/or revivalist conflict—of looking at the nineteenth-century Bengali literati. Initial enthusiasm for radical modernization for women and for Hindu religious life—typified by the outstanding figure of Rammohan Roy (1772/4–1833) and the rebellious Hindu College students of Derozio in the 1830s and 1840s, and then the more sober Brahmo movement for religious and social reform—gradually retreated before a resurgent Hindu revivalism which condemned such changes as denationalizing. The narrative is important. A problem which remains, however, is that this is a predominantly intellectual history, and as such largely separate from the social history that Tithi Bhattacharya and others have attempted without going much into the intellectual aspects.[52] Such separation has not helped the two lines of research.

---

and, later, Anglo-Indians), but Indians could be paid less. As English education spread, notably after Macaulay's Educational Minute of 1835 making English the medium of higher education, Indians with a smattering of English could be recruited for such clerical jobs. Financial benefit may well have been a more crucial motivation behind this shift, not just what the official propaganda presented as an effort to spread more 'civilized' and 'modern' values, and which critics have termed a hegemonizing drive.

[51] Bhattacharya 2005: chapter 1, *et passim*. For an English translation of Kaliprasanna's *Hootum*, see Sinha 2008.

[52] See for instance Sinha 1978.

Veena Naregal's study puts forward a temporal periodization, but along a somewhat different axis: a deepening hierarchical relationship between 'liberal' higher education in English, and the vernacular public sphere.[53] The initial impact of Western learning through, primarily, Elphinstone College in Bombay together with some missionary institutions, she suggests, had a certain openness and emancipatory potential. Two factors, however, distinguished the Bombay situation from Bengal. There was a more extended phase which saw an Orientalist educational policy tilted somewhat in favour of introducing modern 'useful knowledge' through vernacular translation—instead of the Bengal pattern of switching over drastically to English and prioritizing literary rather than scientific education.[54] The caste dimension was also much more prominent in the Bombay–Poona region than in Bengal, perhaps in part because this less elitist Company educational policy allowed a certain entry of intermediate-caste students to the new education, notably the group around Jyotiba Phule. Naregal thinks that there was a brief mid-century moment when a 'caste alliance'—of reformist Brahmins with

[53] A relationship of conflict and domination which I think Naregal somewhat exaggerates, through a parallel with the ways in which, in pre-colonial times, vernacular culture, despite significant advances in the medieval era of languages like Marathi and Bengali, had existed precariously in the shadow of Sanskrit. There are indications that the relationship in late-colonial times of English with the vernaculars was on the whole more productive, perhaps by virtue precisely of its alien character. Vernacular literature, most notably prose, developed rapidly in the nineteenth and early-twentieth centuries, and very largely through the efforts of the English-educated, for whom the vernaculars remained overwhelmingly the mediums for creative and imaginative writing. The 'Indo-Anglian' phenomenon of significant Indian writing in English is, almost entirely, a post-colonial development, which is sometimes illicitly read back to an era during which very few major Indian authors wrote in English: the pioneers of modern Bengali poetry and the novel, Michael Madhusudan Dutt and Bankimchandra Chattopadhyay, both began with English but then quickly switched to Bengali.

[54] The switch to English was what Rammohan had hoped for when he advocated Western education in 1823 in order to open India to new rationalist and scientific ways of thinking, while his friend William Adam was a notable advocate of the worth of vernacular education.

lower-caste elements—seemed possible, for there was in 1849 a split within the Brahmin literati over distribution of the Dakshina Fund that the British had inherited from their Peshwa predecessors. This was an annual sum that could be allocated to select Brahmin scholars. English-educated Brahmins wanted it to be given to modern rather than to old-fashioned Sanskrit scholars, and they were vociferously supported by the lower-caste group headed by Phule. But the quarrel among Brahmins was quickly patched up, and Phule was left alone to pursue his heroic efforts in the cause of extending education to women and to subordinated castes. This happened through his Society for the Promotion of Education of the Mahars and the Mangs; a series of highly subversive anti-Brahmin plays, ballads, and tracts; and eventually the Satyashodhak Samaj he founded in 1873.

Bombay educational policy entered a more aggressively Anglicist phase after the 1840s, and particularly after the foundation of Bombay University in 1857. State funding for the translation of useful texts was stopped, and official patronage through prizes was extended instead to self-consciously literary, high-cultural Marathi-language writings. The educational model was now drawn from Thomas Arnold and entailed a modified classicism where 'the Hindu majority were assigned Sanskrit as the proper linguistic reservoir' of their tradition. There were simultaneous efforts to 'purify' Marathi, insisting on its Sanskrit origins in ways clearly tilted towards high castes. In Bombay, this meant primarily Brahmins, unlike the slightly more open Bengal situation where there was less distinction between Brahmins and the other bhadralok castes of Kayasthas and Vaidyas. The Orientalist emphasis on Sanskrit-based classicism meshed well with the autonomous initiatives of high-caste groups to enhance their prestige and distinguish themselves more clearly from those below them—with an insistence on the purity of their language and social manners.[55] The upshot, in the context of growing intermediate-caste and then Dalit pressures, was a strong Hindu revivalist impulse,

[55] Even the reformist R.G. Bhandarkar could claim in 1877: 'Who is it that speaks good or correct Marathi? Of course, Brahmins of culture. The language of the other classes is not correct Marathi.' Tithi Bhattacharya develops a similar argument about the development of Bengali as a high-literary language.

colouring a whole phase of nationalism in western India through figures like Vishnushastri Chiplunkar and, most notably, the Extremist leader Bal Gangadhar Tilak. Interestingly, Naregal argues, the revivalist turn was associated with the spread of more uncompromising English education, and not the reverse, as has been usually assumed.[56]

Much of the work about the late-colonial middle class tended to assume a third kind of homogeneity as it pays little or no attention to possible internal stratification. Easier access to contemporary high-cultural material, and an assumption that the entire literati was elitist, meant a virtual equation of the literati with well-known and successful government officials, writers, lawyers, prominent teachers, doctors, journalists, and politicians. But below this level there was also another world of genteel, educated poverty, typified by the figure of the clerk, also predominantly high caste, whose smattering of English education had given him access to a poorly paid job in a governmental or mercantile office. The category can be extended to other sections of this high-caste, lower-middle-class world: downwardly mobile older Brahmin literati unable or unwilling to switch over to the new learning,[57] the equivalent of Grub Street printers and hack writers (located principally in the Battala quarter of North Calcutta), struggling journalists, a growing number of the educated-unemployed. This was a world different, however, from its early-modern European equivalents as it did not have connections with artisans—due to the caste barrier. It was also open to the gradual penetration by small sections below it comprising upwardly mobile individuals of lower caste, or of Muslim origin—when the latter could acquire an education.

Print culture has allowed us considerable access to this submerged world. For beneath the world of renowned poems, novels, short stories, essays, and plays, there survives a mass of late-colonial minor writings

[56] Naregal 2001; McDonald 1966.

[57] Such traditional rural literati, high-caste but poor, desperately clinging to their now-disregarded forms of learning and trying to use them for survival in a harsher world, figured very prominently, for instance, in a whole genre of Bengali novels, short stories, and films based on them. A well-known instance would be Harihar in Satyajit Ray's *Pather Panchali* and *Aparajito*.

in the various vernaculars which historians are now exploring. Authors were overwhelmingly upper caste, but by the turn of the nineteenth century an increasing number were published by small presses, usually in small towns, or even in villages, and produced by obscure men of subordinate castes, or Muslims. Here, moods and values could differ significantly from those discernible among the successful and prominent. One path of entry into this world lies through the exploration of their distinct notions and associations of time.

What has seldom been noticed by social historians is that the nineteenth century brought into India not only mechanical print—enabling otherwise obscure men, and fairly soon literate women and then lower-caste men, to write and publish books, quite inconceivable earlier—but also clock time.[58] Around mid nineteenth century, the successful upper layer of the middle class began to perceive their own times in ways that contained the germs of what, in the mid twentieth century, came to be termed a 'renaissance'. The Indian renaissance was seen as akin to its Italian and European prototype, a product of the impact of the modernity brought in through Western learning, and a revival of forgotten aspects of ancient Hindu cultural achievements through the efforts of British and Indian Orientalist scholarship. Early and successful products of Western education, notably in Bengal and Bombay, had in their more optimistic moods a sense of moving forward in consonance with a linear notation of time. Kishorichand Mitra in 1860, for instance, hailed his immediate predecessors in Hindu College, the pupils of the iconoclastic teacher Derozio, as being, like the Kanchenjunga, 'the first to catch the rising sun.' But such self-confidence was quite impossible to achieve for the subordinate layer of the literati, old or new. For them, a modicum of English education brought at best a poorly paid clerical job in a government or mercantile office, where they perpetually lived in terror of foreign bosses whose language of crude command was no more than half comprehensible. This was the world of the 'dasatya of chakri', the bondage of office work governed by the novel institution of clock time, about which a multitude of minor tracts, plays, and farces complained. Such bondage

[58] See 'Kaliyuga, Chakri, and Bhakti: Ramakrishna and the Times', in Sarkar 1997.

became a prominent new component of notions of Kaliyuga, the last and worst of the four eras of the traditional high-Hindu conception of cyclical time, which unexpectedly came to enjoy a new vogue in the lower-middle-class world of Bengal precisely at a time when one might expect that the rapid spread of clock time and modern Western notions of linear progress would banish it completely. Both Kaliyuga and the dasatya or servitude of chakri or paid employment figured prominently in the conversations of Ramakrishna Paramahansa, the saint of rustic poor Brahmin origin who, in the 1880s, cast a strange spell on the Calcutta bhadralok, initially on its clerical underworld. After his death Ramakrishna became through the mediation of his principal disciple, the highly sophisticated and educated Vivekananda, an icon of the entire educated middle class of Calcutta and district towns, his picture adorning banks and offices even in communist-ruled West Bengal in post-Independence times.

It would be wrong, then, to overstress the disjunction among layers of the nineteenth-century middle class. One needs to grasp both the gap and the possibility of a two-way movement, upwards or, much more often, downwards. The same family or kin group would quite often have both—successful, and clerical or unemployed down-and-out—members. As job opportunities shrank steadily over the decades, the ranks of the educated swelled, but offices and professions did not expand in the same proportion. The kerani or clerk in mercantile or government offices came to acquire a much larger role in middle-class social thinking than his actual numbers warranted. For the office was also the point where the respectable, but struggling, Indian directly faced his predominantly foreign bosses, a situation marked by blatant distinctions in pay scales, racism, and insults which compounded the sense of the servitude of new jobs.[59]

[59] A bit of concrete data about the material conditions of Indian clerks, rare otherwise, comes from memorials sent by some of them to the Meston Committee, set up to investigate complaints by Europeans and Indians employed in the imperial departments of the Government of India. Bengali clerks in Calcutta complained that their salaries had remained unchanged over forty years, while prices had gone up by 60 per cent. Rather revealingly, it was also stated that an additional burden they now bore were the higher wages they had to pay to their domestic servants. An appendix to the report

The broad transition from liberal reform to revivalism, chiefly in matters of gender relations and religion, may have had some of its social roots in such phenomena, for certainly the multitude of late-nineteenth-century minor writings was very often marked by a sharper tone of social conservatism. But there were also occasional alternative voices: those of some women, and, slowly, lower-caste writers for whom print culture opened new doors unimaginable before. For Rashsundari Devi, widow of a minor zamindar who would have remained utterly unknown to history but for the unexpected fact of her publishing in the early 1870s the very first Bengali-language autobiography, as well as for the author of a hagiography in verse of a lower-caste (Namasudra) founder of a dissident sect, Kaliyuga was 'blessed' because it brought new opportunities for women and Shudras.[60]

We need now to move towards strands of middle-class activity. A historiographical barrier confronts us here, a strong tendency, common to a variety of approaches, to look at the past through nationalist assumptions, focussing—even fixated—on the single question of attitudes towards foreign rule. This has taken several mutually opposed forms and produced unhelpful polarities—excessive glorification or debunking—of the nineteenth-century literati. The votaries of a Bengal or Indian 'renaissance', looking back with a strong element of nostalgia towards past nineteenth-century cultural greatness amidst the manifold problems of a mid-twentieth-century Bengal torn by war, famine, communal riots, and Partition, were tempted to imagine a linear progress of modernizing reform culminating in anti-colonial

---

gave interesting data about salary differentials in some Calcutta commercial firms. In one, Europeans recruited in Britain began with Rs 300 per month; their counterparts, presumably including Anglo-Indians, Rs 100. The Indians would start with Rs 20. The British could get a maximum of eleven months' leave, plus a free passage home after 5–6 years; Indians 12 days during Durga Puja, and nothing else except for special circumstances. See *Meston Committee Report* 1908.

[60] Sarkar 1999: *passim*. For the lower-caste hagiography, see Sumit Sarkar 'Renaissance and Kaliyuga: Time, Myth and History in Colonial Bengal', in Sarkar 1997.

nationalism. Admirers of Rammohan's rationalistic critique of religious orthodoxies and of his pioneering efforts on behalf of women then felt obliged to hail him also as the Father of Modern India,[61] and so presumably somehow also as a nationalist. The same assumption also produced debunking, as the literati of this period came under radical criticism for their parasitic gentry roots and evident illusions about the providential nature of British rule. Rammohan could on occasion write about a deliverance from 'Muslim tyranny', support a permanent settlement of Englishmen in India as agents of civilization, and, while by no means an uncritical loyalist, confine his criticism to specific policies of the Company. Later, the criticism of the Renaissance model broadened out to suggest that the vocabulary of change was a derivative one, relying entirely on post-Enlightenment Western knowledge.

While the latter, post-colonial strand, uncovered important aspects of political limits and epistemological borrowings from sources of Western knowledge, it relegated to a mere incidental detail the enormous debates on social change, especially the gender debates that went on throughout the nineteenth century. Reformers had to challenge the enormous standing and authority of the conservatives who were respected and feared by the colonial state. In controversies that surrounded widow immolation, widow marriage, age of consent, women's schooling and education, and child marriage, the changes they suggested scandalized entrenched social common sense and religious injunctions.[62]

Languages and Literatures

I have suggested earlier that the belated entry of mechanical print into South Asia in the colonial era was more significant than the coming of English education, though the latter has attracted much more scholarly attention in terms both elegiac and critical.[63] The importance of English as the key hegemonic 'mask of conquest' has been somewhat exaggerated: it looks a bit like an unconscious reading back

[61] A phrase favoured by, among others, Bruce Robertson, for the title of his book on Rammohan: see Robertson 1995.

[62] I will focus more on that in the subsequent companion volume.

[63] In the section of chapter 1 entitled 'Unmasking Conquest', above.

of present-day globalized realities to earlier times. A leading historian of Indian literature's words are more cogent: the main result of the introduction of English, from the 'strictly linguistic point of view, was the replacement of Persian [and to some extent of Sanskrit], without effectively changing the existing relationship between the language of the elite and the languages of the people.'[64] All three—English, Persian, Sanskrit—have been the languages of small minorities, the special positions of which have rested on power. Access to English, however, has been theoretically open (subject of course to important preconditions of opportunity and economic resources), while Sanskrit in its heyday was barred to women and subordinated castes. Significantly, even in colonial times, it was not English but Sanskrit, and in the case of the more refined forms of Urdu it was Persian, that still set the standards of 'purity' and grace for the new vernacular literary activities. Perhaps the very distance of English from South Asian languages helped block any major 'Anglicization' of Indian languages. Only in quite recent times has a certain hybridity of speech become common among urban elite groups. Significant creative writing in English is also much more post-colonial than colonial, and is obviously related to the development of a global market. Early generations of the English-educated did contain people who identified modernity with a superficial aping of Western mores, but they quickly became the objects of ridicule of others whose involvement with the new literary work was serious and not just for pleasure, profit, and fashion.[65] Significant numbers among the latter turned to writing in innovative ways in their respective vernaculars, introducing into their own tongues the ideas and literary forms they were learning about from their reading of English, and occasionally from one or two other European languages. And here the coming of print was decisive, for it made wider markets both possible, through reduced prices, and indispensable, for business success. Such expansion was possible only

[64] Das 1991: 30.

[65] Michael Madhusudan Dutt, steeped in Western values and a master of several European languages, was both the first modern poet in Bengali and the author of a brilliant skit on the blindly Anglicized, *Ekei Bale Sabhayata*: see Dutt 1860.

through the use of the vernaculars which reached a vast readership of ordinary people. The major new development of the colonial era, in the sphere of written culture, was therefore the qualitative advance in vernacular literatures, and, more specifically, vernacular prose.[66]

Print and the Development of Vernacular Languages

An initial puzzle is why print took so long to reach South Asia. Except for existing in one or two port towns within a few missionary printing presses for their Bibles and religious publications, it had very little impact on the rest of the subcontinent. Print became significant only from the closing decades of the eighteenth century in regions conquered by the Company.[67] It then spread rapidly, from around 1800, in the wake of British territorial expansion, but mainly through the initiative of Indians. Yet contacts with Western Europe became both more intensive and extensive from the early sixteenth century, which coincides roughly with the origin and spread of print in Europe. Print had in fact become quite widespread in parts of China and Japan much earlier, and there was no real reason to prevent its spread into South Asia from that direction, too. It had come early to the numerically substantial Jewish and Christian communities in West Asia, and Ottoman Muslims had turned belatedly to it from the early eighteenth century, several generations before Indians did. Explanations in terms of sheer conservative resistance to innovation are hardly satisfactory, for South Asia offers many instances of the quick incorporation of new technologies (gunpowder and cannons, for instance). A somewhat more plausible reason, put forward by Francis Robinson, was the long domination of predominantly oral, person-to-person, forms of transmission of knowledge through the guru–shishya format among Hindus, and murshid–murid among Muslims. These traditions valorized the spoken word, and print may have been construed as a threat to traditional forms of

---

[66] Here there was a marked contrast in the experience of colonialism between South Asia, and much of Africa and Latin America.

[67] For perhaps the earliest such mission, see Singh 1999; and Venkatachala-pathy 2012: Introduction.

authority. Christian missionary challenge to both Islamic and Hindu orthodoxies from the early nineteenth century, disseminated primarily through printed tracts, however, led to the deployment of the new technology 'to compensate for the loss of political power'. Print came to be taken up very quickly, and as much or more by conservatives as by reformists.[68] Among Muslim elites, intense debates among the reformist ulema drove them to project their theological perspectives through cheap and proliferating printed texts and fatwas.

The absence of print had made written material expensive, restricted the number of copies of each title, and often rendered such work valuable more for calligraphic beauty and aesthetic reasons than for functionality and information. Manuscripts, in their South Asian forms, were also quite laborious to read, and to carry from place to place. Manuscript pages were tied together within heavy wooden covers in 'puthis', and often had to be taken out, one by one, while reading—unlike the codex, the book-like form of binding which had been introduced in the West in Roman imperial times, from around the second century of the common era.[69]

Such limitations of South Asian scribal culture did not prevent a substantial development of vernacular languages from around AD 1000, most strikingly in the southern parts of the subcontinent. Sheldon even postulates a 'vernacular millennium', succeeding another era of a thousand years or so marked by the predominance of Sanskrit. In Karnataka, for instance, there was a notable displacement of Sanskrit by Kannada inscriptions between *c.* 750 and *c.* 950, and the first extant Kannada literary work, Pampa's version of the *Mahabharata,* also dates

[68] Robinson 1993: 229–51; Robinson 1996: 62–97. Efforts to maintain controls continued, though: thus, Ashraf Ali Thanawi's *Bihishti Zewar*, written to convey appropriate norms of behaviour to Muslim women, warned: 'Do not read any book without consulting a scholar. In fact, without a scholar, do nothing at all.'—See Robinson 1993.

[69] The greater gap in physical appearance and use between the printed book and the South Asian manuscript, implied by the absence of the codex form, could have been an additional hindrance for the entry of print: Losty 1982; for the codex, see Cavallo 1999: 64–89; for early manuscript and binding technology in South India, see Venkatachalapathy 2012: Introduction, esp. 9–13.

from the mid-tenth century. The history of Telugu literature begins, similarly, with Nannaya's version of that same epic in the mid-eleventh century.[70] The rise of popular devotional (bhakti) movements has often been suggested as a key explanation for this advance of vernacular languages like Kannada, Telugu, Malayalam, Marathi, Bengali, and the early closely related forms of Hindi and Urdu. Pollock, however, argues that the decisive factor behind vernacularization was not so much bhakti as the policies of regional courts eager to assert their independence from the claims of rulers with wider 'imperial' pretensions, and generally operating through Sanskrit.[71]

In several important ways the 'vernacular millennium' was set apart from the vernacularization that came in with print. 'Precolonial vernacular forms existed precariously in the shadow of Sanskrit' insofar as written texts and literary forms were concerned. Contrary to the assumptions common from the nineteenth century of many British Orientalists and the Hindu literati, even the early development of vernaculars seems to have been associated in regions like Maharashtra and Bengal with the weakening of the power of the brahmanical establishments by 'Muslim invasions'.[72] Throughout the pre-colonial and pre-print vernacular millennium, prose was very definitely subordinate to poetry. This testified to the continued importance— given the very limited quantity of available copies—of oral forms of transmission and preservation. Poetry is easier to memorize than prose writings. Texts in prose were generally confined to some specific forms: legal documents and letters, religious texts and pilgrimage

---

[70] Tamil has a much longer history, and is specific in partaking of some of the features of classical (marga) language typified by Sanskrit, while remaining throughout a desi spoken vernacular.

[71] Pollock 1998: 19–28; Pollock 2001: 392–426. A broadly similar approach is elaborated in Kaviraj 2005: 119–42. See also Mantena 2005: 513–34.

[72] Naregal 2001: chapter I, for the general subordination to Sanskrit and the synchrony between the first textual evidence for Marathi, in the 1290s, and the Tughlaq capture of the Yadava capital of Deogiri. The first texts generally associated with Bengali, the *Caryapada*, were produced by a heterodox Buddhist sect, and a leading scholar of Bengali in the early twentieth century, Dinesh Chandra Sen, was a strong advocate of an inverse relationship between brahmanical predominance and the emergence of Bengali literature.

accounts, occasional court chronicles like the Ahom Buranjis, and the Maratha bakhars dealing with Shivaji or other political heroes. Vernacular literature under conditions of scribal culture was quite limited also from the point of view of authorship. This was heavily upper caste or elite Muslim and male—with the notable exception of bhakti devotional poetry which had its lower-caste Chokhamela and Kabir as well as Mirabai. Yet another sharp contrast with colonial and post-colonial times was the absence of a clear distinction between adjoining linguistic groups, as well as of developed notions of loyalty to one's 'mother-tongue'. Both, really, are nineteenth- or early-twentieth-century constructs associated with nationalism, though they invariably try to invent long pedigrees. Earlier apparent eulogies of the vernacular, like *Tamil Vitutu* in the sixteenth-seventeenth century—much used by modern Tamil nationalism—emerge on closer look as significantly different in implications from the cult of tamil tai ('Mother Tamil') in the twentieth century. In the words of a scholar, a South Indian official of the early nineteenth century would have found it perfectly possible and natural to 'compose an official letter in Persian, record a land transaction in Marathi, study music in Telegu, send a personal note to a relative in Tamil, and perform religious ablutions in Sanskrit.' The specific language used would be determined by the task or context, and performed either personally or through experts.[73]

A point-by-point contrast with the situation that eventually appeared in course of the nineteenth century, logically associated with print, grows clear. There was, first, a qualitative leap in the production of vernacular texts, marginalizing Sanskrit fairly quickly everywhere, except among diminishing numbers of pandits. Within that, and again contrasting with scribal times, there was a clear shift to prose forms and an explosion of new genres. These included the novel, everywhere a harbinger of modernity, as indicated by the name. Short stories soon followed, as well as new forms and themes in poetry, while newspaper journalism and essays in periodicals proliferated (both quite impossible in scribal conditions). Plays came to be performed in new ways, while the other genres in print included historical and biographical writings,

---

[73] Ramaswamy 1997; Ramaswamy 1998: 66–92; Mitchell 2005: 445–65.

tracts, manuals, and the farces that made up the new 'low-life of literature' already touched upon briefly. The new literary forms, as well as the spread of silent individual reading, enabled new modes and sites for the exploration of subjectivities. This was the emergence of elements of the 'audience-oriented subjectivity' that Habermas defined as a crucial constituent of the modern public sphere, where private people could come together to constitute a public.[74] While authorship was still heavily upper caste, upper class, and male, women got into the picture surprisingly soon, and so, from mid century, did people of subordinate-caste origins.

Yet another implication of print, with far-reaching consequences extending to present times, was the sharpening of distinctions between neighbouring language communities. Print demanded for every language a more sharply defined, unitary, and 'pure' orthography, lexicon, and grammar, and a single distinctive or standard form in place of the much more fluid boundaries of earlier times. These were dictated by the need for a unified market enabling the sale of publications in a particular language. Along with such developments, a major consequence in course of time was script- or language-associated conflict. That between Hindi and Urdu—breaking the relative peace with which differences in script had long coexisted with a shared vocabulary and syntax—was obviously the most far-reaching, and replete with communal implications. But tensions also developed between Bengali in relation to Assamese and Oriya, and a growing number of regional nationalisms began to emerge around the turn of the century, all based on newly discovered cults of 'mother-tongues': most strikingly, Mother Tamil, for which Tamilians have at times been ready to immolate themselves.[75]

Actual historical developments, though, were not always so tidy or uniform. There are dangers, for instance, in simplifying and overdramatizing the contrast between oral-cum-scribal, and print. This simplified antithesis can quickly degenerate into the positing of technological determinism; it has often produced the opposite tendency—the over-celebration of print culture as progressive and

---

[74] Habermas 1962/1989: chapter 2, *et passim.*
[75] Ramaswamy 1997.

democratic—or arguments, more common nowadays, that print brought new controls and managed a veritable conquest and suppression of 'popular culture'. The transition has never been so simple or neat. There were major time lags, in certain regions and/or languages, in relation to the entry of print. Scribal culture remained dominant till towards the end of the nineteenth century in a fair number of languages: Rajasthani, Maithili, Dogri, Kashmiri, Manipuri. A number of 'tribal' or adivasi regions did not have written scripts, and generally came to acquire them through missionary endeavour, resulting in the use of the Roman font. Manuscript collections reveal that even in the region where print spread most, and earliest, i.e. Bengal, manuscripts were still commissioned and compiled even in the age of print, while Sanskrit remained an important part of education. Nor was print necessarily bound up with the coming of new literary forms and cultural values. As in early-modern Europe, it initially stimulated as much, sometimes more, the production of orthodox, conservative kinds of texts. The relationship of print with orality—quite often equated with the 'popular' though it has not been necessarily or universally so—was also not always conflictual.[76] Older oral forms often continued, even grew, through much of the nineteenth century, and sometimes beyond. Instances would include the recital and singing of poetry by itinerant specialists such as kathaks, bhats, charans, and kirtaniyas, as well as the more prestigious Urdu mushaira and the Telugu avadhani. Several of these forms are in their origin court related, or elite, or at least they were shared in by both elites and the larger public. The making of sharp distinctions between levels of culture is actually highly problematic. It has mostly been given up elsewhere, and, along with a whole series of such binary oppositions, is being increasingly questioned in India.[77]

New studies of particular languages have highlighted the ways in which emergent genres, as well their wider dissemination through print, could be delayed by the considerable conservative resistance from traditional pandits dedicated to Sanskrit and/or very highly

[76] We need only to think of the way in which the Vedas had been preserved down to the nineteenth century, with rote transmission helping to preserve brahmanical control.

[77] Das 1991: chapter 1.

sanskritized forms of the vernacular. A broadly similar chronological pattern seems to be emerging in regional studies which show that the strength of conservative resistance to print varied also with the prestige of particular regional high cultures, and shifting official and non-official British attitudes. In the early nineteenth century there was often an initial period of breakthroughs towards vernacularization in relatively democratic forms. Missionaries provided one major stimulus, as did the needs of colonial officials—before the shift towards the English medium in higher education—for simpler forms of vernaculars that were easier to learn and translate from as well as into. In the Telugu-speaking regions of Madras, for instance, Company administrators like Colin Mackenzie initially patronized the more colloquial form of Telugu prose associated with the karanam (literate village elites; in particular, revenue accountants) which had evolved for the purposes of local administration. This was quite different from the more sanskritized form of classical Telugu that had developed for court poetry in the later phases of the pre-colonial 'vernacular millennium'. The Asiatic Society of Bengal (and Bombay) promoted the systematic study of classical languages in English, but from around 1800 the Fort William College set up by the Company to train its servants contributed significantly towards the development of prose in a number of vernaculars. The latter part of the nineteenth century, however, was marked by a general shift, through which a tacit alliance often developed between 'Anglicism' in higher education and renewed patronage or support for Brahmin or higher-caste efforts at promoting sanskritized and allegedly purer forms of the vernaculars. Karanam Tamil, for instance, was denigrated, as the British could now obtain Indian subordinates with a modicum of English, while the supremacy of classicism was symbolized by the enormous prestige and influence of Chinnaya Suri, outstanding traditional Telugu and Tamil scholar, Telugu pandit in Madras University, and the author of a very influential Telugu Grammar.[78] The development of a more democratic and simpler form of Telugu, as well as of new genres in that language, were thus held back for almost two generations by a tacit alliance of Anglicism of a non-reformist kind, and renewed pandit

[78] Narayana Rao 2004.

power.[79] Only from around the turn of the century, and particularly from the 1910s, was there a renewed growth in a literary-intellectual Telugu closer to the spoken language. This came about through the efforts of social reformers like Viresalingam and figures like Ramamurti and Apparao, in the course of a bitter debate between exponents of a bookish and a vyvaharika vadi ('business') form of Telugu. The basis for this later development lay in the related emergence of a Telugu-based regional nationalism which came to demand a language-based Andhra province.[80]

A broadly similar pattern can be discerned for languages like Marathi (as already seen via Naregal), and Gujarati, where a tacit combination of some British officials like Alexander Forbes and intellectuals of Brahmin or Bania origin worked to 'purify' the language from non-Sanskrit-derived, particularly Persian, terms considered to be smacking of Muslim and Parsi elements. Unlike the Telugu case, however, the resultant, more sanskritized, language did not in these cases delay experimentation in the new genres.[81] Possibly the high level of business activity in that region provides one explanation. The need for quick and regular dissemination of commercial information had been a major early stimulus to the growth of newspapers—as Habermas pointed out in his study of the evolution of the public sphere. The first newspapers in the vernacular by Indians were located in Calcutta or Bombay: Rammohan's *Samvad Kaumudi* in Calcutta in 1821, the Gujarati *Sri Mumbaina Samacar* from Bombay just a year later, and the Marathi *Prahakar* from 1831.

Tamil stood out from the other vernaculars in revealing a very long history, on par with Sanskrit. It was marked in modern times, therefore, by an emphasis on the value of a classical canon. Print was used on a large scale to ensure the longevity, primarily, of old texts written on palm leaves (and frequently ravaged by white ants and termites). The advent of new forms seems to have been slightly

---

[79] Thus, 'printing, which created opportunities for prose, for silent reading, and for the development of a modern subjectivity, was held hostage by the pandits.' Ibid.: 160–1.

[80] Mitchell 2009, esp. chapter 6: 'Martyrs in the Name of Language? Death and the Making of Linguistic Passion'.

[81] Osaka 2002: 1–19; Yashaschandra 2003: 567–611.

delayed, perhaps in consequence: the first novel came out only in 1879, around two decades later than Bengali or Gujarati, and around the same time as in Marathi. But the precise content of the 'classical' canon itself seems to have been a fairly recent construct, constituted around the late nineteenth century. Traditional learning before that had mainly focussed upon high-caste Hindu devotional and religious texts, mainly of the medieval centuries and written in sanskritized forms of Tamil. Emergent Tamil nationalism would by contrast emphasize the greater purity of the Sangam literature of the early centuries AD, which had a non-religious, 'secular' tone, as well as sometimes Buddhist or Jaina associations. The change was related to the emergence of a non-brahmanical, 'Dravidian' strand in Tamil society and, eventually, politics.[82]

Malayalam had a less illustrious past than Tamil, and this perhaps was a stimulus to early innovation. Sanskritized ornate forms and poetry dominated much of the nineteenth century in Travancore, but from the 1850s a 'Venmani' movement developed in the smaller princely state of Cochin, among an elite group of Nambudiri Brahmans who knew little English but still reacted against an excessive dependence on Sanskrit.[83] More significant, ultimately, was the emergence in the last quarter of the nineteenth century of new prose forms, specially the novel. The distinctiveness of the Malayalam situation was that the novels were written largely by members of a caste traditionally subordinated to Brahmins, and, above all the Nayars, along with, quite remarkably, a number of Dalits. *Saraswativijayam* (1893), written by a

---

[82] Venkatachalapathy 2005: 535–53. The Tamil phrase in the caption means 'What is the use', which U.V. Swaminathan Iyer recalled in his autobiography as having been used by a modernistic Tamil official to whom he had tried in his youth to show off his knowledge of what was traditional scholarship. Iyer went on to become through his editing work a major figure in the construction of what today would be considered the Tamil canon, grounded in Sangam literature. For a fuller account of these and related issues in Tamilnadu, see Venkatachalapathy 2012. See also Asher 1970: 179–204. For the history of the shift in society and politics towards non-Brahmanism, see Pandian 2007.

[83] Das 1991: 161. There has been a spate of historical work on late-colonial imaginative literature in Malayalam in relation to lower-caste upthrusts: see the essays by Udaya Kumar, G. Arunima, and Dilip Menon in *Studies in History*, 13, (2), 1997.

Tiyya convert to Christianity, was published only three years after the first major novel in Malayalam, the Nayar Chandu Menon's *Indulekha*. Effective missionary work, in a region characterized by a uniquely gross structure of the upper-caste oppression of 'untouchables'—where not just touch, but even coming closer than a stipulated distance was believed to pollute—had led here to the rapid spread of literacy and the constitution of certain forms of upward mobility.

Bengali was the first to develop a distinctive vernacular prose literature, which quickly became influential in a number of other regions through translations into several Indian languages. Baptist missionaries located in Serampore were the pioneers. William Carey utilized Brahmin pandits and upper-caste literati as native informants and assistants. They were seeking new patrons by moving towards the Calcutta region after the decline of old centres like the Krishnanagar court in Nabadwip. But the domination of Sanskrit forms over vernacular print seems to have weakened here. The Bengali pioneers of somewhat less Sanskrit-bound prose, notably Rammohan Roy, followed by Vidyasagar, were themselves learned Brahmins, and there was bound to be a broad upper-caste bhadralok domination of the new literature that came to be developed in the era of print. An additional factor may have been the presence for a generation in Bengal, after the decline of Orientalist influence from the 1830s, of officials who combined Anglicism in higher education with a reformist thrust. The combination of Anglicism with modernistic reform has often been generalized as characteristic of British cultural policy as a whole from Macaulay on, and made the subject of either eulogy or condemnation. Actually, it was manifested much more in Bengal than in other provinces, and even then evident mainly during the years between the 1830s and 1857.

There was still a lot of pandit resistance to the innovations. Rammohan's daring effort to use the new Bengali prose he was developing to translate and debate brahmanical religious texts, so long the sole domain of Sanskrit, provoked the charge that this was allowing entry into the sacred of 'naked, unchained common language', akin to 'naked, unchaste women'.[84] But the development of modern Bengali prose, quickly coming into use in a wide range of genres, could not

[84] Bhattacharya 2005: 201–2.

be halted by such conservative opposition, though it persisted into the time of the novelist Bankimchandra Chattopadhyay, who set what became the dominant canon for 'sadhu bhasa'—appropriately chaste literary language—down to the early twentieth century. Bankim steered a middle path between the prose of Vidyasagar, still weighed down by Sanskrit, and the experiments in use of colloquial forms by Pyarichand Mitra, who had been a student of Derozio. But Bankim's prose still remained some distance away from colloquial speech, and there would be a further shift from around the 1910s towards the use of 'chalit' (colloquial) forms, with the difference consisting primarily in verb endings. Here the journal *Sabuj Patra,* associated with Pramatha Chaudhuri and Rabindranath, played a key role.

The standard forms, sadhu or chalit, still generally meant an imposition of centralized Calcutta- and bhadralok-based uniformity upon the considerable differences in languages as actually spoken in the various parts of the region. While no doubt associated with power, there was an element of inevitability about the homogenization, given the necessity of a standard orthography and lexicon for print. But tensions persisted: sections of the Muslim literati felt that the bhadralok or respectable upper-caste version had reduced terms of Persian origin and so enhanced the Sanskritic elements inseparable from high Hinduism. They insisted as a reaction on the use of what came to be called Musalmani Bangla, privileging Persian and Urdu terms and sometimes even printing texts back-to-front in pamphlets.[85] Standard Bengali still remains the product of a largely bhadralok world. As against what we have seen in relation to Kerala, the first really significant subordinate-caste novelist in Bengal, Advaita Mallavarman, emerged only in the mid-twentieth century. There was no lack of lower-caste pamphleteering in the region from around the turn of the nineteenth century to the twentieth, but very little imaginative literature.

[85] This would change markedly in the post-colonial years, when the Government of Pakistan attempted to impose Urdu on what was then East Pakistan, leading to a powerful language movement and contributing eventually to the formation of Bangladesh. Here Bengali, in the standard form which had evolved primarily through upper-caste Hindu bhadralok efforts in the nineteenth century, was accepted as the official language, and a patriotic song of Rabindranath eulogizing 'golden Bengal' became the national anthem.

The early presence of the British in Bengal had helped to give Calcutta a head start alike in 'modern' education and the formation of a new intelligentsia. It had led also to a certain temporal priority in new literary forms, and a considerable lead in service jobs, mostly of course clerical, and in the emerging professions of law, teaching, and medicine. The consequent spread of the Bengali 'middle class' outside Bengal, in the footsteps of the British, led to considerable resentment among the emerging literati across much of northern and eastern India at such cornering of jobs. In the areas inhabited by people speaking Assamese and Oriya, this took the form of language conflicts. Some Bengali intellectuals, as well as initially a number of British officials, argued that these were not distinct languages, they were no more than dialects of Bengali. Between 1835 and 1873 Bengali was made the language of the courts in the Assam districts, which was administratively more convenient since they were part of the Bengal Presidency till the latter date. There was also an attempt to make Bengali the medium of instruction in schools. Assamese, by contrast, was promoted by missionary groups like the American Baptists. The resentment at Bengali domination marked the beginning of an Assamese regional nationalism, with Anandilal Dhekian Phukan making a landmark protest in 1852 through a petition criticizing the use of a 'foreign medium' in courts and schools. The situation was complicated by the fact that Anandilal, along with virtually the entire first generation of the Assamese literati, had been educated in Calcutta because of the absence of higher education institutions in Assam. Relations with Bengali intellectual life were therefore ambiguous, with figures like Anandilal sharing a common student life with Bengalis in Calcutta, and sometimes writing also in Bengali. What developed were moods of combined admiration and resentment, akin to those of the highest level of Indian intellectuals with English culture and literature.

But Assamese identity, almost from the beginning, faced another kind of problem, for much of what became a separate chief commissioner's province in 1873 was inhabited by other linguistic-cultural groups with ways of life which, as we have seen, were becoming more distinct through the unwitting fallout of certain British policies. These—in large part in the interest of European tea planters—insisted on a sharp demarcation in land use between the large tracts that had been handed

over to planters virtually gratis, 'peasant' agriculture, and 'tribal' shifting agriculture or hunting-gathering. Partly as a consequence, a variety
of conflicting identity formations began to consolidate and came to
constitute the seedbed of much of the north-east's present-day medley
of regional nationalisms.[86]

There were similar problems in the Oriya-speaking districts of
Bengal Presidency's south-west. Some officials, and certain Bengali
literati—such as the Balasore schoolteacher Kanailal Bhattacharya
and the distinguished scholar Rajendralal Mitra—thought Oriya
was no more than a dialect of Bengali and wanted the latter script
and language to be used in schools and courts.[87] The problem was
aggravated by the fact that while the spoken languages were largely
mutually comprehensible, the Oriya script was similar to those of the
languages of the South and impossible to read for most Bengalis. As
often, the arrival of print culture expanded the frontiers and exacer-
bated the differences. There was in Orissa a further problem pertaining
to borders: two districts, Ganjam in the south-west and Sambalpur
in the north-east, though predominantly Oriya-speaking, were
parts of Madras Presidency and the Central Provinces, respectively.
A movement spearheaded by Madhusudan Das's Utkal Union Conference began to campaign in the 1890s for the reunification of these
districts with Orissa lands. In the early 1900s the British desire to
reduce the influence of an increasingly nationalist Bengali literati led
to some coincidental backing for the other linguistic groups within the
Bengal Presidency. Transferred from the Central Provinces in 1905 as
part of Curzon and Risley's general redrawing of provincial borders,
Sambalpur was merged with the Orissa districts and, in 1912, the
new province of Bihar and Orissa was carved out from Bengal. Orissa
had to wait till 1936 for its constitution as a separate province.[88] But
the language controversy that became the most acute, and pregnant
with consequences, was the one between Urdu and Hindi. In more

[86] Guha 1991: chapters 1, 10; Baruah 1999: chapters 2–5; Baruah 2001:
109–24; Saikia 2005: *passim*.

[87] Another distinguished Bengal intellectual, Bhudeb Mukhopadhyay, took
the opposite view.

[88] Mishra 1997: 207–23. For the provincial reorganizations under Curzon
in 1905, and their revision in 1912, see below.

precise terms, this was a conflict over script rather than language. The paradox was that twentieth-century forms of both Urdu and Hindi were based on refinements of the same Khari Boli—the spoken language of the western UP region—but the scripts which became their vehicles, Persian and Devanagari, were growing mutually incomprehensible to their respective readerships. The subject remains even today a minefield of controversy, turning over and over two questions, both connected with the idea of prior origin: (a) which is older? and (b) which of the two processes—Persianization and the Sanskritic orientation—began earlier? In many ways the debate is futile, the point being that it is already widely agreed that the split came about through these changes; so, depending on one's views, either Hindi or Urdu can be blamed for causing the break.[89] This has happened after centuries during which we have had the phenomena of what have been variously described as twinned languages, multilingualism, and even 'one single language in contradiction'. A series of interrelated vernaculars had begun evolving across a large part of North and Central India from around the thirteenth-fourteenth centuries: Hindavi/Hindi, Avadhi, Brajbhasha, Khari Boli, Maithili, and Hindustani as something like a lingua franca, spoken rather than written.[90] A further complication was added by the fact that the meanings of many of these names were amorphous and changeable over time and regions. Orsini suggests that the processes of refinement of some of these—with Brajbhasha, for instance, becoming the preferred vehicle for poetry, and continuing to be that till the early twentieth century—took place in intermittent ways related often to the existence or otherwise of court links and patronage. The question of prior development and consequent responsibility for rupture, therefore, is decidedly unhelpful. Urdu poetry, having evolved in a slightly different Deccani form in the Hyderabad region, went through a major period of efflorescence in the eighteenth and early nineteenth

[89] How intractable the controversy remains is indicated by the sharply opposed views on the subject by two experts, Shamsur Rahman Faruqi and Harish Trivedi, in Pollock 2003: chapters 14, 17. For a historical overview of the controversy, see King 1994.

[90] A hugely learned though now somewhat forgotten work on the subject was written by Amrit Rai, son of the Hindi novelist Premchand. See Rai 1984.

century through the growing patronage of the later Mughals and then of Nawabi Lucknow, while Urdu printed prose, too, emerged as a developed form earlier than Hindi in Devanagari.

What remains vital, and surprising to many people today, is the fact that, till fairly recent times, the Urdu–Hindi divide had nothing to do with a Muslim/Hindu distinction: Urdu was certainly not, as is so often assumed nowadays, a peculiarly Muslim language. The classic example counteracting this notion has long and accurately been that of the practice of Premchand, the best-known Hindi novelist of the early twentieth century, who wrote and published all his early novels in Urdu. The distinction, in the nineteenth century, was more regional, and to a considerable extent urban/rural, with Urdu for long the dominant form of cultured expression among the literati across a very wide area. It may be mentioned here that the subsequent development of a sanskritized Devanagari Hindi, with its claim to a long pedigree and a unique 'national' content, has had an important homologue with the parallel evolution of modern 'Hinduism', alongside the sharpening of boundaries with the Muslim as 'other' and the subordination of a whole series of vernaculars.[91] The latter came to be seen as derivatives of Hindi, with that language in turn posited as originating in Sanskrit via an intermediate phase of Apabhramsa. A unilinear telos has come to be assumed for both 'Hindi' and 'Hindu' and continues to hold sway—one of the many ways by which notions of history have helped to constitute the ethos of politics as well as, frequently, specific social changes since the nineteenth century.

Company and British policies played a significant role in these developments, though not necessarily always through conscious strategies of divide-and-rule. The efforts of Fort William College from around 1800 to train Company servants in the languages of the country for administrative purposes took the form of a certain division of labour among its staff, with Gilchrist for instance in charge of Hindustani, which he associated with the Perso-Arabic script and assimilated both with Urdu and things Islamic. A Gujarati Brahmin, Lallujilal, was assigned the task of teaching Hindi in Devanagari. The latter has sometimes been considered one of the pioneers of Hindi prose, for which he preferred Khari Boli (the 'upright speech' of the Delhi–Agra

[91] Rai 2000.

region), a decision pregnant with consequences, given the growing impact of print. There was a certain early official preference for Urdu, natural given the considerable contact of Company officials with elite Indian circles in that part of the country, while Hindustani seemed best suited to wider verbal communication. It became the preferred medium, for instance, for the communication of orders to soldiers in the Company and British Indian army. In 1837 Urdu replaced Persian as the language of courts and subordinate government offices in North India. Attitudes began changing, specially with regard to Muslims, in the aftermath of 1857, but there were some interesting straws in the wind even earlier, related probably to the particular language attainments of individual officials. A striking incident took place in 1847, when J.F. Ballantyne, an English professor and later Principal of Banaras Sanskrit College, tried to persuade his students to turn to Hindi: 'It was the duty of himself [a student] and his brother Pundits not to leave the task of formulating the national language in the hands of villagers, but to endeavour to get rid of the unprofitable diversity of provincial dialects—the Pandits of Benares, if they valued the fame of their city, ought to try to make the dialect of the holy city the standard of all India . . .' The Banaras students of 1847 failed to understand this logic: 'We do not clearly understand what you Europeans mean by the term Hindi, for there are hundreds of dialects, all in our opinion equally entitled to the name . . . That you call the Hindi will eventually merge in some future modification of the Oordoo, nor do we see any great cause of regret in this prospect.'[92]

Matters would change dramatically soon. From around the 1860s there was mounting pressure from the upper-caste Hindu literati in Banaras, Allahabad, and other Central and eastern UP cities for the promotion of Hindi in Devanagari, and specifically the replacement of Urdu by Hindi as the language of courts and lower-level government offices of the region. In 1893 this demand acquired an institutional form through the formation of the Nagari Pracharani Sabha in Banaras. The Urdu–Nagari controversy was bound up with the question of employment and helped to sharpen, if not at times initiate, a growing division between the Muslim and Hindu literati. In 1900 Lieutenant Governor Macdonnell granted this demand, much

[92] King 1989: 179–202, esp. 184–5.

to the chagrin of the Urdu-speaking, largely Muslim, intelligentsia. The Hindu–Hindi upthrust could be presented in a populist manner, for the dominant cultural upper crust of North Indian courtly and urban society functioned in Urdu written in the Perso-Arabic script. But that it really represented a vernacular elite, and not the masses in any unqualified sense, is indicated by the way the rise of a 'pure' Sanskritic Hindi simultaneously marginalized a large number of local and regional variants on the one hand, and on the other pushed aside an alternative, the Kaithi script, which had been used in some merchant circles. Meanwhile, Hindi was being transformed into 'shuddh Hindi' (pure Hindi) via increasing its proximity to Sanskrit vocabulary and expression, as well as by cleansing it from 'foreign', i.e. Persian, words. This became the standard of language reform, the agenda of a movement associated in the early twentieth century with influential writers and scholars like Mahavir Prasad Dwivedi and politicians like Madan Mohan Malaviya. Textbooks and histories of Hindi language and literature also played a crucial role in turning the language towards a firmly Sanskritic direction. In the expanding world of North Indian vernacular publications, the once-dominant Perso-Arabic Urdu medium was being steadily displaced by Devanagari Hindi. Between 1915 and 1940, the total number of titles published annually in the United Provinces in Urdu went down from 334 to 209; the corresponding figures for Hindi titles went up from 870 to 1548.[93] Gandhi, particularly during the last decade of his life, made a valiant effort to promote instead the widespread use of the more widely understood Hindustani as the proper language for the whole country, and Premchand also campaigned for it. While never much of a developed literary variant, it was adopted widely in audio-visual cultural forms seeking to address a countrywide popular audience: notably, as we will see, the Bombay-based touring companies of the Parsi theatre in the late-nineteenth and early-twentieth centuries, and then the film industry of Bombay.[94] But the advocates of Sanskritic

[93] The most exhaustive work in book history for North India, dealing with these and related issues by focussing on the career of the pre-eminent post-1857 publishing house of Naval Kishore, is Stark 2007: see esp. chapter 7, 'Hindi Publishing in a Stronghold of Urdu'.

[94] For a good account of Urdu as the language of Bombay cinema, see Kesavan 2008.

Hindi became increasingly influential within Gandhi's own Congress, and after Independence largely dominated the cultural policy of the central government. All India Radio became its most influential instrument, while more colloquial forms lingered on, to a diminishing extent, in Bombay films.[95]

Literatures, High and Low: Poetry, Novels,
Short Stories

The flood of printed materials from the early nineteenth century, we have seen, began with Christian missionary tracts and scripture translations. Other religious groups quickly followed suit, engaging polemically with missionaries and with spokesmen of other communities, but most of all among themselves, as reformist and orthodox positions began to crystallize around particular issues of religious and social change. Much of the early material consisted of print runs of existing manuscript genres, including multiple copies of almanacs. The other basic type consisted of textbooks, whose numbers began to increase exponentially. Statistical confirmation of this early pattern comes from Reverend James Long's three descriptive catalogues for Bengali publications in 1852, 1855, and 1859, while an official directive in the 1860s to send copies of all books published in Indian languages to London laid the foundation for today's invaluable British Library (previously India Office) series of vernacular tracts.[96] Long

[95] The historical literature on Hindi, Urdu, and their relationships is immense and growing. The above account is based mainly on Dalmia 1997/2010: chapters 4–5; Orsini 2002; Freitag 1989; and Pollock 2003.

[96] The material given by Long is conveniently summarized in Roy 1996. A more comprehensive list of publications in Bengali was later compiled by a twentieth-century scholar, Jatindramohan Bhattacharya, and published posthumously in 1993. Roy, along with the other contributors to Chatterjee's volume, emphasizes the dimension of 'surveillance', and certainly there was an element of that, particularly in the wake of 1857. But curiosity and interest about emerging vernacular printed literatures probably also had a role in Long's valuable work. The 'colonial' dimension of surveillance should not be exaggerated, or written about as a mark of 'colonial' difference. There was no lack of censorship in many parts of nineteenth-century Europe—tsarist Russia, and France under Napoleon III, would be two examples—while a general law controlling vernacular publications in India came only in 1878.

confirms that scriptures, mythologies, and religious tracts comprised till *c.* 1850 the largest category of publications, while almanacs and school textbooks had the largest print runs.[97] Newspapers and periodicals also began early, from around the 1820s. By the 1850s, what Long called 'useful books' became more prominent, by which he meant biographies and histories (the latter comprising 5.44 per cent of the books published per year already by 1844–52), ethical and scientific discourses, and translations of the English classics. One might add to these the growing numbers and enormous variety of 'do-it-yourselves' manuals, including for instance domestic manuals, cookery books, and guides to moral conduct and etiquette aimed at wives—these figure quite prominently in catalogues of vernacular tracts. None of this literature would have been conceivable, on any significant scale, in the absence of a rapidly developing print culture.

The other big change from the 1850s, fitting quite well with well-known facts about the 'high' literature of Bengal, is the big increase in works of prose fiction and drama, comprising almost one-fourth of the titles available for sale in 1865. By the late 1850s around 45–50 presses were operating in Calcutta: about 20 in the Battala area. In 1859 a total of 571,670 copies was printed in that city. The number of Bengali presses had gone up to 77 for the whole province by 1877, 61 of them in Calcutta.[98]

Much less is available, or has been found, about early publications in the other Indian languages, in part because of the lag and uneven spread of printing presses in other parts of the subcontinent. Recent book histories, however—in particular by Orsini and Stark for Hindi and by Venkatachalapathy for Tamil—have remedied the lacunae for those languages. One may surmise that Gujarati and Marathi printing took off in line with the other languages, as happened with newspapers and journals in Bombay, while considerable data has been unearthed about the large numbers of religious tracts, manuals, and

[97] For the immense popularity of almanacs in Tamilnadu, Venkatachalapathy quotes C.N. Annadurai as saying in 1950: 'Two books sell the most in our society: one, the almanac; the other, the railway timetable.' See Venkatachalapathy 2012: xviii.

[98] The most detailed account of Battala available so far in English is Ghosh 2006: 118, *et passim*. There have been several Bengali studies, though.

poetry and prose in Urdu from the early days of print. By the turn of the century a flourishing commercial market in Urdu books had developed in a number of North Indian towns, followed by Hindi in Devanagari. The bulk of such now-forgotten ephemera reproduced established genres, but there were also some interesting innovations, as for instance detective stories.[99]

Much of this printed material is scarcely read today except by social historians. There has been a tendency to dismiss it as no more than 'minor', given that literature was for long defined as the work of outstanding writers alone. This 'low life of literature' or the world of 'small books' is now closely studied in many parts of the world,[100] though there is also now an inverse trend: a romanticization of such publications as coming from a 'subaltern' world which is assumed to be rebellious or radical. Much of the appeal of such approaches comes from the prominence of what Long censoriously termed 'erotic' works, as well as the fact that their authors remain obscure. Fear of pornography led to attempts at censoring such material even by 1856, and this attitude was often shared by the bhadralok. Some feminists see in this the attempt to control women's bodies and sexuality, allegedly typical both of Victorian Britain and colonial India, and there can occasionally be in such perspectives the problematic concomitant of a pre-colonial world free of such sexism.[101] The world of small books, while replete with ridicule of educated, Anglicized gentlemen, was even more filled with contempt towards educated women and wives, favouring them as the butt of farces and satirical skits, many of them satirically illustrated.[102] These were very prominent between the 1860s and 1890s, when social reforms centring on widow marriage, the ban

[99] Orsini 2004: 435–82.

[100] Terms used by historians like Roger Chartier, Robert Darnton, and Margaret Spufford, who have studied similar phenomena for France and England in the seventeenth and eighteenth centuries.

[101] An implicit refutation of idealizations of pre-colonial gender sensitivity can be found in the recent work of, among others, Rosalind O'Hanlon: see her essays in the section titled 'Gender between Empires' in O'Hanlon 2014.

[102] Print, it needs to be emphasized, had enabled also the large-scale mechanical reproduction of all manner of visual material, including the now well-known Kalighat paintings (discussed below).

on polygamy, and raising the age of consent were central issues of debate in middle-class life.

The strongly patriarchal note, however, should make us pause, as should the fact that a large proportion of such authors were men with upper-caste surnames—though no doubt often located in a lower-middle-class clerical milieu.[103] Nor should we assume that such books, not least perhaps the erotica, were being read only by humble people, as the very failure of efforts to control them possibly indicates. The tendency sometimes to equate criticism of the ways of the English-educated with an alternative, 'subaltern', 'radical', or even crypto-nationalistic world has little basis. One of the very few early expressions of middle-class patriotism with an anti-colonial slant comes in fact from an article in English in the 1830s by a member of the highly iconoclastic Derozian group. The dividing line between Western or modernist, and traditional or indigenous, values seldom neatly coincided with that between loyalists and critics of British rule.[104]

We move now towards the 'high' literary world, but it would be convenient to highlight at this point two significantly new features that characterized, though often in different ways, high and low publications alike. The first was the spillover into print of the debates around social reform—apart from Western education, this largely

[103] It is true that women may have found it is easier to enter this world, while the development of Musalmani Bangla mentioned earlier can also be placed within the category. By the turn of the century, tracts were also being written in large numbers by members of subordinate castes, generally critical of upper-caste domination. But some within such categories were also able to bring out books and journals that became fairly well known—women in Bengal from the 1860s, some Muslims (writing in more orthodox Bangla), and, in other provinces, lower-caste rebels like Phule by the 1860s.

[104] Such conflations can be seen in Sumanta Banerjee's pioneering works, notably his *The Parlour and the Streets: Elite and Popular Culture in Nineteenth Century Calcutta* (Banerjee 1989), and, more eclectically, in Anindita Ghosh. The Derozian was Kylas Chandra Dutt, whose short story was about an imaginary rebellion against the British in Calcutta in 1845. Quite strikingly, it was published in *Calcutta Literary Gazette* in 1835, a paper edited by an English teacher, D.L. Richardson: one more indication of the occasional porousness of boundaries: Das 1991: 80.

meant questions about the condition of women. This was the dominant concern among educated middle-class groups till right towards
the end of the century. We have already noted the importance of
such issues, mostly presented in anti-reformist ways, in the world
of small books; their presence in a large number of high-culture
journals and literary works is equally evident. Meenakshi Mukherjee
has distinguished a whole category of 'novels of purpose', written as
instruments of religious proselytization or social reform.[105] Nonetheless, the fallout of the concern with gender relations in imaginative
literature was a new centrality for women characters: they tended to
be stronger and more memorable figures in a large number of novels,
short stories, and plays of high quality. The men in the same works,
by contrast, were pusillanimous and much less interesting. This kind
of inversion was apparent even in literature produced by men with
highly conservative views on questions of reform. As the century
moved towards its close, women came to be seen increasingly as the
last bastion of indigenous purity and honour, in contrast with their
menfolk who had meekly surrendered to foreign conquest and cultural
domination.[106]

The other key novelty was the qualitatively new prominence of
history in a multitude of discourses, along with entirely new assumptions about its meaning and patterns. While in the old pathshalas or
primary schools the concentration had been on practical training in
language, arithmetic, and elementary accountancy, history now became a key element in primary and secondary education. Before the
appearance of print, pedagogical manuscripts were predominantly
about religious, moral, or grammatical themes. From being conspicuously absent, history now became an indispensable subject in
schools, increasingly taught as an aspect of other courses too,
particularly of languages.[107] What added to this new importance was
the fact that formal education itself was fast becoming indispensable,
in ways unknown earlier, for respectable jobs, professions, and
services.

[105] Mukherjee 1999.
[106] The thesis for which the best-known source remains Chatterjee 1989.
[107] Shahidullah 1987: *passim*.

But history of what kinds? Marked shifts are noticeable here, especially in the contrast between the work of, on the one hand, an orthodox Brahmin commissioned by the Company to write a historical survey as a language text for their officials, and, on the other, a textbook for schools fifty years later. The first of these two, Mrityunjoy Vidyalankar's *Rajabali* (Chronicle of Kings; Serampur, 1805), began with an exposition of the traditional brahmanic notion of time as cyclical, marked by four eras repeating themselves across aeons of years: Kaliyuga, the last and worst, always located in the present. Such cyclicity did not present any problem—it had never done—for the author's otherwise linear narrative about succession of dynasties. The striking absence, as against the model that would soon become ubiquitous, was of a sense of a major break when Muslim dynasties replaced Hindu ones, or when the latter in turn gave place to Company rule: rulers were simply either good, or bad and tainted and their origins or religion were not important. Misrule was identified as the king's subordination to excessively dominant women, as well as the violation of proper standards of kingship and loyalty. But the second work in question, Nilmoni Basak's *Bharatbarsher Itihas* (History of India; Calcutta, 1857) laid down the parameters for a century or more of the standard textbook periodization of Indian history into ancient, medieval, modern—equated with Hindu, Muslim, and British eras. Soon the medieval 'Muslim' era was identified with retrogression and tyranny as against an earlier Hindu age of glory. The present was sometimes represented as a renaissance, a recovery of past greatness and the notion of greatness involved the reception of Western modernity as well as revival of ancient splendour.

The Muslim literati in northern India, where an elite Urdu culture still flourished, soon appropriated this basic schema, transposing the era of Hindu glory to global Muslim magnificence in medieval times—the glory of the Mughals, the splendours of the Umayyads and the Abbasids, and so on. At more plebeian levels, as we have seen, the Kaliyuga format did not die out for several decades. It was both different and similar; the ideal time was still way back in the past, but thereafter a steady and inevitable decline culminated in the lowest depths, manifest in the present, this nadir being signified by insubordinate women, overpowerful Shudras, and degenerate

Brahmans. Much play was made with the name 'Calcutta', the city of Kali, for negative images of the modern city were characteristic of a lot of literary and visual representations of the times.[108]

These shifts became crucial to the formation of both Hindu and Muslim communalism. It is tempting to read them in terms of the dominant influence of British perceptions, or to attribute them to colonial strategies of divide-and-rule. Certainly those played a part: think of the far-reaching and lasting impact of Tod's highly romantic evaluations of heroic Rajput resistance to 'Muslim' invaders; or of British accounts extolling Shivaji in similar ways; and the ways in which Elliot and Dowson underlined apparently anti-Hindu passages in their post-1857 edition of translated excerpts from Sultanate and Mughal chronicles. Sometimes, vernacular literary representations of such anti-Muslim motifs are explaind in two ways. One sees them, especially Bankimchandra's novels, as coded writing that expected readers to substitute in their minds 'British misrule' for 'medieval Muslim tyranny'. This assumes a continuous and pervasive colonial censorship of middle-class writing, an assumption which is difficult to sustain before the emergence of militant nationalism from around 1905. It is interesting, all the same, that narrative poems, and soon novels, around the theme of Hindu heroic resistance to medieval Muslim tyrants suddenly proliferate in a number of vernacular languages immediately after the 1857 Rebellion and its bloody suppression, events from which the educated middle class had remained entirely aloof—often even publicly proclaiming its loyalism. Therefore, the second explanation: it may not be implausible to suggest that the Muslim tyranny syndrome could to an extent have worked as balm for a sense of guilt, the open expression of which would have been risky in the immediate aftermath of 1857.[109] Loyalism in the present could be justified through the frequent assertion that British rule was a great improvement on the Muslim era.

[108] Sarkar 1997: chapters 1, 5–6, 8. For somewhat different approaches, see Chatterjee1994, and Kaviraj 1995.

[109] The first attempt to write an account of 1857 and its brutal suppression from an explicitly anti-British point of view came only in 1909, in V.D. Savarkar's *First Indian War of Independence*—and that was promptly banned.

There is little doubt that much of the new history became a
major stimulus to the growth of a range of nationalistic identity
formations, putatively anti-colonial, Hindu or Muslim communal,
or regional. These were invariably imagined in linear manner with a
similar pattern of tripartite division into 'periods'. A striking instance
of the multiple uses of this model was the way in which Hindu
social reformers frequently urged improvements in the conditions
of women by attributing social abuses—such as widow immolation,
the prohibition on widow marriage, and child marriages—to the
consequences of Hindu degeneration under Muslim rule: Hindu
women had apparently enjoyed a wonderfully exalted status during
the preceding 'Hindu era'. Very often, the Hindu or anti-Muslim
slant of these readings is ascribed to a cultural nationalism that has
its Muslim counterpart as well. Similarly, orthodox resistance against
reform is projected by some scholars as another variant of cultural
nationalism. The underlying assumption in both readings is a highly
linear teleology: virtually everything in nineteenth-century history
is assumed to lead inexorably towards diverse kinds of twentieth-
century nationalism. I have been arguing against such readings back
of nationalism at various points in this book. Nineteenth-century
literature, we shall see, provides considerable evidence in favour of
contrary arguments. 'Third World literature', contrary to the assumption made in an influential essay by Frederic Jameson, was not always
a 'national allegory'.[110]

The Viewless Wings of Poesy: Poetry and Poetic Forms

The dominant form of pre-print literary expression had been poetry,
and, not unexpectedly, some of the traditional genres persisted into
the new era.[111] Print could often stimulate older forms, both courtly

[110] Jameson 1986: 65–88. For an effective critique, see Ahmad 1987:
3–25.

[111] It should be obvious that my necessarily brief accounts, here and later,
of developments in literature across so many languages cannot even try to be
comprehensive. Any such attempt would become a tedious catalogue, while
remaining utterly inadequate. Those interested in an overall survey should turn
to Das 1991, along with the succeeding volume that covers the years 1911–56.

and 'folk', by expanding their reach. Punjabi kissas and jhaggras, for instance, flourished with print, even reformists coming from the new middle-class literati utilizing their 'vulgar' idioms to popularize novel messages.[112] The story of Hir–Ranjha still circulated in kissa form in 1886.[113] Print facilitated the survival of folk songs and tales, too, enabling subsequent academic studies by folklorists, anthropologists, and historians.[114] It is in some folk ballads, and not in 'elite' forms of literature, that early signs can be detected of patriotic anti-British sentiments. A ballad, written by a court poet of the singular Rajput kingdom that joined the 1857 Rebellion, Bundi, attacked the loyalism of the rest of Rajput's courts. Folk songs glorifying the revolt circulated for a long time in parts of Central India. Over a longer time span, too, tales commemorating the heroism of Maratha warriors, notably Shivaji, were sung in villages as oral ballads or pavadas.[115]

For elite literary continuities with past forms, the Urdu ghazal, which had reached its peak in the poetry of Mirza Ghalib, persisted under the patronage of surviving Muslim courts like Bhopal, Hyderabad, and Rampur. Some literary figures are considered as transitional: Dalpatram in Gujarat and Dasharathi Ray and Ishvar Gupta in Bengal. They had little or no knowledge of English but wrote poems and satires about technological innovations, women's education, and widow marriage.[116]

Three broad phases can be distinguished in the evolution of

There are also, of course, a large number of histories of literature in particular languages, as well as numerous studies of individual writers.

[112] A social historian of the Punjab has made interesting use of such material: Malhotra 2002.

[113] The social history of language and literature in colonial Punjab, including epic tellings and retellings of the Hir–Ranjha narratives, is fulsomely investigated in Mir 2010.

[114] See, for example, Blackburn 2003 for South India.

[115] Or 'powadas': for a detailed recent treatment of these and other historiographical genres in Maharashtra, see Deshpande 2007.

[116] In 1851, for instance, Dalpatram published a long poem entitled 'Invasion of Industry', where 'King Industry' and 'Field Marshall Machinery', preceded by 'General Coarse Long Cloth', conquer the country. The tone, though, is fairly celebratory, with the conquest portrayed as a victory over superstition, ignorance, and idleness: Das 1991: 100–1.

'modern' forms of poetry composed by the new literati over the half century or so between the 1860s and the 1910s. Their temporal manifestations in particular languages varied considerably, but the first phase was dominated by long narrative poems on historical themes, typified for instance by Rangalal Bandyopadhyay's *Padminir Upakshyan* (Padmini's Story; 1858) in Bengali, and Narmadashankar's *Hinduo-na-Padati* (Decline of the Hindus; 1866) in Gujarati. It is in such 'historical' epics that the new assumptions about Muslim tyranny found their most obvious expression. The exact counterpart to this stereotype was presented, memorably, in Hali's narrative poem in Urdu, *Musaddas* (1879).[117] Here the lost golden age was located in the glories of medieval Islam, in India and elsewhere. Some of Rangalal's writings—along with those of other poets in this narrative vein in Bengal like Hemchandra Bandyopadhyay and Nabinchandra Sen—included a corpus of patriotic poetry where an image of the much-bewailed plight of 'Bharat' could be taken fairly easily out of the medieval context in which it was still generally located. Nabinchandra, for instance, wrote a long dirge-like poem on the battle of Plassey (*Palashir Yuddha*: 1876). His hero in that poem, though, was still a Hindu general, depicted as trying to persuade Muslim soldiers not to run away before British cannons. A similar lament for lost glory found expression in Hindi poetry through Bharatendu Harishchandra's *Bharat Bhiksha* (1878).[118]

With Michael Madhusudan Dutt (1824–73) we move to a different level. Dutt, followed soon by the novelist and essayist Bankimchandra Chattopadhyay (1838–94) and then Rabindranath Tagore (1861–1941), constitute the trio that gave Bengali literature a special place in the literary history of the late colonial era. Iconoclastic to the point of bohemianism and Derozian (Derozianism will be discussed in the next volume) by temperament if not strictly in age, Dutt steeped himself in Western literature—English and some European—in a most creative manner. He introduced blank verse into Bengali through *Tilottama* (1860) and *Meghnadbadh* (1861), and the sonnet form (*Chaturdaspadi*

[117] For a modern English translation of this work, see Shackle and Majeed 1997.

[118] Dalmia 1997/2010: esp. 287.

Kavitabali: 1866). Even more daring were his remarkable thematic reversals, using traditional Sanskrit material but inverting values in ways that would seem highly provocative to subscribers of modern Hindutva. For instance, in *Meghnadbadh* he made Ravana and his son Meghnad heroic defenders of their invaded land. Rama, in contrast, seemed to him a weakling: 'I despise Ram and his rabble', he once wrote. To Sita's suffering he was sympathetic, while emphasizing the courage in battle of Meghnad's consort Pramila. In keeping with his quasi-feministic values, his *Birangana Kavya* (1862) rewrote a series of well-known stories from the epic-puranic corpus, deploying the woman's voice, sensibility, and perspective. He carried over this radicalism into writings about contemporary times. While ridiculing the superficial Anglicism of many of his educated contemporaries in the farce *Ekei Bale Sabhyata* (Is this Civilization?; 1860), Dutt also wrote in the same year a devastating exposé of the abuses of patriarchy and class, and of upper-class Hindu communal attitudes, in *Buro Shaliker Ghare Ro* (The Ways of an Old Rake).

Around the 1870s and 1880s poetry began moving from mythological, historical, and quasi-patriotic narratives towards lyrics marked by more subjective, interior, and romantic moods. The city/country dichotomy deepened, and the beauties of nature and unspoiled village life came to occupy the central place. A loose narrative structure was retained at times, but now these long poems were more of a string of lyrics loosely held together by a storyline. An early instance is Biharilal Chakrabarti's *Sarada Mangal* (1879), which inaugurated this turn in Bengali poetry and became a significant influence for a time on the young Rabindranath. Tagore became the towering exemplar of the new era through a plenitude of lyrics and songs from the 1880s, and so he remained, through a diversity of forms, right down to the early 1940s. His verses and lyrics were woven around love, nature, and a very mystical divine being, the three themes so closely associated with each other that it is difficult to know exactly when who or what is being addressed. Nature and love, rather than quasi-historical narratives, now emerged as dominant poetic themes.

Broadly similar changes took place in many other languages, though in varying times, extents, and combinations. To cite a few instances: in Oriya Radhanath Ray established himself as a premier poet of nature through his *Chilka* (1892). He also composed several long narrative poems. Gujarat had Keshav Naik, and Maharashtra had Keshavsut. The latter was of humble background, introduced the sonnet to Marathi, and had unusual socially radical leanings.

A truly exceptional figure, however, was Kumaran Asan in Kerala in the early twentieth century, a singularly major literary figure of lower-caste (Ezhava) origin and prominent disciple of the anti-caste reformer Sree Narayana Guru. A student in Calcutta in the late 1890s—a stay that made him knowledgeable about English poetry—Asan became a highly innovative poet of love and desire. A perceptive analysis has suggested that Asan's major contribution was his bid to move the locus of desire from the charms of the woman's body, often depicted in formulaic ways—as in much of traditional Indian erotic poetry—towards a more individualized, interior self.[119]

Literature in the 1860s and 1870s was implicitly, and occasionally explicitly, political. The next twenty years by contrast saw a certain depoliticization of literary themes, probably connected with the moves under Northbrook and Lytton to enforce restraints on vernacular pub-lications, notably, drama in public theatres. Politics, however, returned, and in far bolder tones, in the first decade of the new century as a vital component of the Swadeshi upsurge and the rise of extremist forms of nationalism.

A Various Universe: Prose, Fiction, Stories

There was a strong link between the coming of mechanical print and the shift to prose in multiple forms. In the world of 'high' literary production, we may briefly glance at five or six different kinds of new publications that print alone could foster, before passing on to a closer look at what was the crucial novelty of the late nineteenth century: the coming of the novel. (The use of that term, in English and sometimes also in some Indian languages, is in itself significant.)

Religious controversies, social reform efforts and their critiques, and emergent nationalist politics all spawned massive numbers of vernacular tracts or pamphlets. These were mostly written at first by high-caste or ashraf men, but women writers emerged fairly

---

[119] Kumar 1997: 247–70.

soon. By the turn of the century, tracts composed by or on behalf of subordinated castes also began to proliferate in some parts of the country. There was also an explosion of newspapers, initially in English but then more and more in vernacular languages. Things were made easier by the relatively low costs of early printing, though at first its inefficiency made weeklies much easier to bring out than daily papers. Periodicals also sprouted, some of high literary quality, constituting sites for the serialization of novels and of debates. In the more serious and sophisticated of these, cultural flows from the modern West, as well as rediscoveries or reinventions of the Indian past, could be conveyed and discussed. Some journals were particularly important for middle-class cultural life: a whole series of such influential monthlies or tri-monthlies in Bengal was, as we noted, often with associated adda groups. Among these, Bankimchandra's *Bangadarshan* (1872) came to occupy a particularly exalted place. Journals began to appear in major cities, and then from mofussil towns and provinces all over the subcontinent. Print also made possible journals directed to, and increasingly edited by, women. A few aimed at lower-caste readers, notably *Dinabandhu* in Maharashtra, associated with the Non-Brahman movement of Jyotiba Phule. And one, the *Bharat Sramajibi* founded by the Brahmo activist and philanthropist Sasipada Banerji, dedicated itself to spreading education and improving the morals of industrial workers in a suburb of Calcutta.

Print brought with it a large number of translations, both from English (and occasionally one or two other European languages), and among Indian languages. Translations of Shakespeare were particularly numerous. The early and wide recognition of Bankimchandra as the first major Indian novelist owed much to such translations, beginning with a Hindi version of his first novel, *Durgeshnandini*, as early as in 1883, followed by one in Kannada in 1885. The Hindi translation was made by Bharatendu Harishchandra of Banaras, the leading poet, dramatist, and writer in Devanagari Hindi of the late nineteenth century.[120]

Another significant modern genre was biographies and autobiographies. The second had been very rare in pre-print times; the first,

[120] And the subject, as noted, of an inspired study: Dalmia 1997/2010.

while less uncommon, had been overwhelmingly about rulers or religious leaders. Now, print made possible the publication of an autobiography by an otherwise totally obscure woman, Rashsundari Devi, as early as *c.* 1875. Among men, the Gujarati writer Narmad had published his autobiography, *Meri Haqiqat,* in 1866, but full-length biographies and autobiographies became numerous only from the 1880s: even a figure as well known as Rammohan had to wait till then for his first biography.[121] Finally, we have a considerable number of travel accounts, including of pilgrimage journeys which were part autobiographical and part travelogue as well. The travels were in India as well as abroad and they vividly show how print, railways, and steamships allowed exchanges of experience across countries and continents. These are often of considerable importance for research on the transmission of cultural influences, and for social history in general. Apart from Rabindranath and Sibnath Sastri who wrote about their travels in England, there was also an interesting Marathi eyewitness account by Vishnubhat Godse of the 1857 Rebellion in Central India, published only in 1907, one of the few Indian descriptions of a cataclysmic event.

Meenakshi Mukherjee's influential study of the novel in India is built around a tension which she considers central, between 'realism' and 'reality'. She assumes that Indian writers tried to take as their model the literary convention of realism, then dominant in the West, but found themselves hamstrung by the fact that there was no counterpart in Indian society then to the marriages for love characteristic in Western literature. Western realism, then would be 'unrealistic' in Indian conditions. Mukherjee's approach assumes attempted imitations of the West. While these influences were often obvious, such as Walter Scott's historical novels on Bankim, for instance, a little too much can be made of such 'derivations'. It is a striking fact that the novels from which borrowings can be detected, Scott apart, were mostly of second-rate quality, by writers then widely

---

[121] 'The Invention of Private Life', the title of Kaviraj 2004, is also a phrase that evocatively captures what was being attempted in early self-descriptive narratives, such as those by Sibnath Sastri. For a variety of analyses of the biographical and autobiographical genres, see Arnold and Blackburn 2004.

read but now virtually forgotten, such as G.W.M. Reynolds. The so-called derivations were considerably superior in literary quality to their alleged prototypes. What was borrowed was often only the skeleton of a plot; what was added constituted the real strength and significance. The remarkable emphasis on women—their amazing activism and independence in driving the narratives—surely had more to do with the centrality of the woman question in middle-class reform and life for much of that century. Even the most daring of novels usually ended with social compromises. But this need not be seen only as a recognition of Indian social realities which were constrictive. Conflicts within that fast changing 'reality', which produced even more pervasive and complex conflicts in the minds of the writers, may have been of greater importance than some putative Western 'model' invoked and then deemed inappropriate.

Mukherjee suggests a threefold classification: novels of purpose; 'historical' novels, sometimes intermingled with fantasy (imaginary history is Kaviraj's term for these); and novels set in contemporary society, written in a realistic vein. Like most typologies, this is of use only as a kind of preliminary scaffolding. More interesting are the ways in which the categories spill over into each other, while it is obvious that the writers themselves felt none of the taxonomic compulsions retrospectively caging them. The contrast between impressive and energetic women on the one hand, and spineless men on the other, could be located in distant times; and social values and associated ambiguities emerge in novels of all three types.

Let me begin with novels in languages other than Bengali, despite the undeniable prominence of Bankimchandra in the writing of both historical and social genres.[122] Novels of purpose include those written by Christian missionaries or their converts, though even in these the central concern was often not so much proselytization as the depiction of the lives and problems of Christian communities. Hanna Catherine Mullens' *Phulmoni o Karuna Bibaran* (1852: subsequently translated into English, Marathi, Telugu, and Assamese), which is sometimes seen as the first Bengali novel, is built around a contrast

---

[122] This may reduce the danger of Bengal-centredness, while also highlighting those literatures where Mukherjee's typology seems more relevant.

between two converted village women. One of them is pious and hard-working, the other lazy and indifferent. Similar contrasts came to be deployed elsewhere to promote the ideal type of new woman, usually a housewife, in other religious communities. A striking instance in Urdu is Nazir Ahmad's *Mirat ul-Arus* (The Bride's Mirror; 1869), where the two poles of Muslim womanhood are symbolized by the spoilt Akbari and the perfect Asghari—educated and an intelligent domestic manager.[123] An interesting set of Christian novels came from what is today Kerala. These foregrounded, quite exceptionally for their times, the lives and woes of untouchable slaves and labourers oppressed by landlords, and remarkably these were among the very first novels in Malayalam. Mrs Collins' *The Slayer Slain*, written in English but translated into Malayalam as *Ghatakavadham* in 1877, was meant to establish the superiority of Protestantism over Syrian Christianity. It depicted an oppressive Syrian Christian landlord who has a change of heart when he witnesses the generosity of his Pulaya slave. Two other early Malayalam novels were written by low-caste Tiyya converts or sympathizers: *Saraswativijayam* (1893) by Potheri Kunhambu, and Joseph Mulayil's *Sukumari* (1897). The first depicted the high-caste Nambudiri landlord who is brought for trial before a Pulaya slave—a slave who had become a judge by converting to Christianity and utilizing new opportunities. The generosity of the latter leads, predictably, to a change of heart in the former. The second is a vivid study of a community of Christians of low-caste origin.[124]

'Historical' novels began from the 1860s, with Bankimchandra one of the initiators, but they became much more numerous from the 1880s. There were obvious links with the growth of a nationalism implicated in Hindu revivalist moods. Recurrent themes were struggles of Rajputs and Marathas against Muslim invaders, portrayed in a large number of literary works, both poetry and fiction. These figured in 'imagined histories' in many parts of the country, including in some that had lately been ravaged by Maratha raiders. The economic historian and Moderate nationalist Romesh Chandra Dutt, to give one instance, published his *Rajput Jivan Sandhya* (Evening in the Lives of Rajputs), based predictably on Tod, and *Maratha Jivan Pravat* or

---

[123] For an English translation of this novel, see Ahmad 2001.
[124] Mukherjee 1999: chapter 2.

The Dawn of Maratha in 1878–9. There were no such publications from Rajasthan itself, but the history of the Marathi novel began with *Mocangad* (1870), dealing with Shivaji's capture of a fort. The first major Marathi novelist, Hari Narayan Apte, wrote a series of novels glorifying Shivaji around the turn of the century, when the Shivaji cult promoted by Tilak was at its peak. The Gujarati novel began with *Karan Ghelo* (1866), about Alauddin's overthrow of the last Hindu ruler of that region. For the decades beginning with the 1880s, major historical novels would include C.V. Raman Pillai's *Martanda Varma* (1891), about the foundation of the kingdom of Travancore; Bhai Vir Singh's *Sundri* (1898), glorifying the Sikh rebellion against the Mughals; and Rajanikanta Bordolai's *Manomoti* (1900), set in the times of the Burmese invasion of the Ahom kingdom in the late eighteenth century. Glorification of medieval Islam was the intent of Abdul Halim Sharar's *Flora Florinda* (1899). It was situated in Spain and was marked by a strong anti-Christian spirit.

Social novels, focusing on human relationships, revolved around issues that were debated at the time. Yamuna, the heroine of Hari Narayan Apte's Marathi novel *Pan Lakshyat Kon Gheto!* (But Who Pays Heed!; 1893), found life suffocating in joint families, before marriage and after. She enters a new world when she moves from the claustrophobic and conservative small town of Poona, to the cosmopolitan big city, Bombay.[125] Women writers sometimes found urban life and modernity liberating while among many of their male counterparts nostalgia for the countryside and indigenous values was growing precisely around these decades. The first Kannada social novel, G.V. Rao's *Indira Bai* (1899), followed the broad trend and depicted traditional customs as oppressive. Govardhanram's four-volume *Sarasvati Chandra* (1887–1901), in Gujarati, depicts the hero's love for a widow who had once been betrothed to him. The intrigues of a wicked stepmother had driven him away from home to embark

---

[125] Much work has been published around Marathi women writers of fiction, memoir, and autobiography, and translated into English over the past decade, notably by Meera Kosambi: see Kosambi 2007, 2008, and 2012. The last of these (Kosambi 2012) includes an excellent introductory overview of Marathi print literature in general and major women's voices over the colonial period in particular.

upon a wandering life. Eventually, he is able to sublimate his love and transform it into service to mankind. The sympathetic depiction of illicit passion—widow marriage, though legal at this time, was still condemned—and the tropes with which radical implications are both expressed and controlled (betrothal in childhood, sublimation), pervaded much of literature of those times. The wandering hero was another common motif which reflects the expansion of space that modern transport enabled.

The 'social' in such novels referred overwhelmingly to middle-class men and women. But there were a few novelists who tried to depict other social levels and relationships. The Oriya novel *Chamana Atha Guntha* (Six Acres and a Third; 1902) by Fakirmohan Senapati is about an oppressive landlord who deprives a poor weaver and his wife of their tiny plot of land. The novel is a strong portrayal of exploitation, police corruption, and judicial heartlessness, and it looks forward to the outstanding social novelists of the 1930s and 1940s—the generation of Premchand, Tarashankar Bandyopadhyay, Gopinath Mohanty, Takazhi Sivasankara Pillai. Another exceptional late-nineteenth-century work was Mirza Mohammad Hadi Rusva's *Umrao Jan Ada,* an early major Urdu novel (1899) dealing with the life of a Lucknow courtesan. Like Apte's *Pan Lakshyat,* it was written as an autobiographical narration by the heroine.

Exceptional in including lower-caste writers very early in its trajectory, as well as in foregrounding caste oppression and the radical impact of Christianity, the novel in Malayalam also had to deal with the special features of marital customs among some communities in Travancore and Malabar: 'sambandham' and matriliny. In the rest of the subcontinent the predominant family form was patrilineal, whether extended or nuclear, and virilocal, the woman moving upon marriage to her husband's house. The themes of social novels, consequently, turned around problems and tensions within such families, the ways in which they could be threatened by extra-marital sexual passion: delineated with sympathy most of the time, in keeping with the new romantic values, yet ultimately sublimated and made respectable. The family among the Nayars of Kerala, who mustered strong among the modern literati, was by contrast often matrilineal, with the woman continuing after her marriage to live in her old jointly held taravad. It was alleged, perhaps without much actual foundation, that the sambandham tradition among Namboodiri Brahmans—the highest caste in Kerala followed by the Nayars—meant their sexual relations with one or more Nayar women through occasional visits. Some interpreters think Nayar women had at one time the freedom to be polyandrous, engaging in relations with more than one male. The degree of female freedom should not be exaggerated, however, for the taravad and its property was really controlled by a male elder, and female-headed matrilineal households were progressively reduced in importance from the late nineteenth century by Anglo-Hindu law and the spread of patriarchal modernist values. The system nonetheless gave Nayar women a certain independence that was unusual in comparison with the rest of the country. By the late nineteenth century, however, the matrilineal, jointly-owned taravad was under pressure from its Western-educated young male members, who felt matriliny was barbaric and who also wanted to break the authority of its male elders, partition the joint estate, and constitute patrilineal nuclear units on their own.

This was the precise context for the first major Malayali novel, Chandu Menon's *Indulekha* (1889). Its hero, the Nayar graduate Madhavan, wants to marry his cousin Indulekha, who lives in the same taravad. But he gets thrown out of the household by its head, the girl's grandfather. Madhavan travels through other parts of the country, visits the new metropolitan cities, but at the end is reunited with Indulekha and is able to set up a nuclear household with her in Madras. The girl herself is depicted as Menon's ideal modern woman; English-educated, possessing modern accomplishments, skilled on the piano, adept at needlework, and pursuing other 'feminine' arts on the model of a properly Victorian lady. At the same time, she is also well versed in Hindu culture, an observer of caste and religious rituals, properly reverential towards her elders. As in several other novels of the time, the device of a peripatetic hero enables a long discussion on contemporary social developments and politics, when Madhavan speaks from a moderately pro-Congress position, criticizes obscurantist practices, and champions a reformed Hinduism.[126]

[126] For *Indulekha*, see particularly Arunima 1997: 271–90.

Well over a century after his death, Bankim remains the subject of abiding literary, historical, and exceptional political interest. The towering figure among writers of both historical and social novels from the 1860s till his death, he was also the author of a large number of brilliant essays—many of them displaying a caustic wit, humour, and satire, as well as numerous analytical pieces. Till the late 1870s he wrote in an extremely radical vein about key matters of gender, caste, and occasionally class, deploying notions of equality that went beyond social reformers of his time. His novels too were dominated by unconventional, active, and often transgressive women, unforgettable characters who dominate plot and narrative and give their names to most of the books. The men, by contrast, are rather colourless and somewhat passive, a clear reversal of the usual norms and expectations.

From the 1880s, a significant break occurs. Radical ideas, rationalistic critiques of social conventions, and even the use of wit and satire gave place to authoritarian preachings of a version of orthodox Hinduism, along with imagined apocalyptic wars against Muslims.[127] *Anandamath* (1882), in particular, in part because of the Bande Mataram hymn that it included, came to occupy a very special but highly ambiguous place in the history of modern times. Starting with the Swadeshi era it became a central anti-colonial nationalist text and symbol, and many nationalists were expelled from schools, whipped, or imprisoned only for singing Bande Mataram or for using it as slogan and rallying cry. But, since the 1920s if not earlier, it has also been an anthem and war-cry for Hindus waging communal riots.

And yet the break was not total, and numerous overlaps make a neat separation of early from late Bankim difficult. The early historical novels were located mostly in contexts of medieval Hindu–Muslim political conflicts where Muslims possessed individualized, human personas: even Aurangzeb in *Rajsingha*. In *Anandamath* and various other writings of the 1880s the Muslims have become demonized hordes instead. Women as primary initiators of action persist into the later phase. The very first novel, *Durgeshnandini* (1865), is deeply

----

[127] English translations of extracts from several of these essays connected with Hinduism are in Sen 2011.

transgressive, for it describes with sympathy a Muslim woman, Ayesha, in love with a Rajput prince. *Kapalkundala* (1866) is unconventional in a very different way. Here the heroine is a Miranda-type figure who has grown up in the wilderness and later finds life in domesticity, even with a husband who sincerely loves her, suffocating. In this novel Bankim seems to be going much beyond the maximum reformist ideal of companionate marriage based on consent. He imagines a woman absolutely free of all encumbrances, even of love and sexual attraction: 'Had I known that marriage means enslavement, I would never have married.' Bankim's novels revolve around two 'inevitabilities' that can never be resolved, the need for a moral order in society and elemental human drives—above all, sexual attraction and love—which press against and often disrupt that order. Both morality and transgression remain unavoidable, constituting the human condition.[128]

In the 1870s Bankim wrote a large number of essays. Some were a remarkable exposure of interrelated exploitation by zamindars, moneylenders, and corrupt court officials, as in *Bangadesher Krishak*. The essay begins with a radical question, which has not lost its relevance even after well over a hundred years. There is a lot of talk nowadays of the prosperity of the country, he says: 'But prosperity for whom?' His answer is a resounding negative, given deliberately from the point of view of 'Hashim Sheikh and Rama Kaivarta', a Muslim and a subordinate-caste Hindu. In *Kamalakanter Darpan* (1873–5), a brilliant and humorous exposure of the foibles of British justice and bhadralok 'radicalism', Bankim's subversive message is conveyed through the persona of a kind of Imagined Other of himself, a disreputable opium addict, undisciplined in actions and words. Opium-induced wisdom allows Kamalakanta, in one essay, to hear a cat preaching egalitarian, socialistic ideas. Similar values are expressed in *Samya* (1879), the zenith of Bankim's social radicalism, comparable among nineteenth-century Indian texts perhaps only with the writings of Jyotiba Phule. Here, a systematic critique is made of the interlocked inequalities of caste, property, gender, and political power (though the last is mentioned only in passing). Buddha, Christ, Rousseau, and some early socialists (Saint-Simon, Fourier, even a passing mention of

---

[128] This is a point made in Kaviraj 1981.

'the International') are mentioned as the great prophets of egalitaria-nism—strikingly, nothing about Hindu traditions. The foundation of this critique is a distinction between inevitable natural inequalities (like different abilities), and unnatural, social, ones. Among these, which Bankim selects for detailed criticism, are the unjust distinctions between Brahmins and inferior castes, zamindars and peasants, men and women.[129]

The paradox of Bankim, even at his most radical, lies in combining enormously subversive ideas with a simultaneous undercutting of all the existing institutions and initiatives for change, however partial. Every reference to Brahmo religious and social reformers, for instance, is contemptuous in the extreme, and he pours similar ridicule on early middle-class nationalists.[130] In the 1870s, however, a charitable interpretation of this combination was possible: Bankim, it has been suggested, was criticizing not reform but the gross inadequacies of its advocates.[131]

A definite change in tone began with the early 1880s, with Bankim's angry refutation of the debunking of Hinduism as mere superstiti-ous idolatry by a Christian missionary, the Reverend Hastie, in 1882. Other, broader factors, in particular the gross racism displayed by many non-official Europeans in the Ilbert Bill furore, probably also contributed. The discourses of the 1880s—*Krishnacaritra* (1886, 1892); *Dharmatattva/Anushilan* (1888), a reading of the Gita—were very different in style and content. Wit, humour, and satire had given place to solemn treatises on Hinduism, replete with quotations from religious texts. But Bankim's still remained a very special perspective on Hindu traditions, far removed from the rising tide of revivalist obscurantism as well as from the resurgence of Vaishnava devotion. His Krishna was emphatically not the naughty prankster nor the

[129] His, then, was a direct challenge to the doctrine of adhikar-bheda (rough-ly, hierarchy), which rested, in its logic of devotional exposition, precisely on such a conflation of natural and social distinctions. The centrality of this concept for nineteenth- and twentieth-century Hindu conservatism will be discussed in the companion to the present volume.

[130] There is a brilliant short piece about a dialogue between Hanuman and a babu, where the latter's political pretensions and enthusiasm about British plans for a limited kind of local self-government is mercilessly ridiculed.

[131] Kaviraj 1988.

irresponsible lover of Radha and other gopis in Brindaban that had
been central to the *Bhagavat Purana* and the bulk of medieval bhakti,
and particularly to Vaishnava devotionalism in Bengal as epitomized
by Chaitanya. Bankim emphasized, rather, the Krishna of the
Mahabharata and the Gita—warrior, statesman, Machiavellian thinker.
Bankim's *Anushilan*, too, was quite a new conception. It elaborated
a training scheme for disciples of a new divinity, the motherland or
nation, elevated now above all other objects of worship.

This explicit collapsing of patriotism with a novel kind of Hinduism acquired its great emotional appeal through Bankim's last novels,
Anandamath (1882), *Debi Chaudhurani* (1884), and *Sitaram* (1887).
Anandamath is about the primarily anti-Company Sannyasi rebellion
of the 1770s, and yet Bankim deliberately focuses it upon the misdeeds
of the Murshidabad nawab, who had become little more than a puppet
of the British, ignoring the conjoint rebellion of the Fakirs, about
which he must have been aware.

Kaviraj and Chatterjee ascribe the change to colonial censorship.
'A mortal fear of the Englishman and the world over which he dominated was a constituent element in the consciousness of the Calcutta
middle class'—and presumably of the nineteenth-century Indian
literati everywhere.[132] I find it a little difficult to accept this thesis
of overwhelming colonial power-knowledge and censorship over the
middle class, still considered by their rulers as basically loyal after
the experience of 1857. Certainly, Bankim was caustic often enough
in his earlier references to Englishmen in India. Censorship—of the
public stage and newspapers, though, not of fiction—did start from
the 1870s, but for its real weight one has to wait till a generation later,
after 1905. And while singing Bande Mataram did often become a
target of persecution from the early twentieth century, *Anandamath*
itself was never banned.[133]

A more 'internal' kind of explanation is suggested by Tanika Sarkar,
who shifts the focus somewhat from colonial constraints. In the

[132] Chatterjee 1994: 57; see also Kaviraj 1986: chapter 3.

[133] From the late 1870s a number of plays were banned, and some
newspapers punished, under the newly passed Dramatic Performances Act,
and Vernacular Press Act, passed under Lytton. In interesting contrast to
Anandamath, Gandhi's *Hind Swaraj* (1909) was banned in India for a decade
from 1910.

1860s and 1870s Bankim had seemed to share many of the concerns of contemporary liberal social and political reform, even sometimes surpassing their limits. But he saw no agency determined or consistent enough to carry out such projects, for he had little or no respect for his own social class—indeed he had a searing contempt for its many weaknesses. He could empathize at this time with the sufferings of peasants but never saw them as potential subjects of their own destiny; they remained for him objects of humanitarian or administrative improvement, and by the 1880s as an incipient mob that could be energized towards violent action if an elite formation of dedicated political sannyasis was available to lead them. Nor did he have much confidence in the bhakti cults, Hindu conservatism, and revivalist nationalism that he could see growing in strength during the last decade of his life.[134] For Bankim the roots of such repeated failures lay in the oft-proven worthlessness, cowardice, and lack of physical strength of the Bengali male, as demonstrated for him above all by the story of the destruction of the last Hindu kingdom in Bengal by Bakhtiar Khalji and his eighteen horsemen. Muslims, he felt, possessed virility and martial valour, despite, or sometimes because of, their other faults. There was, then, for Bankim, what Tanika Sarkar calls the 'impossibility of a political agenda'. Still, Hindus might imbibe Muslim warlike qualities through an apocalyptic war against them. *Sitaram*, his last novel, ends with a strange anticlimax: two peasant bystanders comment in choric cynicism from a distance about what has happened: 'Anyway, we are ordinary people, all this doesn't concern us':[135] the impossibility of a political agenda on a different register.

As in oral and scribal cultures throughout the world, South Asian languages have had an abundance of anecdotes, fables, and tales.

[134] Take for instance his solitary encounter with Ramakrishna Paramahansa, the rustic village Brahmin who by that time (early 1880s) had captivated the educated bhadralok of Calcutta through his simple conversations about bhakti. Bankim clearly tried to shock him through his definition of the aims of life as food, sleep, and sex. See Sarkar 1997: 304.

[135] Sarkar 2001: chapters 4, 5.

What makes the modern short story distinctive is a clearer and closed narrative structure, and a focus around a specific incident, situation, or intense emotional moment. Overlaps have naturally been common: print stimulated the reproduction and collection of old tales, taken for instance from the *Pancatantra* or *Hitopdesh* in Sanskrit and the *Arabian Nights* from Perso-Arabic traditions. These, like the modern short story, were stimulated by the rapid development of monthlies and quarterlies that required novels to be serialized, and therefore often preferred short stories that, being self-contained, were likely to attract more readers. Emergent nationalism also stimulated such collections, particularly of folk tales, a way of returning to its indigenous cultural roots a middle class. In 1907 Rabindranath, for instance, hailed the publication of Dakshinaranjan Mitra Majumdar's collection of folk tales for children, *Thakumar Jhuli* (Grandma's Tales), as a pure swadeshi product.

The modern short story came into its own in many languages roughly from the 1890s, though there have been some earlier claimants, such as a lost story by the Oriya writer Fakir Mohan Senapati, published around 1868. Short stories began in Malayalam in 1891; in Marathi in the pages of a journal edited by Hari Narayan Apte from 1890 (though they were considered for long a form inferior to the novel); in Oriya from the late 1890s; in Gujarati and Hindi from around 1900; in Kannada, Tamil, and Telugu over the next couple of decades. One variant, which was resolutely geared towards entertainment and commercial success and developed quite early, was the detective story.[136] Beginning with Bengali translations of Conan Doyle and other English writers, followed by quick retranslation into several other Indian languages, the detective story seems to have played a significant role in the development of prose fiction in Hindi: a late starter, because of the domination of much of northern India for much of the nineteenth century by Perso-Urdu print culture.[137]

The short story as serious literature received a great stimulus from the large numbers that Tagore wrote in this genre, starting from 1891

[136] Orsini 2004.
[137] Ibid.

and producing some 42 over the next 4 years, with another 21 over the next 15 years. The 1890s stories were mostly set in the central and eastern Bengal countryside, for Tagore then was in charge of the family estates there, and this involved closeness to village life as he travelled by boat. The stunning beauty of the endless fields of paddy and jute, wide rivers fields, and the changing seasons (particularly the onset of the rains) percolated deep into the poetry he wrote over these years, as well as in the short stories. But the stories are even more memorable for their vivid depictions of the lives and simple sorrows and joys of villagers—not exactly peasants, but ordinary folk in the countryside. There is, for instance, a city-bred young man who comes as postmaster to a village and develops a charmingly affectionate relationship with the little girl who becomes his servant, and then his only companion; he is then transferred elsewhere, leaving the girl deserted and forlorn. Subsequent stories begin to shift their location more towards urban life, and explore at great depth domestic and personal relationships within families. One of the best known, *Nashta-neer* (The Ruined Nest), is probably drawn in part from a tragedy involving the author in early youth.[138]

The Indian short story has foregrounded the everyday lives of ordinary people to a greater extent than has either the historical or the social novel, which, in the nineteenth century tended to deal more with dramatic personalities, conflicts, and fundamental moral issues. The realist depiction of both colonial and indigenous class oppression was also thematized from an early date, though in short stories and novels alike such ideas became prominent from the 1920s and 1930s, with the rise of Gandhian and then Left-leaning literature of the 'progressive' kind. Fakir Mohan Senapati's Oriya story 'Rebati' (1898), for instance, was about a village girl torn between her desires and the burden of dominant superstitious values. The first Gujarati short story, remarkably, is about village artisans facing ruin through the flood of imported goods, one of the few instances, prior to about 1905, of the entry of a directly anti-colonial nationalist theme. The

---

[138] I mention these two, among many, in part because through their film versions, made by Satyajit Ray ('Postmaster', in the *Teen Kanya* compendium, and *Charulata*), they would be widely known far beyond readers of Bengali.

early Hindi story 'Eka Tokri Bhar Mitti' (A Basketful of Earth; 1901), by Madhav Rao Sapre, deals with the conflict between a wealthy landlord and a poor widow.

A striking feature of the literary output of the Indian middle class is the way so many major writers have written also for children. In Bengali, for instance, virtually all the famous authors have done this, with the exception of Bankimchandra. The awareness of backwardness, particularly low literacy, led to early efforts to write primers and accompanying material for children. The subsequent emergence of nationalism in different forms contributed to projects for training the next generation in whatever was believed to be the correct patriotic values. But it would be an exaggeration, I feel, as has been sometimes suggested, that writing for children was entirely geared towards producing 'sons of the nation', dutiful and obedient family members with values assumed to be derived from Victorian morality—which itself is often treated simplistically as uniform and unchanging.[139]

It is true that early writings for children began with extreme didacticism and a desire to cram information, as can be seen in Anandiram Dhekial Phukan's *Asamiya Lorar Mitra* (1841), a compendium on various subjects based on an English encyclopaedia; or Vidyasagar's primers and stories for children. The latter were marked by an improvement ideology, wherein the poor boy rises through diligence, hard work, the single-minded pursuit of learning, and disciplined behaviour at home and in school. The diligent Gopal is counterposed in one typical story to the idle and naughty Rakhal. But the famous reformer remained true to his modernist values by steering entirely clear of conventional religious themes and by adopting a basically utilitarian approach. There was also an implicit emphasis on children from the poorer sections of the rural bhadralok, for whom Vidyasagar's programme of strenuous discipline and study would have been particularly appropriate. His perspectives were also extendable in social range over time. Lower-caste movements in Bengal from

[139] For a rather extreme variant of such assumptions, see Bose 1995.

around the turn of the century would take over in their own brand of improvement literature the puritanical virtues and values he had urged for the lesser sections of the gentry.[140]

We need to make a distinction, though, between formal pedagogical methods and the literature written for children. The latter, at least in some parts of the country, soon went beyond the limits of the purely didactic and informative, exploring ways for stimulating the imagination of the young and providing entertainment. In Gujarati, for instance, children's literature began with Navalram's humorous and satirical accounts of the marriage of a baby goat. In Bengali the non-didactic impulse actually peaked from around the turn of the century, precisely when nationalism was coming into its own, and when one may have expected the reverse. There was a succession of remarkable writers for children, like Upendrakishore Raychaudhuri, his son Sukumar Ray, Jogindranath Sarkar, and a number of others. A key role was played by numerous magazines for children, such as *Sakha* (1883), associated with the Brahmos; *Balak* (1885), brought out by members of the Tagore family; and, in the 1910s and early 1920s, Sukumar Ray's *Sandesh*. What was developing was an ability to recognize the child as distinct from the adult, not just as someone who has to be trained into maturity but as a being with an imaginative world of its own which needs to be fostered through humour and imagination. Such efforts could sometimes produce a world which entertained adults, too, at times through a delightful irreverence. Thus, increasingly, not the obedient but the mischievous and naughty child began to be the central figure in some books, in sharp contrast to the Gopal–Rakhal dichotomy. Sukumar Ray wrote wonderful nonsense rhymes (as in his *Abol-Tabol*).

The Visual and Performing Arts

Hybridity and Technological Change: Photography, Theatre, Painting, and the Early Cinema

A marked 'visual turn' began in modern Indian studies from the early 1990s, as historians belatedly entered fields previously left to

---

[140] 'Vidyasagar and Brahmannical Society', in Sarkar 1997: 254–8. See also Hatcher 1996.

specialized scholars and collectors. The new orientation is based on a twofold realization. First, that images are not just reflections or descriptions of reality, and are seldom merely confirmatory evidence for the 'real sources'; they actively help in constituting the 'real', moulding self-perceptions and community identities. Second, a vast expansion in the production and dissemination of images had begun in South Asia from the early nineteenth century and was both available and relatively untapped in historical accounts. The new ubiquity of the visual is now in fact a crucial feature of modernity, however defined.

The visual and performing arts have attracted historians for yet another reason. They provide numerous striking instances of the phenomenon that Homi Bhabha calls hybridity, 'in-between worlds' that repeatedly cross and recross analytical divisions and make untenable the over-distinct polarities which, unfortunately, have for long been rather common in Indian cultural studies.[141] Notions of hybridity have to be extended beyond the realm of colonial–colonized relationships, which have been Bhabha's principal field of interest, to explore many other kinds of porous boundaries between times, genres, social groups, and cultures. They emerge as a mark of modernity in general, and indeed in some ways of all civilizations, none of which have been purely indigenous, authentic, or uncontaminated.

The visual and performative arts, always but more particularly in recent times, tend to bring together written or printed scripts, speech, performance, song, music, and dance. This is most evident in the theatre, and then in that quintessentially modern art form, cinema. Cinema in fact is increasingly considered today to provide a particularly privileged entry point into the phenomena, contradictions, and dynamics of contemporary life. It juxtaposes, like life in the modern city, ephemeral moments with flows of experience—the passing glimpse in a street of a face that rushes by—allowing George Simmels'

---

[141] See Bhabha 1994. Paradoxically, binary oppositions became particularly influential through the wide-ranging impact of *Subaltern Studies*, especially in its later culturalist phase, and through the work of Partha Chatterjee. I speak of 'paradox' here, because the worldwide intellectual trends with which this school is often identified—postcoloniality and postmodernism—have often been sharply critical of binary oppositions. This is evident in thinkers like Bhabha and, indeed, Derrida. See also Gilroy 1994.

analysis of city life to be transposed unchanged into a description of the cinema: 'the rapid crowding of changing images, the sharp discontinuity in the grasp of a single glance, and the unexpectedness of onrushing impressions.'[142] The visual arts cross boundaries in two other, more obvious, ways. Disjunctions between elite and popular, still often made in South Asian cultural studies (though less and less so in other historical traditions), repeatedly demand to be complicated. So, too, do the over-sharp boundaries between traditional and modern, Western and indigenous; and even that most impassable wall, between colonizer and colonized, can be repeatedly undermined, up to a point, through 'mimicry' and 'sly civility'.[143]

Notwithstanding the many continuities, radical transformations in much of visual arts in modern times remain indisputable. The crucial new determinants have been the development of ever-new forms of mechanical reproduction of the work of art. We need to begin, then, with a quick glance at some of these technological innovations. They began in Western Europe—and even earlier in China, followed by Japan—with the arrival of mechanical print. But the major rush of innovations happened in the nineteenth- and twentieth-century West. In sharp contrast to the printing press, these later inventions reached India with surprisingly brief delays, all within a century or so of colonial rule. Our discussion of technological changes will be followed by a closer look at four selected areas: photography, drama and theatre, painting, and the coming of cinema.[144]

Mechanical Reproductions of Art, 'Real Life', and Sound

The coming of mechanical print in Western Europe in the late fifteenth and early sixteenth century was accompanied with efforts at

[142] Charney and Schwartz 1995: Introduction.

[143] The phrases are Homi Bhabha's—see Bhabha 1994: esp. chapter 4, 'O Mimicry and Man: The Ambivalence of Colonial Discourse'; and chapter 5 'Sly Civility'.

[144] The omission of music and dance from this chapter may seem surprising I decided to shift that to a corresponding section in the companion to the present volume, dealing primarily with the post-1914 era, as many of the major changes in these art forms happened from around those times, including times virtual inventions of the 'classical'.

similar mass reproduction of images. Illustrations, often akin to today's cartoons, were a part of many of the early books, the combination of text and illustration being necessitated by the low level of literacy. With increases in print runs and a consequent fall in unit costs, books became much cheaper and managed to remain profitable through an expansion in their markets. Such 'prints' proliferated particularly at moments of major religious and/or political upheaval, such as the Reformation in Germany in the early sixteenth century, and the English Revolution in the seventeenth.

Illustrations or copies of individual works of art had long been made with the application of established artisanal techniques, notably woodcuts and engravings. India, where print came some two centuries later, benefited from an 'advantage of backwardness'. Illustrations accompanied books almost from the beginning, reproduced through the block printing method. The very first print version of a Bengali literary work, Bharatchandra's *Annadamangal* (1816), carried illustrations. Traditional artisanal techniques, with some recent modifications continued to be widely used till the late nineteenth century. Till the late 1870s or 1880s, for instance, multiple handmade copies of cheap Kalighat paintings, and the woodcuts of Battala reproduced through blocks, competed actively for the Calcutta market in religious and mythological pictures. A more advanced technique for reproducing images, lithography, had been invented in Munich in 1798, whereby multiple copies could be made of painted images and designs by pressing these on a greased damp stone block. Subsequent developments in the late nineteenth century, chromolithography and then oleography, enabled the mass reproduction of more and more vivid, lifelike, images in colour. By the late nineteenth century, the three interrelated new techniques had virtually driven out of business both Kalighat 'pats' and Bat-tala woodcut engravings, capturing the biggest mass market in religious and mythological prints. Lithographic techniques also proved very valuable for brand names of manufactured objects and advertisements, vastly developing the world of commercial art. There was a veritable explosion of visual material of the most diverse kinds from around the 1880s that could be increasingly disseminated throughout the country, now by railways. Three major centres of chromolithographic and oleographic production emerged. The Calcutta Art Studio was founded by ex-students of the Government Art School in 1878. V.K. Chiplonkar's Poona Chitrashala Press came up in the 1880s, with a marked thrust towards chromolithographs of Hindu sacred icons and historical-mythological themes, contributing greatly to the emergence of Hindu nationalist extremism in the same region. And in 1894 the leading Indian artist Ravi Varma deliberately crossed the already well-established elite–mass barrier between creative and commercial art, commonplace as separate categories since the European Renaissance. Varma set up an oleograph press with German technical assistance near Bombay to mass produce his famous religious and mythological paintings, deliberately sacrificing some of what Benjamin called the 'aura' of the creative individualized artist and his work of art. Lithography, and more particularly its offshoots permitting colour and realism, enabled the spread of uniform images of the high divinities of Hinduism throughout the subcontinent. Such images considerably modified traditional iconography via the insertion of 'realistic' features, betraying the influence of contemporary naturalist styles in painting modelled on Victorian art—of which Ravi Varma was the leading exemplar. There was also the impact of photographic images. With this were blended elements of mythology and fantasy, producing hybrid 'photos of the Gods', a term Pinney encountered in his fieldwork in Madhya Pradesh.[145] Such proliferating imagery, which spread also through calendar art, proved vital for many forms of twentieth-century Indian nationalisms, particularly, as we shall see, its religious and communal variants.[146]

Meanwhile, the great innovation of the camera, enabled, at least in appearance, a mass reproduction on paper of exact images of life, both natural and human. This began in 1839, simultaneously in France and in England, with Daguerre's 'daguerreotype' on a silver-coated copper plate, and Talbot's paper-based negative/positive process. Many improvements then came apace in the technique of developing photographs, while with the invention by George Eastman of the easily portable hand-held box camera in 1888 (given

[145] Pinney 2004.

[146] Ramaswamy 2003: Introduction; Mitter 2002: 1–32; Guha-Thakurta 1992; Mitter 1994; Pinney 2004.

the brand name Kodak) photography could be individualized and made independent of both studios and heavy tripods. The passage to India of the new technology was remarkably quick, beginning with Calcutta and then spreading to the other two metropolitan cities. Thacker-Spink advertised their import of a daguerreotype camera in January 1840. Around 14 European studios had come up in Calcutta by the 1850s (among them Bourne and Shepherd, the best known), and Indian-owned ones were soon being set up. By 1857 about 30 of the 100-odd members of the Photographic Society of Bengal were Bengalis. Varying deployments of photography by the British Indian state, non-official Europeans, and many Indian social groups have now become the subject of intense study.[147]

There has been less historical work so far on the entry into India of the mechanical reproduction of sound, beginning with the gramophone.[148] The transmission of messages over distance through the conversion of acoustic into electrical waves had begun around the 1840s with the electric telegraph, but that had allowed only the passage of the dots and dashes of Morse. The actual transmission of sound became possible with the discovery of ways of reconversion to sound waves, beginning with the telephone, invented around the 1870s simultaneously by Elisha Gray and Graham Bell, with the latter being the first to patent it. In 1877 Edison made the first 'phonograph', recording sound in round cylinders. Even after the improvements made shortly by Graham Bell's 'graphophone', such cylinders did not allow easy mass reproduction and the quality, too, was poor. The major breakthrough came in 1887 with the German immigrant Emile Berliner's invention of the gramophone in Washington, DC, which used flat discs called records, with the sound data etched in their grooves and playable by the machine's arm which held a needle—a

[147] Karlekar 2005: chapter I, has a helpful brief summary of the development of the camera. See also Pinney 2004.

[148] I have been unable to get hold of a copy of what seems to be the only extant detailed study of the early history of the gramophone in India, Michael Kinnear's *The Gramophone Company's First Indian Recordings, 1899–1908* (Bombay: Popular Prakashan, 1994). But see Dasgupta 2005: 254–84, and for the history of the gramophone in general, the very useful web entries accessible through Google.

primitive form of what was later called a stylus. This form was dominant till the rise of cassettes in the 1970s. The great advantage of Berliner's invention over Edison and Bell was that it enabled real mass production, with multiple copies of discs from a single master recording.

As with the camera, the passage to India was quick, both cylinders (popularly known here as 'bangles', which they resembled), and discs being fairly common by the turn of the century. A Delhi firm, Mahendra Lal, was importing records from 1895 as agent of the Gramophone Company based in London that Berliner had founded. In 1899 the latter made the first recordings, in London, of Indian voices. In typically Orientalist manner, these were of a Hindu reciting from the *Ramayana*, and by a Muslim from the *Koran*. Indian concerns using imported cylinders or discs to make recordings also came up, notably H. Bose in Calcutta during the Swadeshi days. Unfortunately, this stuck to the less efficient cylinder, making hundreds of recordings till around 1910, some of them by Tagore, including his rendering of Bande Mataram. But the discs of the British Gramophone Company came to virtually monopolize the Indian market by the second decade of the twentieth century.

Early gramophone recordings in India had two striking features. First, they helped democratize, to some extent, the world of music, which, with the exception of diverse popular and local forms, had depended on the patronage and audiences provided by the durbars of princes and aristocrats and the mehfils of zamindars. The decline of many such centres in British times made practitioners of instrumental and vocal music—both of which have had very long, rich, and often highly syncretic traditions in the subcontinent—move in search of new sources of patronage. Thus the decline of Delhi, and after 1857 to an extent of Lucknow, led to shifts towards new patrons in Banaras, or among surviving princely courts such as Gwalior and Bhopal, as well as in the new metropolitan cities. The gramophone record brought for the first time the more prestigious forms of music into the homes of ordinary people, and this soon grew enormously popular. Second, there was an important change in the gender dimensions of music.[149]

[149] What ensues in the paragraph is largely derived from Dasgupta 2005.

The 'high' or 'classical' forms had for long been controlled entirely by gharanas that coalesced around particular guru-shishya paramparas, lineages of master performers who passed on their expertise to pupils in what remained an overwhelmingly male world. Women performers were also present in considerable numbers, but, particularly in the nineteenth century with the social inhibitions and prohibitions brought in by 'Victorian' standards, they came to be considered somewhat disreputable as singers and dancers, or denigrated as professional tawaifs or baijis.[150] Such hereditary professions were earlier roughly equivalent to that of the European courtesan, but now tended to be relegated to the status of prostitution. Yet the striking feature of the early gramophone recordings, made from November 1902 by F.W. Gaisberg in Calcutta on behalf of the Gramophone Company of London, was the prominence of women singers. He began with two 'dancing girls' associated with the Classic Theatre of Calcutta, and went on to record, beginning with 11 November 1902, what over time became a very large number of songs by Gauhar Jan, the most popular of the early gramophone artists who acquired an all-India reputation. Gauhar is in fact a fascinating figure; she had an Armenian Jew father and an Indian Jew mother and subsequently changed her religion as well as her name after an affair with a Muslim, making her the exemplar of a hybridity that has characterized the world of the performing artist in general. This, as noted among others by Mukul Kesavan, is clear right down to the Bombay film industry which, even today, is marked by the prominence of Muslims to an extent rare among most elites of today's India.[151]

But to return to the early recordings: the prominence of women related obviously to the initial hesitations of male gharanas about the democratizing tendencies of the gramophone, as they were jealous about their hereditarily preserved secrets. (This changed over time,

---

[150] For works by and discussions of women singers of this period, see Pukhraj 2009; Dhar 2005. Rao 2011 discusses Nilina Sen (Naina Devi), whose training was in the pre-Independence years, and who was born into an elite Calcutta family: she was the grand-daughter of the Brahmo reformer Keshab Chandra Sen.

[151] Kesavan 2008.

beginning with Abdul Karim Khan, who served the court of the
Gaikwad of Baroda.) Gaisberg made 553 recordings in 1902, 230 of
them by women: by 1906–7 the total had shot up to 1402.[152]

Photography: British and Indian

The extraordinarily rapid passage of the totally new technology of
photographs from Britain and France to India indicates a high degree
of interest and involvement, first among the British, and soon among
upper- and middle-class Indians. The sources and expressions of
enthusiasm of the two groups reveal patterns of juxtaposed contrasts
and affinities. As in so many other fields, total disjunctions do not
really work.

As the somewhat unexpected rulers of a rapidly extending and
relatively unknown empire, the British were from the beginning eager
to amass reliable information, and within this knowledge-gathering
visual material was naturally thought particularly valuable. A major
motivation was surveillance-cum-control over previously little-known
spaces and people. But this was accompanied also by genuine curiosity
and interest, a fascination with the almost unknown—aspirations
that cannot be crudely submerged within the power-knowledge
syndrome, the latter being, nonetheless, an undeniable but separable
dimension. Till the coming of the camera, both impulses could be
satisfied only by sketches, drawings, oil paintings, woodcuts, and
lithographs made both by the British as well as by groups of so-
called bazaar artists whom the Company engaged for the purpose of
producing such visual depictions. The camera appeared to represent

---

[152] Dasgupta 2005. Accounts of Gauhar Jan emphasize the rich diversities
of her career and points out her great professional success. She is said to have
charged a fee of Rs 3000 for her first recording, an enormous amount for those
times. Despite her humble and disreputable origins, Gauhar evidently had a
great sense of dignity and independence. She reduced the very large sum she
had initially promised to contribute to Gandhi's Swaraj Fund because Gandhi
failed to keep his promise to come personally to her fund-raising concert. I
intend to take a closer look at the evolving world of Indian music and dance in
my companion volume, for the construction of today's notions of the 'classical'
in both really took place in the era of various forms of well-established cultural
nationalism and identity politics.

a tremendous advance over all such forms in the direction of exact reproduction, an 'indexical' quality unattainable in the other forms.[153] The woodcut depiction of a Toda family in a book about that tribal community (1832), for instance, reveals a suspicious similarity with Biblical images of Jewish patriarchs and are quite different from later photographic representations. In 1857 Joseph Mullins, in an address to the Photographic Society of Bengal, called for 'stern fidelity', as made possible, it seemed, through photographic representation. Other Englishmen indicated the value of the camera in medical and police work—for example, scene-of-the-crime photographs familiar to readers of detective stories. The identifying of criminals as well as the establishing of knowledge-cum-control over diverse and mobile labour forces now began to depend considerably on the camera. This is the 'detective paradigm' that Pinney speaks of, and it is reflected, for instance, in the post-Mutiny People of India series commissioned by Canning. What was being built up were taxonomic dossiers. By the late nineteenth century other techniques had emerged for the effective surveillance of individual subjects. Foremost among these was fingerprinting, a method invented in Bengal.[154]

As mentioned, the colonial photographic record was frequently excited by a fascination with the exotic, leading to what Pinney has called a 'salvage' paradigm, the salvaging being directed at tribes that were thought to be on the verge of extinction and therefore needing to be recorded in their 'purity'.

This led to obvious distortions. A tribal girl of the Andaman islands was photographed in the nude, as was believed to be appropriate when capturing people described as primitives: she was in fact a Christian convert who would normally have dressed in white when going to school or church. But beyond both paradigms, 'indexical' and 'salvagery', there was sheer curiosity, wonder, and pleasure—connected,

---

[153] The term, used by Pinney in his *Camera Indica*, refers to C.S. Peirce's influential distinction between arbitrary 'symbol' (like linguistic signs), 'icon' (with some resemblance to what is being represented), and 'index', which has claims to being the exact reproduction.

[154] A British administrator of Hooghly district, Herschel, had noticed the Indian habit of taking thumb marks as the signatures of illiterate people. By 1880 he had worked this up into an official system for keeping a record of individuals: Ginzburg 1990: 96–127.

obviously, with xenophobic needs. The British repeatedly recorded sites associated with Indian atrocities and their own heroism during the Mutiny, like the Kanpur Well, the Lucknow Residency, and the Kashmere Gate; other favourite subjects of famous mid-nineteenth-century photographers such as Bourne included mountain scenes, hill stations, and views of cities both old and new. The invention of picture postcards was a great asset to individuals and families seeking to maintain their contact with relatives in Britain and other parts of the expanding empire.

Indian appropriations were different—and yet often not so different. A good instance of overlaps can be gleaned from the career of the best-known early Indian photographer, Lala Deen Dayal (1844–1910), who was asked by a British civil servant to photograph Northbrook and cover the visit of the Prince of Wales in 1876. He later became the court photographer of the Nizam of Hyderabad, and towards the end of his life was running a luxurious studio in Bombay with European underlings. This became the favourite photo studio for large numbers of British dignitaries as well as for Indian princes, aristocrats, and other luminaries. But the Indian focus was more on individuals and family groups, not 'types'; and, unlike princes and zamindars who for long preferred portraits in oils as more ostentatious, there was a clear middle-class preference for photographs as these were considerably cheaper. The thoroughgoing Anglicized went to European studios like Bourne and Shepherd in Calcutta, or Higginbotham in Madras; the less exalted preferred the rapidly proliferating and cheaper Indian establishments like the Calcutta Art Studio.

From the 1880s the box camera made possible a privatization of photography, though special occasions might still demand a visit to a studio: newly-weds, new-born offspring, passing an examination, getting a prestigious job. (The post-convocation photograph is still popular.) Photographs of family groups have survived in large numbers from the closing decades of the nineteenth century, providing rich material for social-historical studies. Valuable indications, for instance, of changes in dress habits (like the coming of the modern way of wearing saris), and shifting practices and assumptions are gleaned now from a close look at photographs over time. Bengal threw up quite a galaxy of famous photographers: Rajendralal Mitra, pioneer in the visual and exact recording of archaeological sites; Maharaja Birchandra of Tripura; Upendrakishore Raychaudhuri, whose discovery of an improved technique of half-tone printing vastly improved the quality of illustrations for children's literature in Bengali.

The photographic record expanded over time and the era of high nationalism was particularly rich when photographs were shot by Indian, English, and other foreign cameramen. An unforgettable series records the British police flogging peaceful salt satyagrahis, the rich documentation of leading figures like Gandhi, searing accounts of the Bengal famine of 1943 captured by Sunil Janah, an anguished old Tagore immortalized by Shambhu Saha as he hears the news of the outbreak of the Second World War: Cartier-Bresson's portrayal of Nehru staring out into the darkness and announcing the passing of Gandhi. There were other kinds of appropriations and usages as well and two near forgotten photo-journalists come to mind. Sabeena Gadihoke's research has revealed the pioneering woman photo-journalist Homai Vyarawalla (1913–2012), and the Aditya Arya and Indivar Kamtekar project has showcased that of Kulwant Roy.[155]

Pinney found in his field area of Nagda, a small town in Madhya Pradesh, studios using all the up-to-date techniques of camera-work, montage, and the superimposition of images to produce pictures of the same face in utterly different costumes and in invented settings. Studios have become a 'chamber of dreams' in which a young villager can see himself relocated to places where he will probably never be able to go, or embracing, or sitting close to, his favourite film star. Pinney relates how he too once amused himself by taking a wedding photo with Madhuri Dixit, all done with a camera on a wooden tripod, in a corner of Chandni Chowk.[156]

Play-acting: Theatre and the Movies

Theatre represents the meeting point of script—whether handwritten or printed—and performance on some kind of site or stage. It is often accompanied by music, song, and dance. But the link between literary form and performance could be interrupted by the absence of facilities or resources for the latter, and this seems to have happened

[155] Gadihoke 2006; Arya and Kamtekar 2010.
[156] The above account of photography is based on Pinney 1997; Pinney 2004; and Karlekar 2005.

fairly often in colonial and contemporary times. For on the whole developments of the modern stage lagged behind the writing and publication of plays. The first Oriya stage, for instance, came up only in the 1910s. In late-nineteenth-century Bengal, it seems unlikely that more than a small proportion of the 505 'prahasans' (farces) between 1858 and 1899 that research has unearthed could ever have been performed in the handful of theatres available for playwrights during these decades. Some were possibly enacted in private homes, and the traditional but still flourishing theatrical form of the jatra provided an alternative outlet.[157]

Theatre has a very long and illustrious history in South Asia. Polarities between the old and the new break down when we look at 'traditional' forms, as Kapila Vatsyayan has elaborated in a helpful survey.[158] The traditional or indigenous no longer seems set off so sharply from the Westernized or modern, and the boundaries between elite–classical and popular also become porous. The Sanskrit drama of Kalidas and the courts had long ceased to be a living tradition, but old theatre traditions in more or less sanskritic vernaculars found their abode in the many regional courts of the medieval centuries; these sometimes continued into the colonial era, acting in certain regions as a brake against new theatrical forms. The flourishing genres had for many centuries been among the 'popular', in varying regional and local forms and levels. The hybridity of script, performance, music, song, and dance become evident, though because of the limited circulation of the first in scribal conditions the other elements may have been relatively more prominent in pre-colonial centuries. Vatsyayan warns against any romanticization of a pristine 'popular'. It would be dangerous, for instance, to think of popular theatre, dance, song, and music in India, or indeed anywhere, as emerging somehow in an unmediated manner from the wellsprings of an undifferentiated community or 'the folk', changeless across the centuries. They were performed, most of the time, by specialized and often itinerant groups who sought the patronage of local landlords and village elites. Such specialized troupes were not necessarily of entirely plebeian or low-

---

[157] Goswami 1974.
[158] Vatsyayan 1980.

caste origin either. The Mayurbhanj 'chau' participants, for instance, could range from tribals and lower-caste groups up to the princes of Seraikhela. The itinerant, trained, professional groups of popular culture would also normally exclude women and use boys for enacting female roles: as can be seen for instance in the jatra of Bengal. The major exception to this were tribal or adivasi communities, along with, sometimes, those in the lowest ranks of the caste hierarchy. The adivasi, specifically the Santal, community dances and songs, where women also participated, have stimulated the romantic imaginations of generations of modern Bengali city-bred writers and artists.[159]

Many 'folk' forms were actually derived from the classical epics: the Krishna-lila in the Mathura region and the famous annual Ramlila of Ramnagar near Banaras, for instance. Far from dying out under colonial modernity, these traditions have not only continued but have flourished and expanded with assets provided by print and modern communication. Ramlila, for instance, extending over a number of days every year, happens as a series of performances in which actors and spectators literally move from venue to venue in a kind of microscopic re-enactment of the travels and travails of Ram, Lakshman, and Sita. This is clearly an invented tradition of the late eighteenth century. It was started, and remains dependent on, the patronage of the Raja of Banaras, seeking compensation through theatre after surrendering his political powers to the British—in ways reminiscent of Clifford Geertz and Nicholas Dirks's analysis of Java and Pudukottai, respectively.[160] The Banaras court, along with the coming of print, was crucial also for the dissemination of Tulsidas' sixteenth-century text *Ramcharitmanas*. Collectively, these developments are replete with consequences for the evolution of rural and small-town culture, nationalism, and Hindu communalism throughout the Hindi-speaking regions of North and Central India.[161]

---

[159] Ray's *Aranyer Din Ratri* did include a subtle questioning of such romanticization, through the misadventures of a group of young men out for a weekend in a tribal area.

[160] Geertz 1976; Dirks 1993.

[161] For the Ramlila of Ramnagar, see Lutgendorf 1989: 34–61, and the full-length study by Anuradha Kapur (Kapur 2006). See also Freitag 1989.

More plebeian forms have been interlaced with products from other social strata. They benefited rather than declined with modernity, and repeatedly provided resources for recent political formations. Nautanki, for instance, the most widespread folk entertainment of the Hindi-speaking belt, received a major boost from the spread of print culture. Cheap booklets of Nautanki 'sangeets' proliferated from around the 1860s, Hathras, and then the entirely colonial city of Kanpur, being the main centres both of production, and of the recruitment and training of troupes.[162] Hansen has attempted an analysis of the major themes in the Nautanki, the ways in which they played with and probed recurrent tensions between political power and morality, love and community values, the beauty and sexual dangers embodied in women. Nautanki also provides numerous instances of a quality which the performative genres have repeatedly displayed: the capacity for taking over themes from many different cultural levels. Both the *Inder Sabha* extravaganza, which had originated in the court of Wajid Ali Shah in Awadh in 1853, and the story of Raja Harishchandra, proved particularly adaptable to a very wide range of artistic levels and forms. They have figured repeatedly in Nautanki and on the modern proscenium stage, and the history of the full-length Indian silent film begins in fact with Dadasaheb Phalke's *Raja Harishchandra* (1913). Many other popular forms have shown a similar adaptability and openness to diverse kinds of appropriation. Instances would include the Marathi tamasha, used at different times by Jyotiba Phule, nationalists, and the Left; and the jatra in Bengal and other parts of eastern India. Chronologically closer is the imaginative use made of many folk forms by the Indian Peoples' Theatre Association (IPTA), organized by Communists in the 1940s to propagate messages of anti-fascist People's War, class struggle, and revolution.

But the emphasis on continuities and interpenetrations must not involve any underplaying of the new elements brought in by nineteenth-century drama and theatre. These were in two areas; performative, associated through the basic innovation of the proscenium stage; and the writing of plays of new kinds. The general historiographical

---

[162] Kathryn Hansen has located no less than 470 such Nautanki booklets from the 1860s onwards in the British Library: Hansen 1992.

priority, till quite recently, of the literary over other forms of representation has led to a greater prominence being given to plays over theatre in many historical accounts. But they clearly need to be looked at together, with even a slight pre-eminence at times to the performative whenever evidence can be unearthed on their enactment, or at least about the kinds of sites where they took place. That would be in keeping with the artistic specificities of the theatre form, and suggest an arrangement that begins with the coming of the proscenium stage.

This was an innovation from the West, and it remained the dominant form of the modern theatre till well into the twentieth century, when other types of enactments began to be tried out. The proscenium stage, located indoors and lit by gas and later electricity, was clearly separated from the spectators, sitting in the dark in front of it, by curtains at the end of a scene. A variety of stage props was usual, particularly in the realist or naturalist theatre that had come to predominate in nineteenth-century Europe and which provided the initial model for Indians. Traditional or folk theatre was quite different, as typified by the jatra. Here performances took place on an open ground or slightly elevated temporary platform, the seated or standing viewers surrounding the performers on all sides, with costumes but no stage props, and without much strict separation of actors from viewers. Those among the viewers who were far from the centre sometimes did not manage to see or hear the performance all that clearly.

The proscenium in India began with the Europeans, primarily in the two colonial metropolises of Calcutta and Bombay, as early as 1753–6 in the first, and 1776 in the second (with the Bombay Amateur Theatre, modelled on the famous Drury Lane of London). Calcutta also had the strange episode of Gerasim Lebedeff, a Russian who briefly ran a 'Bengalee Theatre' in Calcutta in the 1790s, with a vernacular translation of an English play and both men and women performers. Shakespeare seems to have been the favourite dramatist of the English stage in both cities, along with eighteenth-century playwrights like Goldsmith and Sheridan. The fascination with Shakespeare passed on to English-educated students, some of whom began enacting excerpts from his plays in colleges and schools. But the big problem was funding, for proscenium stages required much more financial backing than the old kinds of theatre. And this came to be tackled in Bombay and Calcutta in somewhat different ways.

In Bombay, the persistence of considerable collaboration between European and Indian (particularly Parsi) business groups, as well as the much higher level of development of the latter, led to Indian capital quickly entering the field of theatrical production. Jamshetjee Jeejebhoy purchased the leading English theatre when it had to be auctioned in 1835, and he and Jagannath Shankarseth floated in 1846 the Grant Road Theatre, located in 'Black Town' and with cheaper tickets than in the early European theatres in the Fort area. The consequence was the emergence of the Parsi theatre, so called because the ownership was largely by members of that business community. It was the first Indian version of public theatre, in the sense of functioning on a regular and long-term basis through the open sale of tickets, and not by invitations to select individuals. The first such concern was the Parsi Theatrical Company of 1853, and Dadabhai Naoroji, leading Parsi businessman and intellectual—and thirty years later one of the founding-fathers of the Congress—was on its board. The languages used initially were interestingly polyglot: English, dominant at first but then dropping out as English-speaking spectators seldom came to Grant Road; Gujarati; less often Marathi; and the language-complex from which both Persianized Urdu and Sanskritized Hindi had developed, Hindustani. The latter came to dominate for several decades, as Parsi theatre performances outside Bombay through tours by some of the companies became common, attracting big audiences particularly in the cities and towns of North and Central India.[163] Business support and success enabled lavish decorations and props in proscenium performances, as well as a reach that eventually crossed the seas to cater to the tastes of Indians living or settled abroad. The Parsi theatre was both quite crucial for the spread of the proscenium form throughout much of urban India, and for taking Indian performers abroad: by the turn of the century, tours of

[163] Hansen's work on the Parsi theatre is pioneering, her most recent addition to it (Hansen 2011) providing rich biographical detail on India-wide tours by individual actors within these theatre groups and companies.

Parsi theatre companies had extended to Ceylon, Malaya, and other parts of South East Asia, Nepal, and even Guyana and England.

But expansion and resources flowing in from business funding also exacted a certain cost. The writers of plays were relegated to a somewhat secondary role. The hallmark of the Parsi theatre became not so much innovation or any modernizing impulse in themes as what Anuradha Kapur has called a refiguration of old forms. Thus the *Inder Sabha,* here too, became a favourite, repositioning traditional ingredients of fabulous romance, music, and dance—an operatic eclecticism that proved immensely popular largely through familiarity. Its songs came to enjoy an independent circulation, through the coming of the gramophone and Gaisberg's recording of no less than 550 theatre songs. And it should have become obvious already that in several ways Parsi theatre was the real precursor of the Bombay film industry, to which it had to yield primacy after the beginning of sound films from the 1930s. Some of the leading Parsi managers were among its first producers and cinema-owners, such as the business magnate Jamsetji Framji Madan, whose chain included 170 theatres and cinema houses in the 1930s.

But Parsi theatre, once again like Bombay films, where too Hindustani had been the preferred medium, could not in the end remain immune to the pressures and attractions of narrower linguistic nationalisms. With Radheshyam Kathavachak (1890–1963), one kind of Parsi theatre turned towards both a much more sanskritic Hindi, and a predominance of Hindu mythological plays.[164] Around the same time, another group of playwrights, mostly located in the United Provinces and nurtured by Islamic culture, began displacing syncretic Hindustani by Persianized Urdu. Parsi theatre thus anticipated a similar, but mostly post-colonial, transition in Bombay films, through which polyglot Hindustani came to be increasingly displaced by sanskritic Hindi. There was the important difference, though, that by then independent, aggressively Islamic, film producers and directors had become rare in a partitioned India. What has survived of the old 'syncretism' is a presence in Bombay films of a significant number of

[164] Radheshyam Kathavachak's autobiography is one of the four translated in Hansen 2011.

prominent stars and directors with Muslim names, which contrasts with virtually every other kind of Indian elite.[165]

As against Bombay, Dwarkanath Tagore was the only Indian associated with leading English playhouses of early-nineteenth-century Calcutta. This clearly reflects the very different nature of capitalist development in Bengal, after an initially promising phase of indigenous business growth. After the collapse of the Union Bank, the plays that came to be written in Bengali from the late 1850s could be staged only in the lavish private theatres of the proscenium kind that some big zamindars living in North Calcutta had started as symbols of their cultural interests and/or conspicuous consumption. They were private in the sense of admissions being only by invitation. Unlike the Parsi theatre, Bengali plays, particularly in the early years, tackled contemporary issues of widow marriage, polygamy, and even questions of class and racial oppression, at times with remarkable boldness. A number of quite outstanding ones were written in this era of private elite-controlled theatres, more precisely during the 1860s. These included, apart from the already mentioned plays and farces of Michael Madhusudan Dutt, Dinabandhu Mitra's remarkable exposure of the gross exploitation by European indigo planters (*Neel Darpan*, 1860), as well his *Sadhabar Ekadasi* (1866), a brilliant satire of contemporary bhadralok society. Michael Madhusudan Dutt's pieces were staged in the palace of Sobhabazar, while the Jorasanko Tagores (the family of Dwarkanath, Debendranath, and later of Rabindranath and other outstanding luminaries of the nineteenth century), advertised prizes on themes like 'Hindu Females' and 'Village Zamindars'. But everything remained dependent on the grace or inclinations of the landlords; performances usually did not exceed one or two, and the viewers were restricted to the charmed circle of those invited. The impact therefore remained limited—before the rise of the Bengali public theatre in 1872.

The restrictions of the private theatre irritated above all a group of educated youth, drawn generally from somewhat lower levels of the bhadralok, who had no possibility of getting invitations to the plays

[165] My account of the Parsi theatre above is based on Kapur 1995; Hansen 2001: 76–114; Hansen 2003: 381–405; Hansen 2011.

being run by the big men. The emergence of the public theatre was in fact an early instance of the appearance of a class conflict within the bhadralok, between a more conservative and loyalist landlord elite and a group of lesser men who by the 1870s were to lay claims to be of 'madhyabitta' (middle-class) status with patriotic aspirations.[166] The young men began with an amateur group in the north Calcutta locality of Baghbazar, and then in 1872 started a public theatre with a significant name, and initial play: National Theatre, and *Neel Darpan*. Ticket prices were kept deliberately quite low, Re 1 and 8 annas, for the intention was, at least initially, not at all commercial profit. This was not exactly cheap, given the incomes of those times, but still within the occasional range of lower-middle-class purchasers: the Grant Road Theatre in Bombay had also gone in for easier access, but the lowest there, in 1846, was still Rs 2. The proscenium-based public theatre in Bengal could therefore explore certain democratic possibilities, much more than the Parsi stage, and for two reasons. Not only were prices significantly lower, it was also that many of the plays explored very live contemporary issues—unlike the lavish replays through new technology of familiar themes on which the Bombay plays had concentrated, for commercial profit. Such refigurations attracted mass audiences but did not, perhaps, reflect or stimulate much thinking along new lines.

A number of historians have made much of the Parsi stage's use of 'frontality', which seems to have stimulated mutual interaction across the footlights through a carry-over into the new proscenium stage of older 'folk' techniques. What was largely absent here was the Western assumption, at its height in the naturalist theatre of the late nineteenth century, of an invisible fourth wall within which the actors spoke seemingly only to each other in an insulated stage world. On the Parsi stage, as in forms like the jatra and tamasha, by contrast, the performers frequently addressed the spectators in obvious ways, leading to a kind of apparent interchange absent in the contemporary West. This acting style, it has been suggested, was later carried over into the Indian film, and has been a quite noticeable feature right down to contemporary times.

---

[166] This would be also the broad mileu from which the Indian Association

How much of the technique of frontality had been deployed in Bengal does not seem to have been much explored so far, but certainly there did exist interesting patterns of exchange and interpenetration of ideas and emotions. But in Calcutta this could have flowed more from the topicality of the themes and a common hybridity of performers and spectators alike. The initial poverty of the early organizers made them scrounge around for help and talent from an extremely diverse milieu, including the odd down-and-out Englishman and unemployed young men. Given dominant and tightening standards of female respectability, again, the only actresses that could be found when one of the early playhouses, the Bengal Theatre, decided to go in for them, in place of boy actors, were prostitutes from the red light areas of the city. (These happened to adjoin the new theatres, as well as the bulk of colleges and hostels.) The same theatre also encouraged women spectators by concentrating, in partial contrast to the National Theatre and its offshoots, on domestic dramas much spiced up by scandalous tales, many of them based on widely known or rumoured facts. The most striking among these was the Elokesi scandal of 1873, a spate of plays and farces about which made the fortunes of the new and still struggling Bengal Theatre. Elokesi was the wife of Nabin, an employee in a Calcutta press, and had been left in the charge of the Mohant of the leading Saiva temple of Tarakeshwar. She was raped by the Mohant, with or without a degree of consent. Her furious husband murdered her and then surrendered to the police, sparking off a notorious trial and a spate of theatrical and many other kinds of representations.[167] It has been suggested that there ensued, as a consequence of such themes, a complicated and ambiguous exchange of glances, with respectable housewives gazing at glamorous prostitutes playing the part of fallen wives or mistresses. The conventional barriers between these various social categories—wife, mistress, prostitute—could then become unsettled, and the exchange of glances could involve patterns of dangerous attraction, as also might the gaze of men in the audience looking at the prostitutes on the stage.

----

would emerge, challenging the British Indian Association, now attacked for being narrowly zamindar.

[167] For the Elokesi case, and the above paragraph as a whole, see Sarkar 2001: 53–94.

While Michael Madhusudan Dutt was enthusiastic about the turn to actresses, which began with performances of his *Sarmistha* in 1873, other prominent bhadralok more puritanically inclined, most notably the Brahmos, disliked this use of prostitutes and started keeping away from the theatre. The actresses, even the most successful among them, remained dependent on gentlemen patrons, who no doubt often extracted sexual favours from them in return. But a few among them did become quite famous, and gained a degree of respectability, particularly when the saintly Ramakrishna Paramahansa came to a performance of a devotional play about Chaitanya in 1884 and blessed its leading actress, Binodini Dasi. Binodini, as noted already, in later life wrote an autobiography, as well as an unfinished account of her life as an actress.[168]

The striking feature of the early days of the Calcutta public theatre was the hearteningly indiscriminate way in which it forefronted oppression—by English planters, individual Englishmen, Hindu as well as Muslim landlords, religious heads like the Tarakeshwar Mohant. Rape by men in positions of power became a powerful and mobile symbol of exploitation: in *Neel Darpan*; in Dutt's *Buro Saliker Ghare Ro*—where a Hindu landlord who parades his religiosity is shown trying to defraud a Muslim peasant and seduce his wife; in Mir Musharaf Hussain's *Jamidar Darpan* (1873)—where the villain is a Muslim landlord; in the Elokesi plays and farces; and perhaps most dangerously from the British point of view in *Chakar Darpan* (1875)—on Assam tea planters.[169] Along with two other plays of the same year, *Surendra-Binodini* and *Sarat-Sarojini*, both targeting European misbehaviour and their oppression of Indians, this led to the Dramatic Performances Act of 1876 imposing rigorous state control over performances on the public stage. The careful and limited choice of target for repression is significant: not texts, but their enactment on stage; public, not private theatres.[170] Evidently the plebeian and

[168] Bhattacharya 1998.

[169] Indigo had become a declining plantation crop by the late 1860s, and its planters had become targets of criticism of many Englishmen, too, notably missionaries like Long. Tea, in contrast, would be central to British capital in India throughout, along with jute.

[170] *Neel Darpan* itself was not banned, and its author remained an official in the state postal service. What had been attacked through libel charges was

democratic potential of the latter was what worried the authorities, a concern which, incidentally, would be taken over by post-colonial governments for several decades after Independence.[171]

The repression targeted explicitly religious and mythological plays, though religious messages could be covertly filled with political meanings. This became a lasting pattern. Pinney's study of 'popular' printed images in the era of nationalism provides ample indication of more or less deliberate slippages from the religious (largely Hindu) to the political.[172] The formal reason for official forbearance was the policy framework which was set under Warren Hastings in the 1770s, constituting in effect zones of non-intervention, both Hindu and Muslim, in so far as religion, personal and family laws, and social customs were concerned—except, occasionally, when the demand for legal change came from influential and expert opinion among Hindus or Muslims backed up by scriptural texts, as with sati and widow marriage. But the question is why that policy was not modified to take care of new political threats: not all colonial promises were kept so sedulously.[173] There probably was a colonial understanding that even if religious messages carried anti-colonial implications, they would, far more decisively, divide Hindus and Muslims. Reader and viewer reception is after all much more significant than possible author motivation. The 'Muslim tyranny' stereotype may at times have had elements of a surrogate nationalism, but few Muslims were likely to see it in those terms.

---

rather the English translation, which planters feared would consolidate English public opinion against them, both in India and at home. By the mid-1870s it was the rapidly expanding vernacular public that was coming to be feared, and in 1878 Lytton would try to control it through the (short-lived) Vernacular Press Act. More systematic repression, involving books and journals, too, came only with the rise of militant forms of nationalism, from around 1905.

[171] The paragraphs on the Bengal public theatre are based on Mukherjee 1982; Bandyopadhyay 1933/1991; Bhattacharya 1998; and Sarkar: forthcoming.

[172] Pinney 2004.

[173] The promise, conveyed through Victoria's Proclamation in 1858 in the wake of the Mutiny—of non-discrimination in government employment—was emphatically not kept, as generations of early nationalists would repeatedly complain.

Repression was one factor among several in bringing about a change in the nature of the Bengali public theatre from the late 1870s, in some ways bringing it a bit closer to the Parsi theatre. The latter had come to Calcutta for the first time in 1874, but by then the theatre in Bengal was already well developed, and there seems little evidence of any direct influence. As the public theatre became more ambitious about proper halls and décor, the enthusiasm of a motley group of enthusiasts, mostly young and lower middle class, evidently proved financially inadequate. Businessmen, now that the public stage had evidently come to stay, became interested in becoming proprietors of theatres. In 1877 Protapchand Johuri took over a revived National Theatre in Calcutta, which had gone through many vicissitudes and factional disputes, and made the famous Bengali playwright and actor, Girishchandra Ghosh, its manager. Earlier, Ghosh was a senior clerk in a mercantile office, and had only a part-time connection with theatre. Such enrepreneurial proprietors would be interested primarily in box-office success and were unlikely to take political risks.

With Girishchandra a decisive turn towards mythological and Hindu religious themes, along with domestic melodramas with a generally conservative tone, dominated the public stage, sprinkled with the occasional historical romance set invariably safely in the pre-colonial era.[174] The changes fitted well with an overall shift in middle-class mentalities for some twenty years. The dominant mood was now a revivalist cultural nationalism, an opposition to social reform, and a general self-distancing from anti-British politics.[175] Nationalist politics, though, would return with a vengeance with the coming of the Swadeshi Movement, particularly from 1905.

Girishchandra too changed course with the Swadeshi wind. But the preceding era of social conservatism, conveyed through mythological

---

[174] Way back in 1968 the Czech scholar Dushan Zbavitel worked out some interesting statistics about this marked shift in themes. In 1875, 46 per cent of Bengali plays dealt with contemporary themes, only 25 per cent were mythologicals. By 1879, contemporary subjects had gone down to 16 per cent, as against 70 per cent mythological: Zbavitel 1968, cited in Dalmia 1997/2010: 312.

[175] Except on the (extremely rare) occasions when the British were seen to be intervening in religious customs through reform legislation, notably the furore provoked by the Age of Consent Act of 1891.

or hagiographical motifs—had its own compensations. Performances and stagecraft improved. A larger use of operatic elements, alongside an increase in familiar mythological and religious themes, made the theatre more popular, with women who came to watch in much greater numbers. Nor should we exaggerate the sheer conservatism, for certain complexities were apparent even in the many plays that hailed the good traditional housewife, and lampooned the educated Westernized male and female. A subtle modulation can be seen in plays like Girish-chandra's *Prafulla* (1889), which set the tone for numerous less-known pieces, many of them woven around the Kaliyuga theme. Good wives venture a little beyond the model of exemplary and willed suffering typified by Sita in the *Ramayana,* and begin to intervene to check perpetually drunk, brothel-frequenting husbands in a manner that combined subtle self-assertion with overt deference: thus, bringing about a change of heart in their errant husbands. Sometimes they are helped by an old-world servant, and a sub-theme develops, extolling simple peasant virtues and loyalty to the master. Women and class-cum-caste inferiors are thus given a positive role in re-establishing a threatened normative structure. The pattern proved remarkably enduring in many forms of imaginative literature and cinema, right down to a large group of Bombay films in our days. It would not be too far-fetched to see find a distant anticipation of the classic Gandhian methods of non retaliatory resistance to oppression were women and peasants were idealized as perfect satyagrahis.[176]

Our survey of the late-nineteenth-century 'modern' theatre has focussed entirely on its Parsi and Bengal manifestations. The public stage had a much delayed and rocky start in most other provinces. Bombay and Calcutta were cities where Western cultural and dramatic influences, conveyed by plays performed by English men and women, came early. The time lag was also related to the persistence and strength of earlier courtly, and sometimes 'popular', traditions. Sanskrit drama, for instance, remained the model for Malayalam plays till towards the end of the nineteenth century, and the theatre elsewhere in the South

---

[176] This is an argument that I have put forward in several essays: Sarkar 1997: chapters 6, 8, esp. 206–7, 312.

was, for a long time, set in traditional ways. The real breakthrough to modern drama in Malayalam came only around 1909, with the plays of C.V. Raman Pillai.

The new performative form of the proscenium stage and the open sale of tickets to spectators was initiated—except in Bengal—by touring Parsi theatre companies. One of them proved a spectacular success at the Mysore court in 1882, but they could also, by their success, inhibit the development of independent regional formations, as for example the theatre in Karnataka. This happened for Gujarati theatre, as well. Through its Bombay connection, Gujarati theatre had an early start with Ranchodbhai Udayram (1837–1923), who published his first play in 1864. Ranchodbhai mingled Sanskrit-classical and mythological with social reformist themes, in his enormously popular *Lalita Dukh Darsak* (1866), among others. He depicted the sufferings of a wife in an ill-suited arranged marriage. Though the Parsi theatre was a help at first since it used Gujarati in its early years, it subsequently turned to Urdu/Hindustani as it became a pan-Indian phenomenon. Independent Gujarati theatre subsequently languished for several decades. Marathi theatre, however, gained a strong foundation with Anna Saheb Kirloskar (1843–85), who set up a independent troupe in 1880. His themes were based on the Sanskrit classics, which he combined with classical Carnatic and Hindustani music, mingled with folk tunes in a kind of indigenous operatic form. Telugu plays, at first largely on historical and mythological themes and continuing old traditions, turned to social reform issues from the 1880s under the influence of Viresalingam, and in 1897 one such, attacking remnants of the practice of bride-price, by Gurazada Apparao, proved to be a major success. The turn to contemporary themes was associated in Gurazada with a pioneering use of colloquial Telugu, a transition which led to acrimonious controversies between traditionalists and modernists and took some twenty years to accomplish. In regions like Assam and Orissa the absence of the public stage blocked some interesting efforts to write plays on contemporary, mostly reformist, themes: the Assamese *Ramnavami*, written as early as 1857, on widow marriage, and a play about the evils of opium in 1861. There was, in fact, a predominance of social themes in early Assamese play-writing, including one in 1893 about the woes of a clerk in a tea garden. But permanent stages and professional groups did not develop for a long time. Oriya plays were performed before select audiences in royal palaces, for there was no permanent public stage in that province till the 1910s.

The strength of 'popular' traditions of theatre—like Svang or Nautanki in the Banaras region—coupled with the delayed coming of a public stage and frequent visits by Parsi theatre groups, greatly hindered the coming of the new theatre to the Hindi-speaking regions: this despite the emergence of a fine writer of Hindi plays by the 1870s in the endlessly versatile Bharatendu Harishchandra of Banaras. Bharatendu wrote some eighteen plays, including two brilliant skits, *Prem Jogini* (1874–5) and *Andher Nagari,* on contemporary Banaras life, looked at in part from below, as plebeian rogues and charlatans exposed similar behaviour among corrupt Brahmins and other sections of the city elite. Dalmia says that these are at times reminiscent of John Gay's eighteenth-century *The Beggar's Opera,* and even of Brecht. *Andher Nagari* would be revived in a big way in the mid-twentieth century radical theatre of the Indian People's Theatre Association and its successors. This casts some doubts on Hansen's contention that Harishchandra represented elite or 'middle-class' theatre engaged in the suppression of earlier 'popular' traditions. Bharatendu also wrote a proto-nationalistic play, *Bharat Durdasha* (1880), criticizing worsening conditions and numerous abuses associated with foreign rule while at the same time providing the appearance of loyalism. There is remarkably little data on the staging of Harishchandra's plays, though one source does mention that five of them may have been performed—invariably, though, in private theatres, open only to select audiences, organized by the maharaja of Banaras, or sometimes in Bharatendu's own house. A continuous history of the modern theatre in the Hindi belt had to wait for the early-twentieth-century figure of Radheshyam Kathavacak, who, as we have noted, turned to the Parsi theatre for the performances of his plays.[177]

[177] The above paragraphs on theatre outside the Parsi stage and Bengal are based on Das 1991: chapters 9, 13; Hansen 1989: 62–92, and Dalmia 1997/2010: 300–14.

Music, Dance, and Dance-Drama: Devadasis,
Bhatkhande, Paluskar

I venture into the world of Indian music and dance with considerable trepidation. It demands high levels not only of knowledge, but of aesthetic receptivity, and I cannot lay much claim to either. Yet it would be difficult to pass it by. The rich heritage of music and dance was in many ways radically transformed from the closing decades of the nineteenth century, and even the genres today thought to be 'classical' were actually, in large part, constructs of that era.[178]

The intrinsic richness of these traditions that spanned many centuries and regions of South Asia hardly needs reiteration. In addition, the exceptional degree of interanimation among an immense range of genres within the world of subcontinental performative arts makes it difficult to ignore any. Music and dance have often been major components of popular and folk performative genres, of modern drama (e.g. the Parsi theatre throughout; the Bengali stage from about the 1880s), and, strikingly, the cinema. Such intermingling, in particular an abundance of song-and-dance sequences, is seen as a specific characteristic of Indian films, particularly of Bombay and Tamil blockbusters. A separate genre of musicals has therefore not really developed here. More generally Western forms, particularly from the Renaissance on, have been marked by a series of sharp distinctions. Folk and classical; collective participative activity as distinct from an emphasis upon the creativity of the individual artist; a theatre predominantly of spoken words as against musical opera; a distinct upper-class world of symphony orchestra, chamber music, and ballroom dance as contrasted with more folk or popular forms of song, music, and dance—all these have come over time to be clearly demarcated from each other. These divisions have been less evident in subcontinental performative forms. They were not entirely absent: one need only think of the well-established gharanas of Carnatic and Hindustani classical music, made up of lineages of gurus or ustads and

[178] To take one striking instance, Bharatanatyam, so often assumed today to be virtually timeless or at least coming down from ancient times, seems to have been a term that was coined as late as the early 1930s—though of course antecedents of many of its features go back much earlier. Gaston 1996.

their pupils, and generally highly secretive about their specificities. A general marga–desi distinction is also well known. But a notion of numerous interpenetrations across genres and levels is more helpful than assuming sharp elite/popular divisions when approaching the subject.[179]

The intermingling is a striking feature of the *Bharata Natyashastra,* said to be by the eponymous Bharata and dated by scholars between the second century BC and the second century AD. It analysed theatrical spectacle as the amalgam of speech, vocal and instrumental music, gestures, mime, décor, costumes, and inner states of being, and combined in itself a discussion of music, dance, drama, and canons of aesthetic criticism. The ground it covers is wider and more varied than in its nearest ancient Greek counterpart, Aristotle's *Poetics.* The *Natyashastra* was even sometimes acclaimed as a fifth Veda, based on elements of the other four. But any simple top-down transmission of such hybridity to actual forms can be ruled out, for the simple reason that the text was lost for many centuries and was rediscovered only in 1865.[180] Rather, the text itself may have been in significant part an analysis of already existing forms and features of cultural life at many levels and regions of the subcontinent.

[179] This is the theme that runs through Kapila Vatsyayan's very helpful brief survey: Vatsyayan 1980. In keeping with her overall approach, the book includes much else besides 'theatre', narrowly defined. With the possible exception of some tribal or lower-caste songs and dances, for instance, the actual performers in the folk genres are itinerant specialized troupes of professional singers, dancers, musicians, and actors, close to village communities yet distinct in that for them performance has become their vocation. Movements, both downward and upward, of subjects or forms have been equally evident: the best-known 'cycle' or 'miracle' plays, the Ramlila of Ramnagar and the Krishna-lila of Mathura, are obviously based on a shared cultural tradition of the two great epics. Equally evident often is the role of elite patronage, like that of the maharaja of Banaras for Ramnagar or zamindars and gentry for the eastern Indian jatra. Peter Burke's work on early modern European popular culture also focuses on similar plebeian specialized performers as the key producers and carriers of folk traditions.

[180] The first printed version came out from Bombay in 1894, but the text could not be properly understood before the much later publication of a crucial commentary of Abhinavagupta. Vatsyayan 1989: 333–70.

The distinction that did emerge was the well-known North/South division, clearly operative in both music and dance. Even this appeared and became clearer only over time. There was still a fair degree of affinity between Sarangadeva in the early thirteenth century—a Kashmiri Brahmin at the court of the Yadavas of Deogiri who pioneered a systematic analysis of ragas—and the slightly later Amir Khusro, the Delhi Sultanate courtier with a deep knowledge of Persian, Arab, and Indian music to whom is sometimes attributed the invention of the sitar and the tabla. Easier contact with West Asian and Central Asian traditions contributed towards making Hindustani music more dynamic, perhaps, than its counterparts in the South. Certain key new forms had emerged by the fifteenth-sixteenth century. These included kirtan, central to Chaitanya Vaishnavism; dhrupad, with Gwalior as a major centre; its more flexible rival khayal, patronized by the Jaunpur court; and the qawwali, said to have been invented by Amir Khusro. Music became the most striking field of Hindu–Muslim intermingling, as a host of Muslim rulers were patrons and often connoisseurs, Akbar being the best known as patron of Tansen, the creator of many celebrated ragas. Too much cannot be made even of Aurangzeb's notorious antipathy to music. It does not seem to have been total, and in any case music again flourished in the Mughal court soon afterwards. The eighteenth and early nineteenth century were a major epoch for music, and figures like Sadarang, the incorporation of tappas into the classical repertoire (reputedly derived from Punjab camel-drivers' songs), and the development of ghazals and thumris were important markers.

Carnatic music followed different, but equally rich, trajectories. It was much more rooted in temples and religious traditions and was less touched by Islamic influences. But it too received enormous patronage from Muslim rulers, in particular the Deccan Sultans: the North/South divide was not a Muslim/Hindu one. Carnatic music was codified by figures like Venkatamukhi in the seventeenth century and produced great, still much-revered figures—above all perhaps Thyagaraja (1767–1847).[181]

The dance forms that are now considered classical were located

---

[181] The above account is based mainly on Massey and Massey 1993.

primarily in the immense temple complexes of the South, particularly in Thanjavur and Karnataka. Dancers were fairly low-caste devadasis, considered to be married to the deity in their youth, a situation open to exploitation by priests and others, and therefore coming under much attack by the late-nineteenth and early-twentieth century as 'temple prostitution'.[182] The profession was a caste-based hereditary one, the daughters of devadasis following the same vocation, and sons were dance teachers and musicians. As with classical music, this was conducive to preservation and at times significant development, but it kept dance a preserve of certain castes, while its patrons were confined to temples and courts. Both Kathakali and Bharatanatyam developed within this mileu of temples, though there was also a 'secular' variant performed in weddings and courts that was the immediate precursor of modern Bharatanatyam. Combined onslaughts from missionaries, notions of Victorian morality, and middle-class social reform targeted such 'temple prostitution' as immoral. Bharatanatyam became particularly suspect on account of its moods and gestures of sringara—the passion of the lover-devotee for Krishna.

In the North, by contrast, where such temple complexes were less common, courts and mansions of the elites became the principal location of dance and associated music, usually performed by tawaifs and baijis. Distinct forms emerged here, notably Kathak. Tawaifs were often highly cultured women, dispensers of knowledge about etiquette, social norms, and much else that went beyond sexual favours to their predominantly courtly and aristocratic patrons, and functioning virtually as finishing-schools for the young in such families. They were in these respects akin to the cultured courtesans of pre-Revolutionary France, the opprobrium attaching to them as concubines being a gross injustice. Nonetheless, this is how they came to be depicted for a time in the late nineteenth century, prior to fundamental changes, in the South as well as the North. This modified both the composition and the forms of these worlds of music and dance.

What happened from the turn of the century was a varied combination of sanitizing reform, ascent to respectability through changes in form, and the decisive entry of educated middle-class men and

---

[182] An empathetic recent ethnographic and historical study of devadasis over the colonial period is Soneji 2012.

women into a world where earlier such groups—below the old princes and aristocrats but above the lower castes—had had little role. Only a few key developments can be outlined briefly here.

The more reformist—and repressive—dimension of changes in South Indian dance was the passage of a series of laws ending the devadasi system in temples. Some princely states in fact took the lead, and the system was abolished in Mysore in 1910 and Travancore in 1930. Madras, which had had 200,000 devadasis as late as 1927, deeply shocking Gandhi, followed suit immediately after Independence.[183] But change also included more creative aspects, and here a central place came to be occupied by an intense debate within the Bharatanatyam form in the early twentieth century. The two chief protagonists were T. Balasaraswati (1918–84) and Rukmini Devi (1904–86). Rukmini Devi represented the decisive entrance of the respectable urban middle class into a world thus far largely distant from them. Of Brahman origin, unlike devadasis, she drew such elements into the world of classical dance through her organization of her Kalakshetra training centres. Traditional sringara elements were downplayed, songs with explicitly sexual imagery excised, and hand and facial gestures sought to be made devoid of eroticism. The bhakti which was embodied in Bharatanatyam was interpreted by her as essentially spiritual, expressing devotion and supplication to the deity, and not, except metaphorically, the love-play of the gopinis with Krishna. The style of Rukmini's reform was in fact characteristic of much of revivalist cultural nationalism of the early twentieth century: we shall see significant parallels in painting, with the Bengal School of Art. A classicism was being invented through selective processes, and significant change presented as continuity with 'genuine' or 'true' traditions of Indian culture. Balasaraswati, by contrast, was herself once a devadasi, more loyal probably to the earlier tradition. For her, sringara remained crucial to the form, though changing times made her somewhat defensive in her intervention in the debate. The debate was thus associated with contrasting forms of dance, which to some extent continues today. The net result was a decisive shift in the location of the classical South Indian dance from temples (or sometimes, courts)

---

[183] The Madras Devadasis (Prevention of Dedication) Act of 1947 is reproduced in full as Appendix II in Soneji 2012.

to the theatre hall, accompanied by a surge in middle-class performers and audiences. The importance of classical music in the South also led to a major debate on the relative importance of the language of the lyrics, and the 'pure' musical elements. The language had generally been Telugu, and so came under some suspicion in Tamilnadu at the height of the anti-Brahmin Dravidian-cum-Tamil nationalist movement.[184]

Traditions of classical music were preserved in the early decades of colonial rule in more or less traditional ways: princely and zamindari patronage, and gharanas or lineages of gurus or ustads and pupils segregated from each other, jealous of the secrets of their craft and demanding lifelong dedication. This was both a highly fragmented world, and one set apart, on the whole, from that of the new, somewhat westernized, middle class. There were individual enthusiasts and connoisseurs, and sessions of classical or light classical music sometimes formed part of their evening parties.[185] But important changes began from around the turn of the century, at a time when the deepening of nationalist sentiments stimulated a return to imagined or constructed genuinely 'classical' forms of Indian culture. Two key, roughly contemporary, figures were Vishnu Narayan Bhatkhande (1860–1936) and Vishnu Digambar Paluskar (1872–1931), both from Maharashtra. Both sought, though in somewhat different ways, to break down the isolation of the enclosed worlds of individual gharanas, and open classical music to educated middle-class men and women.[186]

Bhatkhande, the greatest modern Indian musicologist, attained an unparalleled knowledge of the practices of the different gharanas by going around the country and listening to them. He then systematized that expertise in a series of publications, like a six-volume *Kramic*

---

[184] Gaston is my principal source for the above para, but I have drawn also from Vatsyayan and the Masseys. For the language debate in classical music, see Weidman 2005: 485–511.

[185] Take for instance the sequence in Ray's *Charulata* where the victory of Liberals in England is celebrated by Bhupati and his friends, initially with a song composed by Rammohan Roy. But then someone requests a light classical piece, a tappa by Nidhubabu.

[186] The most detailed foray into music history, focussing itself almost entirely on this pair, is Bakhle 2006.

Pustak series (1920–37), a *Hindustani Sangeet Padhati,* as well as a historical survey of the music of Upper India in English. He also set up a number of Bhatkhande Music Colleges, helped by traditional princely patrons from Gwalior and Baroda, but he also received support from the Banaras Hindu University. Another achievement was his gradual success in persuading the masters of classical music to record their recitals on the new instrument of the gramophone; earlier, this was much resisted.[187]

Paluskar, in partial contrast, had less in the way of aristocratic, and more in the way of middle-class, connections. He tried to build up an innovative system of musical training through his Gandharva Mahavidyalayas, the first of which was set up in Lahore in 1901. The attempt was to develop an easier and quicker method of learning classical music, where the long traditional learning process through prolonged practice could be somewhat reduced by verbal explanations. Another major innovation was the way in which the mahavidyalayas were able to recruit women singers from 'respectable' middle-class families into a field inhabited previously almost wholly by courtesans. But a total bypassing of the gharana system proved impossible, for the pupils of his mahavidyalayas who wanted to move to higher worlds of music often went on—as they still do—to particular ustads for longer periods of apprenticeship. Paluskar, with help from Bhatkhande, initiated the modern practice of organizing all-India music conferences, the first of them held in Baroda in 1916. Here interaction among gharanas could be stimulated, for the players and singers belonged to many different schools. Princely patrons continued to be vital for organizing the early conferences, but Paluskar also developed contacts with the Congress, with which Bhatkhande had little to do. He sang patriotic hymns at several sessions.

Another figure deserves mention here, though he is seldom included in accounts of classical music: Rabindranath, whose songs attained over time an unparalleled popularity in (mainly) middle-class circles in Bengal. The scale of his experiments in the thousands of songs he composed, taking in elements from Western, but more often from folk melodies (particularly the Baul tunes), introducing the chorus

---

[187] Reasons for the resistance are offered in Dhar 2005: 'Fear of Recording: The Non-Westernness of Hindustani Music'.

form in his musical-and-dance dramas, and freely combining elements from different ragas was seen by most experts in classical music to have seriously reduced the rigour and purity of its structures. It did not help that Tagore had had no really serious classical training, though he was fairly knowledgeable about it. But it is still interesting that he belonged to the same generation as Bhatkhande and Paluskar, and some rough parallels are fairly obvious: the way in which he flouted puritanical prejudices, particularly prevalent in his Brahmo community, to encourage the girl students of Santiniketan to act, sing, and dance in public theatres, from the 1920s onwards. It was around the time when Paluskar recruited women from similar social groups for his mahavidyalayas.[188]

Technological innovation in sound films and the radio would substantially transform the worlds of music and dance from the 1930s. There would also be a notable 'folk' revival, in significant part through the efforts of the Left-initiated IPTA in the 1940s. But that is another story, and too long to be told here. The next volume, which will discuss Leftist politics, will be a better place for it.

Picturesque: Painting and the Fine Arts

The colonial era was marked by a series of major changes in the world of fine arts, above all in painting. The taxonomy considered most normal today, whereby the fine arts—painting, sculpture, architecture— become distinct from artisanal crafts, is a post-Renaissance separation. It attained its full development in the image of the romantic artist in the nineteenth-century West and came into India as part of the Western cultural baggage. Not that pre-colonial South Asian art had no conception of some distinctions at different levels. The richly varied world of village-level arts and crafts was certainly quite different from the 'karkhanas' (workshops) that kings and aristocrats maintained, where artists worked under close supervision to turn out products for their masters. Such institutions, like the well-documented Mughal

---

[188] Massey and Massey 1993; Bhagwat 1987: 109–15. See also the more detailed work on Bhatkhande and Paluskar in relation to nationalist feeling: Bakhle 2006.

karkhanas, however, employed what would today be called artisans or craftsmen as well as painters, and there were only a few signs of the artistic individualism that became from the Renaissance onwards a key feature of Western art. Some painters had begun signing their works, and the lives of a few (like Daswanth and Basawan, under Akbar) attracted the attention of court historians. Nor were village or tribal artists sharply distinct from craftsmen or specialists in theatre or song. The patua scroll-painters of West Bengal, for instance, who became well known after their nineteenth-century migration to Calcutta as the creators of the interesting Kalighat paintings, had earlier been an itinerant group displaying their scrolls alongside recitation and song, and they had close connections with potters and carpenters.

Monumental and domestic architecture, we have seen, was for the British in India the major field of art investment, these being expressions of power and splendour and representing efforts to find ways of living comfortably in an unfamiliar climate. Indian artistic creativity, in sharp though understandable contrast, prioritized painting. There was a fair amount of largely imitative palace and mansion construction by Indian princes and zamindars, as for instance the Marble Palace in Calcutta modelled on classical Renaissance Palladian style. In tune with the changing fashions of their rulers, there was also a partial late-nineteenth-century shift towards 'Hindu', and 'Muslim' or Saracenic forms. But significant architectural investment was well beyond the resources of the middle- and lower-middle-class strata which became the major creators of what would come to be recognized as modern Indian art. They preferred new and changing styles of painting, and, to a lesser extent, sculpture.

In general terms, two major transformations stand out in the terrain of Indian painting. There was, first, the transition from karkhanas, tightly supervised by court officials, to the independent 'gentleman-artist' with his studio, producing for an open art market. The artist consequently became distinct from the artisan: the shilpi as distinct from the karigar or mistri.[189] This paralleled the European transition from the Renaissance till the nineteenth century, but with certain specificities. In particular, as we have seen in several other fields, there

---

[189] Chatterjee 1990.

was a certain conflation of phases, as oil painting came here around the same time as the entry of developed techniques of mechanical reproduction, such as lithography and chromolithography. An interesting consequence was that the distinction between elite and popular was repeatedly undercut, as studio artists, both the less successful and sometimes the best known, turned to mass production: Ravi Varma being the most striking instance.

The second crucial novelty was a persistent desire, in artistic styles, to somehow combine the modern with the 'authentic', true to 'Indian' traditions. Both imperatives had been absent earlier, in so far as there was not that constant presence of an Other who was identified with 'modernity': worthy of imitation and 'catching up' with, and yet a dominant and oppressive presence. It was also an Other whose artistic forms were appealing, particularly the new techniques of oil painting on easels and perspective. Some Mughal artists had already shown an interest in post-Renaissance forms, despite their limited acquaintance.

Yet a sense of unease and guilt became increasingly difficult to avoid in the colonial era, as nationalistic moods intensified. The resultant dual imperative stimulated claims to being more authentic than the preceding forms. This, it is now recognized, considerably distorted the history of modern Indian art. To anticipate briefly a point that will require elaboration later: the 'Bengal school' headed by Abanindranath Tagore that developed in the era of Swadeshi-Extremist nationalism condemned Ravi Varma and other artists painting in the naturalist mode as purely imitative and denationalized. Yet what was now thought to be genuinely indigenous was actually in very large part a recent invention heavily derived from one strand of Orientalist scholarship and art thinking in the contemporary West. An interesting consequence, as the Swadeshi moods receded, was a series of discussions about art which ran parallel to important debates about the meanings and value of cultural nationalism.[190]

The decline of the Mughal and its successor courts was accompanied by the total collapse of karkhanas in course of the eighteenth century. In

[190] Guha-Thakurta 2005: 71–107 provides a helpful introduction to this subject.

Bengal, the first region that passed under the control of the Company, artists earlier employed in the official enterprises at Murshidabad and Patna were pushed down to the level of what the Europeans termed bazaar artists. Some of them managed to get Company employment, for the new rulers wanted pictorial descriptions of flora and fauna, topography, archaeological and historical remains, social customs, and the everyday lives of the newly acquired land and people for effective rule and the satisfaction of their curiosity alike. Before the mid-nineteenth-century inauguration of photography there was a need therefore for accurate drawings, and this provided the initial impetus to the turn towards the naturalist representations which would characterize Indian art for much of the nineteenth century. But the origins and trajectory of the first major kind of art in colonial times were very different, and more autonomous, than the work of such 'Company artists'.

Kalighat Paintings

Around the middle of the nineteenth century the humble low-caste patuas who had migrated to Calcutta and settled in the environs of the bustling temple centre of Kalighat developed a remarkable genre of paintings. Pilgrims and visitors to the temple provided a ready market for these highly portable canvases. Europeans of various kinds—missionaries, seekers of Oriental curiosities, tourists who wanted mementos, and eventually scholars of art—contributed to the preservation of many specimens of this art, after it had vanished in the early twentieth century, in a number of Western museum collections. Traders and travellers also took with them Kalighat 'pats', and rich collections developed—for instance at Shekhavati, the home of many of the Marwari businessmen of Calcutta.

Kalighat provides a particularly striking instance of the interpenetration of times and forms that makes conventional polarities unworkable, a point emphasized by Jyotindra Jain in what is the best study of the entire genre.[191] Artists migrated from villages in south-west Bengal, pursuing their traditional caste occupation in new ways and contexts.

---

[191] Jain 1999. My account draws heavily from his work.

The satirical criticism of urban 'babu' culture evident in some of their paintings has been read at times as a popular, indigenous, or traditional rejection of the new culture of the westernized elite. But a closer look reveals that Kalighat paintings were hardly 'traditional' or 'rural'; in many ways they were distinctively modern, constituting perhaps the first modern school of Indian art. The patuas who moved to the city (others remained itinerant artist-singers in the villages, where they can sometimes still be seen) abandoned the old practice of narrative scroll paintings accompanied by recitation and song, which would be unfolded and displayed rather than simply sold. They became sellers of their wares, moving to single drawings or paintings on the new medium of cheap, mill-made paper, along with an accompanying shift from tempera to watercolour. The first had been prepared by the village artists themselves, mixing earth with other material to produce opaque colours, while watercolour was a more expensive, imported article which added considerably to brightness. Sitting on the roadside, watching diverse kinds of passers-by go, selling their wares to them, the Kalighat artists have some claim to be considered the first among the Indian artists who produced entirely for an open market and not at the behest or orders of patrons—yet another mark of modernity.

Jain's study moves from specific details of artistic form to their possible connections with equally specific social circumstances. One striking feature of Kalighat art, for instance, was the illusion of three-dimensionality that painters had produced in its figures, though no attempt was made to achieve perspective for the entire picture. This illusion of volume was achieved not through any noticeable imbibing of Western techniques, but through a vision and method akin to sculptural modelling. Two alternative views about the origins of Kalighat have been propounded. T.N. Mukherjee in the 1880s had emphasized its continuities with rural patua art; William Archer in the 1950s stressed Western influences entering through imports of English reproductions and prints. Jain's opinion differs from both. He analyses the specific manner of creation of an illusion of volume. Patuas—painters—often simultaneously made clay figures of divinities and lived, both in their earlier village homes and in the city, in close proximity with potters (kumors) and wood carvers (sutradhars). Such groups were also close to stone carvers (bhaskaras). Kalighat painters also had to work at great speed to catch purchasers. Jain suggests that this actually became an asset, and helps to explain another feature of the art. Speed made for a confident sweep and tension of lines and forms, producing bold and dynamic, not inert and laboured, paintings.

Kalighat 'pats' were very much part of the rapidly changing patterns of urban life in Calcutta and much of this worked its way into its themes. It was a time of massive proliferation of new visual images, from varied kinds of print and engraving to photography and Western-style proscenium theatres. As keen observers of such novelties, the patuas introduced rippling curtains on the top border of many of their paintings so that the scene depicted resembled a tableau, seeming to be set on a proscenium stage with curtains; or it could resemble a studio photograph. Ignorant of classical art canons, Kalighat painters sat in bazaars, 'watching the vendors of *paan*, vegetables and sweetmeats, the nouveau riche babus, the fashionable bibis, courtesans, or fisher-women', and went on to create vivid galleries of street figures.[192] Sacred and profane figures repeatedly crossed and recrossed: a painting of Shiva, Parvati, and Ganesh resembles a middle-class family on an outing, divine nuptials appear like wedding photographs. Once again, there are parallels with other cultural forms, for the domesticated, homely Shiva had been a common image already in eighteenth-century Bengali poetry.

As in contemporary farces with which they had many similarities, the themes were often satirical but the targets lampooned were extremely varied. The henpecked husband bullied by his wife or mistress was a common motif, stereotypical in so much contemporary literature of the degeneration of modern times; the corrupt, pot-bellied Brahman or sadhu was also often a target. What seems missing, though, is the figure of the educated, reformist bhadralok, or the educated woman. The principal object of caricature is, instead, unre-formed babu culture, not the world of the educated, reformist middle-class literati. Predictably, and once again running parallel with contemporary plays and farces, the Elokesi scandal of 1873 became a favoured subject, with a whole crop of 'pats'. These bring together

[192] Ibid.: 19.

corrupt sadhu, cuckolded husband, and a wife who has gone astray, the resemblance to contemporary theatre being evident. Both love to depict, for instance, courtroom scenes, which in themselves include many elements of the theatre.

Kalighat painting was at its peak between the late-1850s and 1870s, as pilgrims and visitors poured into Calcutta in unprecedented numbers to take advantage of new railway networks. This was followed by a slow but irreversible decline in the face of an expanding range of other forms of cheap methods of production, increasingly mechanical. Early competition came from woodcut and metal engravings located in Battala, also the centre of the Calcutta printing world and therefore of the growing enterprise of book and magazine illustrations. From about the 1880s Battala engravers in turn began to lose control over the market for bazaar art to lithographs, oleographs, and chromolithographs, which demanded more initial investment than either they or the Kalighat painters could usually afford. The hour of the gentlemen painter had arrived, that of Kalighat had passed, the last of their painters dying in the 1920s and 1930s. Paradoxically, it was only then that the elite world, in India and in the West, began discovering their merits. Jamini Roy, a Calcutta-based artist who was an icon for middle-class art lovers, for instance, modelled himself at times on the rediscovered heritage.

Gentlemen Artists, Realism, and Ravi Varma

From the 1850s the British introduced forms of art education. The Calcutta School of Art was set up in 1854 and counterparts developed soon in Bombay and Madras. These were brought under the supervision of the Director of Public Instruction in 1855. There seems to have been a dual motivation, the emphasis shifting over time. Art education—comprising some acquaintance with European masterpieces and methods through copies, and, more importantly, imparting basic skills of drawing and draughtsmanship—would hopefully provide alternative channels of employment to educated youth through low-level technical jobs in government departments such as surveying, where such techniques were in demand. A second motive, which grew in importance over time, emerged from concern for traditional Indian artisans buckling under the onslaught of competition from British machine-made goods. Interest in the vanishing craft products of India was stimulated by the collections brought over to London for the Crystal Palace Exhibition of 1851, and this concern fitted well with late-Victorian moods of disillusionment about the aesthetically shoddy products of industrial civilization and the related rupture of 'high' art from everyday crafts: William Morris, the most outstanding figure in this trend, would eventually develop an aesthetic medievalism into a distinctive kind of socialism. An early consequence was the emergence of two kinds of art-teaching methods and theories in Britain—the Royal Academy (along with the British Museum and the National Gallery) as the centre for 'high' or 'fine' art, and a Central School of Industrial Art founded in the alternative, slightly more plebeian, cultural centre of South Kensington. The contrast persists, for South Kensington is today the site of the Victoria and Albert Museum, with its rich collection of Indian and other craft products and everyday articles, as well as of a number of science museums. It is significant that the teachers of the government art schools in India were drawn heavily from South Kensington ex-students: Henry Locke, John Lockwood Kipling (father of Rudyard), and E.B. Havell. A new kind of Orientalism was emerging, one of admiration tinged with patronage, rather than condemnation, and in the early twentieth century this would have a very major impact on the trajectory of Indian art through the key figure of Havell.

The objective of training skilled artisans in the new government schools was not realized. There was a great lack of material resources among the artisans, declining rapidly because of foreign competition. For them, continuing in established forms of family-based apprenticeship was much more advisable rather than investment in a new kind of training. Even where free admission was promised, as initially in Bombay, the requirement of prior knowledge of elementary arithmetic and geometry effectively excluded them. The schools therefore became an alternative channel of upward mobility for the less academically motivated sons of elite or middle-class families. In 1872–3, 81 out of 94 students of the Calcutta Art School came from middle-class families. In a few cases, they did become successful artists, constituting the first generation of gentlemen painters, and gradually winning a toehold in salon exhibitions at Simla and Calcutta, long monopolized by Europeans. They included M.V. Dhurandhar in Bombay, and Annada Prasad Bagchi, Sashi Hesh, and Bamapada Banerjee in Calcutta. Such men took to oil painting, using perspective and realist representation. In social terms, they represented a new category. They were very different from the old court painters as they worked not for royal or noble patron-employers, but for an art market sought through periodic exhibitions where connoisseurs would hopefully gather. The realist methods they had adopted, however, were generally used to depict fairly traditional themes, above all mythological scenes. Some British officials had hoped that accurate drawing and realist representation would dispel what they thought were mythic clouds in Indian minds. The kind of 'surrogate realism' (Geeta Kapur's term) adopted by Indian painters in the late nineteenth century actually had a reverse effect, for the gods, previously depicted in metaphorical terms, now became objects of a kind of photographic realism. Pinney underlines the emergence of such 'photos of the gods', conflating the mythic past with the present. Realism applied to icons made mythic figures more easily understandable and popular, and contributed over time to uniformity, gradually ironing out many regional and local specificities.

Realism, at its finest, had been deployed in the West to penetrate below surfaces and bring to light hidden dimensions of the real. In late-nineteenth-century India (with the possible exception of Ravi Varma at his best) it was a technology to better depict conventional themes. It was very different, for instance, from the work of the European realist painter closest in time to the work of these Indian artists, Gustave Courbet. A further problem, for Indian artists seeking to paint in Western modes, was that knowledge of the latter came entirely through British instances of academic art. The new worlds being opened up from the latter part of the nineteenth century by the Impressionists and their successors passed Indian art by, till well into the twentieth century.

Gentlemen artists wanted to project a self-image of superiority over the bazaar painters of Kalighat and Battala. But in practice the rapid development and profitability of the new techniques of mechanical reproduction led to the repeated breakdown of such distinctions.

The less successful of the products of the art schools, and soon even many of the most exalted of them, found the easy profits promised by multiplication of images impossible to resist. The consequence was an important development of a series of Indian studios that specialized in the mass printing of art objects. Annada Prasad Bagchi and three other Art School graduates set up the Calcutta Art Studio in 1878 with a very successful early series of what it called 'Hindu mytho-pictures', sold in multiple lithographic copies. It sought a multi-level market, selling hand-tinted lithos for Rs 1–2 and so capturing much of the Kalighat and Battala demand, as well as more highly priced photographic and oil portraits. The Poona Chitrashala Press was founded the same year. Unlike its Calcutta contemporary, the Poona press quickly developed a marked Hindu-nationalist tone, in many ways preparing the ground for Extremism in Maharashtra. It was started by Vishnukrishna Chiplunkar, a mentor of Tilak, who had launched in 1874 the journal *Nibandha Mala*. He would also extend in the 1880s printing facilities for *Kesari* and *Mahratta*, famous journals edited by Tilak. Chitrashala combined Hindu mytho-pictures with evocations of the glorious history of the Marathas, combining implicit anti-British messages with overt anti-Muslim readings of the past.

The third major centre of mass art production was the Ravi Varma Fine Art Lithographic Press set up in 1894 in Girgaum, in the city of Bombay, and later shifted to nearby Lonavla. The finest and best-known painter of the time thus also turned to commercialized mass production, with the superior technology of chromolithograph and oleograph imported from Germany. He produced precise and glossy copies of the oils he had painted, or at least allowed to pass under his name. As with Jamini Roy a generation later, or for that matter Rembrandt, it is sometimes difficult to establish the precise artist: some are willing to attribute to Ravi Varma only around ninety of the much larger number carrying his imprimatur.

Ravi Varma (1848–1906) embodied yet another kind of intersection of different worlds. Born in a Kerala aristocratic—not urban middle class—family, with some connections with the courts of both Tanjore and Trivandrum, Varma, after his early and remarkable success, cultivated a self-image of romantic self-made artist without formal art training who miraculously mastered the new techniques of oil painting. The self-image may not correspond exactly with reality. Varma's uncle had connections with the tradition of Tanjore court painting, his brother with whom he often collaborated was also an artist, and so, it seems, was his sister, who predictably had little chance to reveal her talents. Ravi Varma probably had some training under a visiting European artist as well. His leap to fame began in 1873 when he received a gold medal at an exhibition organized by the official Madras Art School. Varma, like contemporary gentlemen painters in Bengal such as Bamapada Banerjee, began with portraits, akin to photographs, of distinguished figures, and went on to a series of more impressive and realistic depictions of Keralan and eventually Indian types—such as the 'Nair Lady' that got him the 1873 award, or the ten oils sent to the Chicago Exhibition of 1893 which were praised for their 'ethnographic value'. His real fame, along with sumptuous patronage from a number of princes, came through the amalgam, typical for the times, of 'historical' with puranic and mythological themes, such as the series he did for the palace of the Gaekwad of Baroda. But unlike most others in this genre, Varma was able to depict his mythological figures, particularly the heroines, not as statuesque icons but as 'palpable, desirable, human beings'.[193] The voluptuous figures he clearly loved to paint, as for instance in *Sakuntala's Love Epistle to Dushyanta,* or *Arjun and Subhadra* (where the couple are evidently moving towards a kiss), would be denounced in the heyday of cultural nationalism and the Bengal School as both immoral and denationalized. Actually they were more in conformity with much of classic Hindu art tradition than later effete and desexualized depictions, for ancient Hindu mythological literature and art had been seldom shy of sexual and physical frankness. These had shocked many Christian missionaries and upholders of Victorian morality, whose prudery was, paradoxically, internalized by Hindu cultural nationalism in the twentieth century.

The charge of denationalized imitation of Western art commonly made against Varma after the turn of the century assumes that all influence is necessarily imitative, and, in colonial conditions, that would indicate a surrender to power. The approach ignores the genuine

[193] Mitter 1994: 202.

appeal of the new: novel artistic techniques like oils and perspective.[194] Actually, cultural nationalist elements are evident often enough in the themes of Varma's historical-cum-mythological paintings. In this, as well as in the overwhelming predominance of Hindu imagery and myths, there were in fact many continuities between Ravi Varma and his successors at the Bengal School, despite the major shift in artistic style. In common with many of his generation, Varma's patriotic cultural leanings were combined easily with loyalism and closeness to the rulers. The 1903 Madras session of the Congress had an exhibition of Varma's paintings around the same time as the British awarded him the title of Kaisar-i-Hind (1904), the only Indian artist to be thus honoured.

Almost from the beginning, Varma provided an image of the artist as successful entrepreneur, even before he turned in the 1890s to mass mechanical reproduction of his paintings. Together with his younger brother Raja Raja Varma, also a painter of merit, he was able to charge as much as Rs 1500 for full-length portraits by the 1880s, this being more than any English artist then working in India could hope for. Mechanical reproduction through the press he had founded then led, in yet another coming together of elite and popular levels, to the uniquely widespread popularity of his prints, or at least prints carrying his name. This was associated with a certain loss of aura in elite circles, and may have contributed to the sharp attacks on him that would follow a few years later. Ravi Varma images proliferated commercially everywhere—as decorations on porcelain figures manufactured in Germany, matches, English baby food, to mention only three among innumerable instances. The images of Hindu gods and goddesses as standardized and spread by Varma have links also with calendar art today.[195]

[194] In an article of 1961 cited with approval by the art critic Geeta Kapur, Asok Mitra pointed out that the adoption of similar criteria in the history of nineteenth-century literature could have led to the placing of writers like Ishwar Gupta, free of any Western influence, above Bankimchandra. Mitra argued that Varma's was not 'a cheap or pointless imitation' of European technique but a struggle 'to look around himself through his European equipment—modified to suit his vision.' Mitra 1961, cited in Kapur 1989: 59–80.

[195] Pinney however thinks that this has been exaggerated. The gods and

Ravi Varma's art, finally, had close connections with other kinds of visual production in his time. He and his brother were avid theatre-goers, and Varma's paintings show strong theatrical elements. A link with Indian cinema, which would soon emerge, is also obvious. The connections are both artistic and institutional, for D.G. Phalke, the first Indian maker of feature films (once again, like so many of Varma's paintings, on mythological themes), was connected for some years from 1901 with the Lonavla Press that had been founded by Varma.

Till the Swadeshi-Extremist era, the combination of Western artistic models and forms with indigenous themes was regarded as an asset rather than otherwise. This was shown also by the leap to fame in the 1890s of Ganapatrao Mhatre, the first major Indian academic sculptor. Mhatre was the son of a Poona army clerk whose fame for a few years rivalled even that of Varma. His *To the Temple* (1896) was acclaimed precisely for this combination, for Mhatre followed a Graeco-Roman form for an obviously indigenous and traditional theme.

The Bengal School—and After

A new kind of nationalism was emerging in some regions of India, notably in Bengal and Maharashtra, from the turn of the century. Then came Curzon's Partition of Bengal in 1905, and the widespread middle-class anger it evoked vastly strengthened the new moods and the quest for new methods. In this Swadeshi era, what came to be called 'Extremism' condemned the older 'Moderates' as ineffective 'mendicants', insufficiently patriotic, denationalized, and not adequately Hindu in their culture. The counterpart in the world of art was a sudden fall in the prestige of Ravi Varma and the entire realist or naturalist genre, and the rise of a group of painters, headed by Abanindranath Tagore, that came to be termed the Bengal or Calcutta School. This became the artistic counterpart of the Hindu national-

---

goddesses of calendars really are connected much more with the devotional aesthetic developed in the 1920s and 1930s in the Nathwara region of Rajasthan, where the realism and perspective associated with Ravi Varma came to be much attenuated. Pinney 2004: chapter 5.

ism of these years. It proclaimed, often in somewhat exaggerated ways, that it had brought about a total rupture with the older forms of late-nineteenth-century art. This was necessary to achieve true nationalism and cultural authenticity. The Ravi Varma era had already taken many of its themes from Hindu religious traditions and literature. But now the use of realistic techniques, imported from the West, amounting to 'photos of the gods', to depict traditional Hindu religious divinities and narratives—which had only the other day ensured Ravi Varma's popularity and reputation as a patriot—were no longer considered sufficient. What was now demanded was a more valid 'Indianness', equated as before mainly with Hindu (really, in the main, upper class or sanskritized) themes and values. The key term became authentic bhava—roughly, truly indigenous emotions and sentiments, associated with the exaltation of the allegedly 'spiritual' Orient over crassly materialist Western civilization and culture.

In practice, elements of prudery invaded the new style of painting, and Ravi Varma's women were often condemned as sensual and voluptuous. A good indicator of changing conceptions of art is provided by the excellent reproductions of contemporary Indian painting that became an important feature of the two influential monthlies edited by Ramananda Chatterjee, *Prabasi* from 1901 and *Modern Review* from 1907. The paintings of Ravi Varma, M.V. Dhurandhar, and other realistic artists had been carried prominently by *Prabasi* in its early years, and not thought of as incompatible with some by Abanindranath or with reproductions of Western art. As late as January 1907, the first issue of *Modern Review* could still hail Ravi Varma as the 'greatest painter of modern India'. But the same issue also carried an article by Sister Nivedita (close associate of Vivekananda) which was characteristic of the new mood that would dominate the art world in the immediate future. She violently condemned Varma's *Arjun and Subhadra* for its un-Indian vulgarity, as compared with Abanindranath's *Bharatmata*. The latter had a vaguely defined outline of the female figure put forward as symbol of the motherland, and thereby firmly excluded any hint of sexuality.

Discussions on art now acquired an overtly literary quality. A category like bhava, or an appropriate mood culled by meditations on holy matters, mainly pertained to the world of literature, and often had little to do with the more technical aspects of the work of professional artists. The articles on art in Ramananda's journals were thus very different from the emphasis on the teaching and training of art as a vocation that had dominated an earlier journal, *Shilpa-pushpanjali* (1885), the first exclusively art magazine in Bengal. An associated change was the effort to elevate the 'true' artist totally above the world of popular or commercialized art. Not everyone even in the era of the Bengal School could live up to this ideal, of course, but the new role model was an aristocrat like Abanindranath.

There had been occasional anticipations of the moods characteristic of post-1900 art forms, just as there were precursors of Extremism and Hindu nationalism going back to the 1870s. Shyama Charan Srimani in 1874, for instance, had called for a recovery of the ancient heritage of art in the service of the motherland, and projected the chaste Hindu woman as the true symbol of that heritage. He was a teacher at the Government School of Art but had left it to join the National School of Nabagopal Mitra which came up in the wake of the Hindu Mela. Meanwhile, much more was learnt about this ancient heritage through the work of Orientalist scholars and archaeologists, both European and Indian. Early Orientalist scholarship had been mainly linguistic and literary in its interests and discoveries, but from around the mid-nineteenth century archaeologists and art historians became more prominent, typified by figures like James Prinsep, Alexander Cunningham, James Ferguson, and John Griffiths (the first to explore the Ajanta frescoes). An Indian counterpart was not too slow in coming. As early as 1834, Ram Roz wrote an essay on early Indian texts on architecture. From around the 1860s, Rajendralal Mitra became a key figure in the Asiatic Society of Bengal. Between 1875 and 1880 he organized a group of Government School of Art students to prepare illustrations of the monuments of Orissa. This became a part of his major work on that area. For Rajendralal Mitra, Orissa was a privileged region for the study of 'Hindu' architecture, for it had remained largely untouched by 'Muslim' invasions. His *Indo-Aryans* (1881) also revelled in the artistic achievements of the Aryan race from which Hindus had allegedly sprung. His scholarship, incidentally, led to a violent and at times openly racist attack on him by Ferguson in his *Archaeology of India with Special Reference to the Works of Babu Rajendralal Mitra* (1884).[196] Ferguson accused Rajendralal of rank incompetence. The controversy in part turned around the question of the extent of Greek influence on ancient Indian art. Ferguson emphasized such influence; Mitra, and later many other Indian scholars, stressed their fundamentally indigenous roots. The coincidence in time between this virulent attack on the competence of a leading Indian intellectual and the Ilbert Bill furore was not accidental. Some passages of Ferguson make it evident that he was passing on to the Indian scholar some of the anger he felt at the babus daring to claim equality with Europeans as judges.[197]

The strand within Western Orientalism that appreciated the artistic heritage of India—in contrast with violent denunciation by missionaries and others—went through two phases. The first we have already encountered: an interest in the declining decorative arts of the subcontinent. This had emerged as an offshoot of anti-industrial moods in the West, and had manifested itself in constituting the curricula of the various Government School of Art in Calcutta and elsewhere on the model of the South Kensington alternative to the Royal Academy. What stimulated and deeply influenced the rise of the Bengal School was, however, a selective admiration for some of the 'high' traditions of South Asian art, along with appreciation of the spiritual and philosophical content which was seen in that heritage and hailed as far superior to the materialism of Western culture. This spiritual /material and East/West contrast had always been a crucial element in Orientalist thinking, the Orient alternately denounced for its otherworldliness and hailed for the same reason.

The key figure in the founding of the Bengal School, from this point of view, was E.B. Havell (1864–1937), who came to India as head, successively, of the Madras and then the Calcutta School of Art (1896–1906). Beginning like preceding teachers there with admiration for Indian craft skills,[198] Havell successively became appreciative of

---

[196] The Mitra–Ferguson controversy is deployed as the starting point of a history of colonial archaeology by Upinder Singh: see Singh 2004.

[197] For some details about this clash, see Guha-Thakurta 2004; and Singh 2004: chapter 9.

[198] Havell, for instance, initially interested himself in improving Indian

Mughal miniatures, Abanindranath (whom he met around 1902–3, and claimed as his protégé before Western audiences), and then increasingly the specifically 'Hindu' heritage. Even the *Handbook* he published in 1904 for Agra and the Taj Mahal tried to separate the 'Persian' external influences from the genuinely 'Indian' central core of Hindu features in Mughal art. Admiration for the allegedly spiritual qualities of authentically 'Hindu' elements deepened in his *Benaras, the Sacred City* (1905), and in later books like *The Ideals of Indian Art* (1911). Havell emphasized Indian spiritualism in art, rather than mere technical or archaeological interpretation. It is this spirituality that he thought he had discovered at its deepest in Abanindranath, even though the artist himself had already experimented with several distinct kinds of paintings, and would resume such experimentation in old age after the wave of neo-Orientalism had receded. For the moment, though, it is possible that the heads of Abanindranath, and of the pupils who gathered around him, were somewhat turned by extravagant praise from an influential Englishman. Havell insisted on making him vice-principal at the Government School of Art. Three other figures from abroad added to this chorus of praise. I have already referred to Nivedita's assessment of the latter in 1907. This influential associate of Vivekananda contributed significantly to the alignment during the Swadeshi years of Hindu revivalism and nationalism with what became for several decades the dominant discourse on Indian art. There was a major input also from Japan, then beginning on an era of resurgent nationalism, which came to be enormously admired in Indian patriotic circles because of its unexpected victory over a European power, Russia, in 1905. The link was made by visits of Okakura beginning in 1902. He was introduced to Abanindranath and his brother Gaganendranath by Nivedita. Okakura was a towering figure in the Japanese Nihonga art movement which stressed Japanese cultural identity and which had rebelled against the earlier domination of Westernized artists like Kuroda. Okakura's *Ideals of the East* (1903) held out a perspective of Asian unity against the West, within which India and its ancient culture were promised an important place.

---

handlooms through introducing the fly-shuttle—a not unimportant component in the Swadeshi Movement.

Even before Okakura's first visit, two Japanese artists, Taikan and Shunso, had visited Calcutta and inspired Abanindranath to adopt the technique of wash painting, creating the smoky shadows and hazy and wispy contours of figures that became characteristic for a time of Abanindranath and his disciples. These rarified images were hailed as expressive of inner meaning, *Bharatmata* being a leading instance. Finally, there was the figure of Ananda Coomaraswamy, who developed over time into the most important art commentator among these admirers of the Bengal School. Of mixed Sinhalese-English parentage, living in England in his youth, Coomaraswamy, during a brief stay in Ceylon (1904–7), became a nationalist ideologue increasingly enthusiastic about the Swadeshi Movement in India. This went through two phases, his initial enthusiasm having been for traditional Sinhalese and Indian crafts. Later this was supplanted by eulogies of the sublime value of Hindu India's fine art and spiritual values. Coomaraswamy's texts, particularly *Essays in National Idealism* (1909) and *Art and Swadeshi* (1912) were extremely influential, and the *The Deeper Meaning of the Struggle,* a slightly earlier pamphlet published in 1907, located the real meaning of Swadeshi nationalism not in any material gains but in the propagation of the 'great ideals of Indian culture'.

The neo-Orientalist art of the Bengal School often found the true repository of Indian values, bhava, in the figure of the ideal Hindu woman, depicted most famously in *Bharatmata* and hailed by Nivedita as the 'first masterpiece of Indian art'. Other famous works of Abanindranath in this era included *Sita in Captivity in Lanka,* and another celebrated painting in the same vein was his pupil Nandalal Bose's *Sati,* in which widow immolation was the symbol of suffering, self-sacrifice, and devotion. Art during the Swadeshi period thus became imbued with dominant strands of Hindu revivalist thinking regarding the ideal Indian woman. It needs to be added, though, that even if it went along with the contemporary political upsurge and contributed to it to some extent, this phase of art was also shot through with a cultural as distinct from political nationalism. Artists like Abanindranath stayed away from active political involvement,[199]

---

[199] In his delightful reminiscences, *Gharoa* (Viswabharati, 1941) and *Jorasankor Dhare* (Viswabharati, 1944), Abanindranath recalled how alarmed

and, correspondingly, the rulers found nothing to fear and much to encourage in the work of the Bengal School. A notorious critic of Extremist politics like the *Englishman* praised *Bharatmata* for its 'non-political quality' and the ways in which it brought nationalist excesses under the 'controlling influences of both art and religion' (30 July 1907).[200] The main institutional base of the Bengal School, the Indian School of Oriental Art (1907), received official and big landlord patronage. Prominent supporters included Kitchener, Woodruffe, and two successive lieutenant governors of Bengal, Carmichael and Ronaldshay. It would be unfair to treat the Bengal School as an unchanging bloc. Nor did it ever entirely dominate the entire world of Indian painting, even at its point of greatest influence.

Bombay artists centred around the J.J. [Jamshetji Jeejebhoy] School of Art stuck with rare exceptions to the traditions of Academic Realism, and Dhurandhar was still the dominant influence. An exception was a younger painter, Ravi Shankar Rawat, from Gujarat, who became a votary of Gandhi, sent some of his students to Santiniketan, and later painted the Haripura Congress panels jointly with Nandalal Bose. Abdur Rahman Chugtai, one of the first of modern Muslim painters, was influenced for a time by Abanindranath, but tried to depict similar moods to portray Muslim themes and was attracted by the Ajanta frescoes.

The changes within the Bengal School were themselves quite striking. Abanindranath, contrary to his cult image, which identified him totally with his Swadeshi era work, was in fact a notably eclectic and creative painter. His initial inspiration had come from Mughal art, and, particularly in his later days, he seemed at times impatient with the constraints imposed by the cult that had gathered around him. Already by 1909 he was interested in folk traditions and was one of the first to rehabilitate the Kalighat bazaar artists after several decades of denigration by all types of gentlemen painters, naturalists,

---

he had been when his uncle Rabindranath insisted on taking him along to put rakhis on the wrists of Muslims at Nakhoda Masjid on 16 October 1905, Partition Day, in a gesture of Hindu–Muslim unity, the response to which was uncertain.

[200] Guha-Thakurta 2004: 279.

and Orientalists. In old age, the impatience took the form of a retreat into a private world where painting became indistinguishable from play through completely free creation, unrelated to Hindu nationalist models. He spent his time carving wooden toys. His brother Gaganendranath was even more experimental, and painted brilliant political and social caricatures. In the early 1920s he was clearly attracted to contemporary non-realistic Western art, notably Cubism. Some of the pupils of Abanindranath also moved away from the forms imposed by the straitjacket of Swadeshi nationalist ideology. Two study tours of Ajanta led by Asit Haldar around 1910 proved a revelation, for there the Bengal artists encountered an indisputably ancient Indian tradition marked by its firm contours and colours, very different from the vague outlines of the Bengal School at its height. Nandalal Bose, the most outstanding among Abanindranath's students, progressively moved closer to Rabindranath, whose ideas on art as they developed in the poet's late life were utterly different. Nandalal travelled around the Bengal countryside and then went to Japan as Tagore's companion in 1915–16, and these seem to have contributed to a decline in his work of the elements of veneration of an idealized past so evident in the early painting of *Sati*. Even mythic figures now began to be drawn from everyday visual facts about peasant and tribal life: a village archer figured as Arjuna; Krishna again became a cowherd; Sabari a tribal woman. The Haripura panels of Nandalal and Rewat at the Congress session emphasized medieval bhakti themes that had often cut across Hindu–Muslim divides, and presented them in forms drawn from rural life, in keeping with the dominant ethos of the Gandhian national movement of the 1930s. Nandalal headed the Santiniketan Kala Bhavan for a generation from the early 1920s, which became famous as well as significantly different from the Bengal School of Abanindranath.

Non-Indian admirers who had contributed much to the casting of the Bengal School in a neo-Orientalist mould also evolved over the years. The later work of Coomaraswamy, in particular, attained greater solidity of scholarship after he moved in 1916 to head the new section on Indian art at the Boston Museum of Fine Arts. He produced an impressive two-volume work on Rajput painting, which also paid much attention to Kangra art, and eventually to his magnum opus, *History of Indian and Indonesian Art* (1916). What persisted in Coomaraswamy, however, was a dichotomy between 'Muslim' and the more 'authentically' Indian art identified with Buddhist or Hindu culture and embodied in Ajanta, Rajput, and Punjab hill court paintings. In contrast, later works of Nandalal, as well as the paintings of Rabindranath, moved in a very different direction. Tagore's paintings coincided in time with the paintings of the brilliant young artist trained in Paris who died young, Amrita Sher-Gil.

It must be emphasized also that the Bengal School had never lacked its critics even at the height of its influence. And once again there was an important ideological and political link between the critique of Extremist Hindu nationalism from around 1907–8 and artistic debates. As the efforts at developing a mass movement against Partition through appeals to revivalist Hinduism dissolved in Hindu–Muslim riots in parts of East Bengal, a disillusioned Rabindranath led the first kind of attack, amounting at times to a kind of auto-critique. The close look at art debates in the pages of contemporary Bengali periodicals, by Tapati Guha-Thakurta and Partha Mitter, has recently discovered a major arts theory counterpart to this turn away from Extremist forms of nationalism.[201] This took a number of different forms. Already in August 1910 an anonymous disciple of Ravi Varma had pointed out that the charge of denationalized sensuality against Varma was no more than a carryover of alien Victorian standards. Contemporary advocates of indigenous values were thus writing from 'an European standpoint'.[202] The artistic controversy came to mingle with journalistic rivalry, with a number of Bengali monthlies, notably Sureshchandra Samajpati's *Sahitya* (along with *Bharatbarsha*), defending the values of Academic Realism as typified by Ravi Varma. Even earlier, a section of Government Art College students had condemned Havell's sale of its European art collection as a damaging

[201] My full-length study of the era (Sarkar 1973/2010) had missed out this dimension.

[202] *Modern Review*, August 1910. The famous English monthly started in 1907 by Ramananda Chattopadhyay, the editor of *Prabasi*, was, like its Bengali counterpart, a powerful advocate through articles and prints of the turn brought about by Havell and Abanindranath. But it was open-minded enough to also publish dissident views.

excess of Orientalist zeal, and had started an alternative organization. A number of successful artists in the early twentieth century continued to adhere to the methods of naturalism, including figures like Hitendranath Tagore, Hemendranath Majumdar, and Atul Bose. Some of the latter also followed the late-nineteenth-century gentlemen artists, combining elite portraits and oils with commercial sale of printed copies, and bridging the gap between elite and popular markets on the model of Bamapada Banerjee and Ravi Varma. Most Bombay artists produced by the J.J. School of Art, as we have seen, also remained loyal to the earlier art traditions.

Post-Swadeshi debates were occasionally suggestive of modernistic values that helped to contribute to the sea change in Indian art from around the 1920s. In June 1907, in the pages of the *Modern Review,* Upendrakishore Raychaudhuri, inventor of improved methods of half-tone reproduction, argued that there was no necessary contradiction between patriotism and a critical receptivity to external values and methods. Patriotism needed to combine 'legitimate and affectionate pride in all that is noble in our national life and traditions' with 'sincere regret for our shortcomings and eagerness to remove them . . .' His son Sukumar Ray refuted the charge of illicit 'cosmopolitanism' brought against Upendrakishore by O.C. Ganguli, a leading advocate and patron of the Bengal School, in brilliantly sarcastic polemic where he ridiculed the dreamy ethereal faces, spineless gestures, and dependence on literary rather than properly artistic standards that characterized the Bengal School. He had no patience with the hollow claims to superior indigenous spirituality: they were, he argued, marked by a 'smokescreen of mysticism'. His criticisms are in tandem with Rabindranath's contemporary denunciations of Extremist methods and values in his post-1907 essays, the closing parts of *Gora,* and *Ghare Baire.*

In 1922 came the first real encounter of Indians with contemporary modern European art, when the Bauhaus exhibition in Calcutta brought over original paintings of artists of the stature of Klee, Kandinsky, Munch, and various German Expressionists. Meanwhile Benoy Sarkar, who had been prominent in the Swadeshi days, wrote essays from abroad arguing that ancient Indian culture (what he liked to call the 'Positive Background of Hindu Sociology') had often been imbued with materialistic rather than otherworldly mysticism, and condemned the chauvinistic shutting out of 'Young India' from the 'aesthetic revolution of contemporary Europe'. The Bauhaus exhibition, in possible connections as yet unexplored, may have been an incentive for Gaganendranath's 1920s experimentations with Cubism. The art world was fast changing, with Nandalal and the new star, Jamini Roy, virtually displacing the old kind of Orientalist Bengal School in the avant-garde taste of middle-class Bengalis by about 1930.

Rabindranath, along with Amrita Sher-Gil, blazed the trail for Indian artistic modernism. But it needs to be added immediately that for most artists and art critics, then and down to recent times, there would remain an imperative, in ever-changing forms, of combining modernity with some conception of being true to 'national' traditions. The precise meanings of both 'modernity' and 'tradition' would necessarily go on changing, but among them the art forms developed by the Bengal School would remain an important component.

The Beginnings of Indian Cinema

The development of Indian cinema has had many remarkable features. These include a very early start; an enormous output (1313 recorded silent feature films in the two decades from 1912–13, shooting up to around 28,000 by 2000 in the era of sound); a significant number of directors of world stature; and above all the blending of many different art forms and genres. Ashish Rajadhyaksha sees in the mythological feature films of the 'father' of the Indian cinema, Dadasaheb Phalke (1870–1944), a bringing together of 'tendencies simmering in painting, music, and theatre'—and to this list one could add other genres and traditions. The feature film that is usually taken to be the crucial breakthrough, Phalke's *Raja Harishchandra* (1913), set a trend that still continues for a significant number of Indian films. Up-to-date technology is brought in from the West and deployed to present traditionalist or revivalist Hindu narratives and values, which are thus popularized in new ways. There can be little doubt, then, about the importance of the cinema for understanding the specifics of South Asian modernity. And yet it is only quite recently, over the last

15–20 years, that the subject has come to attract scholarly and historical attention. The turn in history-writing today towards the study of visual dimensions has produced a growing mass of research and insights which we can expect to expand rapidly in the coming days.[203]

After their first 'cinematographe' showing in Paris on 28 December 1895, Louis and Auguste Lumière sent agents to display their 'views', *Arrival of a Train* and *Leaving the Lumière Factory* in a number of major cities of the world. The Bombay Watson's Hotel show took place on 7 July 1896, five months after London, less than two after St Petersburg, and actually before New York. It is said that in some early Western showings spectators had panicked at the sight of a train apparently hurtling towards them. No such reaction is recorded for India, possibly because spectators here were more used, through puppet shadow plays for instance, to seeing moving images of a sort. But some revealing special features were introduced in Bombay: a broad price range, between 4 annas and Rs 2, as well as 'reserved boxes for *Purdah* Ladies and their Families'. Despite such incentives, early audiences seem to have comprised mainly Europeans and educated Indians. But the mass appeal of films, cutting across class and gender, did not take much time to manifest itself, as a glance at the kind of silent shorts and methods of displaying them would reveal—even before the stunning popularity of *Raja Harishchandra*.

A number of Indians took to the new technology very quickly. The basis had been laid by the developed techniques of photography, introduced a half-century earlier. Short silent films made by Indians, of the order of newsreels, started in 1898 with Sakharam Bhatvadekar, who had had a photographic studio in Bombay from around 1880. Hiralal Sen began making similar shorts in Calcutta the same year, turning to the reproduction of scenes from the popular public stages in the city, occasionally with an accompaniment of gramophone recordings of their songs. Most of the subjects of the early shorts

[203] I take these statistics from Barnouw and Krishnaswamy 1963; see also Thoramal 2000; Rajadhyaksha 1987: 44–77; Vasudevan 2010; Mazumdar 2007. Dass (2014) shows new public spaces being created around film screens and examines the cinema's role in reshaping the public sphere.

were public events or spectacular action sequences: the reception of a successful Cambridge graduate, excerpts from the Imperial Durbar of 1903, wrestling or circus scenes. For a few years after 1905, major political demonstrations connected with the Swadeshi upsurge were also filmed. Sadly, not one of these early shorts have survived.

There were, of course, no cinema houses for some time, but the early makers turned that to an advantage by developing low-cost and itinerant forms of display that could reach large numbers. Shorts were shown during intermissions in public theatre performances, in tents, or in the open air, and primitive low-cost projectors allowed them to be easily carried around and displayed before small-town or even village audiences. The best-known and successful of the early distributors was Jamshetji Framji Madan (1856–1923), a Parsi businessman resident in Calcutta who showed 'bioscopes' in tents and in the open on the Calcutta Maidan in 1902. Like the slightly later Abdulally Esafally, Madan progressed from tents to 'palaces', opening the Elphinstone Picture Palace in Calcutta in 1907, and owning 37 theatres all over the country by 1907. In the early 1920s, he controlled 50 per cent of Indian film distribution and owned 172 of 265 Indian cinema halls. Esafally at times was even more adventurous, touring with a big tent parts of South East Asia too. The world career of Indian films thus began early, often following in the tracks of the Parsi theatre companies already described.

Silent films had certain advantages. Language was not a barrier, as it became with sound, and brief subtitles in several different languages could be inserted for instant communication. There was thus potentially unrestricted access to any film for all the language communities of India. The lead in films made in some languages, especially in Hindi, therefore still lay in the future. The flip side, for Indian film-makers and distributors, was that there was no language bar to films in Western languages also. The era of silent film, and shorts followed quickly by full-length features, constituted therefore a very international scene. The French Pathe Company was in the forefront in the early years, but there were also large-scale imports of American, British, Italian, and German films in the years before the First World War, with London companies as the principal distributors. The war for a time reduced European imports, and contributed to the near-domination in the 1920s of Hollywood. Only 15 per cent of the films shown in 1927 were Indian, while American films comprised 90 per cent of the rest.[204]

The unprecedented mass appeal of Phalke and his mythologicals ended the possibility of a virtually total capture of the Indian market by imported films, even before a language barrier came up with the early 1930s shift to sound. Audiences for foreign films then became confined to a small (though growing) English-knowing elite. Phalke epitomized, both in his biographical trajectory and the films he eventually made, the mingling of diverse strands characteristic of Indian (and in some ways all) films, making the latter perhaps characteristic of modernity in general. Born in a Nasik village (Maharashtra) in a Brahman pandit family, Dhundiraj Govind ('Dadasaheb') Phalke was trained initially as a Sanskrit scholar, like his father, but quickly developed a greater interest in such un-Brahman arts as painting, play-acting, and magic. Moving with his father to Bombay, where the latter had become a teacher in Elphinstone College, he learned photography and painting at the J.J. School of Arts there, followed by a spell at the Baroda Kalabhavan. The professions he tried out were equally diverse: painter of dramatic props at Baroda, draughtsman and photographer at the Poona Archaeology Department, running a photographic studio at Godhra, even a magician after being briefly trained by a visiting German. More significant perhaps was Phalke's connection with Ravi Varma in the 1890s at the latter's lithographic and oleographic press. For Varma was 'the direct cultural predecessor' of Phalke and the entire mythological genre of Indian films, as he was also of a whole series of industrial arts—calendars, posters, packages of small consumer goods, film advertisements, etc.

Phalke's venture into full-length feature films—Indian cinema had thus far functioned merely as a recording device for spectacular or significant events—was motivated by a strongly revivalist-nationalist impulse, in tune with the dominant mood of the Maharashtrian

---

[204] Statistics from Barnouw and Krishnaswamy 1963, who used the data collected by the Indian Cinematograph Committee of 1927. The report of that committee found 20 theatres showing films in Bombay, 13 in Calcutta, 9 in Madras, and 6 each in Poona and Delhi.

high-caste elite of the 1900s. An essay he wrote in 1917 recalled his response to a Western film about the life of Christ. He decided to make a feature film about an Indian (Hindu) divinity. Watching the scenes of *Life of Christ*, Phalke recalled: 'I was mentally visualizing the gods Shri Krishna, Shri Ramachandra, their Gokul and Ayodhya . . . Could we, the sons of India, ever be able to see Indian images on the screen?' Krishna, his first choice, proved too ambitious for the first venture, so Phalke turned to Harishchandra, the mythological king who was put through dreadful ordeals, to be vindicated in the end by the assurance that everything had been to prove his merits. The subject, we have seen, had been central to the Parsi stage already for fifty years or more. With his chequered and adventurous early life, Phalke had little in the way of financial resources, and he and his family had to sacrifice a lot to make *Raja Harishchandra*, his wife even pawning her jewellery. But for Phalke any failure to finish the film would have been 'a permanent disgrace to the swadeshi movement . . .' Luckily for him the film proved a runaway success from its release on 21 April 1913, with subtitles in Hindi, Urdu, and English, and eventually eight languages. Mythologicals had much that suited the silent era, and their appeal, in televised forms, persists into our own time. The stories and characters were widely known and required no effort to understand. They attracted huge crowds, including many women for the first time, amidst an atmosphere of devotion and fantasy. Men and women sometimes prostrated themselves before the screen on seeing Rama and Krishna as living figures. The English-knowing literati largely kept away, but in terms of numbers and commercial success their absence was more than compensated for by the appeal to more plebeian audiences in cities, small towns, and eventually villages—Phalke sometimes took his films there, with a projector on a bullock-cart. At every step, the traditional was being mingled with the modern and the state of the art, for Phalke had learned his new trade during a trip to England, from where he brought back the apparatus that he needed for his film.

He went on to make around a hundred silent films, all in the mythological genre, including *Lanka Dahan* (1917), *Shri Krishna Janma* (1918), and *Kaliya Mardan* (1919): this last has survived the best, for only a small part of *Raja Harishchandra* can be seen today. Getting women to perform was a problem initially, as it had been in the early days of the public stage. Phalke's daughter had to play the part of the boy Krishna in one of the early films. The enterprise as a whole was in large part a joint family enterprise, which Phalke kept under tight patriarchal control: the era of less personalized studios would come only from the 1920s and 1930s. He continued to make films even into the 1930s, including one sound film which proved a flop. The great era for Phalke and for the total domination of the mythological genre was really the 1910s. After that, in a changed atmosphere probably not unrelated to the rise of different forms of nationalism less bound up with Hindu-revivalist values, other genres of 'social' and 'historical' films began, with a new generation of film-makers from different parts of the country—even before the transition to sound that would be inaugurated for India by *Alam Ara* (1931).

During the 1920s Chandulal Shah took advantage of the flood of black market money made in the War years to venture into social comedies very different in tone from the mythological-devotional, often with Anglo-Indian or westernized actresses in the more risqué roles. His *Guna Sundari,* for instance, depicted the problems of an over-dutiful and conventional wife whose husband gets involved with a dancing girl. The wife gets her own back by turning modern herself, though, pertly replying to her husband's query about where she has been with the response he had always made to her question earlier: 'Such questions should not be asked nowadays!' In Bengal, Dhirendranath Ganguly, who had studied at Calcutta University and Santiniketan, also explored the modern milieu in comedies like *England Returned*, making fun of the excesses of anglicized and ultra-conservatives alike. Debaki Bose, a great name in the sound era, also began his long career through silent films in the 1920s. These were three among the many who began coming up then, extending the genre of Indian films beyond the limits of Phalke.

Phalke died an almost forgotten man in 1944, and with the rise of the realist genre in Satyajit Ray's *Pather Panchali* (1955)—the film and its director had a meteoric rise to international fame—the whole era of silent films and sometimes of popular Bombay films in general came to be rather neglected and treated with disdain by the serious film criticism that developed in the wake of Ray and Ritwik Ghatak.

There has been, however, a major revival of interest in recent years with the rise of historical studies of the Indian cinema, and important work has been done on Phalke in particular. Attention has been given in particular to the links between his film techniques and the paintings of Ravi Varma, along with the contemporary public theatre, Parsi and Marathi, for Phalke had been deeply interested in these genres and had had many opportunities for learning from them. The proximity of theatre is particularly striking in *Raja Harishchandra*. Not only was the subject very common on the Parsi stage: the film opens with a tableau-like still of king, queen, and son, distinct spaces are marked out for family scenes and the 'outside', and in the last scene the gods appear on the horizon and assure the audience that the sufferings of the king had been only to test his merits.

The more crucial theme, notably developed by Ashish Rajadhayksha and Anuradha Kapur, carries echoes of the public stage as well as of Ravi Varma's portraits. This is the device of 'frontality', which periodically interrupts linear narrative with iconic stasis, the hero staring out at the spectators in a way that has remained common with big box-office heroes till recent times. The imaginary fourth wall which separates action on stage or in film in the mode of realism, where the actors behave as if oblivious of any audience, is thus breached in many Indian films. This, it has been suggested, in effect deploys modern film technique to retain and enhance the traditional qualities of darshan, the gaze and blessing which gods/heroes impart to believers. Realist depiction thus strengthens devotion to the supramundane. The magic in a way has continued, with the tremendously successful *Ramayana* Doordarshan serial and its direct role in promoting the Ramjanmabhoomi movement, at once apparently traditional and high-tech.

In 1998, Madhava Prasad made an interesting (if at times slightly reductive) effort to link the frontality/movement, traditional/modern blend so often typical of popular Indian cinema with its social foundations. Extending to culture the distinction between 'formal' and 'real' subsumption of labour to capital—which Jairus Banaji, deployed in the study of agrarian relations—Prasad argued that the combination reflects the nature of Indian capitalist development till recently. It drew sustenance from pre-capitalist production relations in place of a total rupture with them. The hybridity that resulted is sought to be linked to the production techniques and studio organization that have dominated the Indian film industry. Whatever the problems with this analysis, it represents an important pioneering effort at exploring a crucial theme: the mode of production of films as a form of industrial technology.

Bibliography

Ahmad, Aijaz, 'Jameson's Rhetoric of Otherness and the "National Allegory"', *Social Text*, 17, 1987

Ahmad, Nazir, *The Bride's Mirror (The First Urdu Bestseller: Mirat ul-Arus)*, translated by G.E. Ward, with an Afterword by Frances W. Pritchett (Delhi: Permanent Black, 2001)

Ahuja, Ravi, 'The Bridge-Builders: Some Notes on Railways, Pilgrimage and the British "Civilizing Mission" in Colonial India', in Harald Fisher-Tine and Michael Mann, eds, *Colonialism as Civilizing Mission: Cultural Ideology in British India* (London: Anthem, 2004)

Anantha Murthy, U.R., *Samskara: A Rite for a Dead Man*, trans. from the Kannada by A.K. Ramanujan (Delhi: Oxford University Press, 1979)

Arnold, David and Stuart Blackburn, eds, *Telling Lives in India* (Ranikhet: Permanent Black, 2004)

Arunima, G., 'Writing Culture: Of Modernity and the Malayalam Novel', *Studies in History*, 13 (2), 1997

Arya, Aditya, and Indivar Kamtekar, *History in the Making: The Visual Archives of Kulwant Roy* (New Delhi: HarperCollins, 2010)

Asher, R.E., 'The Tamil Renaissance and the Beginnings of the Tamil Novel', in T.V. Clark, ed., *The Novel in India: Its Birth and Development* (Berkeley: University of California Press, 1970)

Bakhle, Janaki, *Two Men and Music: Nationalism in the Making of an Indian Classical Tradition* (Delhi: Permanent Black, 2006)

Bandyopadhyay, Brojendronath, *Bangiya Natyashalar Itihas 1795–1876* (Calcutta: Bangiya Sahitya Parishad, 1933; rpntd 1991)

Banerjee, Sumanta, *The Parlour and the Streets: Elite and Popular Culture in Nineteenth Century Calcutta* (Seagull Books: Calcutta, 1989)

Barnouw, Erik, and S. Krishnaswamy, *Indian Film* (New York: Columbia University Press, 1963)

Baruah, Sanjib, *India Against Itself: Assam and the Politics of Nationality* (Delhi: Oxford University Press, 1999)

————, 'Clash of Resource Uses in Colonial Assam: A Nineteenth Century Puzzle Revisited', *Journal of Peasant Studies,* 23 (3), 2001

Bayly, C.A., *Rulers, Townsmen, and Bazaars: North Indian Society in the Age of British Expansion, 1770–1870* (Cambridge: Cambridge University Press, 1983)

Bhabha, Homi, *The Location of Culture* (London: Routledge, 1994)

Bhagwat, Neela, 'Vishnu Digamber Paluskar', *Journal of Arts and Ideas,* 14–15, 1987

Bhattacharya, Rimli, ed. and trans., *Binodini Dasi: My Story and My Life as an Actress* (New Delhi: Kali for Women, 1998)

Bhattacharya, Tithi, *The Sentinels of Culture: Class, Education and the Colonial Intellectual in Bengal* (New Delhi: Oxford University Press, 2005)

Blackburn, Stuart, *Print, Folklore, and Nationalism in Colonial South India* (Delhi: Permanent Black, 2003)

Bose, Pradip Kumar, 'Sons of the Nation: Child Rearing in the New Family', in Partha Chatterjee, ed., *Texts of Power: Emerging Disciplines in Colonial Bengal* (Minnesota: University of Minnesota Press, 1995)

Breman, Jan, *The Making and Unmaking of an Industrial Working Class* (New Delhi: Oxford University Press, 2004)

Cavallo, Guglielmo, 'Between *Volumen* and Codex: Reading in the Roman World', in Guglielmo Cavallo and Roger Chartier, eds, *A History of Reading in the West* (Cambridge: Polity Press, 1999)

Chakrabarty, Dipesh, '*Adda*: A History of Sociality', in Dipesh Chakrabarty, *Provincializing Europe* (Princeton: Princeton University Press, 2000)

Chandavarkar, Rajnarayan, *The Origins of Industrial Capitalism in India: Business Strategies and the Working Class in Bombay, 1900–1940* (Cambridge: Cambridge University Press, 1994)

Charney, Leo, and Vanessa R. Schwartz, 'Introduction', in Leo Charney and Vanessa R. Schwartz, eds, *Cinema and the Invention of Modern Life* (California: University of California Press, 1995)

Chatterjee, Partha, *Nationalist Thought and the Colonial World: A Derivative Discourse* (New Delhi: Oxford University Press, 1986)

————, 'The Nationalist Resolution of the Women's Question', in Kukum Sangari and Sudesh Vaid, eds, *Recasting Women* (New Delhi: Kali for Women, 1989)

————, *The Nation and its Fragments* (Princeton: Princeton University Press, 1994)

Chatterjee, Ratnabali, *From the Karkhana to the Studio: Changing Social Roles of Patron and Artist in Bengal* (New Delhi: Books and Books, 1990)

Chaudhuri, Sukanta, ed., *Calcutta: The Living City,* 2 vols (Calcutta: Oxford University Press, 1990)

Dalmia, Vasudha, *The Nationalization of Hindu Traditions: Bharatendu Harishchandra and Nineteenth-century Banaras* (1997; rpnt Ranikhet: Permanent Black, 2010)

Dalrymple, William, *White Mughals* (Delhi: Viking/ Penguin, 2002)

———, 'White Mughals: The Case of James Achilles Kirkpatrick and Khair un-Nissa', in Indrani Chatterjee, ed., *Unfamiliar Relations: Family and History in South Asia* (Delhi: Permanent Black, 2004)

Das, Samarendranath, ed., *Kolkatar Adda* (Calcutta: Mahajati Prakashan, 1990)

Das, Sisir Kumar, *A History of Indian Literature, Volume VIII, 1800–1910: Western Impact: Indian Response* (New Delhi: Sahitya Akademi, 1991)

Dasgupta, Amlan, 'Women and Music: The Case of North India', in Bharati Ray, ed., *Women of India: Colonial and Post-Colonial Periods, History of Science, Philosophy, and Culture in Indian Civilization*, vol. IX, pt 3 (New Delhi: Sage, 2005)

Dass, Manishita, *Outside the Lettered City: Cinema, Modernity, and the Mass Public in Late Colonial India* (New York: Oxford University Press, 2014)

Datta, Partho, *Planning the City—Urbanization and Reform in Calcutta c. 1800–c. 1940* (New Delhi: Tulika, 2012)

Deshpande, Prachi, *Creative Pasts: Historical Memory and Identity in Western India 1700–1960* (Ranikhet: Permanent Black, 2007)

Dhar, Sheila, *Raga 'n Josh: Stories from a Musical Life* (Ranikhet: Permanent Black, 2005)

Dirks, Nicholas B., *The Hollow Crown: Ethnohistory of an Indian Kingdom* (Wisconsin: University of Michigan Press, 1993)

Dossal, Mariam, *Imperial Designs and Indian Realities: The Planning of Bombay City, 1845–1875* (Delhi: Oxford University 1991)

———, 'Signatures in Space: Land Use in Colonial Bombay', in Sujata Patel and Alice Thorner, eds, *Bombay: Metaphor for Modern India* (Bombay: Oxford University Press, 1996)

Dutt, Michael Madhusudan, *Ekei Bale Sabhayata* (Is This Civilization?, Calcutta, 1860)

Evenson, Norma, *The Indian Metropolis: A View Towards the West* (Delhi: Oxford University Press, 1989)

Freitag, Sandria B., ed., *Culture and Power in Banaras: Community, Performance and Environment 1800–1980* (Delhi: Oxford University Press, 1989)

Gadihoke, Sabeena, *Camera Chronicles of Homai Vyarawalla* (Ahmedabad: Mapin, 2006)

Gaston, Anne-Marie, *Bharata Natyam: From Temple to Theatre* (Delhi: Manohar, 1996)

Geertz, Clifford, *The Religion of Java* (Chicago: University of Chicago Press, new edition, 1976)

Ghosh, Anindita, *Power in Print: Popular Publishing and the Politics of Language and Culture in a Colonial* Society (New Delhi: Oxford University Press, 2006)

Ghosh, Siddharta, *Koler Sahar Kolkata* (Calcutta: Ananda Publishers, 1991)

Gillion, Kenneth, *Ahmedabad: A Study in Indian Urban History* (Berkeley: University of California, 1968)

Gilroy, Paul, *The Black Atlantic* (Cambridge, Mass.: Harvard University Press, 1994)

Ginzburg, Carlo, 'Clues: Roots of an Evidential Paradigm', in Carlo Ginzburg, *Myths, Emblems, Clues* (London: Hutchinson Radius, 1990)

Goswami, Jayanta, *Samajcitre Unabingsha Satabdir Bangla Prahasan* (Calcutta, 1974)

Guha, Amalendu, *Medieval and Early Colonial Assam: Society, Polity, Economy* (Calcutta: K.P. Bagchi & Co., 1991)

Guha, Ramachandra, *An Anthropologist among the Marxists and Other Essays* (Delhi: Permanent Black, 2001)

———, *A Corner of a Foreign Field: The Indian History of a British Sport* (London: Picador, 2002)

Guha-Thakurta, Tapati, *The Making of a New 'Indian' Art: Artists, Aesthetics and Nationalism in Bengal, c.1850–1920* (Cambridge: Cambridge University Press, 1992)

———, *Monuments, Objects, Histories: Institutions of Art in Colonial and Postcolonial India* (Delhi: Permanent Black, 2004)

———, 'Lineages of the Modern in Indian Art: The Making of a National History', in Kamala Ganesh and Usha Thakkar, eds, *Culture and the Making of Identity in Contemporary India* (New Delhi: Sage, 2005)

Gupta, Narayani, 'Military Security and Urban Development: A Case-study of Delhi, 1857–1912', *Modern Asian Studies*, 5 (1), 1971

———, *Delhi Between Two Empires, 1803–1931* (Delhi: Oxford University Press, 1981)

———, 'Urbanism in South India, 18th–19th century', in Indu Banga, ed., *The City in Indian History* (Delhi: Manohar, 1987)

Habermas, Jürgen, *The Structural Transformation of the Public Sphere* (1962; English translation, Cambridge: Polity Press, 1989)

Habib, Irfan, *The Agrarian System of Mughal India 1556–1707* (1963; 3rd edn Delhi: Oxford University Press, 2013)

Hall, B., *Fragments of Voyages and Travels* (Edinburgh: Robert Cadell, 1832)

Hansen, Kathryn, 'The Birth of Hindi Drama in Banaras, 1868–1885', in Sandria Freitag, ed., *Culture and Power in Banaras: Community, Performance, and Environment, 1800–1980* (Delhi: Oxford University Press, 1989)

———, *Grounds for Play: The Nautanki Theatre of North India* (Berkeley: University of California Press, 1992)

———, 'The Inder Sabha Phenomenon: Public Theatre and Consumption in Greater India', in Rachel Dwyer and Christopher Pinney, eds, *Pleasure and the Nation: The History, Politics and Consumption of Public Culture in India* (Delhi: Oxford University Press, 2001)

———, 'Languages on Stage: Linguistic Pluralism and Community Formation in the Nineteenth-Century Parsi Theatre', *Modern Asian Studies*, 37 (2), 2003

———, *Stages of Life: Indian Theatre Autobiographies* (Ranikhet: Permanent Black, 2011)

Hatcher, Brian, *Idioms of Improvement: Vidyasagar and Cultural Encounter in Bengal* (Calcutta: Oxford University Press, 1996)

Jain, Jyotindra, *Kalighat Painting: Images from a Changing World* (Ahmedabad: Mapin Publishing Pvt. Ltd, 1999)

Jameson, Frederic, 'Third-World Literature in the Era of Multinational Capitalism', *Social Text*, 15, 1986

Joshi, Chitra, *Lost Worlds: Indian Labour and its Forgotten Histories* (Delhi: Permanent Black, 2003)

Joshi, Sanjay, ed., *The Middle Class in Colonial India* (Delhi: Oxford University Press, 2010)

Kanwar, Pamela, *Imperial Simla: The Political Culture of the Raj* (Delhi: Oxford University Press, 1990)

Kapur, Anuradha, 'The Representation of Gods and Heroes in the Parsi Mythological Drama of the Early Twentieth Century', in Vasudha Dalmia and Heinrich Stietencron, eds, *Representing Hinduism: The Construction of Religious Traditions and National Identity* (New Delhi: Sage, 1995)

———, *Actors, Pilgrims, Kings and Gods: The Ramlila of Ramnagar* (Calcutta: Seagull, 2006)

Kapur, Geeta, 'Ravi Varma: Representational Dilemmas of a Nineteenth-Century Indian Painter', *Journal of Arts and Ideas*, 17–18, 1989

Karlekar, Malavika, *Revisioning the Past: Early Photography in Bengal, 1875–1915* (New Delhi: Oxford University Press, 2005)

Kaviraj, Sudipta, *A Taste for Transgression: Liminality in the Novels of Bankim*

Chandra Chattopadhyay, Occasional Paper XLVI (New Delhi: Nehru Memorial Museum and Library, 1981)

————, 'Humour and the Prison of Reality: *Kamalakanta* as the Secret Autobiography of Bankimchandra Chattopadhyay', Occasional Paper, Second Series, IV (New Delhi: Nehru Memorial Museum and Library, 1988)

————, *The Unhappy Consciousness: Bankimchandra Chattopadhyay and the Formation of Nationalist Discourse in India* (New Delhi: Oxford University Press, 1995)

————, 'The Invention of Private Life: A Reading of Sibnath Sastri's Autobiography', in David Arnold and Stuart Blackburn, eds, *Telling Lives in India* (Ranikhet: Permanent Black, 2004)

————, 'The Sudden Death of Sanskrit Knowledge', *Journal of Indian Philosophy*, 2005

Kennedy, Dane, *The Magic Mountains: Hill Stations and the British Raj* (Berkeley: University of California Press, 1996)

Kesavan, Mukul, 'Urdu, Awadh, and the *Tawaif*: The Islamicate Roots of Hindi Cinema', in Mukul Kesavan, *The Ugliness of the Indian Male and Other Propositions* (Ranikhet: Permanent Black, 2008)

Pukhraj, Malika, *Song Sung True*, ed. and trans. Salim Kidwai (Delhi: Zubaan 2009)

King, Antony D., *Colonial Urban Development: Culture, Social Power, and Environment* (London: Routledge and Kegan Paul, 1976)

King, Christopher R., 'Forging a New Linguistic Identity: The Hindi Movement in Benaras, 1868–1914', in Sandria B. Freitag, ed., *Culture and Power in Banaras: Community, Performance, and Environment, 1800–1980* (Delhi: Oxford University Press, 1989)

————, *One Language, Two Scripts: The Hindi Movement in Nineteenth Century North India* (Delhi: Oxford University Press, 1994)

Kinnear, Michael, *The Gramophone Company's First Indian Recordings, 1899–1908* (Bombay: Popular Prakashan, 1994)·

Kosambi, Meera, *Bombay and Poona: A Socio-Economic Study of Two Indian Cities, 1650–1900* (Stockholm: University of Stockholm, 1980)

————, *Crossing Thresholds: Feminist Essays in Social History* (Ranikhet: Permanent Black, 2007)

————, *Feminist Vision or Treason Against Men: Kashibai Kanitkar and the Engendering of Marathi Literature* (Ranikhet: Permanent Black, 2008)

————, *Women Writing Gender: Marathi Fiction Before Independence* (Ranikhet: Permanent Black, 2012)

Kumar, Nita, *The Artisans of Banaras: Popular Culture and Identity, 1880–1986* (Princeton: Princeton University Press, 1988)

Kumar, Udaya, 'Self, Body, and Inner Sense: Some Reflections on Sree Narayana Guru and Kumaran Asan', *Studies in History*, 13 (2), 1997

Lewandowski, Susan J., 'Urban Growth and Municipal Development in the Colonial City of Madras, 1860–1900', *Journal of Asian Studies*, 34 (2), 1975

Llewellyn-Jones, Rosie, *A Fatal Friendship: The Nawabs, the British, and the City of Lucknow* (Delhi: Oxford University Press, 1983)

Losty, Jeremiah P., *The Art of the Book in India* (London: British Library, 1982)

Lutgendorf, Philip, 'Ram's Story in Shiva's City: Public Arenas and Private Patronage', in Sandria B Freitag, ed., *Culture and Power in Banaras: Community, Performance and Environment 1800–1980* (Delhi: Oxford University Press, 1989)

Maclean, K., 'Making the Colonial State Work for You: The Modern Beginnings of the Ancient Kumbh Mela in Allahabad', *The Journal of Asian Studies*, 62 (3), 2003

Majumdar, Boria, *Twenty-Two Yards to Freedom: A Social History of Indian Cricket* (Delhi: Penguin Viking, 2004)

Malhotra, Anshu, *Gender, Caste, and Religious Identities: Restructuring Class in Colonial Punjab* (Delhi: Oxford University Press, 2002)

Mantena, Rama Sundari, 'Vernacular Futures: Colonial Philology and the Idea of History in Nineteenth Century South India', *Indian Economic and Social History Review*, 42 (4), 2005

Massey, Reginald, and Jamila Massey, *The Music of India* (New Delhi: Abhinav Publications, 1993)

Mazumdar, Ranjani, *Bombay Cinema: An Archive of the City* (Ranikhet: Permanent Black, 2007)

McDonald, Ellen E., 'English Education and Social Reform in Late 19th Century Bombay: A Case-study in the Study of a Cultural Ideal', *Journal of Asian Studies*, 25, 1966

McLane, J., *Indian Nationalism and the Early Congress* (Princeton: Princeton University Press, 1977)

Meston Committee Report (1908), Oriental and India Office Collections (British Library), file no.V/26/210/25, 1908

Metcalf, Thomas, *An Imperial Vision: Indian Architecture and Britain's Raj* (London: Faber and Faber, 1989)

Mir, Farhana, *The Social Space of Language: Vernacular Culture in British Colonial Punjab* (Ranikhet: Permanent Black, 2010)

Mishra, P.K., 'Language Agitation in the 19th Century', in J.K. Samal, ed., *Comprehensive History and Culture of Orissa*, vol. II (New Delhi: Kaveri Books, 1997)

Mitchell, Lisa, 'Parallel Languages, Parallel Cultures: Language as a New Foundation for the Reorganization of Knowledge and Practice in Southern India', *Indian Economic and Social History Review*, 42 (4), 2005

———, *Language, Emotion, and Politics in South India: The Making of a Mother Tongue* (Ranikhet: Permanent Black, 2009)

Mitra, Asok, 'Forces behind the Modern Movement', *Lalit Kala Contemporary*, 1, 1961

Mitter, Partha, *Art and Nationalism in Colonial India 1850–1922: Occidental Orientations* (Cambridge: Cambridge University Press, 1994)

———, 'Mechanical Reproduction and the World of the Colonial Artist', *Contributions to Indian Sociology*, 36 (1–2), 2002

Mukherjee, Meenakshi, *Realism and Reality: The Novel and Society in India* (New Delhi: Oxford University Press, 1985)

Mukherjee, Soumen, *Calcutta: Essays in Urban History* (Calcutta: Subarna-rekha, 1993)

Mukherjee, Sujit, *Forster and Further: The Tradition of Anglo-Indian Fiction* (Hyderabad: Orient Longman, 1994)

Mukherjee, Sushil Kumar, *The Story of the Calcutta Theatre, 1753–1988* (Calcutta: K.P. Bagchi, 1982)

Nandy, Ashis, *The Tao of Cricket: On Games of Destiny and the Destiny of Games* (New Delhi: Penguin, 1989)

Narayana Rao, Velcheru, 'Print and Prose: Pandits, *Karanams*, and the East India Company in the Making of Modern Telugu', in Stuart Blackburn and Vasudha Dalmia, eds, *India's Literary History: Essays on the Nineteenth Century* (Delhi: Permanent Black, 2004)

Naregal, Veena, *Language Politics, Elites, and the Public Sphere: Western India under Colonialism* (New Delhi: Permanent Black, 2001)

O'Hanlon, Rosalind, *At the Edges of Empire: Essays in the Social and Intellectual History of India* (Ranikhet: Permanent Black, 2014)

Oldenburg, Veena Talwar, *The Making of Colonial Lucknow, 1856–1877* (Princeton, N.J.: Princeton University Press, 1984)

———, 'Lifestyle as Resistance: The Case of the Courtesans of Lucknow', in Douglas Haynes and Gyan Prakash, eds, *Contesting Power: Resistance and Everyday Social Relations in South Asia* (Delhi: Oxford University Press, 1991)

Orsini, Francesca, *The Hindi Public Sphere: 1920–40* (New Delhi: Oxford University Press, 2002)

———, 'Detective Novels: A Commercial Genre in Nineteenth Century North India', in Stuart Blackburn and Vasudha Dalmia, eds, *India's Literary History: Essays on the Nineteenth Century* (Delhi: Permanent Black, 2004)

Osaka, Riho, 'Language and Dominance: The Debates over the Gujarati Language in the Late Nineteenth Century', *South Asia*, 25 (1), 2002

Pandian, M.S.S., *Brahmin and Non-Brahmin: Genealogies of the Tamil Political Present* (Ranikhet: Permanent Black, 2007)

Patel, Sujata and Alice Thorner, eds, *Bombay: Mosaic of Modern Culture* (Delhi: Oxford University Press, 1995)

Pinney, Christopher, *Camera Indica: The Social Life of Indian Photographs* (Chicago: University of Chicago Press, 1997)

————, *'Photos of the Gods': The Printed Image and Political Struggle in India* (London: Reaktion Books, 2004)

Pollock, Sheldon, 'The Cosmopolitan Vernacular', *Journal of Asian Studies*, 57 (1), 1998

————, 'The Death of Sanskrit', *Comparative Studies in Society and History*, 43 (2), 2001

Rai, Alok, *Hindi Nationalism* (New Delhi: Orient Longman, 2000)

Rai, Amrit, *A House Divided: The Origin and Development of Hindi/Hindavi* (Delhi: Oxford University Press, 1984)

Rajadhyaksha, Ashish, 'The Phalke Era: Conflict of Traditional Form and Modern Technology', *Journal of Arts and Ideas*, 14–15, 1987

Ramaswamy, Sumathi, *Passions of the Tongue: Language Devotion in Tamil India, 1891–1970* (Berkeley: University of California Press, 1997)

————, 'Language of the People in the World of Gods: Ideologies of Tamil before the Nation', *Journal of Asian Studies* 57 (1), 1998

————, ed., *Beyond Appearances: Visual Practices and Ideologies in Modern India* (New York: Sage, 2003)

Rao, Vidya (2011). *Heart to Heart: Remembering Naina Devi* (New Delhi: HarperCollins, 2011)

Raychaudhuri, Siddharta, 'Colonialism, Indigenous Elites, and the Transformation of Cities in the Non-Western World: Ahmedabad (Western India), 1890–1947', *Modern Asian Studies*, 35 (3), 2001

Risley, H.H., *Tribes and Castes of Bengal, Volume I* (Calcutta: Bengal Secretariat Press, 1891)

Robertson, Bruce, *Raja Rammohan Ray: The Father of Modern India* (Delhi: Oxford University Press, 1995)

Robinson, Francis, 'Technology and Religious Change: Islam and the Impact of Print', *Modern Asian Studies*, 27 (1), 1993

————, 'Islam and the Impact of Print in South Asia', in Nigel Crook, ed., *The Transmission of Knowledge in South Asia* (Delhi: Oxford University Press, 1996)

Roy, A.K., *A Short History of Calcutta: Town and Suburbs* (Calcutta: Rddhi India, 1902)

Roy, Tapti, 'Disciplining the Printed Text: Colonial and Nationalist Surveillance', in Partha Chatterjee, ed., *Texts of Power: Emerging Disciplines in Colonial Bengal* (Minnesota: Minnesota University Press, 1995)

Saikia, Yasmin, *Assam and India: Fragmented Memories, Cultural Identity, and the Tai-Ahom Struggle* (Ranikhet: Permanent Black, 2005)

Sarkar, Sumit, *The Swadeshi Movement in Bengal 1903–1908* (1973; 2nd edn Ranikhet: Permanent Black 2010)

———, *Writing Social History* (Delhi: Oxford University Press, 1997)

Sarkar, Tanika, *Words to Win* (Delhi: Kali for Women, 1999)

———, *Hindu Wife, Hindu Nation: Community, Religion, and Cultural Nationalism* (Delhi: Permanent Black, 2001)

———, 'Performing Power: Political Imaginaries in the Early Bengali Public Theatre' in *Rebels, Wives, Saints: Designing Selves and Nations in Colonial Times* (Ranikhet: Permanent Black, 2009)

Sarma, Rani Siva Sankara, *The Last Brahmin: Life and Reflections of a Modern-day Sanskrit Pandit*, trans. from the Telugu by D. Venkat Rao (Ranikhet: Permanent Black, 2007)

Sartori, Andrew, *Bengal in Global History: Colonialism in the Age of Capital* (Chicago: The University of Chicago Press, 2008)

Sen, Amiya, *Bankim's Hinduism: An Anthology of Writings by Bankim Chandra Chattopadhyay* (Ranikhet: Permanent Black, 2011)

Shackle, Christopher, and Javed Majeed, ed. and trans., *Hali's Musaddas: The Flow and Ebb of Islam* (Delhi: Oxford University Press, 1997)

Shahidullah, Kazi, *Pathshalas into Schools: The Development of Indigenous Elementary Education in Bengal* (Calcutta: Firma KLM, 1987)

Singh, Brijraj, *The First Protestant Missionary in India: Bartholomaeus Ziegenbalg 1687–1719* (New Delhi: Oxford University Press, 1999)

Singh, Upinder, *The Discovery of Ancient India: Early Archaeologists and the Beginnings of Archaeology* (Delhi: Permanent Black, 2004)

Sinha, Kaliprasanna, *The Observant Owl: Hootum's Vignettes of Nineteenth-century Calcutta—Hootum Pyanchar Naksha*, trans. from the Bengali by Swarup Roy, foreword by Partha Chatterjee (Ranikhet: Permanent Black/Black Kite, 2008)

Sinha, Pradip, *Calcutta in Urban History* (Calcutta: Firma KLM, 1978)

Soneji, Davesh, *Unfinished Gestures: Devadasis, Memory, and Modernity in South India* (Ranikhet: Permanent Black, 2012)

Spodek, Howard, 'The Manchesterization of Ahmedabad', *Economic Weekly*, 17, 1965

———, *Ahmedabad: Shock City of Twentieth Century India* (Bloomington: Indiana University Press, 2011)

Srinivas, S.V., *Politics as Performance: A Social History of the Telugu Cinema* (Ranikhet: Permanent Black, 2013)

Stark, Ulrike, *An Empire of Books: The Naval Kishore Press and the Diffusion of the Printed Word in Colonial India* (Ranikhet: Permanent Black, 2007)

Thompson, Edward, *An Indian Day* (London: Ernest Benn, 1927)

Thoramal, Yves, *The Cinemas of India* (Delhi: Macmillan, 2000)

Vasudevan, Ravi, *The Melodramatic Public: Film Form and Spectatorship in Indian Cinema* (Ranikhet: Permanent Black, 2010)

Vatsyayana, Kapila, *Traditional Indian Theatre: Multiple Streams* (New Delhi: National Book Trust, 1980)

——, 'The *Natyashastra*—A History of Criticism', in Anna Dalla-piccola, Christine Walter-Mendy, and Stephanie Zingel-Avé Lallemant, eds, *Shastric Traditions in Indian Art*, vol. I (Stuttgart: Steiner, 1989)

Venkatachalapathy, A.R., '"Era Prayacanam": Constructing the Canon in Colonial Tamilnadu', *Indian Economic and Social History Review*, 42 (4), 2005

——, *The Province of the Book: Scholars, Scribes, and Scribblers in Colonial Tamilnadu* (Ranikhet: Permanent Black, 2012)

Vernède, R.V., *British Life in India: An Anthology of Humorous and Other Writings Perpetrated by the British in India 1750–1947* (Delhi: Oxford University Press, 1995)

Weidman, Amanda, 'Can the Subaltern Sing? Music, Language and the Politics of Voice in Early 20th Century South India', *Indian Economic and Social History Review*, 42 (4), 2005

Williams, Raymond, *The Country and the City* (Oxford: Oxford University Press, 1973)

Yagnik, Achyut, and Suchitra Seth, *The Shaping of Modern Gujarat: Plurality, Hindutva and Beyond* (New Delhi: Penguin, 2005)

Yalland, Zoe, *Boxwallahs: The British in Cawnpore* (Norwich, 1994)

Yashaschandra, Sitangshu, 'From Hemchandra to *Hind Swaraj*: Region and Power in Gujarati Literary Culture', in Sheldon Pollock, ed., *Literary Cultures in History: Reconstructions from South Asia* (Delhi: Oxford University Press, 2003)

Zbavitel, Dushan, 'The Beginnings of Modern Bengali Drama, 1852–80', *Archiv Orientalni*, 36, 1968

Index